FANTASTICAL IMAGINATIONS

FANTASTICAL IMAGINATIONS

The Supernatural in Scottish History and Culture

Edited by

Lizanne Henderson

First published in Great Britain in 2009 by
John Donald, an imprint of Birlinn Ltd

West Newington House
10 Newington Road
Edinburgh
EH9 1QS

www.birlinn.co.uk

ISBN: 978 1 906566 02 9

Copyright © The editor and contributors severally 2009

The right of the editor and contributors to be identified as the authors
of this work has been asserted by them in accordance
with the Copyright, Designs and Patents Act, 1988

All rights reserved. No part of this publication may
be reproduced, stored, or transmitted in any form, or
by any means, electronic, mechanical or photocopying,
recording or otherwise, without the express written
permission of the publisher.

The publishers gratefully acknowledge the support of the
Strathmartine Trust towards the publication of this book.

British Library Cataloguing-in-Publication Data
A catalogue record for this book is available on request from the British Library

Typeset by Hewer Text UK Ltd, Edinburgh
Printed and bound in Britain by Bell and Bain, Glasgow

In loving memory of Padea
– 24 September 2008 –
an extraordinary wee soul

Contents

List of Contributors   ix

List of Abbreviations   xi

Acknowledgements   xii

Introduction:
   Studying the Supernatural History of Scotland   xiii
Lizanne Henderson

1. The Discovery of the Future: Prophecy and
   Second Sight in Scottish History   1
   Edward J. Cowan

2. 'Away with the fairies'   29
   Louise Yeoman

3. Seventeenth- and Eighteenth-Century Astrology
   and the Scottish Popular Almanac   47
   George M. Brunsden

4. From Natural to Supernatural:
   The Material Culture of Charms and Amulets   70
   Hugh Cheape

5. The Scottish Enlightenment and the Supernatural   91
   Colin Kidd

6. 'Nathaniel Gow's Toddy': The Supernatural in Lowland
   Scottish Literature from Burns and Scott to the Present Day   110
   Douglas Gifford

7. Witch, Fairy and Folktale Narratives in the Trial of Bessie Dunlop   141
   Lizanne Henderson

8. Stories of the Supernatural: From Local Memorate to Scottish Legend   167
   Margaret Bennett

9 The Church and Traditional Belief in Gaelic Society   185
   John MacInnes

10 Lewis Spence: Remembering the Celts   196
   Juliette Wood

11 The Wicker Man: Virgin Sacrifice in Dumfries and Galloway   212
   Valentina Bold

   Index   221

Contributors

Dr Margaret Bennett is a singer, storyteller, broadcaster and one of Scotland's foremost folklorists. She has published several articles and is author of The Last Stronghold: Scottish Gaelic Traditions in Newfoundland (1989), Scottish Customs from the Cradle to the Grave (1998), and Oatmeal and the Catechism: Scottish Gaelic Settlers in Quebec (1999; 2004). She was a lecturer at the University of Edinburgh School of Scottish Studies until 1995 and is a highly sought after lecturer and performer on both sides of the Atlantic.

Dr Valentina Bold is Senior Lecturer in Scottish Studies at the University of Glasgow Dumfries Campus. She is the author of several articles on Scottish literature and culture and her recent books include Smeddum: Stories, Poems and Essays by Lewis Grassic Gibbon (2001), James Hogg: A Bard of Nature's Making (2007) and editor of Robert Burns's The Merry Muses of Caledonia (2009).

Dr George Brunsden, a PhD graduate of the University of Glasgow, currently teaches English Grammar at University of Waterloo (Renison campus). His most recent publication is Orkney's Ultimate Viking, Earl Thorfinn the Mighty (2009).

Dr Hugh Cheape is a Course Leader at Sabhal Mòr Ostaig, the National Centre for Gaelic Language and Culture, teaching a postgraduate programme 'Cultar Duthchasach agus Arainneachd' (Material Culture and Environment). He was formerly Principal Curator in the National Museums Scotland and specialist in Scottish and European material culture. He has published widely in the subject fields of ethnology and musicology, including other papers on charms, amulets and talismanic belief in Scotland. His books include Periods in Highland History (1987) (with I. F. Grant), Tartan: the Highland Habit (1995), Witness to Rebellion (1996) (with I. G. Brown) and The Book of the Bagpipe (1999). He has edited Tools and Traditions: Studies in European Ethnology (1993) and 'A very civil people': Hebridean Folk, History and Tradition by John Lorne Campbell (2000).

Professor Edward J. Cowan is Professor of Scottish History at the University of Glasgow, and Director of the University's Dumfries Campus. He has written extensively on various aspects of Scottish history and is a prominent broadcaster and public speaker with an international reputation. His most recent books are *For Freedom Alone: Scotland's Declaration of Independence* (revised edition 2008), *Folk in Print: Scotland's Chapbook Heritage 1750–1850* (2007) and *The Wallace Book* (2007).

Professor Douglas Gifford is Professor Emeritus Scottish Literature at the University of Glasgow. Among his publications are *James Hogg: A Critical Study* (1976), *Neil Gunn and Lewis Grassic Gibbon: A Critical Study* (1983), and *The Dear Green Place? The Novel in the West of Scotland* (1984). He has co-edited *A History of Scottish Women's Writing* (with D. McMillan) (1997), *The Polar Twins: Scottish History and Scottish Literature* (with E. J. Cowan) (1999), and *Scotlands: Poets and the Nation* (with A. Riach) (2004). He is Honorary Librarian of Sir Walter Scott's Library at Abbotsford and is Director of the Abbotsford Project.

Dr Lizanne Henderson is a Lecturer in History at the University of Glasgow Dumfries Campus. She is author of Scottish Fairy Belief: a History (with E. J. Cowan) (2001; 2007), and has several articles on such topics as the Scottish witch-hunts, charmers, and supernatural beliefs. She is a board member of The Folklore Society (London) and has lectured on supernatural belief and cultural history in Europe, North America and Australia.

Professor Colin Kidd is Professor of Modern History at the University of Glasgow. He is the author of Subverting Scotland's Past (1993), British Identities before Nationalism (1999) and The Forging of Races (2006). His latest book is Union and Unionisms: Political Thought in Scotland 1500–2000 (2008).

Dr John MacInnes was Senior Lecturer at the School of Scottish Studies, University of Edinburgh, until his retirement in 1993. He is a native Gaelic speaker, with expertise on the oral tradition of the Scottish Highland and Islands, and is author of numerous articles on various aspects of Scottish folklore, music, Gaelic language and literature. A collection of his essays has recently been edited by Michael Newton, Dùthchas Nan Gàidheal: Selected Essays of John MacInnes (2006).

Dr Juliette Wood is Associate Lecturer in the Department of Welsh, University of Cardiff, and Secretary of The Folklore Society (London). Her most recent books include The Celts: Life, Myth and Art (1998), The Celtic Book of Living and Dying (2000), and Eternal Chalice: The Enduring Legend of the Holy Grail (2008).

Dr Louise Yeoman, now a radio producer at BBC Scotland, was a curator in the Manuscripts Division of the Department of Special Collections at the National Library of Scotland from 1992 to 2001. A specialist in sixteenth- and seventeenth-century history, she completed a PhD on the Covenanters in 1991 at St Andrews University. She was also co-director of the University of Edinburgh's Survey of Scottish Witchcraft project.

Abbreviations

AT	Antti Aarne and Stith Thompson, *The Types of the Folktale* (Helsinki: Academia Scientiarum Fennica, 1961)
DOST	W. H. Craigie, *Dictionary of the Older Scottish Tongue* 12 vols. (1937)
EUL	Edinburgh University Library
NAS (formerly SRO)	National Archives of Scotland, Edinburgh
NLS	National Library of Scotland, Edinburgh
NMS	National Museums of Scotland, Edinburgh
NSA	New Statistical Account
PSAS	*Proceedings of the Society of Antiquaries of Scotland*
Pitcairn (ed.), *Trials*	*Ancient Criminal Trials in Scotland, 1488–1624*, 4 vols., ed. Robert Pitcairn. Edinburgh, 1833.
ROSC	*Review of Scottish Culture*
RPC	*Register of the Privy Council of Scotland*, 38 vols., ed. S. I. Gillon and J. I. Smith. Stair Society, 1954–74.
RPS	*Records of the Parliaments of Scotland to 1707*, ed. K. M. Brown *et al.* (St Andrews) online
SHR	*Scottish Historical Review*
TGSI	*Transactions of the Gaelic Society of Inverness*
Thompson, *Motif-Index*	Stith Thompson, *Motif-Index of Folk Literature*, 6 vols. 1955–8; Bloomington, Indiana: Indiana University Press, 1966.

Acknowledgements

I am indebted to several friends and colleagues for their advice and support during the preparation of this book and assistance with the conference that originally inspired this collection. A big thank you to Professor Richard Finlay (University of Strathclyde), Professor James MacMillan (University of Edinburgh), Mrs Anne-Marie Baran, Dr Kirsty McAlister, and the ever-helpful staff at the National Archives of Scotland. Gratitude must also be extended to the Strathmartine Trust for financial support, and to everyone at Birlinn, especially Mairi Sutherland and Hazel Reid. My greatest debt of thanks is to Ted Cowan for sharing his extensive knowledge and wisdom with me, if not always delivered with his characteristic good humour and patience!

Lizanne Henderson

Introduction
Studying the Supernatural History of Scotland

Lizanne Henderson

. . . it is declarit that all ydle personis ganging about in ony cuntrie of this realme using subtill, crafty and unlauchfull playis, as juglarie fast and lowis, and sic utheris, the idle people calling thame selffis Egyptianis [gypsies], or ony utheris that fenyeis thame selffis to have knawlege of prophecie, charmeing or utheris abusit sciences, quhairby they persuaid the people that they can tell thair weardis [fate] deathis and fortunes and sic uther fantasticall imaginationes.[1]

The term 'folklore' has been a problematic one, since it was coined in 1846 by William Thoms,[2] for it has been 'predicated on the death of tradition'.[3] What many of the pioneering folklorists forgot to mention was that as quickly as one tradition dies, another is born, and so folklore goes on refreshed and renewed. However, whatever the drawbacks of the word, it caught on quickly in the British Isles and was cemented with the creation of The Folk-Lore Society (1878) in London, of which prolific Scots writer Andrew Lang was a founding member.[4] Elsewhere other terms were adopted instead of, or as well as, 'folklore'; for instance, the German *volkskunde*, French *traditions populaires*, Italian *storia delle tradizioni populari* and Swedish *folklivsforskning* (folklife research). The Irish have *Béaloideas* (*béal* 'mouth' and *oideas* 'instruction') which carries the

---

1. *RPS* (27 Oct. 1579) 'For punishment of the strang and ydle beggaris'. Similar legislation was passed in 1575.
2. William Thoms, using the name Ambrose Merton, wrote to *The Athenaeum* in 1846 to suggest that instead of the definition 'Popular Antiquities, or Popular Literature' a better terminology might be found 'by a good Saxon compound, Folklore – *the Lore of the People*'. *The Athenaeum* No. 982 (22 August 1846) 862–3, reprinted as William Thoms, 'Folklore', in *The Study of Folklore*, ed. Alan Dundes (Englewood Cliffs, NJ: Prentice-Hall, 1965) 4–6.
3. Diarmuid Ó Giolláin, *Locating Irish Folklore: Tradition, Modernity, Identity* (Cork: Cork University Press, 2000) 8.
4. Other founding members, often referred to as the 'Great Team', included G. L. Gomme, Edwin Sidney Hartland, Edward Clodd and Alfred Nutt.

sense of orally communicated tradition.⁵ Folklore is understood to embrace all aspects of folk activity such as belief, custom, expressive forms and behaviours, folktale and story-telling, ballad, music and song, folk drama, crafts and material culture, calendar customs, courtship, marriage, and child-rearing, indeed all facets of culture in the widest sense. However, it could be argued that the retreat from folklore began almost at the moment of its discovery as the everyday assumptions and understandings of the subordinate classes were gradually degraded, dismissed and demonised by the learned as 'fantastical imaginations'.

The folklorist William Henderson, a native of Durham, expressed some of the difficulties of the task he faced in the introduction to his study of the borderlands between England and Scotland. 'It is difficult, while living on the surface of society, so smooth, so rational, so commonplace, to realise what relics of a widely different past linger in its depths'. He was, like many of his contemporaries, both in England and Scotland, concerned that many of the customs and pastimes, stories and legends, were 'fast fading away and perishing', thus it was up to collectors like himself to shoulder the responsibility of preserving the memory of these traditions for future generations. Henderson remarked that his nineteenth century contemporaries both celebrated and lamented the disappearance of folklore: 'I for one will frankly acknowledge that I regret much which we are losing, that I would not have these vestiges of the past altogether effaced'. Paradoxically, Henderson further noted that those 'who mix much among the lower orders, and have opportunities of enquiring closely into their beliefs, customs and usages, will find in remote places – nay, even in our towns and larger villages – a vast mass of superstition, holding its ground most tenaciously'.⁶

The collecting of folklore could have other motives. Rev. James Napier, who gathered his materials primarily from the Glasgow region, did so in order to 'exhibit' the 'degrading influence on society' that superstitions continued to have in the latter half of the nineteenth century. Napier was not convinced, like others of his day, that the superstitions of the eighteenth century had died out, that 'when we speak of the Folk Lore of our grandfathers and great-grandfathers, we believe that we are speaking of beliefs which have passed away, beliefs from which we ourselves are free'. A reconsideration of the matter revealed to him that 'we will find that in many respects our beliefs and practices, although somewhat modernised, are essentially little different from those of last century'.⁷ Setting aside Napier's professional desire to take the high moral ground, his collection is

---

5 Roslyn Blyn-LaDrew, 'Geoffrey Keating, William Thoms, Raymond Williams, and the Terminology of Folklore: "*Béaloideas*" as a "Keyword" ', *Folklore Forum* 27/2: 5–37.
6 William Henderson, *Notes on the Folk Lore of the Northern Counties of England and the Borders* (London: Longmans, Green and Co., 1866) vii, xvii.
7 James Napier, *Folk Lore in the West of Scotland* (1879; Wakefield: EP, 1976) vi–vii.

an invaluable source of traditions and beliefs from his parish, though, at times, his struggle to reconcile folk belief with his own worldview can be erratic and idiosyncratic to say the least.

Folklorists have, like William Henderson, intentionally preserved folkloric material for posterity, while men such as Napier have, no doubt unintentionally, contributed to the survival of the very customs and beliefs that gave such offence. The process of writing down 'folklore' had two curious effects. On the one hand, the information was disseminated to a much wider audience, and thus had the effect of keeping a tradition or belief going for longer than perhaps it might have otherwise. But, on the other hand, the traditions and beliefs became 'frozen in time', encapsulations of either days gone by, examples of quaintness, or worse, barbarism.

The process of using folkloristic material to enhance a particular argument has, of course, a much earlier history than that of the age of the folklorist proper. Just as John Francis Campbell of Islay collected, in the nineteenth century, copious Gaelic folktales and legends, in part to preserve aspects of his culture that he feared were dying out,[8] so too, in the later seventeenth century Robert Kirk recorded incidents of fairy belief and second sight, though in his case, his motives were to protect his religion. The latter's concern was to defend religion against the ravages of atheism. In his view to demonstrate the reality of spirits, demons, fairies, second sight and the rest was to prove the existence of God.

One might justifiably ask why we need to continuously define the genres we study, but as Roger Abrahams points out, 'how we define folklore has an important effect on the way we practice the discipline'.[9] While the dictionary has defined 'folk' as 'a people, nation, race; people of a particular group or class; people in general; one's family or relatives',[10] folklorist Alan Dundes took this one step further when he said 'the term "folk" can refer to any group of people whatsoever who share at least one common factor'.[11] Neither of these definitions is particularly new as a reading of Raymond Williams' *Keywords* reveals. 'Folk' was a common variant in old Teutonic languages. It held a general meaning of 'people', 'in a range from particular social formations, including nations, to people in general . . . it is typically friendly and informal, people seen by one of themselves rather than from above or outside'.[12]

8 J. F. Campbell, *Popular Tales of the West Highlands*, 2 vols. (1860–1; Edinburgh: Birlinn, 1994) and *More West Highland Tales*, 2 vols. (1960; Edinburgh: Birlinn, 1994).
9 Roger D. Abrahams, 'Personal Power and Social Restraint in the definition of Folklore', *Journal of American Folklore* 84 (1971): 16.
10 'Folk', *Funk and Wagnalls Standard Dictionary*, 2 vols. (New York: Collins, 1970).
11 Alan Dundes, 'What is Folklore?', in *The Study of Folklore*, ed. Alan Dundes (London: Prentice-Hall, 1965) 2.
12 Raymond Williams, *Keywords* (London: Fontana Press, 1976) 136.

There have been many scholarly attempts made to define and explain folk belief.[13] In the Early Modern period, when popular culture and folk belief were under threat as never before, the quest often involved distinguishing supernatural or magical beliefs, as held by the folk, from supernatural or magical beliefs, as expressed in religion. Separation of these two ideas was a painful, and often a fruitless exercise.

Fundamentally, a folk belief is something that is communally held to be true. The level of belief may vary in degree or intensity, or alter from time to time, or situation to situation. But why, one might reasonably ask, does one person or societal group, interpret a given event as a natural event, while another opts for a supernatural explanation. It is easier to accept that a person may have good reason to give a paranormal interpretation when they have personally been the object of the occurrence. It is perhaps more difficult to explain why someone who has not personally been involved in 'unexplained' phenomena should adopt the supernatural as a hypothetical explanation. Such a person could, in other words, believe that fairies were capable of the abduction of humans without ever having been abducted themselves, or even having known someone who had been so 'taken'. Culture, and what is regarded as culturally acceptable and/or viable, has much to do with how a person interprets, or comes to terms with, a given event. The man who insists that his child, or his wife, was stolen by the fairies will only be believed by his peers if such an explanation seems credible to them also.

Two major belief narrative genres are legend and memorate.[14] The distinction between the two is the level of belief expressed both in the narrative and by the narrator. William Bascom defines legend as a prose narrative generally accepted as true by both the narrator and the audience. Legends are set in the recent past, in a world not far removed from today. More often the attitude is secular as opposed to sacred and the principle characters are human.[15] The believability of the legend is, according to Linda Dégh, the cornerstone of this genre.[16] The memorate is essentially a personal experience narrative. As the legend is believed because it

---

13 A particularly interesting study is that of David Hufford, who concentrates on the 'Old Hag' tradition in *The Terror That Comes in the Night: An Experience-Centered Study of Supernatural Assault Traditions* (Philadelphia: University of Pennsylvania Press, 1982). For Scotland, see Lizanne Henderson and Edward J. Cowan, eds, *Scottish Fairy Belief: A History* (2001; Edinburgh: John Donald, 2007). An attempt to study the psychological reasons behind current 'superstitious' beliefs is Stuart A. Vyse, *Believing in Magic: The Psychology of Superstition* (Oxford: Oxford University Press, 1997).
14 The exemplar is similar to legend, is told as an instructional tale and usually is about saints. The dite does not generally deal with any particular individual.
15 William Bascom, 'The Forms of Folklore: Prose Narrative', *Journal of American Folklore* 78 (1965): 3–20.
16 Linda Dégh, 'What is the Legend After All?', *Contemporary Legend* 1 (1991): 23–5.

happened to someone else, the memorate is believed because it happened to the narrator. A memorate can in time develop into a legend.[17] The major difference between the memorate and the legend lies in the level of interpretation given. Memorates rarely offer statements of personal interpretation. Conversely, legends have a tendency to stress interpretation. The fact that memorates are accounts of an individual's actual experience makes them the most vibrant belief form. Recovering memorates, or first person accounts, is problematic but not impossible in an historical context. They may be preserved, for example – even at one remove – in witch trial statements, which can sometimes offer the closest thing to the true voice of the folk if the material is handled carefully and with caution.[18] Margaret Bennett's contribution to this volume discusses the relationship between memorate and legend, specifically in a Gaelic context.

Folk custom is an integral part of culture. It operates as an invisible framework which guides and supports nearly every other aspect of folk belief and practice. When someone made a journey to a holy or healing well, it was customary practice that took them there, which might or might not have involved belief in the magical attributes of the well water.[19] After about 1650 scholars began to make distinctions between popular or folk culture and elite culture. Though folk beliefs and practices were largely rejected they nevertheless continued to fascinate. John Aubrey, who derived a significant amount of his information from Scotland through correspondence, opined that 'old customs and old wives-fables are gross things: but yet ought not to be quite rejected: there may be some truth and usefulness be elicited out of them: besides, 'tis a pleasure to consider the errors that enveloped former ages: as also the present'.[20] It should be understood, however, that in earlier centuries the term, 'custom', embraced much of what is today carried by the word culture. In the works of Scottish historians from the sixteenth- to the eighteenth- centuries the sense was conveyed by the word 'manners'. It has been said that sixteenth-century historians such as Hector Boece and John Leslie were at their most interesting when discussing 'the auld Scottis maneris'.[21] Francis Bacon, much read and respected in Scotland,

17 Lauri Honko, 'Memorates and the Study of Folk Beliefs', *Journal of American Folklore* 1 (1964): 12.
18 Arguments in defence of using witch trial testimonies are found in the work of Carlo Ginzburg, *Ecstasies: Deciphering the Witches' Sabbath*, trans. R. Rosenthal (New York: Pantheon, 1991). See also Henderson and Cowan, *Scottish Fairy Belief*, and chapter 7 below.
19 Lizanne Henderson, 'Charmers Spells and Holy Wells: The Repackaging of Belief', *Review of Scottish Culture* (April 2007) 10–26.
20 John Aubrey, 'Remains', in *Three Prose Works* (Fontwell, 1972) 132, quoted in Peter Burke, *Popular Culture in Early Modern Europe* (New York: Harper, 1978) 283.
21 Edward J. Cowan, 'The Discovery of the Gàidhealtachd in Sixteenth Century Scotland', *TGSI* 60, 1997–8 (2000): 259–84.

described custom as induced and habitual inertial behaviour; 'Men Profess, Protest, Engage, Give Great Words, and then Doe just as they have Done before. As if they were Dead Images, and Engines moved onely by the Wheeles of *Custome*'. For Bacon, custom was a conceivable way to encourage better habits early on in life; 'Since Custom is the principal Magistrate of Man's Life, let Men, by all means, endeavour to obtain good Customs . . . Custom is most perfect when it beginneth in young Years; This we call Education, which is, in Effect, but an early Custom'.[22]

The folklorist G. L. Gomme, described folklore as customs, rites and beliefs belonging to the people:

> And oftentimes in definite antagonism to the accepted customs, rites and beliefs of the State or the nation to which the people and the groups of people belong. These customs, rites and beliefs are mostly kept alive by tradition . . . They owe their preservation partly to the fact that great masses of people do not belong to the civilisation which towers over them and which is never of their own creation.[23]

It could thus be said that custom, from the eighteenth century onwards, was the rhetoric of legitimisation for almost any usage, practice, or demanded right and, hence, was continually subject to change. By the late nineteenth and twentieth centuries, the understanding of custom began to fall under the sway of anthropological and sociological influences. Custom is used to apply to the 'totality of behaviour patterns which are carried by tradition and lodged in the group, as contrasted with the more random personal activities of the individual'. Anthropological definitions state that custom is 'a habit which is socially learned, socially performed, and socially transmitted'. Sociology also adopted the term as meaning, 'social practice or usage that is shared in the group as tradition and learned by the individual as habit. The group within which it is shared may be a society or a sub-group of society'.[24]

Jan Harold Brunvand claims to integrate a variety of terms, concepts, and points of view in his pursuit of a suitable definition of custom. Unfortunately, he falls back on the safety net of 'tradition' to explicate the complexity of folk custom: 'a custom is a traditional *practice* – a mode of individual behaviour or

---

22 Francis Bacon, quoted in E. P. Thompson, *Customs in Common* (London: Merlin, 1991) 2.
23 Thompson, *Customs in Common*, 6.
24 E. Sapir, 'Custom', in *Encyclopaedia of the Social Sciences*, ed. E. R. A. Seligman (New York: MacMillan, 1930); J. Gillin, *The Ways of Men* (New York: Appleton-Century, 1948); 'Custom', *A Dictionary of the Social Sciences*, ed. J. Gould and W. L. Kolb (New York: Free Press, 1964).

a habit of social life – that is transmitted by word of mouth or imitation, then ingrained by social pressure, common usage, and parental or other authority'.[25] Perhaps a more stable, descriptive encapsulation of folk custom occurs in the following:

> Customs do things – they are not abstract formulations of, or searches for, meanings, although they may convey meaning. Customs are clearly connected to, and rooted in, the material and social realities of life and work, although they are not simply derivative from, or re-expressions of these realities. Customs may provide a context in which people may do things it would be more difficult to do directly . . . they may keep the need for collective action, collective adjustment of interests, and collective expression of feelings and emotions within the terrain and domain of the coparticipants in a custom, serving as a boundary to exclude outsiders.[26]

The central purpose of folk customs is hard to pinpoint, though it would seem that they reinforce and promote social cohesion within a group or society. While there are no hard and fast definitions for folk custom, it is, for the most part, based on tradition and repetition – and is temporally or spatially located. It must be borne in mind, however, that custom is not a static repetition of tradition.

It has been noted that human beings have consistently organised their lives around many 'fields of symbolic action'. What differentiates present day behaviour from that of our predecessors is not so much that our way of thinking 'is grounded on science and theirs on symbolism', for 'our behaviour also carries symbolic meaning'. Rather,

> the real difference is that we do not bring forward from one context to the next the same set of ever more powerful symbols: our experience is fragmented. Our rituals create a lot of little sub-worlds, unrelated. Their rituals create one single, symbolically consistent universe.[27]

With hindsight, it can be seen that Scottish people from around 1740 were no longer operating within a 'symbolically consistent universe' but were in the process of creating several different galaxies, each competing and jostling

---

25 Jan Harold Brunvand, *The Study of American Folklore: An Introduction* (New York: Norton, 1986) 328.
26 Thompson, *Customs in Common*, 13.
27 Mary Douglas, *Purity and Danger: An Analysis of the Concepts of Pollution and Taboo* (1966; London: Ark Paperbacks, 1984) 69.

for position with the next. The belief, or unbelief, in supernatural phenomena such as second sight, fairies, witches, witchcraft and charming, was just one of many realms of Scottish intellectual, social and political life to experience the full brunt of a meteor shower. The various contributors to this book explore aspects of folk belief and folk culture both before and after the fallout. Chapters which deal with either the earlier period or the lengthy era of transition are Ted Cowan's erudite discussion of prophecy and second sight, Louise Yeoman's insightful investigation of prophetesses during the time of the Covenanters, George Brunsden's fascinating essay on astrology and almanacs, Hugh Cheape's important contribution on the topic of charms and amulets, and Lizanne Henderson's intriguing exploration of witch narratives and folktale.

Historians have generally viewed the eighteenth century as a period when customary practices were in decline, a phenomenon illuminated by Colin Kidd in his essay, in this collection, on the Scottish Enlightenment and the supernatural. Pressures to 'reform' popular culture were coming from above; oral tradition was being displaced by literacy; enlightenment (it is supposed) was filtering down from the elite to the common folk. However, the historian E. P. Thompson has argued that customary consciousness and customary usages were especially robust in the eighteenth century and attempts to 'reform' customs were stubbornly resisted.[28] What is certain is that the century witnessed a profound alienation between the culture of the aristocracy and the common folk. The social historian Peter Burke suggested this emergent gulf was a European phenomenon, and that one consequence was the birth of folklore. Early folklorists, holding much the same view as that expressed by John Aubrey, went in search of the 'Little Tradition' of the plebeians, to record their strange customs and rituals. Aside from the patronising tone, what is significant here is the notion of customs as 'survivals' from a bygone era, in desperate peril of vanishing into the mists of time, if left unrecorded.[29]

The widespread view that early modern Scotland was culturally divided into two main competing aggregations of belief may well be convenient for the sake of clarity but is, to say the least, problematic. In one we find the literati, the men of learning, of superior education and high culture, members of a circle which revolved around universities, literary and scientific societies, political, legal and medical institutions, and the church. It was, in proportion to the population, a small, but nonetheless, powerful group. The other party, or commonalty, to which

---

28 Thompson, *Customs in Common*, 1.
29 Barbara Myerhoff, 'Rites of Passage: Process and Paradox', *Celebration*, ed. V. Turner (Washington DC: Smithsonian, 1982) 116. Victorian anthropology had an ethnocentric bent, valued its own usages as the measure of all things, and sought for the origins of customs with a vested interest in establishing the phases of human evolution.

the vast majority of the people belonged, comprised 'the folk', the unlettered, those of inferior, or at least of limited, education. Family life, occupation, the church, and possibly the parish school, were the fundamental institutions in their lives. This group largely depended on an oral culture and while its numbers were greater, it was increasingly subordinated by the purveyors of the written word. This recognisable division between 'high' and 'low' culture is cognisant of only the extreme differences presented by the two cultures and pays little attention to the many instances and occasions of overlap and integration, when two worlds or mentalities collide and form a sort of 'middle' culture, for lack of a better word. The problem for the historian or the folklorist is that people's thoughts, attitudes and aspirations cannot easily be pigeon-holed, categorised or labelled. It is, after all, human individuality that makes us interesting, if not a little challenging.

It was said of Britain in general that 'in the tranquil mood of the nineteenth century, the wars of church and state safely behind, and the battle of reason over superstition clearly won, Victorian gentry could smile at vulgar antiquities as the heritage of the unlettered and the unknowing'.[30] The veracity of this statement is questionable, though it does, perhaps, capture the mood of the times it describes, to some extent. The average household of an early nineteenth century gentleperson would almost certainly have contained a copy of John Brand's *Observations on Popular Antiquities* (1777; revised 1813), which was a truly monumental achievement and has been described as having 'laid the foundations for the science of folklore'.[31]

The fascination with 'things that go bump in the night' was far from cleansed from the supposedly 'enlightened' minds of a new generation of commentators and increasingly avid readers. One of the most well-read and influential of these figures was Sir Walter Scott. His Waverley novels are lavishly embellished with supernatural elements.[32] He also printed a large number of ballads in the *Minstrelsy of the Scottish Borders* (1802)[33] and penned *Letters on Demonologie and Witchcraft* (1830). Like many writers before him, Scott distanced himself

---

30 Richard Dorson, *The British Folklorists: A History* (London: Routledge and Kegan Paul, 1968) 19.
31 John Brand, *Observations on Popular Antiquities: chiefly illustrating the origin of our Vulgar Customs, Ceremonies and Superstitions*, 2 vols., revised with additions by Henry Ellis (Newcastle on Tyne, 1777; London, 1813); Dorson, *British Folklorists*, 17.
32 See Coleman O. Parsons, *Witchcraft and Demonology in Scott's Fiction, with chapters on the Supernatural in Scottish Literature* (Edinburgh and London: Oliver and Boyd, 1964) and chapter 6 below.
33 Sir Walter Scott, *Minstrelsy of the Scottish Borders: Consisting of Historical and Romantic Ballads*, 3 vols. (Kelso: James Ballantyne, 1802–3; London: Thomas Tegg, 1839; 4 vols. Edinburgh, 1932).

from his material by placing it within the eighteenth-century framework of such perceived opposites as credulity/incredulity, belief/unbelief, savage/civilised, ignorance/enlightenment, black/white, and all leavened with a heavy dose of sympathetic criticism. And yet, for all his seeming efforts, his deep fascination and intrigue with the occult and invisible worlds shines brightly from each page. Scott died in 1832 but his fame and popularity continued to live on; he was just as likely to be consulted as Brand's *Popular Antiquities*, on questions relating to folklore and the supernatural. Douglas Gifford shows the perennial appeal of the supernatural and the occult in Scottish literature in his discussion of 'Nathaniel Gow's Toddy'.

A good friend of Scott's was Robert Chambers, born in Peebles but who moved to Edinburgh as a young lad of eleven years. Aged only twenty-two, Chambers produced the first study of urban folklore, *Traditions of Edinburgh* (1824) which revelled in such tales as those surrounding the infamous Major Weir and his less famous, but nevertheless sinister, younger sister Jean. The second volume he respectfully dedicated to Scott who had supplied him with some of his material. Scott was also a helpful contributor to Chamber's second enterprise, *The Popular Rhymes of Scotland* (1826; 1841), and a third publication, *Scottish Jests and Anecdotes* (1832) included many stories from one of Scott's chief informants, Mrs. Keith. Chamber's *pièce de resistance* was *The Book of Days* (1862-4) which based its framework not only on that established by other prolific antiquarians such as John Brand, John Aubrey and William Hone, but also on the groundbreaking work of men such as the Gaelic collector, John Francis Campbell of Islay, who produced his four volume *Popular Tales of the West Highlands* (1860-2).[34]

William Grant Stewart introduced a fresh approach by classifying supernatural phenomena into distinct categories in *The Popular Superstitions and Festive Amusements of the Highlanders of Scotland* (1823), a format still in vogue today. Stewart worked hard to delineate the differences between the ghost and the fairy, the fairy and the witch, while other writers, such as Scott's *Letters* (which came out seven years later) tended to stress the overlap between these traditions. Stewart claims to have collected many of his tales and anecdotes from oral tradition though he confesses to having edited them down for ease of publication;

---

34 Robert Chambers, *Traditions of Edinburgh*, 2 vols. (Edinburgh, 1824), *The Popular Rhymes of Scotland* (Edinburgh and London, 1826; Edinburgh, 1841), *Scottish Jests and Anecdotes* (Edinburgh, 1832) and *The Book of Days*, 2 vols. (London and Edinburgh, 1862-4); J. F. Campbell, *Popular Tales of the West Highlands*, 2 vols. (1860-2; Edinburgh: Birlinn, 1994) and *More West Highland Tales*, 2 vols. (1940; 1960; Edinburgh: Birlinn, 1994).

the length of those primitive relations is necessarily much abridged, but a strict regard has been had to their original style and phraseology. The language is almost entirely borrowed from the mouth of the Highland narrator, and translated, it is hoped, in a manner so simple and unvarnished, as to be perfectly intelligible to the capacity of the peasant, for whose fireside entertainment this little volume may, perhaps, be peculiarly adapted.[35]

In another part of the country, Hugh Miller, the famed geologist and all-round polymath, was amassing the first ever collection of folkloric and oral narrative materials from Cromarty and the Black Isle. Miller's vast canon, and in particular *Scenes and Legends of the North of Scotland* (1835)[36] has received limited acknowledgement as an early, if not the first, contribution to the folklore of the area. An exception was Richard Dorson, who praised *Scenes and Legends*, as exceeding 'all expectation for a pioneer collection of local narratives and merits a recognition it has never received, as a superb record of folk traditions seen in their full context of village society and history'.[37] There must be many reasons why Miller decided upon a collection of local and personal tales and legends, but the most apparent was his obsession with the idea that such traditions were dying out and it was essential to record them before they were gone altogether.

The field methods employed by John Francis Campell of Islay, when he set out to collect the traditional stories of the *Gàidhealtachd*, were unique for the times. While other commentators had concentrated their efforts within the libraries and archives of Edinburgh, Campbell tried out something new and truly innovative; he employed and sent out a trained team of Gaelic speakers to interview informants over the entire Highland and Western Isles region. The sheer quantity of material amassed by Campbell and his team was so great that most of it still languishes in the National Library of Scotland, as yet unpublished. The stories that made it to publication in the *Popular Tales* represents a fraction of what was

---

35 William Grant Stewart, T*he Popular Superstitions and Festive Amusements of the Highlanders of Scotland* (Edinburgh: Constable, 1823) xv–xvi.
36 Hugh Miller, *Scenes and Legends of the North of Scotland or the Traditional History of Cromarty*, ed. J. Robertson (1835; Edinburgh: B and W, 1994).
37 Dorson, *British Folklorists*, 138, 140. On Hugh Miller as folklorist see Lizanne Henderson, 'The Natural and Supernatural Worlds of Hugh Miller', in *Celebrating the Life and Times of Hugh Miller: Scotland in the Early 19th Century*, ed. L. Borley (Cromarty Arts Trust, 2003) 89–98. See also David Alston, 'The Fallen Meteor: Hugh Miller and Local Tradition', in *Hugh Miller and the Controversies of Victorian Science*, ed. M. Shortland (Oxford: Oxford University Press, 1996), James Robertson, 'Scenes, Legends and Storytelling in the Making of Hugh Miller', in *Hugh Miller in Context*, ed. L. Borley (Cromarty Arts Trust, 2002).

actually collected. A notable modern collector, John MacInnes, demonstrates in his contribution, the relationship between Gaelic folk tradition and the church.

As the nineteenth century drew to a close, the church-driven desire to expunge all remnants of 'pagan' or 'popish' relics began to recede from the texts to be replaced with an ethnographic, anthropological and historical approach to 'survivalisms'. There were a few exceptions, such as James Napier's already mentioned *Superstitious Beliefs in the West of Scotland* who defined superstition as 'beliefs and practices founded upon erroneous ideas of God and nature'.[38] But, for most collectors, the main concern resided in the preservation of tradition from a position of academic interest. One such was Lewis Spence, whose underrated achievement in the field of folk studies is assessed by Juliette Wood. The phenomenon of modern, supposed, folk revivals is considered in Valentina Bold's exploration of the cult movie 'The Wicker Man'.

---

38 Napier, *Folk Lore in the West of Scotland*, 4.

ONE

The Discovery of the Future: Prophecy and Second Sight in Scottish History

Edward J. Cowan

And it shall come to pass afterward that I will pour out my spirit upon all flesh; and your sons and your daughters shall prophesy, your old men shall dream dreams, your young men shall see visions.   Joel II: 28

'They are millenarians sprung from the millenarian demon, who have skills for leading a thousand astray', proclaimed Walter Bower, in the 1440s. 'They are dragons in the air, flying across the countryside, on earth creeping with earthly things . . . accursed children . . . inveterate liars, deviants from the pathways of the law through whom Satan has sought to sift us like wheat.' These supposed fiends were Wycliffites, despicable heretics who were no doubt, to some extent at least, motivated by notions of the apocalyptic. They denied that the pope was the vicar of Christ and they claimed, sensibly enough, but erroneously, that no unsaintly man could ever hold papal office.[1] Some 250 years later, partially inspired, we may think, by similar ideas about the Last Days, a group of prominent Scots were to turn their minds to the possible scientific basis of prophecy and second sight – people like Robert Kirk, at different times minister of Balquhidder and Aberfoyle, a man who spent much time and energy in the production of an Irish bible, George Sinclair, Professor of Natural Philosophy at Glasgow, Robert Wodrow, historian of the sufferings of the Church of Scotland, George, third Lord Reay of Durness, Lord Tarbat, later first Earl of Cromarty and Sir George Mackenzie of Rosehaugh sometime Lord Advocate of Scotland, among a host of others, many of whom were associated with the Royal Society in London. Ideas about prophecy of course abounded long before the time of Bower but from the fourteenth- to the seventeenth-centuries the reality and efficacy of prognostication were widely accepted, when it was assumed that the future was, in certain respects, as knowable as the past, and when prophecy entered the mainstream of Scottish political culture. While historians have

---

1 Walter Bower, *Scotichronicon*, ed. D. E. R. Watt, 9 vols. (Aberdeen and Edinburgh: Aberdeen University Press, 1989–98) vol. 8, 69–71.

often debated when the Middle Ages in Scotland ended, the group of scholars known as the 'Scottish Medievalists'[2] long ago agreed on the terminus of 1638, a date which might be rather too optimistic. An alternative may be offered with the opponents of Sadduceeism (materialistic unbelief) in the late seventeenth-century, on the very eve of the Scottish Enlightenment. That even this view might be somewhat over-sanguine may be suggested by Marjorie Reeves' observation that 'perhaps we might say that only when intelligent and educated men ceased to take prophecy seriously were the Middle Ages truly at an end'.[3]

In Scotland this subject, along with the supernatural in general, has been unaccountably ignored by mainstream historians, and thus one huge chunk of human experience, interest and concern, has been excised.[4] There has been a pretence that it was a non-issue, irrelevant, or at best an aberration. God himself is, of course, the ultimate 'supernatural', a word first used in the sixteenth century. However the study of the providential, of God's role in history, despite its undoubted importance, is not of present concern. Rather the aim is to explore the 'fantastical imaginatiounes' which involved and informed almost all aspects of Scottish history and literature and which are generally assumed to represent the exact opposite of the godly, namely those beliefs which are generally described as 'superstition' – Bower's *supervacuitas* – and which impacted upon all classes of society at almost all periods of history, Scottish or otherwise.

Thanks to the severe and oft-expressed reservations of Enlightenment writers concerning superstition, such matters, if they were mentioned at all, were mainly dismissed as the crass and craven delusions of a barbarous era, or, when confronted contemporaneously, as evidence of monstrous ignorance.[5] Such attitudes embraced the rejection and negation of the experience and beliefs of

---

2 The Scottish Medievalists meet annually in January for a weekend conference. An early version of this paper was first presented to that conference in 2000 and it has had several outings since, for example at the universities of Sydney and Tasmania and elsewhere.
3 Marjorie Reeves, *The Influence of Prophecy in the Later Middle Ages: A Study in Joachism* (1969; London and Notre Dame: University of Notre Dame Press, 1993) 508. See also Marjorie Reeves, *Joachim of Fiore and The Prophetic Future: A Medieval Study in Historical Thinking* (Stroud: Sutton, 1999).
4 I have greatly profited from Athol Gow, *Prophetic Belief in Early Modern Scotland*, unpublished MA thesis, University of Guelph 1989. For a popular treatment of the subject see Elizabeth Sutherland, *Ravens and Black Rain: The Story of Highland Second Sight* (London: Constable, 1985). Among useful recent publications are T. Thornton and B. Taithe, *Prophecy: The Power of Inspired Language in History 1300-2000* (Stroud: Sutton, 1997) and Lesley A. Coote, *Prophecy and Public Affairs in Later Medieval England* (York: York Medieval Press, 2000).
5 Edward J. Cowan, 'Burns and Superstition', in *Love and Liberty. Robert Burns: A Bicentenary Celebration*, ed. Kenneth Simpson (East Linton: Tuckwell Press, 1997) 229–38.

a majority of the population, even in the eighteenth century, much of whose history was thus consigned to oblivion.

The supernatural appears to take central stage in the sixteenth and seventeenth centuries, the era of the witch-hunts in which healers and seers, as well as alleged witches, were sucked into the vortex of persecution. The notorious sabbat at North Berwick kirk, on Halloween 1589, launched the demonic pact upon Scotland, revealed in a colourful and confused amalgam of legal testimony, folk tradition, learned lore, pamphleteering, pornography, magic, folk medicine, spells, conjurations and political conspiracy.[6] We are only just beginning to accept that what have previously been regarded as the deluded rantings of tortured victims are actually meaningful texts, which can be deconstructed to reveal much of great value about folk or popular belief.[7] James VI, the target of the North Berwick conspiracy, basking as he did in the title of 'the greatest enemy the Devil hath in the world', looked for a time as if he was about to become involved in a kind of cosmic struggle with the powers of darkness, but after penning his *Demonologie* (1597), he backed off. His withdrawal, however, did not save hundreds of poor wretches from the stake, and popular accusations of witchcraft survived well into the nineteenth century.[8]

Describing the 'dark and drublie days' just at the outbreak of the Montrose wars in 1644–5 Patrick Gordon of Ruthven noted in his *History* 'divers prodigies' indicative of the catastrophes to come. Strange motions were seen in the air 'as of armed men in battle ranged to fight'. Near Banff phantom armies were observed to be engaging in hostilities; panic-stricken, neighbourhood people, hearing the thundering shot and the clash of arms, buried their valuables, in nearby bogs. The sun in a clear sky was seen only dimly or appeared as a pool of blood. At Ellon the minister roused some of his parishioners to witness the sun shining brightly between midnight and one in the morning, a prodigious omen interpreted to signify that just as the sun shone when night was darkest, so, 'when the obscurest and darkest plots of the Covenant shall reach their zenith or greatest height, God, pitying our extreme afflictions, shall raise to

---

6 Edward J. Cowan, 'The Darker Vision of the Scottish Renaissance: The Devil and Francis Stewart', in *The Renaissance and Reformation in Scotland*, ed. Ian B. Cowan and Duncan Shaw (Edinburgh: Scottish Academic Press, 1983) 125–40.
7 Lizanne Henderson and Edward J. Cowan, *Scottish Fairy Belief: A History* (2001; Edinburgh: John Donald, 2007) *passim*. See also Edward J. Cowan, 'Witch Persecution and Folk Belief in Lowland Scotland: The Devil's Decade', in *Witchcraft and Belief in Early Modern Scotland*, ed. J. Goodare, L. Martin and J. Miller (Basingstoke: Palgrave Macmillan, 2008) 71–94.
8 Edward J. Cowan and Lizanne Henderson, 'The Last of the Witches? The Survival of Scottish Witch Belief', in *The Scottish Witch-Hunt in Context*, ed. Julian Goodare (Manchester: Manchester University Press, 2002) 198–217.

us the true sun or light of true religion'. Elsewhere in Buchan, on consecutive days at the time of morning prayer, a choir accompanied by organs and other instruments was heard to produce music of a ravishing sweetness in the upper loft of a kirk. The musicians were invisible but the music ended on a long note, 'or stroke of a *viola da gamba*'. Most remarkable of all, a piece of heaven-mounted ordnance,

> did ring in the eares of everie man, woman and child throughout the whole kingdome, as if it had beene levelled and shote at themselfes, as well in the houses as in the fieldes, and in all the partes or corners of the kingdome, not only in one day and one houre, but at one moment of tyme.

At that precise instant Alasdair Mac Colla landed in the west to drown the covenant in oceans of blood.[9]

For the rest of the century portents, omens, apparitions, and prophecies were to abound. Montrose and the royalists might have taken some comfort from a prophecy which stated that a squint-eyed, red-haired Earl of Argyll would be the last of his race while that same Argyll, the leader of the Covenanters and by far the most powerful clan chief in all of the *Gàidhealtachd*, had his own spin doctors who were on hand in 1640–41 to reassure their patron, in a Gaelic poem, of a glorious future. Only the translation has survived.

> I gave Argyll the praise
> because all men sees it is treuth;
> for he will tak geir from the lawland men;
> and he will tak the Croun per force;
> and he will cry King at Whitsonday.[10]

Patrick Walker, writing of 'that good, ill-time of persecution', the 1670s and 1680s when government dragoons exploited state terror to hunt down and slaughter those who adhered to the covenant, noted many a portent of future calamity, including moors covered with the apparitions of men, women and tents, where one day conventicles (open air services of worship) would be held. Other places resounded to the chorus of ghostly psalm singing. Near Falkirk a phantom congregation on a hillside was seen and heard to sing the

---

9 All references on portents in the North-East, an area opposed to the Covenanters, are drawn from Patrick Gordon of Ruthven, *A Short Abridgement of Britane's Distemper from the yeare of God M.DC.XXXIX. to M.DC.XLIX* (Aberdeen: Spalding Club, 1845) 62–3.
10 Edward J. Cowan, *Montrose For Covenant and King* (1977; Edinburgh: Canongate, 1995) 94.

121st psalm, while nearby stood a milk-white horse with a blood-red saddle on his back. Showers of swords and bonnets outside Glasgow were thought to predict the advent of the Highland Host in 1678. After the battle of Bothwell Brig a comet appeared. In the bitter winter of 1683–4 graves were found on moors frozen hard as iron, presaging deaths to come. Walker himself visited Crossford on the Clyde near Lesmahagow, hoping to witness various reported prodigies, which included such phenomena as showers of weapons and protective headgear, and sightings of opposing armies which seemed to march through one another before falling to the ground and disappearing, only to reform and repeat the process. He saw nothing, though he conversed with many who did. 'I have been at a loss ever since what to make of this last: however a profane age may mock, disdain, and make sport of these extraordinary things, yet these are no new things, but some such things have been in former times'.[11]

Scotland's most neglected folklorist, Robert Wodrow, laboriously recorded numerous portents associated with the suffering bleeding remnant during the 'Killing Times'. Dozens of condemned Covenanters made dying predictions on the gallows, their utterances taken so seriously that the government introduced the practice of drum-rolls to drown out their potentially subversive farewells.

During the eighteenth century, numerous travellers visited Scotland hoping to hear first-hand accounts of supernatural experiences. In 1815 the learned world headed by Sir Walter Scott was electrified by the Brahan Seer's reported prophecy concerning the 'Doom of the Seaforths'.[12] As popular as those of the Seer, known in Gaeldom as Coinneach Odhar, were the predictions of Rev. John Morrison, 'The Seer of Petty' who died about 1774. In 1861 John Kennedy recorded many of the words of *Na Duine*, or 'The Men', evangelical lay preachers, including the prophecies of his own father, the minister of Killearnan.[13] Elsewhere in this book John MacInnes provides several more recent examples of those in possession of the gift.

Yet even Walter Bower in the fifteenth century had a tendency to suggest that the more outlandish examples of superstition (which derives from Latin *superstitio*, quite simply a term for any non-Roman belief) occurred in the dim and distant past. Indeed most chroniclers, such as Fordun and Wyntoun as

---

11 Patrick Walker, *Six Saints of the Covenant*, ed. D. Hay Fleming, 2 vols. (London: Hodder and Stoughton, 1901) vol. 1, 32–8.
12 Alexander Mackenzie, *The Prophecies of the Brahan Seer (Coinneach Odhar Fiosaiche)* (1899; Golspie: Sutherland Press, 1970) 89–93, 99–108.
13 John Kennedy, *The Days of the Fathers in Ross-shire* (1861; Inverness: Christian Focus Publications, 1979) 129–98.

well as the poet, Barbour, were concerned to eschew the fabulous in favour of 'suthfastness' or truth, and almost all are explicit on the point.[14] There are several potentially rewarding research projects in the medieval supernatural. Bower describes mystical stones, *lapides mistici*, standing and inaugural. He subscribes to the old legends of Britain as a Land of Giants. He has a lengthy and fascinating discussion of the heathen gods and the process of euhemerism that produced them. In this context Bower approvingly quotes Petronius; 'it was fear that first caused gods to appear in the world', and, it might be added, much else to appear as well. He describes simultaneous or synchronic visions – people beholding distant events while they are taking place. Other topics include an example of the living dead, dragons and portents, bloody rain, comets, numerous miracles, and a woman with a musical posterior, but the chronicler affects to remain the dispassionate and objective reporter.

> What ridiculous stupidity to think that a historian should address his pen to such stories – I will not call them apocryphal, but also pure inventions vainly and gratuitously conceived! Anyone in his senses would refuse to believe them.

Although guilty of the practice himself he condemned historians who took the trouble to insert old wives' tales or 'silly tales of old men'. He agreed with Seneca that such nonsense was best left to the poets, 'whose purpose it is to charm men's ears and weave a pleasant tale'. Those, on the other hand, 'who wish to heal minds and keep faith in human affairs and to inculcate in men's minds remembrance of the past, speak seriously and strive mightily to proclaim the truth.'[15] Yet Bower does not for one moment doubt the efficacy of prophecy. He is much taken with Merlin and Arthur, the prophecies of Bede and St. Columba, as well as others proclaimed in recent memory.

Prophecy was the triplet sibling of poetry and history in the Greek and Roman worlds, the Judaic world, as well as that of the Celts and, indeed, of all that had not yet learned to forget the future. It is a moot point whether prophecy and second sight are the same thing but both are manifestly concerned with the discovery of the future. Second Sight is perhaps best characterised as premonition or even precognition, often, but not invariably, with reference to a single event, such as an individual's death. Throughout the medieval era it was believed that, just as certain characteristics of human beings could reappear from generation

---

14 Edward J. Cowan, 'Competing Pathways to the Past', *Tayside and Fife Archaeological Journal* 14 (2008) 100.
15 Bower, *Scotichronicon*, vol.2, 325.

to generation, so the events of past time prefigured those of the present. To a certain extent history was thus predictive. To cite a modern analogue a person looking today through a powerful space telescope can retrieve, across millions of light years, a picture of how this planet was formed and that person can also recover, by the same means, an impression of how the world will end. For the chronicler historiography was the telescope of Time.

Amongst the learned these matters were, historically, highly complex. Since most were motivated by providential history, great minds as far apart as those of Bede and Isaac Newton tried to calculate the length of the Last Age, while making the usual noises about how such things were known only to God. Prophecy in religious terms, whether we are discussing Joachim of Fiore or John Knox, meant revelation of the word of God. There was also a good knowledge throughout the Middle Ages, reinforced by the Renaissance, of Sybilline prophecy. Most important of all, perhaps, in a political sense, was the tradition of secular prophecy, for example, *The Prophecies of Merlin* which became quite familiar due to their popularisation by Geoffrey of Monmouth in the late twelfth-century, though there are tantalising indications that they had been known, in Scotland and elsewhere, for several hundred years before Geoffrey's time. For example a Welsh poem, *Armes Prydein Vawr, The Great Prophecy of Britain* was composed, it is claimed, to inspire the confederation of Welsh, Scots and Norsemen who fought the English at Brunanburh in 937:

> the Irish of Ireland and Anglesey and Scotland,
> the men of Cornwall and of Strathclyde will be made welcome among us.
> The Britons will rise again
> ...
> the Men of the North will be in place of honour about them,
> they will advance in the centre of their van of battle.[16]

Herein there were obvious antecedents of, later to be echoed in, Merlin's vaticination:

> Albany [Scotland] will be angry; calling her near neighbours to her she shall give herself up entirely to bloodshed ... The mountains of Armorica [Brittany] shall erupt and Armorica itself shall be crowned with Brutus's diadem. Kambria [Wales] shall be filled with joy and the Cornish oaks

---

16 *Armes Prydein: The Prophecy of Britain From the Book of Taliesin*, ed. Ifor Williams (Dublin: Dublin Institute for Advanced Studies, 1972) 3.

shall flourish. The island shall be called by the name of Brutus and the title given to it by the foreigners [i.e. English] shall be done away with.[17]

By the sixteenth century religious and secular prophecy came together as in Italian prophecies about Emperor Charles V, the second Charlemagne, 'the great king who would arise in the north', involving millenarian elements, buttressed with the prophetic utterances of such luminaries as St Bridget and Merlin.[18] Such awesome predictions had previously been applied to Charles VIII of France (1470–98). That the prophecies concerning both rulers named Charles proved untrue did not affect their actual validity since, as has been neatly observed, prophecies might be disconfirmed but they were not thereby discredited.[19] It was always the interpretation which was deemed to be at fault; prophecies themselves could be stored up for future application and, in any case, no one person would ever be in a position to absolutely affirm whether or not every single detail of a prediction had been borne out.

John Barbour included an interesting 'discourse' on prophecy in his poem *The Bruce* following a passage in which the king's hostess predicted the future success he was to enjoy after overcoming considerable adversities. Robert I is made to express his doubts that anyone could know for certain of future events other than through divine inspiration. Folk, however, were so curious, so keen to obtain knowledge of future events, that they would resort to astrology or devilry. Barbour doubted the efficacy of the former and condemned the latter, though he well understood that individuals always dreaded things of which they had heard tell, 'namely of things to come', until they were certain of the outcome. He who claims to know of future events, says Barbour, is guilty of great lies. Nonetheless he clearly considered the inclusion of prophetic material to be worthwhile; whether a certain prophetess knew what she was talking about or not, it could not be doubted that everything she predicted came to pass.[20]

Walter Bower is as useful an authority as any on medieval perceptions of prophecy. He discusses Merlin who was responsible for many utterances difficult to comprehend, 'scarcely ever or not at all understood by anyone until the events actually happen; but light is more readily thought to be shed upon them as

---

17 Geoffrey of Monmouth, *The History of the Kings of Britain*, ed. Lewis Thorpe (Harmondsworth: Penguin, 1966) 174–5. See Cowan, 'Myth and Identity in Early Medieval Scotland', *SHR* 63 (1984) 111–35.
18 Ottavia Niccoli, *Prophecy and People in Renaissance Italy*, trans. Lydia G. Cochrane (Princeton: Princeton University Press, 1990) 173–5.
19 Howard Dobin, *Merlin's Disciples: Prophecy, Poetry, and Power in Renaissance England* (Stanford: Stanford University Press, 1990) 76.
20 John Barbour, *The Bruce*, ed. A. A. M. Duncan (Edinburgh: Canongate, 1997) 182–9.

they happen or after they have occurred'.[21] Merlin had correctly predicted the expulsion of the Britons by the Saxons who, in turn, would be subjugated by the Danes whom the Normans would replace. However he foresaw that the Britons (or Welsh) would seize power from the Normans in alliance with the Bretons and the Scots. At this point Bower makes a pious and memorable disclaimer:

> Whether the events described in prophecy of this kind are either about to happen, or bound to happen and which, as it is thought, are not yet happening, will actually come to pass or not, lies in the will of Him to whom both past and future alike are continually present.[22]

In other words such matters are known only to God.

He also quotes Gildas, the ninth-century demented Welsh monk who perpetually confused venomous propaganda and historiography:

> The posterity of Brutus allied with the Scots will press hard
> On the Anglian kingdoms with war, hardship, slaughter.
> Rivers will flow stained with enemy blood.
> The treacherous nation subdued by all kinds of dispute will perish.
> The youth of Britain united with the Albans will overthrow it.
> The earth will turn red, dyed with Saxon blood.
> The Britons' friends of the Scottish race will rule.
> The whole island will bear its ancient name.
> As the eagle speaking from the old tower proclaims,
> The Britons along with the Scots will rule their ancestral kingdoms.
> They will rule equally in peaceful prosperity
> Till Judgement Day, once the enemy is driven away.[23]

The Venerable Bede, best known as England's first great historian, is invoked to warn that a 'town upon the Tweed' would be a prey to the English, appropriately enough since the ownership of Berwick was a matter of contemporary concern. The English are characterised as an evil homicidal, deceitful, drunken and gluttonous race, 'greedy for wealth, wicked in its progeny', which would be overcome by the French, or Normans, followed by the Scots, a prophecy also recorded by the English chroniclers, Ranulf Higden and Henry of Huntingdon.[24] Bede was not historically a prophet, a status which he may have received because

---

21 Bower, *Scotichronicon*, vol. 2, 45.
22 Bower, *Scotichronicon*, vol. 2, 47.
23 Bower, *Scotichronicon*, vol. 2, 59.
24 Bower, *Scotichronicon*, vol. 2, 61–3, 391.

of the supposed truthfulness of his *History*, or possibly through his work on *Time*; he it was who introduced the *anno domini* dating of the years.

As Bower's editors note, Bede's supposed prophecies actually belong to the reign of Edward I, as did those of Gildas and Merlin, but the point is that they were frequently reworked in later generations and interpreted, for example, with reference to the Albany regency following the battle of Flodden in 1513. Bower assures his readers that it is commonly believed that Arthur, 'the once and future king', is still alive and that songs anticipate his return to lead the Britons.[25]

The chronicler reports Thomas Rhymer's prediction about the death of Alexander III:

> Alas for tomorrow, a day of calamity and misery! Because before the stroke of twelve a strong wind will be heard in Scotland the like of which has not been known since times long ago. Indeed its blast will dumbfound the nations and render senseless those who hear it; it will humble what is lofty and raze what is unbending to the ground.

The courtiers assumed that Thomas was crazy but, of course, news of Alexander's death was duly received, the doubters discovering 'by experience that the prophecies of the said Thomas were to become all too credible'.[26] From Fordun Bower borrowed the inspirational prophecies, dated by M. O. Anderson to 1307,[27] concerning the alliance of the Welsh and the Scots. Moving closer to his own day he records both the prediction and the comet indicating the death of David Duke of Rothesay in 1402.[28] He cites Merlin's prophecies concerning Joan of Arc[29] without comment or qualification, probably because both Joan and the prophecies were manifestly anti-English. Both Fordun and Bower had no problems with prophecy as such and doubtless they believed that simply by recording or repeating those about the Scots and the English they would somehow hasten their fulfillment.

Sceptics about the subject had been around since the time of the Greeks, while Cicero's *De divinatione* acquired a new lease of life during the Renaissance. The great Montaigne drew heavily upon the Roman in his essay *On Prognostications*. Of prophets he asked, 'Who can shoot all day without hitting the target

---

25 Bower, *Scotichronicon*, vol. 2, 69.
26 Bower, *Scotichronicon*, vol. 5, 429.
27 Marjorie O. Anderson, *Kings and Kingship in Early Scotland* (Edinburgh and London: Scottish Academic Press, 1980), 67.
28 Bower, *Scotichronicon*, vol.8, 41.
29 Bower, *Scotichronicon*, vol.8, 131–3.

occasionally? Nobody keeps a record of their erroneous prophecies since they are infinite and everyday; right predictions are prized precisely because they are rare, unbelievable and marvellous'. Cicero and Montaigne also latched on to a couple of points that have often been made about vaticination. First, there is no divining like divining about the past – once things have happened we can find some interpretation of them which turns them into prophecies. As was said of Epimenides, he always prophesied backwards.[30] Second, Montaigne noted that when people were in a state of bewilderment – through civil disturbance, plague or whatever, they resorted to almost any superstition,

> including seeking in the heavens for ancient portents and causes for their ills . . . those who have been inducted into the subtle art of unwrapping portents and unknotting them would be able to find anything they wish in any piece of writing whatsoever: but their game is particularly favoured by the obscure, ambiguous, fantastical jargon of those prophecies, the authors of which never supply any clear meaning themselves so that posterity can give them any meaning it chooses.[31]

Such criticisms might be applied with equal force to the Book of Revelations or *The Prophecies of Merlin*.

Robert Wedderburn's *Complaynt of Scotland* (1550) might seem at first sight to share Montaigne's cynicism when he warns against 'diverse prophane propheseis of Merlyne and uthir ald corruppit vaticinaris', because popularly, more faith is placed in these imaginary works than in the prophesies of Ezekiel, Jeremiah or the Evangel, which have affirmed 'in rusty ryme', that Scotland and England would be ruled by one king, to which 'inglismen gifis ferme credit'.[32] He was not, however, objecting to the truthfulness of the prophecy but rather to the interpretation; a Scottish slant was perfectly acceptable while an English one was not. Even Lord Hailes, at the height of the Enlightenment, was compelled to remark, 'Let it be considered that the name of Thomas the Rhymer is not forgotten in Scotland, nor his authority slighted even at this day'. Recently his prophecies and those of other soothsayers had not only been reprinted but had been 'consulted with a weak, if not criminal curiosity'.[33] But, just as today there are people around who are reluctant, for reasons of spiritual insurance, to

---

30 Michel de Montaigne, *The Complete Essays*, trans. M. A. Screech (London: Penguin, 1993) 808.
31 Montaigne, *Essays*, 44–5.
32 Robert Wedderburn, *The Complaynt of Scotland (c.1550)* (Edinburgh: Scottish Text Society, 1979) 65.
33 David Dalrymple, Lord Hailes, *Remarks on the History of Scotland* (Edinburgh, 1773) 3.

completely relinquish a belief in God, so for many centuries there were those who were agnostic about prophecy, as undoubtedly many still are.

When James Charles Stewart became king of England in 1603 he ordered his printer Waldegrave to publish *The Whole Prophesie of Scotland, England, & some part of France, and Denmark, Prophesied bee meruelous Merling, Beid, Bertlingtoun, Thomas Rymour, Waldhave, Eltraine, Banester, and Sibbilla, all according in one. Containing many strange and meruelous things*. In the 1615 edition Ireland was added for good measure. The collection prints at length, in verse, the prophecies of Bede, Merlin, Berlington, Thomas Rhymer, Waldhave abbot of Melrose (the longest) and Gildas. It interjects a popular and much quoted prose fragment to the effect that the English for their drunkenness, treason, and carelessness of God's house shall be overcome and vanquished in turn by the Danes, the Normans, and, thirdly, by the Scots, at which point, it is asserted, since this was originally an English prophecy, 'the world will be unstable'. It is followed by the Prophecy of Sybilla and Eltraine (in verse) and by another prose fragment attributed to Sibylla, *Regina Austri*, allegedly composed for king Solomon, which predicted two noble princes and emperors who would subdue and overcome all earthly princes to their crown and diadem, and also be glorified and crowned in Heaven among the saints. The first of these was Constantine the Great; the second, with breathtaking arrogance, was confidently identified as 'the sixth king of the name of Stewart of Scotland, the which is our most noble king'. The collection closes with a long rigmarole in prose which, like so many of the verse prophecies, is full of animal imagery sometimes convincingly interpreted through heraldry, but just as often not, because a rich store of animal symbolism also derived from biblical and classical lore. The piece appears to refer to James IV, 'he shall be drawne to a place of Battel, where he shall get great discomfort, by the which he shall die'; and James V, 'in his time shall the Church tremble as an aspen leaf and great trouble in all manner of estates',[34] but we can never be too certain about such matters. 'Aside from the deliberate obscurity of the prophecies, our confusion comes from trying to figure out just where and how they fit into an understanding of the past.'[35] The following passage seems to be predicting the downfall of Henry VIII at the hands of a Scottish ruler, in robust rhetoric highly suitable for re-application to James VI at a later date. The nameless hero was possibly the Frenchman, John Duke of Albany, heir-presumptive to the Scottish throne during James V's minority and sometime 'Lord Governor' of Scotland:

---

34 *Whole Prophesie*, 48–9.
35 Sharon L. Jansen, *Political Protest and Prophecy under Henry VIII* (Woodbridge: The Boydell Press, 1991) 6.

Soone after there shal come out of the North, a Dragone and a Wolfe, the which shal bee the helpe of the Lyon, and bring the Realme to great rest and peace with glorie, with the most joy and triumphe, that the like was never seene these many yeares before: for by the sweete smel of the Lillie and the flowredeluce, there shal a Chiftane of the kith choose forth himselfe: stable as a stone, stedfast as the Christall, firme as the Adamant, true as the Steele, immaculate as the Son, without all treason, he shal saile on the sea with walls on every sid; and that with all gloire and joy to deliver the kith out of all thraldome and dolour, for he shal be as strong as the Wolf, wise as the Serpent, humble as the Lambe, simple as the Dove, Victorious as the Lyon, Prince of justice, the weil of this nation...[36]

Prophetic language represented a great and complex code deliberately designed to be at best ambiguous, and at worst incomprehensible, even after it was deconstructed.

In the second edition of *Whole Prophesie*, published by Hart in 1615, a translation was supplied of 'The Old Scottish Prophecies' which appeared only in Latin in the first. For the curious or those intrigued by the possible fulfillment of such vaticination the prophecies are supplied in an appendix to this chapter. In the Hart edition they are followed by the famously inspirational HEMPE text, not produced in Latin and not in the 1603 version:

> When HEMPE is come and also gone.
> SCOTLAND & ENGLAND shall be one.
> Praised be God alon, for HEMPE is cum & gon
> And left us old *Albion*, by peace joined in one.

The acronym signifies the succession of Henry VIII, Edward VI, Mary Tudor, her husband Philip of Spain, and Elizabeth.[37]

What must be understood herein is that *The Whole Prophesie*, was a compilation of material that went all the way back to medieval times, and that much of it was English in origin. Indeed some of it was copied by Fordun and Bower, made more palatable to a Scottish audience by the inclusion and substitution of familiar place-names such as Caithness, Lothian, Tweed, the Bass Rock, Dumbarton, Govan and the Lomond Hills. *The Whole Prophesie* continued to be reprinted in chapbook form well into the nineteenth century.

---

36 *Whole Prophesie*, 49.
37 *Whole Prophesie*, 63.

There is thus a virtually unbroken tradition of Scottish prophetic literature extending over a period of some five hundred years, and that half millennium can easily be extended backwards. Adomnán's *Life of Columba*, for example, completed in 697, reveals a man who appears to have been as much of a seer as a saint.[38]

There was one passage in the *Prophecies* which caused a great sensation at the time even among those who were disinclined to believe in their veracity.

> From the North to the South Sey
> A French wife shal beare the son
> Shall rule all Bretane to the sey
> that of the Bruce's blood shall come
> As neere as the ninth degree.

Quibblers might argue that James VI was not quite the ninth in succession to Robert Bruce but there was little doubt that the French wife, bride of the Dauphin, was Mary Queen of Scots, the mother of James. Archbishop Spottiswood was astounded by the accuracy of the prophecy which, like several others, he attributed to Thomas Rhymer who had lived in the late thirteenth century:

> The prophecies yet extant in Scottish Rithmes [*sic.* Rhymes], whereupon he was commonly called Thomas the Rhymer, may be justly admired, having foretold, so many ages before, the union of England and Scotland, in the ninth degree of Bruce's blood, with the succession of Bruce himself to the crown, being yet a child, and other divers particulars which the event hath ratified and made good . . . Whence or how he had this knowledge, can hardly be affirmed.

It was reported that the whole commons of Scotland were discussing Thomas's predictions. John Colville mentioned them in his funeral oration for the late Queen Elizabeth; at one time he had laughed at the prophetic lines which now turned out to be serious and authentic.[39]

Thomas Rhymer or Learmont was a real person who lived at Earlston, or Erceldoune, in the Borders. The romance, *Tomas Off Ersseldoune*, has been dated to about 1440. It is clearly the inspiration for the prophecies which occupy

---

38 John MacQueen, 'The Saint as Seer: Adomnan's Account of Columba', in *The Seer in Celtic and Other Traditions*, ed. Hilda Ellis Davidson (Edinburgh: John Donald, 1989) 37–51. Adomnán of Iona, *Life of St Columba*, trans. Richard Sharpe (London: Penguin, 1991).
39 These references are conveniently gathered in *The Romance and Prophecies of Thomas of Erceldoune*, ed. James A. H. Murray (London: Early English Text Society, 1875) xl–xli.

the first two fittes of the poem. The ballad may have originated at about the same time, or have had a parallel existence, although, curiously, while it tells of Thomas meeting with the Fairy Queen under the Eildon Tree, and of his sojourn in Fairyland, it does not mention specific prophecies.[40]

Even in England doubters such as Francis Bacon were impressed that the trivial prophecy concerning HEMPE, which he had heard as a boy, had actually been fulfilled. Sir John Harrington purportedly translated a prophecy out of Welsh and rewrote it in English to the effect that an individual would appear who would be: 1. a babe crowned in his cradle, 2. marked with a lion on his skin, 3. shall recover again the cross, 4. shall make the Isle of Brutus whole and unparted, 5. the new kingdom to grow henceforward better and better. The part about recovering the cross aside – an error of one in five was impressive in the circumstances – all other points appeared true, the Archbishop of York stating that James VI and I was 'said to have a mole like a Lyon'.[41] In the prophetic world James definitely had such a mole whether he knew it or not! He had no option.

All of this is the more surprising in that as recently as 1574 the Scottish parliament had legislated against persons claiming knowledge of 'prophecie, charming or utheris abusit sciences quhairby they persuaid the people that they can tell thair weirdis, deathes and fortunes and sic uther fantasticall ymaginatiounes'.[42] James himself, in his *Daemonologie*, opined that second sight was a trick of the devil though he offered some guidance as to how second sight differed from prophecy since it functioned at a popular, and thus uncontrollable, level while prophecy enjoyed 'the sanction of Time and Antiquity', at least in theory.[43] Needless to say the supposed efficacy of prediction received a great boost as a result of the publication of *The Whole Prophesie*. As already indicated the entire seventeenth-century especially around the signing of the Covenant and the consequent wars, as well as the later persecutions culminating in the 'Killing Time' was prophetically imbued. What might be described as prophetic chapbooks, which had been circulating in Italy since the early sixteenth century, first appear in Scotland in the 1670s. Another phenomenon which Scots shared with Italians and other Europeans, apart from comets, portents, prodigies, phantom armies and the rest, was the exhibition of freaks of nature, both animal and human such as Siamese twins or tragic, horribly deformed individuals who attracted paying audiences. The Canadian novelist Robertson Davies has

---

40 Henderson and Cowan, *Scottish Fairy Belief*, 142–51.
41 Dobin, *Merlin's Disciples*, 113–14.
42 *Records of the Parliaments of Scotland to 1707*, ed. K. M. Brown et al. (Online) [A1575/3/5][1]
43 James VI, *Daemonologie in the forme of a Dialogue, 1597* (London: The Bodley Head, 1924).

taught his readers time and again that they view those sad creatures in order to reinforce their own normality but in past centuries such unfortunates were seen as prefiguring the future, their deformities reckoned to be symbolic of present, or yet to be realised, calamities.[44]

It was to transpire, however, that although state-sponsored prophecy was considered inspirational, that of the folk emphatically was not. During the seventeenth century many poor women were burned for uttering predictions of one sort or another. Interestingly Ottavia Niccoli, in her investigation of Italian vaticination, has concluded that it fell into disfavour at around the same time as it came to be monopolised (or such, at least, was the perception) by women; the denial of prophecy was the concomitant of a rise in misogyny.[45]

Political prophecy, so far as we can tell, first truly surfaces during the Wars of Independence. The English chronicler Langtoft appears to have been the source of the idea that Edward I was the subject of *The Prophecies of Merlin*. The identification made sense for he could indeed be seen as a second Arthur after the conquest of Wales and (as he thought) of Scotland. Edward, however, had two friars executed in 1307 for proclaiming that Robert Bruce was Arthur *Redivivant*. Certain contemporary prophetic propaganda that year encouraged the Scots and the Welsh to unite against the Plantagenet usurper. If the dating is correct, 1307 was also the year in which Robert Bruce wrote his famous letter to the Irish stressing the common ancestry of the Scots and the Irish. After Bannockburn Edward Bruce followed through to Ireland and he was in touch with Llewellyn on the Welsh March. Bruce actually seems to have attempted to manipulate the prophecies to his own ends.[46] And here a most interesting point arises which can be sustained right through to *The Whole Prophesie*. The English, in their propaganda, concentrated on the end result – the second Arthur, or Cadwallader, or the nameless monarch who would one day rule over the united kingdoms of Britain. Everyone must have been aware that Merlin's prophecies were not English in origin but Welsh, that the English were the target of the prophecies, and that Welsh, Scots, Irish, and Bretons would league against them. The English extracted the monarchical, or even the imperial, thread but the Scots developed a racial prophecy, the idea of a prophetic people, embracing not only Scots but also the other Celtic peoples. As *The Whole Prophecie* put it, 'Scotland! . . . out of thee shall people rise up with divers happiness . . . then shall the Scots sword sweat with blood/ and slaughter

---

44 Niccoli, *Prophecy and People*, 30–60.
45 Niccoli, *Prophecy and People*, 190–5.
46 Edward J. Cowan, *'For Freedom Alone' The Declaration of Arbroath 1320* (Edinburgh: Birlinn, 2008) 68–9.

which they make".[47] The English could not know it but in prophetic terms they were on a hiding to nothing – they did not even understand the prophecies!

In the later fifteenth and in the sixteenth centuries the verbal conflict heated up. Henry Tudor manipulated some of the Welsh prophecies to his own advantage and he christened his eldest son Arthur, he who, upon his demise, left his wife to his brother Henry, with devastating consequences. But both James IV and James V also named their oldest sons Arthur in order to hasten prophetic fulfillment. Throughout the sixteenth century the prophecies became part of the propagandist war of words that raged between the two kingdoms, embracing not only the prophecies but the Brut myth similarly inspired, or at least popularised by Geoffrey of Monmouth.[48]

The Reformation spawned a whole new obsession with, and fashion for, prophecy. David Lindsay in *Monarche* warned that God alone knew the date of Doomsday but pointed out that it could be discovered:

> be divers conjectouris
> And principal Expositouris
> Off Daniel and his Prophecie
> And be sentence of Elie.

John Knox announced that 'the prophetis of God sumtymes may teache treasone aganis Kingis' and yet not offend God. In 1565 he preached that 'God hath revealed unto me secretes unknown to the worlde; and also that he made my tongue a trumpet, to forwarne realms and nations, yea certain great personages, of translations and changes'. Two of the great personages he upset were Mary Tudor and Mary Queen of Scots, as presaged in his *First Blast of the Trumpet Against the Monstrous Regiment of Women*. In 1558 he tried to reassure Elizabeth, another Deborah, 'a judge in Israel at a time when there were no kings', that his attacks did not include her personal regiment, or government.[49] It was precisely because of Elizabeth's lack of a secure position, like that of Henry VIII before her,[50] that successive legislation explicitly banned 'any fonde fantasticall or false Prophecye' utilising heraldry, banners, animals, badges or any such others as

---

47 *Whole Prophesie*, 63.
48 Roger A. Mason, 'Scotching the Brut: Politics, History and National Myth in Sixteenth-Century Britain', in *Scotland and England 1286–1815*, ed. Roger A. Mason (Edinburgh: John Donald, 1987) 60–84.
49 John Knox, *History of the Reformation in Scotland*, ed. William Croft Dickinson, 2 vols, (Edinburgh: Thomas Nelson, 1949) vol. 1, 285, 290–95. See also Dobin, *Merlin's Disciples*, 43–4.
50 Jansen, *Political Protest*, 35ff.

signs or signifiers, including specific years, days or times, in order to justify rebellion, insurrection, dissension or any other kind of disturbance.[51] James VI thus inherited a kingdom which was as familiar with, and as paranoid about, prophecy, as his own.

In his *Daemonologie* King James asserted that second sight, the 'fore-telling the death of sundrie persones', was a deception the Devil played upon an individual's imagination, 'a kinde of vision wherein he commonly counterfeits God among the Ethnicks (pagans or common people)'.[52] James in the same publication showed himself to be part of what would become a much bigger debate when he fulminated against Dutch sceptic Johann Weyer and the Englishman Reginald Scot who denied the existence of witchcraft 'and so mainteines the old error of the Sadducees, in denying of spirits', while applauding the work of demonologist Jean Bodin, who argued that witchcraft was an exceptional crime against God – *crimen exceptum* – 'a crime which involves every wickedness imaginable'.[53] During the following century and later, many Scots were to engage in the fierce debate concerning Sadduceeism. Quite simply, to deny the reality of spirits in the manner of the Sadducees, the Jewish sect which rejected resurrection and immortality as well as angels and spirits, was to deny the very existence of God himself, a challenge reiterated by the new 'mechanical philosophy' of René Descartes, Thomas Hobbes and Baruch de Spinoza. So far as the devout were concerned the best defence against scepticism, atheism and deism, against the very concept of 'Enlightenment', was to demonstrate the actuality of spirits, fairies, second sight and the rest in order to prove the existence of God.[54]

The debate, which gripped the whole of the British Isles, as well as several other countries, is perhaps best epitomised in the highly influential tract *Saducismus Triumphatus* (literally *Agnosticism Overcome*) jointly authored by Joseph Glanville and Henry More, a work which set out to prove two main propositions, first, that immaterial spirits exist and are known to humankind, and second that witchcraft, like other forms of demonic activity, actually occurs. In gathering evidence the net enveloped Scotland, particularly that part inhabited by Gaelic speakers, the Highlands and Islands, the *Gàidhealtachd*. Especially fascinating was the phenomenon of second sight, or *taidhbhse*, to

---

51 Dobin, *Merlin's Disciples*, 24.
52 King James the First, *Daemonologie (1597)* ed. G. B. Harrison (London: The Bodley Head, 1924) 75.
53 *Daemonologie*, xi–xii; Jean Bodin, *Démonomanie des Sorciers* (1580) *On the Demon-Mania of Witches*, trans. R. A. Scott and J. L. Pearl (Toronto: 1995).
54 Henderson and Cowan, *Scottish Fairy Belief*, 176–81.

which several investigators devoted their attention.[55] It has been suggested[56] that such enquiries were initiated by Robert Boyle of the Royal Society, in advancing supposed scientific explanations for Scottish folk beliefs, including second sight, a view which is, to some extent, supportable, but it is quite likely that Boyle first heard of second sight from his close associate, Sir Robert Moray, a Scot, a freemason and the first president of the Royal Society, whose work on tides was mentioned by Martin Martin.[57] An overwhelming number of informants were Scots[58] who had doubtless considered explanations of the phenomenon themselves.[59]

Among these were Robert Kirk author of *The Secret Commonwealth* (1691). His tract contains many pages associating second sight with fairies, while citing numerous examples which demonstrate to his satisfaction that 'the things seen by the Seers are Real Entities, the presages and predictions found true'. He believes that the creatures of the invisible world seek to convince humankind, in opposition to Sadducees and atheists, of the existence of a deity and of spirits, 'of a possible and harmless method of correspondence betwixt men and them, even in the Lyfe'.[60] He quotes a letter of Lord Tarbat, later first earl of Cromarty to Robert Boyle the noted scientist and translator of the Irish bible, relating that a seer might see the object of his vision as far away as America, though Gaels who went there lost the ability. Tarbat 'truly related' matters of fact concerning deaths and military activities during the Cromwellian occupation, but he could hazard no conjecture as to the cause of the phenomenon.[61]

Other interested parties included George Sinclair of Glasgow University who designed water pumps for the coal mines and who wrote *Satan's Invisible*

---

55 For modern statements on the phenomenon see two articles in *The Seer*, ed. Davidson: John MacInnes, 'The Seer in Gaelic Tradition', 10–24 and Eilidh Watt, 'Some Personal Experiences of the Second Sight', 25–36. I first encountered current accounts of second sight in South Uist in the early 1970s. I am grateful to my informants at that time. I believe, beyond question, that they believed what they were telling me.
56 Michael Hunter, *The Occult Laboratory Magic, Science and Second Sight in Late 17th-Century Scotland* (Woodbridge: Boydel Press, 2001) 2–3.
57 Martin Martin, *A Description of the Western Islands of Scotland* (1703; London: 2nd edn, 1716) 44.
58 Henderson and Cowan, *Scottish Fairy Belief*, Chapter 6.
59 Hunter is keen on the idea that the enquiring minds of the Royal Society sought to explain second sight while the Scots took it for granted, *Occult Laboratory*, 1,9, but acceptance does not necessarily imply that it was unquestioned by people like Moray and his Scottish associates.
60 Robert Kirk, *The Secret Commonwealth*, ed. Stewart Sanderson (Cambridge: The Folklore Society, 1976) 82. The most recent edition of Kirk's *Secret Commonwealth* is in Hunter, *Occult Laboratory*, 77–106.
61 Kirk, *Secret Commonwealth*, 73–80. For Boyle's notes on his meeting with Tarbat in 1678 see Hunter, *Occult Laboratory*, 51–3.

World Discovered (1685), a collection of supernatural phenomena, and Robert Wodrow, the tireless historian of, and apologist for, the Church of Scotland, particularly its extreme wing, but who also penned *Analecta or a History of Remarkable Providences*, not published until 1843. Sir George Mackenzie, known to the Covenanters as 'the Bluidy Advocate' also entered the debate, as did John Fraser, minister of Tiree and Coll, who unhelpfully explained in his *Deuteroscopia* (1707) that the seeing of the seer was 'nothing else but the Transition of the intentional Species thro' the chrystallin Humour to the retiform Coat of the Eye, and judged by the common Sense, and conveyed the optic nerve to the Fancy'.[62] The moving finger writes and having writ moves on, leaving us none the wiser! Fraser's editor, Andrew Symson, author of *A Large Description of Galloway* (1685), dedicated the minister's posthumous work to Lord Tarbat, perceptively remarking that the subject of the discourse should more accurately be described as 'First Sight, because it for the most part sees Things before they are'.[63]

One of the most illuminating commentators on the phenomenon was Martin Martin, a native of Skye and one of the first of very few Gaelic speakers who ever wrote about their people and their culture, from the inside. He defined second sight as 'a singular faculty of seeing an otherwise invisible object, without any previous means us'd by the person that sees it for that end'.[64] The ability was not inherited or communicable. Sometimes the same object was seen by different people living at some distance from one another while the time of day or night might determine the length of time it would take for the premonition to be realised. Like others who wrote on the subject most examples concerned imminent deaths but some indicated a future spouse. Martin was one of the few individuals to relate that he had himself been the object of visions:

> I have myself been seen by Seers of both Sexes at some hundred miles distance; some that saw me in this manner, had never seen me personally, and it happened according to their Visions, without any previous design of mine to go to those Places, my coming there being purely accidental.[65]

---

62 John Fraser, *A Treatise Containing A Description of Deuteroscopia, commonly called the Second Sight* (1707; Edinburgh: reprinted 1754) 13; reprinted in Hunter, *Occult Laboratory*, 187–204.
63 Fraser, *Deuteroscopia*, xi.
64 For this and what follows see Martin, *Description of the Western Islands*, 300–35. For a useful annotated reprint see *Curiosities of Art and Nature: The new annotated and illustrated edition of Martin Martin's classic A Description of the Western Islands of Scotland*, ed. Michael Robson (Port of Ness: The Island Book Trust, 2003).
65 Martin, *Description of the Western Islands*, 303.

A chair which appeared to be empty presaged the death of the unfortunate who actually occupied it at the time. Ghostly funeral processions were common. A seer could share his vision by touching a person near him. A loud banshee-like cry, widely heard, foretold a death. Some seers employed second smell, detecting the odour of fish or meat in the fire though neither commodities were in the house. Children, horses and cows also experienced second sight. Children would cry out on seeing a corpse without necessarily knowing what it was; horses would refuse to pass certain places on the road having instead to be led a long way round; cows would flee in fright if the woman milking them experienced a vision.

Martin refutes those critics who have recently denied the reality of second sight, for example the assertion that seers are melancholics who only imagine they see things. On the contrary, seers of both sexes are completely free from madness or any kind of hysterical or convulsive disorder. A drunk man cannot experience the sight. To the objection that since the learned cannot explain the visions they are not to be believed he responds:

> If every thing for which the Learned are not able to give a satisfying account be condemn'd as impossible, we may find many other things generally believed, that must be rejected as false by this Rule. For instance Yawning, and its influence, and that the Loadstone attracts Iron; and yet these are true as well as harmless, tho we can give no satisfying account of their Causes. And if we know so little of natural Causes, how much less can we pretend to things that are supernatural?[66]

To the third charge that seers are imposters imposing upon the credulous, he defends both the power and his people. Seers were not born to deceive; they are well-meaning and honest. None of them are enriched through their abilities. 'The people of the Isles are not so credulous as to believe implicitly, before the thing is accomplished; but when it actually comes to pass afterwards, it is not in their power to deny it, without offering violence to their Senses and Reason.' If seers were frauds it is unreasonable to assume that all of the islanders would be

---

66 Martin, *Description of the Western Islands*, 308–9. This passage may be presumed to have inspired Samuel Johnson's later repost to Mr Macpherson of Sleat who announced that he was resolved not to believe in second sight since it was founded on no principle. 'There are many things then, which we are sure are true, that you will not believe. What principle is there why a loadstone attracts iron? why an egg produces a chicken by heat? why a tree grows upwards when the natural tendency of all things is downwards? Sir, it depends on the degree of evidence that you have', *Johnson's Journey to the Western Islands of Scotland and Boswell's Journal of a Tour to the Hebrides with Samuel Johnson, LL.D*, ed. R. W. Chapman (Oxford: Oxford University Press, 1970) 262.

complicit in deceit. Many respectable folk believe. It is not credible that 'children, horses and cows could be pre-ingaged in a Combination (or conspiracy) to persuade the World of the Reality of the *Second Sight*'.⁶⁷ Those who deny the visions will accept strange developments in the distant past based upon ancient histories, yet they deny contemporaries, 'the liberty to believe their intimate Friends and Acquaintances, Men of Probity and unquestionable Reputation, of whose Veracity they have greater certainty, than we can have of any ancient Historian'.

Martin supplied many illustrations which proved, to his satisfaction, that the reality of second sight was demonstrable. But, though the 'faculty of seeing visions enjoyed the sanction of antiquity', it had declined by some 90 per cent during the previous twenty years. Furthermore it was not confined to the Hebrides but was experienced in many other places such as Holland and the Isle of Man. One other point re-iterated in the secondary literature is that the power was often regarded as a curse. It was not pleasant to be endlessly witnessing death omens or indications of sickness. On the island of Coll it was believed an individual could rid him/herself of the ability by the gift of alms to the poor followed by prayer. A seer was seriously troubled by visions of his two sons currently serving abroad in the army. Having shed the ability he asked a practising seer to report on his seeing. The latter sat beside the central fireplace because visions were best seen through fire. Severe sweating indicated a painful vision of the two sons' deaths in combat.⁶⁸

The year 1763 saw the publication of *A Treatise on The Second Sight* by one, Theophilus Insulanus, now thought to have been a Skye minister named John MacPherson.⁶⁹ His intention was to defeat the preposterous views of 'atheists, deists and freethinkers' by proving the immortality of the soul, his chosen medium of proof the phenomenon of second sight, which was universally believed by people of all ranks in the Hebrides from earliest times to the present.⁷⁰ The author thought that since second sight was an immaterial phantom it could not be seen by the eye. Rather it was communicated by a supernatural agent:

67 Martin, *Description of the Western Islands*, 309–10.
68 John Gregorson Campbell, *Witchcraft & Second Sight in the Highlands & Islands of Scotland* (Glasgow: James MacLehose, 1902) 180. For a characteristically mystical account of the subject see Lewis Spence, *Second Sight Its History & Origins* (London: Rider and Company, 1951).
69 There is a boring debate about the identity of Theophilus, see Hunter, *Occult Laboratory*, 47, and Sutherland, *Ravens and Black Rain*, 92. Various competing ministers have been suggested rendering an expectant world none the wiser. The debate is somewhat irrelevant since all of them were like-minded anti-Sadducees and all complicit in the same polemic.
70 Theophilus Insulanus, *A Treatise on The Second Sight, Dreams and Apparitions: several instances sufficiently attested and An Appendix of Others Equally Authentic* etc (Edinburgh: Ruddiman, 1763) xxiii, 2.

> And if we believe in the existence of spirits, agreeable to the sense of the generality of mankind, there is nothing in the Second Sight, or dreams, shocking to our reason or understanding: otherwise, how could it happen, that what severals dreamed, were fulfilled in all their circumstances?[71]

One man was informed by a voice at his bed-head that Charles Edward Stewart had been defeated at Culloden. Allan MacDonald of Flodigarry, 'a gentleman of good sense and free of superstition', believed in second sight after enquiring into many incidences thereof. Many prophecies were associated with the Forty-five Rebellion. A remarkable example of the exploitation of prophecy for political, propagandist and confirmational purposes is furnished by the Jacobite victory at Prestonpans, on 21 September 1745, when, after the fact, the site of the battle was moved six miles away to Gladsmuir, in order to comply with the medieval prediction that a memorable victory would be accomplished at Gladsmoor, 'the great Armageddon of the prophecies':

> The battle of Gladsmoor, it was a noble stour,
> And weel do we ken that our young prince wan;
> The gallant Lowland lads, when they saw the tartan plaids.
> Wheel round to the right, and away they ran.[72]

This was not the first time that Gladsmuir's prophetic significance had been exploited for it was there that the Scottish army optimistically mustered in 1547 before the battle of Pinkie, which, despite the omens, proved a cruel defeat.[73]

Theophilus found much convincing evidence in the bible and in the works of Scottish historians; for him the multiplicity of examples proved his thesis, as did endless repetition:

> From the certainty of dreams, Second Sight, and apparitions, follows the plain and natural consequence of the existence of spirits, immateriality and immortality of the soul: a truth that is acknowledged by the most barbarous nations, as well as by the most civilized, and carries its own

---

71 Insulanus, *Treatise*, 34.
72 *Romance and Prophecies*, ed. Murray xlii. See also Edward J. Cowan, 'Prophecy and Prophylaxis: A Paradigm for the Scotch-Irish?', in *Ulster and North America Transatlantic Perspectives on the Scotch-Irish*, ed. H. Tyler Blethen and Curtis W. Wood (Tuscaloosa: University of Alabama Press, 1997) 15–23.
73 Marcus Merriman, *The Rough Wooings: Mary Queen of Scots, 1542–1551* (East Linton: Tuckwell Press, 2000) 5.

conviction in every human breast; unless sensual appetites, and rampant lusts sink the man, and make the brute predominant.[74]

The journey to the Western Isles of the terrible twosome, Johnson and Boswell, in 1773 generated more interest in the phenomenon; both were influenced by Martin Martin's *Description* and by Thomas Pennant's accounts of his Scottish tours. The latter recounted the case of William Sinclair of Freswick in Caithness, wrongly supposed to be the last to possess second sight, who allegedly feigned the gift in order to impress his clansmen, and, according to another account, to scare off potential thieves. However, he came to believe that he actually had real powers, the knowledge of which rendered the last years of his life truly miserable.[75] The story is of interest as signifying a period when belief in the phenomenon was crumbling, at least in Caithness.

Some prophetic utterances employed the device of seemingly impossible conditions that must be fulfilled before the prophecies could come to pass. One such recorded by Pennant was a prophecy of Coinneach Odhar, the Brahan Seer:

> Whenever a Maclean with long hands, a Frazier with a black spot on his face, a Macgregor with the same on his knee, and a club-footed MacCleod of Raasay, should have existed; whenever there should have been successively three Macdonalds of the name of John, and three Mackinnons of the same Christian name; oppressors would appear in the country, and the people change their own land for a strange one.[76]

Emigration was thus anticipated and, indeed, already underway, but the wording is interesting because it was echoed in Coinneach's most famous prediction concerning the doom of the Seaforth Mackenzies. He was unusual among seers because, according to traditional accounts, he employed a magic stone with a hole in it when having a vision. It has been shown that the historical personage, Kenneth Ower, was a convicted witch executed at Chanonry Point on the Black Isle in 1578.[77] Tradition advanced him a century to the reign of Charles II. It tells how he was forced to relate the content of a synchronic vision to Lady Seaforth who, incensed by the seer's disclosures about her husband's

---

74 Insulanus, *Treatise*, 42.
75 Thomas Pennant, *A Tour in Scotland 1769* (1771: Perth: Methven Press, 1979) 179; Robert Mackay, *History of the House and Clan of Mackay* (Edinburgh, 1829) 547.
76 Thomas Pennant, *A Tour in Scotland and Voyage to the Hebrides 1772* (1774, 1776: Edinburgh: Birlinn, 1998) 319.
77 William Matheson, 'The historical Coinneach Odhar and some prophecies attributed to him', TGSI vol. 46, 66–88.

infidelity, condemned Coinneach to be burned in a barrel of tar. Before he died he pronounced the 'doom':

> I see into the far future, and I read the doom of the race of my oppressor. The long-descended line of Seaforth will, ere many generations have passed, end in extinction and sorrow. I see a chief, the last of his house, both deaf and dumb. He will be the father of four fair sons, all of whom he will follow to the tomb. He will live careworn and mourning knowing that the honours of his line are to be extinguished forever, and that no future chief of the Mackenzies shall bear rule at Brahan or in Kintail. After lamenting over the last and most promising of his sons, he himself shall sink into the grave, and the remnant of his possessions shall be inherited by a white-coifed (or white-hooded) lassie from the East, and she is to kill her sister. And as a sign by which it may be known that these things are coming to pass, there shall be four great lairds in the days of the last deaf and dumb Seaforth – Gairloch, Chisholm, Grant and Raasay – of whom one will be buck-toothed, another hare-lipped, another half-witted, and the fourth a stammerer. Chiefs distinguished by these personal marks shall be the allies and neighbours of the last Seaforth; and when he looks around him and sees them, he may know that his sons are doomed to death, that his broad lands shall pass away to the stranger, and that his race shall come to an end.[78]

It is reported that the last of the Seaforths, Francis Humberstone Mackenzie, was rendered deaf through a childhood attack of scarlet fever. He was allegedly struck dumb when the last of his four sons predeceased him. He died in 1815, the four contemporary highland lairds confidently identified by those who cared to do so. This part of the story was memorialised by Walter Scott in verse and a version mentioned by Elizabeth Grant in her *Memoires*, which appeared, like Scott's poem, in 1815. Scott noted that Mary Frederica Elizabeth Mackenzie succeeded her father and he alluded to the prophecy that the family would fall with a deaf Mackenzie, though he failed to mention that she had any further part to play in its fulfillment. Mary was the widow of Admiral Sir Samuel Hood, and thus Lady Hood; she returned to Scotland from India – and thus 'from the east' – where her husband died. She was thus supposedly 'hooded' by her marriage, or (doubtfully) by her widow's weeds, though the pun does not work in Gaelic in which 'hood' is *clonnabharr*. No contemporary seems to have known anything about her role in the prophecy. While driving her sister Caroline in a

---

78 Mackenzie, *Brahan Seer*, 92.

trap on the Brahan estate the ponies bolted. Both ladies were injured when they were thrown out of the carriage, Caroline fatally. Thus Mary could have been said to have killed her sister.

Herein we can see a prophecy in the making. Coinneach was an historical figure transposed to the following century, but there was no Seaforth title in 1578. There appears to be no trace of the Seaforth prophecy until 1815, many new details being furnished by Alexander Mackenzie's book, *The Prophecies of the Brahan Seer* published in 1899 and reprinted several times since. Even in the context of second sight much of the material does not ring true. Seers had no need of magic stones. In the story Coinneach exults in his power or gift, using it for mischievous or malignant purposes in a manner claimed, the Freswick case aside, to be alien to the tradition. The Brahan Seer continues to fascinate because his prophecies are allegedly still coming true, but the doom of the Seaforths is a classic example of prophesying backwards, or after the fact. Prophecy provides confirmation of unusual events or developments. When it ought to exist but does not, it is manufactured. John MacInnes was told in the 1980s that 'when two women rule this land the kingdom is approaching its end',[79] an achievement so far unattributable to either Queen Elizabeth or sometime prime minister Maggie Thatcher.

There is perhaps a type of historical satisfaction in the appropriateness of tradition situating the Brahan Seer in the period of the Royal Society and the Scientific Revolution since prophecy and second sight, like science, sought to probe the boundaries of knowledge and the depths of the unknown. Just why Scots, like most of humankind, seem to have always been so insistent in knowing about a future that must often have proved perilous and unwelcome is something of a mystery, but the possibility that the unknown was potentially knowable was a notion on which the popular and learned traditions were at one. They differed in that science questioned, and then attempted to destroy, a long-standing traditional belief which at least some of the folk continued to nurture.

---

79 MacInnes, 'The Seer', 22. MacInnes shows, as does Watt, 'Some Personal Experiences of Second Sight', that the debate on the subject is far from over. See too John L. Campbell and Trevor H. Hall, *Strange Things: The Enquiry by the Society for Psychical Research into Second Sight in the Scottish Highlands, the story of Ada Goodrich Freer and the Ballechin House ghost hunt, and the stories and folklore collected by Fr. Allan McDonald of Eriskay* (London: Routledge and Kegan Paul, 1968).

APPENDIX: THE OLD SCOTTISH PROPHECIES

(Extract from *The Whole Prophesie*, 61–3)

Scotland be sad now, & lament, thy child whom thou has lost
Bereft of Kings falsely undone, by thy own kindlie host.

Alace the free bond is become, and deceit is thy fall,
The falshood of the brutish race, hes broght thee into thrall.

The grave of the most noble Prince, to all is great regrate,
Noght subiect to law, who doth leave, the kingdom & estate

O anguish great, where every kind and age doeth lament,
Whom bitter death hes tane away, shall Scotland sore repent

Latelie a land of rich increase, a Nation stout and true,
Hes tint their former dear estate, which they did hold of due.

By hard conflict, and by the chance, of mobile fortuns force,
Thy hap and thy prosperitie, is turned into worse.

Thou wont to win, now is subdewd, and come in under yoke
A stranger reigns & doth destroy, what likes with swords strok

The English race whom neither force, nor manners do approve
Wo is to thee, by guile and slight, is onlie win above.

The mightie Nation was to fore, invincible and stout,
Hes yeelded low to destinie, great pitie is but doubt.

In former age the Scots renown did flourish goodlie gay:
But now alace is overcled with a great dark decay.

Then mark and see what is the cause, of this so wondrous fall
Contempt of faith, falshood deceit, the wrath of God withal

Unsaciable greed of worlds gaine oppression cryes of poore,
Perpetuall a slanderous race, no justice put in ure.

The hautie pride of mighty men of former vice chief cause
The nurriture of wickednesse, an unjust match of Lawes.

Therefore this case ye Prophets old of long time did presage
As now hes hapned every point into this present age.

Sen fate is so, now Scotland learne in patience to abide,
Slanders, great feares, & sudden plagues, & dolors mo beside.

For out of thee shall people rise, with diverse happinesse,
And yet a pen can scarcely write, thy hurt, skaith & distress.

But yet beware thou not distrust, although overwhelmed with grief
Thy straik is not perpetuall, for thou shalt find relief.

I do suppose although too late, old Prophecies shall hold,
Hope thou in Gods goodness ever, and mercies manifold,

For thou that now a patient is, and seemeth to be bond,
At libertie shall free be set, and with empire renownd.

From high above shal grace come down, & thy state Scotland be
In latter end more prosperous, nor former age did see.

Old prophecies foretell to thee, a warlike Heire bees borne,
Who shal recover new his right, advance his kingdoms horn

Then shall the Scots sword sweat with blood, and slaughter which they
    make:
The King himself revenger shall the guilty troops down wrack

The English Nation shal invade but not escape a plague,
With sword, with thirst, with teares and pest, with feare, and suchlike ague.

And after enemies thrown down, & mastered by weir
Then Scotland in peace quietly, passe joyful dayes for ever.

TWO

'Away with the fairies'

Louise Yeoman

In 1639, Archibald Johnston of Wariston, no mean wonder worker himself, was uplifted by the 'heavenly speeches' of a Covenanting prophetess – Margaret Mitchell, whom he invited to stay with him and whom he introduced to the entire Covenanting leadership to answer their questions.[1] She exhorted the leadership of the Covenanters to go forward in their cause and assured them that God was on their side. Unfortunately, no detailed record of her speeches and predictions survives. Her appearance was not a peculiarity of Scottish Calvinism, for example she also had a contemporary Catholic counterpart: Sister Anne Marie de Jesu Crucifi who had a vision of Louis XIII being led around the battle fields by the saints. She reported the results of this supernatural aerial reconnaissance to Cardinal Richelieu via her spiritual director Père Joseph du Capuchin and Richelieu took her predictions very seriously, especially as they were validated by her spiritual director.[2] These were prophetesses who sat at the top table – like the prophets of the Bible. They were state-sanctioned oracles drawing on Biblical examples, but prophecy in Scotland also had much humbler manifestations too.

Over the period 1651–1685, when the Presbyterian party was out of power, Scotland produced no fewer than five female prophetic visionaries: Barbara Peebles, Grizell Love, Jonet Fraser, Donald MacGrigor's daughter in Monzie and the Glenluce visionary. These women were mostly from the west of Scotland and mostly from the middling sort of people who formed the backbone of Covenanting praying societies – although two of the group came from much lower class families. Female visionary prophecy is not something normally associated with seventeenth century Scottish Calvinism.

Though prophecy was supposed to have ceased with the end of apostolic times, this was subverted by the strong emphasis on spiritual experience which characterised the devout in both reformation and counter-reformation countries. Since intimacy with God was being heavily stressed through prayer

---

1 George M. Paul, ed., *Diary of Sir Archibald Johnston of Wariston, 1632–1639*, Scottish History Society, First series (Edinburgh: T. and A. Constable, 1911) 395–9.
2 C. Cupples, 'Testing visionaries in early modern France', unpublished paper, Sixteenth Century Studies Conference, Toronto, 23 Oct. 1998.

and sacraments, it was no surprise that some people became so intimate with God that they believed he had started speaking to them.

The earliest surviving narrative of the five, and also the shortest, dates from 1651 and was an account of a vision had by the wife of Robert Jameson in Glenluce (referred to hereafter as the Glenluce visionary). She was unable to write, so the vision was recorded by the local minister, John Scott. The woman had spent the most part of the previous night in prayer. At about the break of day she fell into a trance and 'continued till 11 o clock without sense or motion but as in a lethargy'. The result was a vision of 'the Lord sitting on his throne and the lamb walking before the throne and with him a little flock all clothed in white'.[3] She went in and out of trances during which the vision developed. Next, she saw a bloody throne streaming blood from all four corners and a great black cloud covering the throne. The trances lasted for periods ranging from several hours to three-quarters of an hour. Finally, she began to interpret the visions and to prophesy. The cloud was the cloud of the Lord's indignation against the shedding of the blood of the saints, deliverance would come, but not yet. Most radically of all she stated 'all your heads, your noblemen most of their purses are stuffed with the blood of the saints, they are undone with treachery'.

This was the kind of utterance commonly heard from English civil war prophetesses such as Anna Trapnel or the early Quaker women.[4] Yet Robert Jameson's wife was clearly not a member of such a sect. The minister who was called to attend her, John Scott, was a prominent radical Presbyterian – one of the Commission of Assembly of 1649. He was also clearly interested in the supernatural: he took a leading part in attempting to exorcise the Devil of Glenluce – a poltergeist described in George Sinclair's *Satan's Invisible World Discovered*.[5] These Scottish visionaries were Presbyterians and not Quakers.

It is easy to see why this vision might appeal to a Presbyterian minister. With its apocalyptic imagery the Glenluce vision was highly scriptural (as were Quaker and Baptist visions). It had a strong emphasis on prayer. This also gave it credibility – the Devil was unlikely to be speaking in someone who called for more prayer. The visionary discoursed much on the excellence of Christ. This would seem highly edifying to a minister – they tended to do this themselves. The whole process of her trances, speeches and admonitions took place in public before a local audience. It was not a private experience. Such public witness to God could seem attractive to a clergyman as it could play a role in converting

---

3 Lord Polwarth (Scotts of Harden), Glenluce vision, 1651. NAS, GD157/2637/1.
4 Phyllis Mack, *Visionary Women: Ecstatic Prophecy in Seventeenth century England* (Berkeley: University of California Press, 1992) 77–9, 90, 122, 131–3.
5 Hew Scott, ed., *Fasti Ecclesiae Scoticanae* (Edinburgh: Oliver and Boyd, 1915) vol. 2, 348; George Sinclair, *Satan's Invisible World Discovered* (London, 1815) 54.

others. This would tend towards a minister evaluating this as the work of God and not of the Devil – an important consideration as demonic activity was always to be feared in such manifestations. The demonologist Jean Bodin, who often featured as an authority in Scottish witch trials may be cited here.[6] Bodin radically distrusted apparitions and raptures. Wolfgang Behringer notes how in Bodin's section on divination in his *De Magorum Daemonomania*, he discussed various sorts of dreams, visions and the apparition of angels and emphasised strongly the importance of enquiring whether the phenomenon was sent by God or the Devil – putting particular emphasis on the personal quality of the person involved and the orthodoxy of the sentiments.[7] So a prophetess who had spent most of the previous night in prayer would be a more convincing visionary than a local ne'er do well after a few drinks. In fact, all the prophetic visions recorded over this period fitted these criteria: the visionary came from a godly background and expressed godly sentiments. If this was not so, they would probably never have been recorded.

If godliness was one common factor, then timing was another; visions seemed to come either at or just after times of crisis. The Glenluce visionary had her revelation on 5 October 1651, a month after the battle of Worcester and the final victory of Cromwell and in the middle of the Protestor-Resolutioner controversy which split the Church of Scotland. As apparently a devout Presbyterian, the rise and fall of the Presbyterian cause would have exercised her greatly. In all probability, she also heard a great deal of these events from the pulpit in the shape of 'preaching to the times', the preaching on contemporary events to keep congregations aware of national events. Pious Protestants were expected to note (in the words of Archibald Johnston of Wariston) how 'his [God's] kingdom goes on and Satan's kingdom is borne doun.'[8] Thus it would be a godly exercise to examine the workings of the current events of this world for the working out of God's providence.[9]

Note, however, that the vision came after the crisis and not before it. Other visions also showed links to times of crises. Barbara Peebles recorded two revelations: the first on 20 July 1660, nearly two months after the Restoration of Charles II. The second, she had on 4 December 1666 a week after Rullion Green and the crushing of the Presbyterian party in battle. Grizell Love, the Paisley

---

6 For example, the trial of Geillis Johnston for witchcraft (1614), NAS, High Court of Justiciary, court books – old series, Regality of Dunfermline, JC1/38. This trial has been edited by Louise Yeoman and Michael Wasser, *Scottish History Society Miscellany XIII* (Edinburgh, 2004) 83–145.
7 Wolfgang Behringer, *Shaman of Oberstdorf*, trans. H. C. Erik Midelfort (Charlottesville: University Press of Virginia, 1998) 93–4.
8 Behringer, *Shaman of Oberstdorf*, 93–4.
9 'Diary of Archibald Johnston of Wariston', transcript, 1655–60, NLS, MS 6248, (Dec. 1655 – Mar. 1656) 57.

prophetess, commented on a wide series of events: the Dutch war, the activities of General Turner in Dumfries and Galloway, Rullion Green, Bothwell Bridge, the Indulgences and the Highland Host.[10] Jonet Fraser, a Cameronian, had visions that coincided with the Killing Times.[11] Donald Macgrigor's daughter 'at the time of the town's persecution' was 'desired to enquire at Christ if it were best for some who were of intention to pass out of the country to escape the persecution that then was. It was answered that they needed not pass forth of the country but wait for God's deliverance'.[12] These were crisis revelations.

On the whole, the prophetic revelations seemed to follow or coincide with, rather than precede significant events. It was almost as though the visionaries were asking the question – what does this mean? They seemed to be telling their communities how to react to it. Prophets, to use a contemporary reference, are almost like God's spin doctors. They tell their audience what God wants them to think of major events. This is a role which we might expect to see confined to the ministry, but just as someone has to guard the guards, so someone has to give guidance to the guides. Ministers and lay saints sought guidance not only through their own experiences in prayer, but through interpreting providences and hearing what God was saying through other people. For instance, one of northern minister Thomas Hogg's star pupils was a Gaelic tinker, John Card, who 'knew the old catechism very exactly'. Despite his shaky grasp of English, Card was considered to be so gifted in attaining guidance in prayer that Hogg would often go to consult him, or he would be put to prayer by the local godly community to determine what would happen in a crisis.[13] Similar occurrences could be found in prayer groups all over Scotland in which ministers listened to what others received in prayer and took note of it. Mr. Daniel Douglas's wife, Margaret Hutcheson was given to staying in prayer until 'ten hours at night'. Neighbouring Borders minister, David Hume duly recorded some of the answers she received.[14] Barbara Peebles and the other visionaries may have been part of that sort of guidance mechanism.

Barbara Peebles' trances survive in the papers of ministers whose collections came into the hand of the Rev Robert Wodrow – the Presbyterian historian of the later Covenanters who collected so many of their surviving documents.[15]

10 'The exercise of Grizell Love', NLS Wod.Qu.LXXII, fos. 110v., 114, 115, 152, 194.
11 Thorbjorn Campbell, *Standing Witnesses* (Edinburgh: Saltire Society, 1996) 18.
12 'Admiranda et Notanda', EUL, Dc.8.110, fo.19r.
13 Matthew Leishman, ed., *Robert Wodrow's Analecta: or materials for a History of Remarkable Providences*, 4 vols. (Edinburgh: Maitland Society, 1842–3) vol. 2, 164.
14 David Hume's diary, NLS, Wod. Oct. XV, 23, 29.
15 One appears in a volume of papers belonging to Glasgow minister Neil Gillies and Professor James Wodrow, another in a volume which may have come from ministers Thomas and Robert Wyllie, NLS Wod.Qu.XXVI, fo.283, Wod.Qu.XXXV, fo.144.

Barbara was not the only visionary whose narrative was copied and recopied by such circles. The Glenluce Visionary was even more popular. The probable reason was her last statement: that the days would come when ministers would only get leave to meet with their flocks in mosses and brae sides. In Cromwellian terms, of course, that was wrong. The regime was tolerant of Presbyterian worship at a local level. However, in the context of 1660 and the ensuing ejections of Presbyterian ministers, these words seemed truly prophetic. Her work survived in at least four versions. Two of them appear in the papers of hard-line Presbyterian exile Robert MacWard and one in the hand of his fellow exile, John Brown, suggesting that the text circulated amongst the more radical Presbyterian exiles in the Netherlands.[16] To survive and be copied and re-copied in this way, visionary narratives like these must have had a strong appeal. Three out of the four copies of the narrative appear in the papers of Presbyterian ministers, indicating that they found this manuscript interesting and relevant. Perhaps they were its intended audience, after all one of their number had taken it down in the first place. For graduate ministers to take such a phenomenon seriously was no surprise. Only ten to twenty years previously, Cardinal Richelieu, Argyll and the Covenanting nobles also took such visions seriously – as noted at the beginning of this paper. Women with the correct lifestyles and sentiments could clearly get their visions accepted by educated men.

The dependence of female visionaries on male patronage, was noted by Phyllis Mack in her book *Visionary Women*.[17] Female prophecy meant venturing dangerously close to the male public sphere – and that raised anxieties for women about their visions becoming public. Mack notes that the English prophetess Grace Cary circulated her work in manuscript to avoid it falling into the hands of 'the meaner sort, of vulgar people' who presumably might ridicule it as the production of a woman.[18] Scottish women had similar anxieties. The two Scotswomen who wrote their visions themselves – Grizell Love and Barbara Peebles certainly had concerns about their mission. Grizell Love, for instance, worried about her revelations becoming 'too publick and friends to whom it was committed as a secret had proven unfaithful in communicating it so folk were likely to misconstruct it.'[19] She evidently worried about what people would

---

16 Lord Polwarth (Scott of Harden), Glenluce vision, 1651, NAS, GD157/2637/1; NLS, Wod. Qu.XCIX, fo.50, fo.52, note, these two versions differ from each other and are probably not both copied from the same source. Fo. 50 (in John Brown's hand) is probably the earliest version. It follows Wod. Oct.XV, fo.22 more closely. Wod. Oct.XV, fo.22 is a very inaccurate copy (due to Wodrow's problems with transcription) but is taken from a much older, probably contemporary manuscript, apparently similar to Wod. XCIX, fo.50.
17 Mack, *Visionary Women*, 97.
18 Mack, *Visionary Women*, 99.
19 'The exercise of Grizell Love', NLS, Wod. Qu.LXXII, fo.148v.

say – and perhaps how this would affect her reputation as a woman venturing into an 'unwomanly' activity of meddling with divine revelation on national events. Barbara Peebles talked about being 'forced to go and manifest the vision to the ministry'; she felt the need to make a point that it was not her idea to stray into the public sphere. 'God made me do it' was her excuse.[20] Both these highly literate women felt the need to apologise for themselves – perhaps because they were their own scribes. Their visions were not supplied to the public clothed in the handiwork and credibility of a male interpreter. They themselves had chosen to write down their experiences and to communicate them – it is notable that they show more anxiety about how their visions will be received than the women who had male amanuenses to take down their words.

The words of the other women, the Glenluce visionary, Jonet Fraser and Donald Macgrigor's daughter were communicated via the educated men who transcribed their words (see below). They make no self-justifications. Their visions are validated and publicised by learned men, so presumably they did not feel the need to apologise. In this they may bear out Mack's observation that women seemed to be more acceptable to their contemporaries if they were 'babbling with glazed eyes', rather than talking rationally as activists.[21] Although Grizell and Barbara both had visions, they were communicating them in the tranquillity of the written page, not in the drama of a fit. They were thus aware that they were moving into the male public sphere where many might think they had no business to be. They knew that was what they were doing and that they could be attacked by others for doing it.

However, gender could help as well as hinder a visionary. For a woman, a weak vessel, to be chosen for such a revelation strengthened its supernatural character. There was a tradition in Presbyterian circles that God might turn away from unsatisfactory conventional instruments of his work such as nobles and lairds, and turn to unconventional channels such as women, the lower classes and children.[22] A contemporary of the Glenluce visionary, John Edington, a protestor Presbyterian in the Merse, pleaded that the Lord 'would raise up poor contemptible ones to preach himself and to teach masters of Israel. Even poor lasses and lads to teach these that esteemed themselves Rabbies in this age'.[23] In a crisis situation God might reject the normal channels of authority. From 1650 to 1689, the Presbyterian Church was in just such a crisis situation, and it is over this period that the five visionary

20 'The exercise of Grizell Love', NLS, Wod. Qu.XXVI, f.289v.
21 Mack, *Visionary Women*, 107.
22 R. Thomson Martin, ed., *Sermons, Prayers, and Pulpit Addresses by Alexander Henderson, 1638* (Edinburgh, 1867) 335–6.
23 David Hume's diary, NLS, Wod, Oct XV, 83.

narratives come. When a church loses its status as an established church, then it loses much of its vested interest in upholding the normal structure of church authority, but it can still claim that God is speaking to it directly through holy members of its flock – despite being disowned by the state. So the female visionary phenomenon may have seemed like a sign of God's approval to the radical wing of Presbyterianism which produced firstly the Protesters and secondly the Dutch exiles.[24]

The two literate women, Grizell and Barbara, were strong supporters of that radical Presbyterian ministry and they are best examined together. Grizell Love was a Paisley woman, probably unmarried and of burgess rank, as there were other Paisley burgesses of that name. She wrote her own copious prophetic text, 180 pages in length, narrating her encounter with first of all witches, and then angels.[25] Grizell had waking visions which she insisted were not trances and did not happen while she was asleep.[26] She saw representations of events such as a communion, or of men up to their armpits in blood waving the covenant, or fiery chariots over the parliament house of Westminster, the meanings of which were revealed to her in successive visions.[27] In this, her prophetic experiences seem to be modelled on the Biblical example of the Book of Revelation and of the Book of Daniel – in which visions were revealed and interpreted by angels. She condemned the Indulgences (the toleration of Presbyterian ministers acceptable to the Government in certain areas) and predicted that God would take the Kingdom away from the King and that the Church would be delivered.[28] Like Barbara, Grizell was self-conscious about her role and felt the need to state that she was 'afraid of presumption' in writing these things down and that she did so only because the Lord told her to write it down.[29] She worried about her mission but reassured herself with Exodus 3:24, the Lord speaking to Moses out of the bush. She recorded 'the Lord's speaking by vive voice[30] being now ceased, the Lord had spoken to me out of these representations by the scriptures and uses from these scriptures which were given to everyone of them, to clear and confirm them and was God's way of speaking now viz. by the scripture'.[31] Thus Grizell, while using Biblical prophetic models for her experiences, cleverly disclaimed any accusations of setting herself up as a prophet. Her visions were in accordance with scripture and they were shared with her friends, who against

---

24 See below for discussion of manuscript provenances.
25 'The exercise of Grizell Love', NLS, Wod.Qu.LXXII, fos. 107–97.
26 'The exercise of Grizell Love', NLS, Wod.Qu.LXXII, fo. 110.
27 'The exercise of Grizell Love', NLS, Wod.Qu.LXXII, fo. 97.
28 'The exercise of Grizell Love', NLS, Wod.Qu.LXXII, fos. 158v, 194.
29 'The exercise of Grizell Love', NLS, Wod.Qu.LXXII, fo. 110v.
30 Orally, by direct speech.
31 'The exercise of Grizell Love', NLS, Wod. Qu.LXXII, fo. 122.

her wishes shared them with some 'eminent Christians'. Therefore, although she enquired into matters of state and public business, she carefully avoided setting herself up in a public role.

Barbara Peebles was very different in this respect. She did think that her visions should be public. Barbara was married and she was probably a close female relation of Protester minister of Lochwinnoch, Hugh Peebles from Mayneshill, in the parish of Beith.[32] One of her main messages was the singular importance of the Presbyterian ministry – which would make sense if she was a close relation of a radical minister. Her visions, unlike Grizell's were aimed at the King. The Lord wanted her to 'show salvation to the King'. The King was not to touch 'these tender grapes and clusters' of the vines, which were those 'upon whomsoever I power out the Holy Ghost from the King to the beggar'. The true government of the church was, according to the Almighty, synods, presbyteries and sessions. If the King ignored these instructions and maintained episcopacy then he would be 'rooted out root and branch' and would go to hell.[33] These instructions came from Barbara's post Restoration vision of 20 July 1660, but she returned to the theme in December 1666 in the wake of Rullion Green. This time she had a unique vision of the King's repentance. In contrast to the apocalyptic theme of all the other visionaries she reached for the parable of the prodigal son and produced her own version of the prodigal King. 'And I thought Christ weeped tears of blood over him and when the King saw the tears of blood he fell downe and none could comfort him ...'. Christ said to him 'My prodigall king, great shall be the day of Israel and my prodigal kingdome, turne o Shunamite ... and I (Barbara) thought he turned his face to the Kirk and answered the prayers of his people and cast open his prison doors and there was great joy in Heaven for the turning home of the prodigal King'.[34] According to her vision there should be no more armed resistance but only the standard protest weapons of prayer and fasting which would bring about the repentance of the King and restoration of the Covenant.

Barbara may even have believed that she should eventually testify to the King. In the postscript to her vision she writes: 'Lord will thow bring me out and I shall manifest it to the greatest of them ... Then said I, O Lord bring me forth

---

32 Hugh Peebles had a sister-in-law named Barbara, married to his brother John Peebles; however, given the Scottish habit of women keeping their maiden names, she is an unlikely candidate. A more likely person would be Hugh Peebles's daughter who married local laird Matthew Hamill of Roughwood, see *Fasti*, also NAS, Register of Sasines, RS13/3, fo.499r, 21 Feb 1660.
33 Barbara Peebles' visions, NLS, Wod. Fol.XXVII, No. 71.
34 Barbara Peebles' visions, NLS, Wod. Fol.XXVII, No. 72.

and I shall avow it to the greatest of them ... so I am everyday upon my wing to come forth and avow this great manifestation the Lord manifests to my soule in the vision'.[35] The emphasis on revealing her visions to the 'greatest of them' showed that Barbara may have envisioned herself as another Margaret Mitchell who would inspire the Scottish nobility and perhaps eventually get to reveal her message to the King himself – along the lines of Hulda, the Old Testament prophetess, who prophesied to King Josiah. Female prophets were well-known from the Bible – the most famous of them being Miriam, Deborah, Hulda, Anna the daughter of Phanuel and the prophetess denounced in Revelation – Jezebel. Ministers would have been particularly aware of Hulda because she appeared in two key Old Testament passages associated with the doctrine of national covenanting. When good King Josiah discovers the forgotten book of the law and decides that the people must repent and make a new covenant with God, the rediscovered law book is taken to Hulda the Prophetess for validation (2 Kings 22:14; 2 Chron. 34:22). Hulda prophesies wrath upon Judaea because of their idolatry (burning incense to other Gods), but says that the King will be spared because his heart was tender. Applying this text to Restoration Scotland would also have been quite natural. In fact Barbara's visions seem to indicate that the two Hulda texts were probably in her mind, particularly where her vision spoke of the King sending out 'the good covenant'; this could well be a reference to Josiah – the original covenanted King. 'Blest are they that persuaded the King to take on the Covenant' says the Lord to Barbara, indicating that she may have seen Charles II, as a covenanted King in Josiac terms. The implication to anyone who knew the passage, and any Covenanting ministers could be expected to know it, would be to read Hulda as a scriptural precedent for Barbara.

The differences between the three versions of Barbara's first visions are sometimes revealing. In one version a unique detail survives in the preface, she says 'my husband rebuked me and bade me be quiet, to whom I replied, not so, for when the Lord God did speak who then can but prophecie?'[36] Barbara identifies what she is doing as prophesying and under the authority of God answers back to her husband. One other text shows her husband bidding her to be quiet but omits her answer back to him.[37] This has the ring of something likely to be dropped to make her central Presbyterian message more acceptable.

The preface to Barbara's vision is interesting for another reason. It gives her account of her calling, her initiation to her visionary career. It is this account, which blends conversion narrative with distant echoes of witch confessions,

---

35 Barbara Peebles' vision, NLS, Wod. Qu.XXVI, fo. 289v.
36 Barbara Peebles' vision, preface, NLS, Wod. Qu.XXXV, fo.144 r. On the verso is a poem by James Stirling against Sempill of Beltrees. Stirling may have collected the preface.
37 Barbara Peebles' vision, NLS, Wod. Qu.XXVI, fo. 284.

which may give some clue as to how christianisation had influenced the gift of prophecy in Scotland. Barbara was sick and sleep-deprived when she had her first visionary experience. She tells us that she was in the 'last three nights of my sicknesse, after a fortnight's fasting and waking'.[38] In her sickness Barbara records how after her first communication with God 'all the power went out of my body'. A friend prayed with her and a biblical text affected her so that 'presentlie all the strength of my body returned againe'. She also talked of 'falling dead', and 'speechlesse' and 'dumb', and later fell dumb for four days. This was not all. Lying one night in her bed Barbara thought she was caught up to heaven and was 'all night in glory' until she was woken up in the morning and found herself in her body.[39] She had her key first experience after a life-threatening illness which took all the power out of her body and left her with a tendency to fall into trances. She was not alone in this: Grizell, whose first angelic visitation came after she had been for two days 'looked on as sick unto death' had a very similar experience.[40] When these attributes are compared with sixteenth and early seventeenth century witch confessions then some very interesting similarities can be found.

Sickness and loss of power from the body prior to the supernatural experiences was a common theme from early witch-confessions involving the fairies. John Stewart the vagabond in the Irvine witches case of 1619, temporarily lost the power of tongue and eye; Alison Peirson, a convicted witch from Fife in 1588, lost the power of her left side. This is not unlike Barbara Peebles observation of how the 'power went out of my body'. Convicted witches Issobell Haldane from Perth, Bessie Dunlop from Ayrshire, Alison Peirson and John Stewart all record how their traumatic experience after their illnesses resulted in meeting a supernatural entity and being gifted with prophecy. Issobell Haldane, burned as a witch in Perth, was taken out of her bed and off to another world just like Barbara but she entered a fairy hill. Covenanting women experienced sleep deprivation and sickness, fell into trances, met supernatural beings and were gifted with prophecy, but the other world they went to was not Elphame but Heaven. They did not meet fairy characters such as Mr. William Simpson and Christsonday like the witch suspects, they met Christ! And nobody offered to burn them for this. Witches, Bessie Dunlop and Andrew Mann, met people they knew or knew of who had gone to the otherworld.[41] Barbara Peebles met someone she knew in heaven and

---

38 Barbara Peebles' vision, NLS, Wod. Qu.XXVI, fo. 283v.
39 Barbara Peebles' vision, NLS, Wod. Qu.XXVI, fos. 283v.–286v.
40 'The exercise of Grizell Love', NLS, Wod. Qu.LXXII, fo. 108v.
41 Robert Pitcairn, ed., *Ancient Criminal Trials in Scotland*, 3 vols. (Glasgow: Maitland Club, 1833) vol. 1, 51–8; J. Stuart, ed., 'Trials for witchcraft MDXCVI–MDXCVII', *The Miscellany of the Spalding Club* (Aberdeen: Spalding Club, 1841) 119–24. On Bessie Dunlop see chapter 7 below.

reported 'There was one which appeared unto me whom I knew upon the earth and shee was cloathed with the righteousness of the lamb and I thought shee was more glorious than I . . . and I thought kent hir not as naturall but as she was redeemed through the blood of the lamb and glorified'.[42] Issobell Haldane used her visits to fairy and her information from her fairy friend to predict whether people would live or die.[43] Grizell Love obtained angelic intelligence about the illness of her minister and his eventual death.[44]

Two other Covenanting female visionaries of this period left visionary narratives: Jonet Fraser of Closeburn in Nithsdale and the unnamed daughter of Donald MacGrigor in Monzie. These two women could read but not write – their visions (like that of the Glenluce visionary) were dictated to men. It is (perhaps unsurprisingly) in the visions of the two less literate women that the strongest traces of the earlier traditions can be found.

Janet Frisell or Fraser was 20 years old. She lived with her father Thomas 'a weaver more than ordinary exercised with God'.[45] Her narrative was recorded by Hew Maxwell of Dalswinton, a connection of the Maxwell of Pollock family.[46] Maxwell described her as a 'serious Christian' who could 'read print' but could not 'write herself'. Her sympathies appear to have been staunchly Cameronian.[47] Janet's account records how on 5 November 1684, while she was at prayer, three persons dressed in white appeared to her 'and did goe round about me the way the sun goeth'.[48] She records falling into trances and having visions either at night or at the significant hour of 12 noon when fairies often appeared.[49] She recorded further strange circumstances. Her first 'holy' as opposed to demonic vision happened outdoors where she had fallen asleep near a bush – fairies were associated with appearing near thorn bushes – but Janet's vision was of a dove and of 'lightenings' playing round the bush. This seems to have been using the motifs of John's baptism (the Dove) and Moses and the burning bush.[50] Traditional

---

42 Barbara Peebles' vision, NLS, Wod. Fol.XXVII, fo. 153v.
43 *RPC*, series 2, xiii, 353.
44 'The exercise of Grizell Love', NLS, Wod. Qu.LXXII, fo. 110r.
45 'Admiranda et Notanda', EUL, Dc.8.110, p. 3.
46 'Admiranda et Notanda', EUL, Dc.8.110, another incomplete version (to 16 July 1685) with only the vision and no biographical information; Lord Polwarth (Scott of Harden) Jonet Fraser's vision, NAS, GD157/1880.
47 'Admiranda et Notanda', EUL, Dc.8.110, p. 32.
48 'Admiranda et Notanda', EUL, Dc.8.110, p. 9.
49 'Admiranda et Notanda', EUL, Dc.8.110, (at 11 at night to 1 am) p. 32, (at 12 noon) pp. 36, 38. See also Bessie Dunlop's vision of Thom Reid who died at Pinkie and lived with the fairies, Pitcairn (ed.), *Trials*, vol. 1, 56, 'that at the twelfth hour of the day was his commoune appearing'.
50 Lord Polwarth (Scotts of Harden) Jonet Fraser's vision, NAS, GD157/1880, fo. 1. Fairies and thorn bushes, for instance the case of Bessie Dunlop, Pitcairn (ed.), *Trials*, vol. 1, 52.

elements that could be found in witch confessions were 'christianized', they took on Christian interpretations and references. The closeness of such visions to material which might spark a witch trial can also be seen in the way they could be demonised by Church courts when they fell out of fashion.

Far from bringing respectability and acceptance for Jonet's beloved 'suffering remnant', the Cameronians, the Church settlement of 1690 led to a resurgent Presbyterian church of more moderate views which had jettisoned the Covenant. The United Societies stayed out of this new church. Instead of being an inspirational prophetess, Janet now seems to have been seen as a potentially demonic embarrassment. She was summoned in 1691 before the Presbytery of Dumfries where she confessed that: 'She had pretended to prophecying and seeing of visions and that she had sinned greatly in being deluded by Satan.' Her 'book' as they termed it (presumably the narrative described here or additions to it) was examined by two of the ministers, and on her second appearance before the Presbytery, she acknowledged that 'she was possessed by some evil spirit and humbly besought the prayer of the ministers and of all others'.[51] Acknowledging the authority of the ministers and no longer going over their heads for direct revelation from the Almighty seems to have been enough to save her from the danger of witch trial, but the case shows how easily a visionary could be reinterpreted as a demoniac. Local regime change itself could be enough.

Also functioning close to that edge was Donald MacGrigor's daughter, a ten-year old girl in the Highland Perthshire parish of Monzie, who had angelic visitors in the years 1683–84. Her visions also showed traces of the older tradition in a christianised form. Her visitors came at night and 12 noon. She was attracted by unearthly and beautiful music, so beautiful that her 'spirit fainted', a characteristic of the fairies, but as she was a godly young woman, in her case it turned out to be little children from heaven singing psalms.[52] Compare this with the characteristics of Early Modern European fairies or night people described by Wolfgang Behringer in the *Shaman of Oberstdorf*. Fairies were associated with music of unearthly beauty which gave people a yearning to follow it. In the upper pastures of the Alps they were said to sing psalms too, which the herdsmen overheard.[53] She tasted the local water in heaven which everyone drank there. It was in a golden stand and tasted sweeter than sugar and honey – again a characteristic of going with the fairies is that

---

51 J. Maxwell Wood, *Witchcraft and Superstitious Record in South West Scotland* (1911; Kessinger Publishing, 2003) 130–1. See also Lizanne Henderson, 'The Survival of Witchcraft Prosecutions and Witch Belief in South-West Scotland', *SHR* (April 2006) 52–74.
52 'Admiranda et Notanda', EUL, Dc.8.110, fo. 5v.
53 Behringer, *Shaman of Oberstdorf*, 37.

fine drink is available although it is more usually wine.[54] The matter of the fate of the dead discussed earlier, arose in this case too – her mother asked her to find out what became of young children who died unbaptised and she returned the rather callous angelic answer that they might go to hell as well as others.[55] She was also asked to find out whether a minister who had murdered a child was guilty or not – those who consulted the fairies were often asked to obtain supernatural knowledge of a similar nature.[56] The family's fellow villagers were quite forthright in their analysis of these events: 'several of her neighbours said to her that she was taken away with the fairies and that it was but the Devil that was dealing with her'. Thus, they combined the traditional view with what they were increasingly being taught by the Kirk.[57] Such manifestations were from the fairies but as a century of state witch-hunting had taught them, the fairies were also demonic.

So folkloric elements, as well as being christianised, were also demonised which in many ways amounts to the same thing. In witch-hunt cases, encounters with the fairies were assimilated to the notion of demonic pact.[58] The demonic also features in the visionary narratives, but it features only to be overcome. Grizell Love, Jonet Fraser and Donald MacGrigor's daughter all spoke of being assaulted by witches. They came in the night into Grizell's bedroom and one of them danced all the time. Satan also assaulted her by making a noise like a pistol shot near her.[59] Donald MacGrigor's daughter heard a cry like an owl, and then saw witches and the Devil. The Devil later appeared in the shape of a black man and an ox.[60] Jonet Fraser saw the Devil over the space of eight years in the form of a bee and a black man and a bony hand.[61] In this 'terrors' phase' of fear of the Devil, witches and Hellfire, these three narratives closely resemble both possession cases and conversion narratives.

In my article 'Devil as Doctor', I have already explored the parallels between demonic possessions and conversion experiences in both Reformed and

---

54 'Admiranda et Notanda', EUL, Dc.8.110, fo. 11r
55 'Admiranda et Notanda', EUL, DC.8.110, fo. 8v.
56 'Admiranda et Notanda', EUL, Dc.8.110, fo. 22v, 23r.
57 'Admiranda et Notanda', EUL, DC.8.110, fo. 12v.
58 See Lizanne Henderson and Edward J. Cowan, *Scottish Fairy Belief: A History* (2001; Edinburgh: John Donald, 2007).
59 'The exercise of Grizell Love', NLS, Wod. Qu.LXXII,fo. 108r&v.
60 'Admiranda et Notanda', EUL, DC.8.110, fo. 3r&v.
61 Lord Polwarth (Scotts of Harden) 'Jonet Fraser's vision', NAS, GD157/1880 fo. 1r. Christian Shaw, the possessed adolescent discussed below, also saw the Devil in these shapes; see Alexander Gardener, *The Renfrewshire Witches* (Paisley, 1877) 109–10. See also Hugh V. McLachlan, *The Kirk, Satan and Salem: The History of the Witches of Renfrewshire* (Glasgow: The Grimsay Press, 2006).

Counter Reformation contexts.[62] The possession cases start like conversion cases with a terrors' phase, but instead of the simple terror of going to Hell, the possession cases start with demonic visions and apparitions of witches and issue into witchcraft accusations, which classic conversion cases do not. Like the classic conversion experience, the demonic possession resolves itself when assurance is reached. In fact, the demonic possession may simply be a specialised sub-set of the classic conversion experience in which an exorcism ritual is used. This can be either by Puritan methods of fasting and praying or Catholic methods of ritual and liturgy to bring about assurance of salvation and contact with the holy, and to rescue the sufferer from the power of the Devil. These five prophetic visionary narratives seem for the most part to be a special sub-set of the conversion narratives: Barbara Peebles, Grizell Love, Jonet Fraser and Donald Macgrigor's daughter all seem to pass from a demonic terrors' phase through a crisis to a phase of assurance of election and positive supernatural experience. Donald MacGrigor's daughter was challenged that her visions were not proof of election and she then strove to show other marks of being elect, however her own words showed that she thought the vision gave assurance, for Christ told her in it that places were prepared in heaven for her and her mother.[63]

The visionary narratives also show affinities with demonic possession cases. Demonic possession cases involved children, like Christian Shaw of Paisley, falling into speechless fits, in which they saw apparitions only visible to them. The visionary narratives share this feature of trances, all the five women (including the Glenluce visionary) fell into trances (although Grizell denied that what she experienced were trances). Prior to her visionary experiences Donald MacGrigor's daughter, aged about ten years old, fell into what were described as 'fitts', the more usual description of what happened in a demonic possession.[64] MacGrigor's daughter's case initially followed the normal path of demonic possession: fits leading to witchcraft accusations, relieved by an exorcism, except that a visionary phase followed upon this. However, the witches who assaulted her were never named and we have no record of trial following. Perhaps this was because her family were covenanting dissenters who refused to hear the curates. In such circumstances they may well have experienced difficulty in getting an unsympathetic regime to take any witch-accusations forward. Another aspect of demonic possession is that it can often be a bid for attention and indulgence by a child in an otherwise unyielding environment. Christian Shaw was able to obtain

62 Louise Yeoman, 'The Devil as Doctor – Wodrow, Witchcraft and the Wider World', *Scottish Archives: Journal of the Scottish Record Association*, i (Glasgow, 1995).
63 'Admiranda et Notanda', EUL, DC.8.110, fos. 13r, 20v.
64 'Admiranda et Notanda', EUL, DC.8.110, fo. 4r.

the sympathetic and indulgent attention of a learned adult audience through her fits and declamations.[65] In the case of Donald MacGrigor's daughter her angelic visitors were very insistent that she must be kept at school and taught to read and write — something which might otherwise have been out of the question for her.[66] Demonic possession plus exorcism could certainly lead to a visionary and prophetic phase, if it was allowed to do so. There are parallels for this both in English and French cases of demonic possession and exorcism.[67] But the key for moving out of the phase of terrors and fits and into the phase of visions and trances was obtaining freedom from the power of the Devil and assurance of salvation. Demonic possession narratives were narratives of transformation.

All five Scottish narratives are about transformation, four show transformations to assurance, the fifth is too sketchy for its circumstances to be adequately known. When we look back to the older fairy tradition too, we are also looking at narratives of transformation: women and men who pass from being sick, marginalised and distressed to being healed, having access to another world and acquiring the power of prophecy. The similarities of structure may in fact be more important than the differences.

This becomes clearer when we compare the Scottish narratives with Wolfgang Behringer's study of the *Shaman of Oberstdorf*. Chonrad Stoeckhlin, a horse wrangler in the Upper Valais, made a pact with his friend Jacob Walch that whichever of them predeceased the other would come back from the grave and tell his friend about the hereafter. When Walch reappeared, he had a stunning message for his friend. He had to give up drink, behave well to God, the world and magistrates and give up all sorts of sins so that he did not end up walking the Earth or in Purgatory.[68] The effect of this message was not surprisingly electrifying. Chonrad stopped his bad behaviour at once. This purification was so effective that he received a visit from an angel. The angel was even harder on him. He and his family had to pray thirty-thousand ave marias each ember season[69] as well as attending mass eagerly and honouring the sacrament.[70] The reward however was that Chonrad was allowed to fly with the angel and travel with the local version of the fairies – the night people. He could attend their banquets, enjoy their music and find out all sorts of things from his angel. Chonrad was

---

65 Gardener, *The Renfrewshire Witches*, 91.
66 'Admiranda et Notanda', EUL, DC.8.110, fos.5v,23r.
67 D. P. Walker, *Unclean Spirits* (London: Scolar, 1981) 19, 43.
68 Behringer, *Shaman of Oberstdorf*, 12–13.
69 Ember Days, the three days of fasting prescribed by the ecclesiastical calendar in the first week of Lent (Ember season of spring); in the Octave of Pentecost (Ember season of summer); in the third week of September (Ember season of autumn); and the third week of Advent (Ember season of winter).
70 Behringer, *Shaman of Oberstdorf*, 20.

very satisfied with his symbiosis of counter-reformation conversion and fairy belief and the prestige it brought him, until on the basis of a discussion with his angel, he accused a local woman Anna Enzensbergerin as one of the witches who had caused a dangerous epidemic.[71] But, when the news came to the local Bishop's magistrates, they took a very dim view of this. Chonrad was arrested as a witch, tortured, convicted and burnt. His transformation narrative was not considered to be orthodox enough to be accepted.

Here we see a transformation narrative synthesising catholic religiosity and fairy belief and leading to the stake. This is very similar to what we see in the Scottish witch trials of the sixteenth century. Fairy beliefs of witch suspects such as Bessie Dunlop, Alison Peirson and Andro Mann show the imprint of Christian beliefs about purgatory, heaven and hell and a belief in the efficacy of blessing. However, such narratives of fairy transformation were not orthodox enough to satisfy the reformed ministers who were interrogating them.

What we are seeing in the demonic possession, conversion and especially the visionary narratives of the seventeenth century would seem to be a synthesis of these experiences which was actually acceptable to the graduate ministerial elite of the Scottish Presbyterian church. By that point Scotswomen had learned to have acceptable possessions in the form of Calvinist conversion. By using apocalyptic imagery, some of them had even learned how to make angelic visitors, prophetic powers and visits to other worlds acceptable to the more radical parts of the learned elite. It is probably no accident that the most radical forms of Presbyterianism, those most likely to accept visionary accounts, drew their strength from precisely the kind of peasant population where fairy belief was likely to be strongest.

The common denominator *par excellence* which makes these prophetic narratives rather than conversion narratives or demonic possession narratives, is their journeying to heaven and bringing back apocalyptically-charged messages of public import from Christian supernatural beings. In this, their transformational experiences differed from normal private conversion narratives. Like the women and men who met the fairies, they had been on a journey to the other side where they had met beings of great authority who gave them privileged messages to take back to the people of this world.

All of the visions appear to have been associated with times of crisis for Covenanting Presbyterianism. Prophecy as a means of empowerment, practised by women, at times of crisis in which the male establishment

---

71 Behringer, *Shaman of Oberstdorf*, 85.

may feel that it has lost its way, is a well-known phenomenon documented throughout Western Europe.⁷² The phenomenon crossed denominational and national boundaries: French Calvinist prophetesses of the Camisard, English Quaker prophetesses, and Counter-Reformation nuns, such as Soeur Jeanne Des Anges and Sister Anne Marie de Jesu Crucifi all had messages for the authorities, either praise or denunciation. What seems to define this kind of prophecy is individuals whose own private religious crises seem to have coincided with times of national or denominational crisis. Just as crises in the state could lead to upsurges of witch accusations, so times of crisis or change could lead to an increase in prophecy.

Such prophecy depended for its authority on the belief that these women in that day and age visited other worlds or received visitors from them. In this sense, it was the mirror image of witchcraft. Instead of entertaining devils, it required the belief that they were visiting heaven or talking to angels or members of the trinity. Furthermore it required believing that this kind of rare experience was available to lower or middle class women, while properly-qualified men with university degrees rarely had or owned up to such experiences. It was not only women who could have these experiences. In France at the height of anti-Calvinist persecution, lower class Camisard prophets both male and female had similar experiences, falling into prophetic trances for hours on end.⁷³ There were also reasons (as discussed above) why women and children might be thought more likely to have these sorts of experiences.⁷⁴ However it is notable in Scotland that only female visionary accounts have survived the period of persecution, raising the possibility that it was not acceptable for Scottish men to fall into trances and produce visionary accounts like this. Perhaps women were found more credible as trance-visionaries in Scottish society.

There are obvious reasons why people disadvantaged by traditional hierarchies should seek authority from a supernatural world, bypassing the disabilities of sex, age and social class. There are indeed obvious reasons why a radical Presbyterian Church in crisis might turn to this kind of extraordinary providential buttressing, which if accepted, proved direct favour from God for their cause. However, the question remains why did the Grizells and Barbaras and Jonets and their ilk produce these visions and produce them in the form that they did? The obvious answer is that they used the Calvinist conversion

---

72 For example the Camisards, see P. Joutard, *Journaux Camisards 1700–15* (Paris, 1965) 21. At Nimes 'Les femmes aussi bien que les hommes expliquent le onzieme chapitre de Apocalypse' (The women as well as the men explained/ expounded the eleventh chapter of the Book of Revelation).
73 Compare L. Crété *Les Camisards* (Paris: N.p, 1992) 52–66.
74 Martin, *Sermons, Prayers, and Pulpit Addresses by Alexander Henderson*, 335–6.

experience as their springboard and that they used biblical models from prophetic books such as Daniel and Revelations. The less obvious factor is that they may also have been unconsciously building on a much older foundation: a tradition of cunning women and men who were transported to another world, met supernatural beings and who were vouchsafed wisdom by the fairies.

In the late sixteenth century, the fairy tradition was in the process of being demonised in Scottish witchcraft trials. By the seventeenth century it overlaps with the first conversion narratives and the first recorded Covenanting women's visionary accounts. This is just at the point where we would expect the impact of christianisation through the reformed ministry in Scotland to be arming ordinary people of limited formal education with sophisticated biblical and theological concepts with which to describe unusual events in their inner lives. Visions induced by fever, sleep deprivation, illness or anxiety could now be conceptualised without recourse to fairy lore and could even be seen as important in interpreting public affairs.

The Bible itself functioned as a useful handbook for how to describe these states and what it was acceptable to see in them. Processes like exorcism (in Scotland this amounted to becoming the centre of attention and counselling in a prayer group), transformed traditional manifestations of bewitchment into conversion crises from which acceptable spiritual inspiration and experience could follow. Increased teaching of reformed doctrine combined with witch-hunting, taught peasants to keep their mouths shut about encounters with fairies, and to concentrate on sermon attendance, Bible reading and learning to pray in the approved emotive fashion, if they wanted to have encounters with the supernatural. The existence by the 1680s of visionary material from weavers' daughters and the daughters of tenant farmers shows that this process had gone very far, but the apple does not fall far from the tree. The traces of the earlier traditions are there to be found in the conversion experiences and visions of the Covenanters, as well as in the confessions of the accused witches. This could be developed further by using sources such as the Reverend Robert Wodrow's *Analecta* which shows how similar beliefs persisted into the early eighteenth century, but for the seventeenth century, it is perhaps not going too far to suggest that the role of the local wise-woman who had access to the wights of middle earth was being gradually taken over by the Calvinist saint who had access to supernatural knowledge in prayer. Sometimes this access took the form of female prophetic visions which bore traces of the earlier traditions.

THREE

Seventeenth- and Eighteenth-century Astrology, and the Scottish Popular Almanac

George M. Brunsden

When they had heard the king, they departed; and, lo, the star, which they saw in the east, went before them, till it came and stood over where the young child was. When they saw the star, they rejoiced with exceeding great joy. (Matthew 2:9–10)

And I saw another sign in heaven, great and marvellous, seven angels having the seven last plagues; for in them is filled up the wrath of God. (Revelations 15:1)

Celestial bodies have long provided inspiration and guidance in understanding the real and ethereal. The gifted could interpret heavenly omens and take precautionary measures, while likewise instructing others. The aforementioned biblical excerpts attest to astrology's frequent proximity to Judeo-Christian thought, though the relationship between mainstream religion and the 'cosmology' of astrological prediction was often uneasy. Certainly, this was the case in early modern Scotland. Yet prognostication was a sought after tool, providing the believer with a perceived edge in counteracting fate or random chance.

Early modern astrological prognostication was chiefly spread through the almanac. However, the popularity of astrology itself was never constant, as scepticism was always present. Furthermore, official and intellectual condemnation of the practice endured throughout Britain, being especially prevalent in Scotland. Yet Scotland's almanacs overcame these obstacles, emerging as something recognisably Scottish, despite sharing many characteristics with their English siblings.

Astrology depended upon the accurate charting of celestial movements, possible only after the maturation of mathematical astronomy.[1] Thus astrology was the first discipline embodying psuedo-scientific processes, offering

---

1 S. J. Tester, *A History of Western Astrology* (Woodbridge: Boydell, 1987) 11.

humanity some theoretical self-determination.² It was 'the most ambitious attempt ever made to reduce the baffling diversity of human affairs to some sort of intelligible order.'³ However, astrology was not solely science (or religion, magic, or alchemy). Instead it 'was only itself: a unique divinatory and prognostic art embodying centuries of accreted methodology and tradition'.⁴

Astrology and religion uneasily coexisted, as often one seemingly encroached upon the other's territory. In Britain, early Christianity – itself 'sometimes . . . taken for a solar religion'⁵ – often tried to distance itself from popular astrology. A more elitist form of astrology seems to have won favour with early churchmen, however. Studied at seventh-century Canterbury,⁶ this form probably sprang from tradition integrated into western religion. It was argued that since the length and breadth of Creation was God's doing, He had placed the stars to provide humanity with 'a source of divine guidance',⁷ a belief derived from familiar biblical narrative:

> And God said, 'Let there be lights in the firmament of the heaven to divide the day from the night; and let them be for signs, and for seasons, and for days, and years . . .' (Genesis 1:14)

Genesis's contention that celestial motion was God's way of providing humanity with the concept of time, stems as much from sheer pragmatism, as any religious speculation. For shepherds 'keeping watch over their flock at night', observing phenomenon like the moon's phases was a practical method of calculating the passage of time.

Eventually in Scotland (and likely elsewhere) these latter principles induced a certain outcome, prompting 'The Complayner' to recognise the importance of comprehending astral events:

> Siklyik phisic astronomye and natural philosophie var fyrst prettikit and doctrinet be vs that ar schephirdis for our faculte knauis the natur and

---

2 Bernard Capp, *Astrology and the Popular Press. English Almanacs 1500–1800* (London: Faber, 1979) 15–16.
3 Keith Thomas, *Religion and the Decline of Magic. Studies in Popular Beliefs in Sixteenth- and Seventeenth-century England* (Harmondsworth: Weidenfeld and Nicolson, 1971) 340.
4 Ann Geneva, *Astrology and the Seventeenth Century Mind. William Lilly and the Language of the Stars* (Manchester: Manchester University Press, 1995) 9.
5 Thomas, *Religion and the Decline of Magic*, 456.
6 Henry Mayr-Harting, *The Coming of Christianity to Anglo-Saxon England* (1972; 3rd edn, London: B. T. Batsford, 1991) 196–8.
7 Patrick Curry, *Prophecy and Power. Astrology in Early Modern England* (Cambridge: Polity Press, 1989) 3.

the vertu of the steris and planetis of the spere and circlis contenit in the samyn for throucht the lang studie and contemplene of the steris, ve can gyf ane iugment of the diuerse futur accedentis, that ar gude or euyl, necessair or domageabil for man or beyst . . .[8]

Emphasised again is astronomy's utilitarianism, related to the belief in God's omnipotence over natural events, and His willingness to share knowledge of His plan with the faithful observer. All noted early modern British astrologers were adherents of one Christian creed or another – they would claim their art was compatible with their religion, believing 'that the heavenly bodies were merely instruments of God's will'.[9] We might therefore conclude that astrology and mainstream religion happily coexisted. But in reality, the situation was not uniformly harmonious.

Consultation with heavenly bodies certainly was acceptable under specific circumstances. Yet the observer's sincerity, and the significance he might attach to an astrological phenomenon, could be scrutinised. The Old Testament warned its Judeo-Christian audience that the application of knowledge gained through divination of any sort was reproachable:

If there arise among you a prophet, or a dreamer of dreams, and giveth thee a sign or a wonder. And the sign or the wonder come to pass, whereof he spake unto thee, saying Let us go after other gods, which thou hast not known, and let us serve them; Thou shalt not harken unto the words of that prophet, or that dreamer of dreams . . . (Deut. 13:1–3)

This 'dreamer of dreams' stood as the antithesis of loyalty towards God. Yet presumably a prophet who channelled people toward Him was desirable, as numerous such persons regularly materialise in the Old Testament's books. Prophecy thus was acceptable, or non-threatening, when it did not unsettle standing political, religious, and social values. Exacerbating tensions was that the term 'other god' could be fairly liberally interpreted: Galileo's 'other god' was his seemingly innocuous telescope, and belief in its 'wonders' earned him the unenviable label of heretic.

Concurrently, astrologically-derived prophecy caused anxiety within certain circles, contending that it mitigated Providentially granted free will.[10] This provided the basis for Robert Henryson's critique of astrology's sagacity:

---

8 Robert Wedderburn, *The Complaynt of Scotland* (c.1550), *by Mr Robert Wedderburn*, ed. A. M. Stewart (Edinburgh: Scottish Text Society, 1979) 36.
9 Thomas, *Religion and the Decline of Magic*, 456.
10 Curry, *Prophecy and Power*, 10.

> ... O man, recleme thi folich harte!
> Will thow be God and tak on the his parte,
> To tell thingis to cum that neuir wilbe,
> Quhilk God kepit in his preuetie?
> Thow ma no mair offend to God of micht,
> Na with thi spaying reif fra his richt.[11]

Knowledge of future events was thus God's exclusive purview, a thought reasserted by early protestants. Emphasising individuality, and an unfettered relationship between God and mankind, the reformers' doctrine reinforced the threat astrology posed to free will. Astral prognostication was deemed idolatrous by Martin Luther and (especially) Jean Calvin, as it apparently clouded the direct relationship between God and His people.[12]

In one of his numerous religious tracts, distributed in Britain, Calvin lashed out at astronomy as 'diuelish superstition'.[13] The Franco-Genevan theologian's attack was specific, emphasising astrology's division into two main branches. The first was *judicial astrology*, which attempted to draw links between astral phenomenon and the specific fortunes of individuals, institutions, and nations. Typically, the signs sought-out by judicial astronomers were the spectacular, such as comets and eclipses – though commonplace events sometimes figured. Existing concurrently was *natural astrology*, normally concerned with forecasting general weather patterns, useful for farmers, herders, and mariners. Events such as eclipses held a general, rather than specific importance for natural astrology, sometimes referred to as 'low' or popular astrology.

Calvin believed that the true demon was judicial astrology. Natural astrology was less worrisome. God, he argued, had illuminated both day and night so that mankind could reckon planting and harvesting times, know the seasons, ascertain general weather patterns and learn navigation.[14] In this respect, the reformer's ideas resemble Henryson's, who recognised the value of 'trew astronomy'.[15] Calvin held that overly clever men had perverted this God-granted science. Such perverse individuals were false prophets, claiming knowledge

---

11 Robert Henryson, 'Orpheus and Eurydice', *The Poems of Robert Henryson*, ed. Denton Fox (Oxford: Clarendon, 1987) 151 (ll. 579–84).
12 Curry, *Prophecy and Power*, 11; cf. Joseph Klaits, *Servants of Satan: The Age of the Witch Hunts* (Bloomington: Indiana University Press, 1985) 35. This concern that the stars could stand between the Almighty and His people may have been shared by pre-Reformation religious men.
13 Jean Calvin, *An admonicion against astrology iudiciall and other curiosities the raigne now in the world*... (London, n.d.) 12.
14 Calvin, *An admonicion*, 15–16.
15 Henryson, 'Orpheus and Eurydice', 152 (l. 596).

of the time and place of His final vengeance. However, Calvin concedes he is powerless in converting such men. Rather, he desires to caution the multitude, and instruct them in the 'difference bet-wirte the right Astrologie and these superstici[ou]s of charmers and sorcerers'.[16]

Calvinism's lasting potency as a societal modifier is well known. Little surprise then that it could work to fetter astrology, years after the Reformation. As the relationship between prognosticator and protestant soured, several seventeenth-century English astrologers came under fire.[17] Noteworthy was the struggle between prominent almanac author William Lilly, and Puritan Thomas Gataker. However, with the latter's 1654 passing – supposedly induced by an eclipse – adherents could rejoice in judicial astrology's 'vindication', undeterred that death was likely attributable to the deceased's advanced age of 80 years!

Calvin's apprehensions notwithstanding, the contention emerged that under certain circumstances, judicial prophecy was acceptable. In Scotland the practice might escape condemnation if observed omens appeared providentially sent and illuminated the godly path. Thus upon Catholic Queen Mary's return in August 1561, John Knox noted that:

> The very face of heaven, the time of her arrival, did manifestly speak what comfort was brought into the country with her, to wit, sorrow, dolour, darkness, and all impiety . . . that day of the year was never seen a more dolorous face of the heaven than was at her arrival . . . That fore-warning gave God unto us; but alas, the most part were blind.[18]

Apart from transparent attempts at bolstering protestant propaganda, Knox's readiness to interpret astral and meteorological phenomena is a comment upon sixteenth-century power structures, and the freedom they had in employing judicial astrology. However, the nation at large was still predisposed toward prophecy of all types,[19] despite official condemnation.[20] Perhaps the authorities recognised that any attempt to extinguish belief in astrology would be fruitless

---

16 Calvin, *An admonicion*, 14.
17 Capp, *English Almanacs*, 154–5.
18 *John Knox's History of the Reformation in Scotland*, ed. William Croft Dickinson, 2 vols. (London: Nelson, 1949) vol. 2, 7.
19 Thomas, *Religion and the Decline of Magic*, 456, describes parts of the English and Irish countrysides stubbornly adhering to astrology well into the seventeenth century.
20 This refers to the familiar 1574 and 1579 parliamentary edicts against prophecy (APS, III, p. 140). Athol Gow, 'Prophetic Belief in Early Modern Scotland, 1560–1700' (Unpublished MA thesis, University of Guelph, Canada, 1989) 193, suggests the thrust of these laws was not to stamp out prognostication as much as to restrict wandering beggars, of whom itinerant fortune-tellers were but one element.

(Calvin's earlier message suggests this). This realisation possibly helped to prompt them to control and exploit the medium to their own advantage.

Such an environment, however, produced seemingly inconsistent attitudes toward astrology. Though James VI scoffed at the 'vaine' astrologer, studying the 'course of the stares' for self-serving reasons, he initially thought there was little sinister about the art itself.[21] Yet with the commencement of Scotland's infamous witch-hunt, arguably furthered by James for political purposes, many forms of prophecy increasingly became linked with diabolism. The art's practitioners and patrons then literally risked their lives, being condemned for seeking out the stars' messages not by God's prompting, but rather that of Satan.[22]

Scotland's treatment of alleged diabolism affirms that prophecy could arouse deadly suspicion, possibly causing almanac authors to avoid judicial prophecy altogether. This characteristic has prompted opinion contending that the 'Scottish almanac was an almanac only, without a true prognostication', characterised by a 'rather colourless' nature.[23] Certainly there is truth to this, though it overlooks those factors contributing to the Scottish almanac's relative 'colourlessness'.

Therefore very few Scottish almanacs featured judicial prophecy, the isolated examples mostly emerging during the 'safer' eighteenth century. These included Dublin-printed *Doctor John Whaley's Strange And Wonderful Prophecy For . . . 1721*, essentially a pro-mercantile piece lauding allegedly better trade opportunities within a united Britain. Similarly, there was the bizarre *Wonderful Vision . . . revealed to William Rutherfoord, Farmer . . . Upon the 19th of March 1719*, not strictly an almanac, but a tract greatly influenced by colourful reading and interpretation of Revelations, describing imminent dreadful events. A few fully-fledged Scottish almanacs also finally venture into the field:

> A mighty fight shall foughten be,
> Which many of your Eyes shall see . . .
>
> The place as Constellations say,
> In a plain Field benorth the Tay . . .
>
> A knight shall jump before his fall,
> And fight the Adverse General.

---

21 King James VI, 'Basilicon Doron' *King James VI and I, Political Writings*, ed. Johann P. Sommerville (Cambridge: Cambridge University Press, 1994) 44.
22 The 1622 trial of the doomed Margaret Wallace (doubtless among others), serves to illustrate this; see Pitcairn (ed.), *Trials*, vol. 3, 508.
23 Capp, *English Almanacs*, 275.

> But ah a Rogue with subrile Wheels
> Shall suddenly turn upon his Heels.
> Two myter'd Heads shall long-contend,
> Their Monarch safely to defend
> But he and they shall go to wrack,
> And be laid flat upon their back.
> King, Knights and Men of meaner Rank,
> Shall all be buried in one stank,
> This Fight shall be surviv'd by none,
> But the Two Generals alone.[24]

Certainly a vaguely worded prophecy, such as this, stood a greater chance to be 'proven' correct than a more exacting one. Yet this prophet's discomfiture probably also stems from rumours of uprisings supportive of James Francis Edward Stewart. Four years later these apprehensions were realised, when, during the 1715 uprising, the Tay was over-run by the Old Pretender's followers. Yet prior to that, in 1711, the judicial prophet cautiously approached the subject of Jacobitism – the movement possibly enjoying its strongest support around the time of the 1715 uprising. Thus during a time when the outcome of the Hanoverian/Stewart struggle was problematic, the prognosticator thought it prudent to couch his language in ambiguity. Aberdeen's almanac for 1711 explicitly identifies no specific individual, contrasting with Englishman John Partridge's almanac for the same year, in which the author mentions Queen Anne by name, albeit in complimentary fashion.[25]

Therefore a few Scottish almanacs, mostly of the eighteenth century, did dabble in some basic judicial astronomy. Yet these were greatly outnumbered by serials predicting the commonplace. The most regular feature of the latter was elemental plant and weather lore based upon astral projection. Natural astrology of this nature was generally the most encountered form in many lands, not just Scotland, being less apt to incur official anger, while enjoying wide popularity.[26]

Thus popular almanacs abounded in early-modern Scotland, its printers happily producing copy after copy, year after year. These publications assumed two or three basic guises, while adopting the chapbook's layout. As probably the most common

---

24 *Gloria Deo in Excelsis. Good News from the Stars, 1711; Or, Aberdeen's New Prognostication* ... (Aberdeen, Edinburgh reprinted, J. Reid, 1711) 16.
25 *Dr. Partridges ... Prophecy for the year 1711 ... Containing his astrological judgements on the Twelve Months ... what will happen throughout Europe, and the Downfall of the French King ...* (London, Edinburgh reprinted, 1711) 3. A short biography of him is found in Curry, *Prophecy and Power* 79–82.
26 Curry, *Prophecy and Power*, 4 and 11.

chapbook, almanacs were chiefly distributed by chapmen during the seventeenth century.[27] From the late seventeenth century onwards, there appeared to be no shortage of almanacs in Scotland. In 1619, Andrew Hart of Edinburgh printed one of Scotland's first popular almanacs.[28] An important early printer, Hart produced translated bibles, popular editions of the Bruce and Wallace, and the General Prognostication for ever. The popularity of this, or any other early seventeenth-century Scottish almanac, cannot be ascertained. However, it is estimated that 400,000 almanacs were printed annually in England during the 1660s.[29] It is unlikely that Scottish numbers matched those of England during a comparable period, due to a dearth of printing presses north of the border. But, if opinion can be formed around surviving examples, then large numbers were produced in Scotland, since they are frequently encountered in various archival collections today.

As a result, it is no exaggeration to say that from c.1680–c.1750 the Scottish market was flooded, with two or more rival almanacs often printed for the same year. For example, in 1686 no fewer than five different almanacs were issued simultaneously.[30] This is in spite of the growing level of scepticism directed toward astrology, thus giving rise to the argument that the almanac might have been more readily regarded as entertainment. However, late in the seventeenth century, several factors contributed to the Scottish almanac's popularity. Previously, there seems to have been but one almanac from one printer per year. But for the first time in 1681, multiple almanacs were issued, the number specific to that year being three. This might partially be due to generally greater output from Scottish printing-presses starting c.1680.[31] In fact the number

---

27 W. R. McDonald, 'Scottish Seventeenth-Century Almanacs', *The Bibliotheck*, vol. 4 (1963–66) 260. See also Edward J. Cowan and Mike Paterson, *Folk in Print: Scotland's Chapbook Heritage, 1750–1850* (Edinburgh: John Donald, 2007).
28 See Harry Gidney Aldis, *A List of Books Printed in Scotland Before 1700* (Originally printed 1904; reprinted with continuation including 1700, Edinburgh: National Library of Scotland, 1970).
29 Margaret Spufford, *Small Books and Pleasant Histories. Popular Fiction and its Readership in Seventeenth-Century England* (London: Methuen, 1981) 2. Thomas, *Religion and the Decline of Magic*, 348–9, believes 'it is clear that the figure of 3,000,000 to 4,000,000, which is sometimes suggested as the total production of almanacs in [England during] the seventeenth century, is a distinct under-estimate; the ten years after November 1663 alone nearly reached that total. Not even the Bible sold at this rate'. Recently, such figures have found favour among people like Curry, *Prophecy and Power*, 21.
30 Aldis, *Books Printed in Scotland Before 1700*, 126, relates that the *Everlasting Prognostication* was printed in Aberdeen; there were three distinct *New Prognostications* printed in Aberdeen, Edinburgh and Glasgow respectively; while J. Paterson also issued an almanac in Edinburgh.
31 R. H. Carnie, 'Scottish Printers and Booksellers, 1668–1775: A Study of Source Material', *The Bibliotheck – A Scottish Journal of Bibliography and Allied Topics*, vol. 4 (1963–66) 213. My thanks to Professor E. J. Cowan, Glasgow University, for this reference.

of Aberdeen's almanacs annually sold during the 1680s topped the 50,000 mark.³² But the numbers produced by this burgeoning industry is a curious development, given early eighteenth-century scepticism. At that point when the Scottish almanac's popularity seemed to increase, astrology itself was falling into disrepute. Yet it was precisely because of this waning that almanacs enjoyed healthier sales. Early modern astrology's last bastion was indeed the almanac. During the eighteenth and nineteenth centuries the almanac was the last place where astrology still garnered a measure of respectability.³³

Most Scottish almanacs mimicked formats established by their English counterparts. The unanswerable question remains as to whether they were direct copies of English examples, or whether they represent a parallel development.³⁴ Owing to unmistakable similarities between English and Scottish almanacs, and since the former was readily found in Scotland, probably northern almanac writers did directly copy formulae established in England. This applies only to the almanac's format, not to its actual content. Scottish almanacs were not mere reprints of equivalent English examples. In terms of content, Scotland's almanacs were specifically tailored to its own tastes, particularly that of select Lowland locales.

Thus the content of Scottish almanacs can be established in relation to their English counterpart, which contained:

1. A calendar of church festivals, markets, and fairs, as well as a selective chronology of world events.
2. A listing of phenomena for the upcoming year, minimally including eclipses, lunar phases, and solar ingress.
3. Astrological predictions for such things as the weather, crops, and general health – 'this category nearly always embraced political and religious predictions (as discreetly worded by the author as possible)'.³⁵

Many of these features were also present in early modern Scottish almanacs, one being that of 'J. A. Mathe[mat]'.³⁶

Like numerous other astrologers, J. A. desired anonymity and recognition as 'mathemat'. Widespread *noms de plume* also included 'professor of mathematics',

---

32 Capp, *English Almanacs*, 275.
33 Tester, *A History of Western Astrology*, 241.
34 Briefly grappling with this question, McDonald, 'Seventeenth-Century Scottish Almanacs', 257, arrives at few definitive conclusions.
35 Curry, *Prophecy and Power*, 21.
36 *A New Prognostication for . . . 1667 . . . By J. A. Mathe[mat]* (Edinburgh: Society of Stationers, 1667).

and 'Philomath' (lover of learning). Many other authors were identified through their initials alone. In the case of many seventeenth-century Aberdeen examples, however, it might be that these initials were spurious, the true 'authors' being the printers.[37] Typical of early modern almanacs, J. A.'s comprised sixteen pages or eight leaves octavo. If an author desired to surpass this, rather than increase pages, the accepted solution was to reduce type size and cover 'all available space with little regard to the appearance of the finished article'.[38] Clearly the goal was to save paper, and thus reduce costs. Select eighteenth-century examples were reduced to eight pages or four leaves octavo: the acerbic Merry Andrew lamented during his 'last speech' how 'From town to Town they banish'd Me, | Diminish'd to half a Sheet'.[39]

After cordially greeting his dedicated readership – the inhabitants of 'the most Honorable City of Edinburgh' – J. A. presented 'A Succinct Computation of Memorable things to this present Year of God, 1667'. Such chronologies began to appear in English almanacs early in the seventeenth century,[40] and most Scottish popular almanacs followed this trend. Some commonly cited events noted by J. A. include, the Creation and Great Flood, Fergus I's crowning, the construction of Edinburgh Castle, Scotland's adoption of Christianity, and the invention of guns and printing. J. A. repeats several less mentioned events like Guy Fawkes's gunpowder plot, the births of Charles I and Charles II, and the latter's coronation at Scone. Occurrences of initially local significance are occasionally encountered, such as J. A.'s inclusion of 'The great fire in Glasgow'.

Following his chronology, J. A. indexes upcoming 'common or vulgar notes', including dates for such seasonal markers as Pasche (Easter) and Whitsunday. This preceded a list of upcoming solar and lunar eclipses, accompanied by a proviso:

> Having Typically represented to thy view the form of this Eclipse, thy eye may afterwards be both judge and witneße if I have deceived thee: as for the Predictions therefrom, I have not attain'd the confidence of some young Prophets, who adventures to determine Things and times in particulars, wherein their very Teachers are in doubt . . .[41]

This mitigating note, though non-typical in its wording, actually echoes similar cautionary statements that occasionally creep into Scottish almanacs. The author

---

37 Capp, *English Almanacs*, 275.
38 McDonald, 'Scottish Seventeenth-Century Almanacs', 257.
39 *Aberdeen's New Almanack . . . for the Year 1752 . . . By Merry Andrew . . .* (Belfast, 1752) 1.
40 Capp, *English Almanacs*, 215.
41 *A New Prognostication*, 1667, 4.

wishes it known that his list of forthcoming eclipses is for general interest's sake alone, and that no greater significance should be inferred from them. Such statements of non-culpability are common at least in the seventeenth century, and likely formulated with the hope of calming both the critics and authorities.

Following this, J. A. lists 'The exact day, hour and minute of The New moon, her Full and Quarters: With the daily disposition of the Weather; with the whole Fairs in Scotland for the Year, 1667', ending with tables furnishing the sun's rising and setting, the length of days, times of high and low tide, and moon's waxing and waning. As stated earlier much of this information would appeal to farmers, herders, and seamen. However, the general public was also fascinated by meteorological data. In seventeenth-century England, many people changed their clothes with the new moon, while others put off trimming their hair and nails until the moon's waxing.[42] Possibly this was a carry over from times when calendars were unknown, and other means were used to calculate times of social ritual, and certain aspects of personal hygiene and appearance. Nevertheless Scottish almanacs produced by J. A. and his successors, by including material of the type outlined, readily betray a utilitarian intent. However, intentions were not always satisfactorily realised.

Important though they may have been, advertisements for such events as fair days were rarely researched by the almanac's author. Rather, most non-astrological and non-chronological data was compiled by the printer.[43] Yet, according to a late seventeenth-century advertisement, printers were not always fastidious in this latter enterprise:

> One special use of Almanacks being to give notice of Fairs & Mercats, & for the most ther's [sic] no other Au[t]hority for inserting of the said Fairs . . . but what the Printer Coppies of others which is Optional to him to take in, or leave out: So that many Fairs . . . are either altogether Omitted, or wrong placed in most Almanacks. This is . . . to give notice to all concerned that An Almanack with a true and plain Account of all the Fairs of the Kingdom, is intended to be published by the first of October next.

---

42 Thomas, *Religion and the Decline of Magic*, 352.
43 McDonald, 'Scottish Seventeenth-Century Almanacs', 267. Capp, *English Almanacs*, 216, also suggests that much of the chronological data contained in any English almanac was probably lifted from earlier editions, and thus also came under the printer's purview. The yearly similarity of chronologies found in various Scottish almanacs, supports the same theory. However, Capp does assert that at some early juncture, perhaps standard histories were consulted in formulating almanacs' chronologies.

The same notice then called for interested persons to meet at the Caledonia coffee house (in Edinburgh?) to discuss having their fair listed in the new almanac.[44] No doubt helping the almanac survive the eighteenth century, accurate market announcements remained an essential component. Thus after a twenty-year 'death', Merry Andrew was 'resurrected' so that he might write *Aberdeen's New Prognostication For . . . 1772*, featuring information on fairs and markets more accurate and 'fuller than in any other Almanac'.

Similarly, though forecasting natural events was generally not considered inflammatory – as it dealt with either the obvious (as the sun's rising and setting) or the subjective (notwithstanding major meteorological disturbances, the definition of a 'nice day' was variable) – weather prediction was an art no more infallible 300 years ago than today. The 'unwavering' stars regularly revealed contradictory messages to different weather prognosticators. For the year 1705, Merry Andrew predicted that March would start 'unconstant & windy to the 9th; fairer to the 18th; ends with bad weather'.[45] However, 'G. C. Mathemat' offered this prediction for March 1705: 'good weather to 8; stormy & rains to 14; cold, wind with light rain to 20; good seed weather ends'[46] – in other words, virtually the exact opposite of Andrew's forecast! But in this case, the two almanacs' expressed differences reflect their respective printers' disagreements. James Watson was Andrew's printer; whereas G. C. came from rival Mrs Anderson, widow of, and 'heir and successor' to, Andrew Anderson.

After his death in 1676, Mrs Anderson sought to extend her husband's rights as printing monopolist. Unfortunately, she was less interested in maintaining his production standards, and the 'atrociousness of her work' has been described.[47] Watson on the other hand took a progressive stance toward printing, trying to bring improved continental methods and equipment to Edinburgh. In so doing, he challenged Mrs Anderson's position, the court proceedings not to be reproduced here. Watson, however, was well familiar with not only a courtroom's interior, but also that of a gaol. In 1700, the pro-Jacobite, episcopalian Watson was incarcerated for printing the anti-government piece *Scotland's Grievance Respecting Darien*.[48]

---

44 *Edinburgh Gazette*, no. 50 (14–17 Aug., 1699).
45 *Merry Andrew, 1705* . . . (Edinburgh: James Watson, 1705) 5.
46 *An Almanack . . . for . . . 1705 . . . by G. C. Mathemat* (Edinburgh: Heirs and Successors of Andrew Anderson, 1705) 5.
47 William Ferguson, *Scotland: 1689 to the Present* (Edinburgh: Oliver and Boyd, 1968) 98. For James Watson's personal account of these, and related issues, see W. J. Coupar, ed., *Watson's Preface to the 'History of Printing' 1713* (Edinburgh 1913), *passim*, but especially pp. 49–59 (Watson, 11–24).
48 Watson remained imprisoned until 15 July 1700. Upon release, he was banished from Edinburgh, to maintain a minimum distance of ten miles for one year, before summarily paying his bail. See *The Edinburgh Gazette*, no. 140 (Mon. 24 June–Thurs. 27 June 1700).

As their printers disagreed, so too did almanacs over weather predictions. The outcome (as today) was a high level of scepticism regarding any forecast's exactitude. Thus in this instance, the entire art was scorned, rather than an individual. While the disdained judicial prophet might risk more, the bogus weather forecaster endangered only his professional credibility, being subject to the ridicule of various wits and competing authors.[49]

Certain almanac authors were especially vulnerable to professional criticism. The practitioners of insubstantial prophecy were especially disadvantaged, a problem which might have plagued Scotland's almanacs. Owing to their desire to avoid serious astrological-based prediction, and reliance on established English forms, certain seventeenth-century Scottish authors deliberately moved into the direction of ambiguity. One adopted form was especially indistinctive:

> Erra Paters Observations for this Year 1671
> In the Year that January shal enter on the Sunday,[50] the Winter shal be cold and moist,[51] the Summer shal be hot and rainy, with great abundance of Corn, Wines, and other grains, and of all garden fruits and herbs: there shal be little oyl, abundance of all manner of flesh: some great news shal men hear spoken of Kings and Prelats of the Church, and also of great Princes: great wars and robberies shal be made, and many young people shal die.[52]

The author of this equivocal piece consciously copied the style of an ambiguous seventeenth-century form known as the 'perpetual prognostication'. Often called Erra Paters, these cheap publications were aimed at the market's basic level, and so listed such mundane events as upcoming lucky and unlucky days, and prophecies of the most transparent variety. The title Erra Pater might also recall the name of the type's alleged originator, Kinki Abenezrah, the 'wandering Jew' – a sobriquet alluding 'to the ancient legend of the Jew condemned to roam the world for ever in atonement for his cruelty to Christ at the crucifixion'.[53] Despite their popularity, certain English astrologers contemptuously regarded the Erra Paters for their light-weight prophesies. Of course 'erra pater' literally translates as 'wandering father', but wits were quick to corrupt it into 'erring father' or

---

49 Thomas, *Religion and the Decline of Magic*, 353.
50 Apparently 1671 *was* such a year, but then so was 1672, and, it goes without saying, numerous other years.
51 A fairly safe bet for a typical Scottish winter!
52 *A New Prognostication For . . . 1671 . . . by M.D.L. Professor of Mathematics in Aberdeen* (Glasgow: Robert Sanders, 1671).
53 Capp, *Astrology and the Popular Press*, 31 and 395n. Several Scottish almanacs fashioned themselves 'Everlasting Prognostication'.

'father of lies'. Hence, competing almanac authors might abusively designate one another Erra Pater, as did Englishmen John Booker and George Wharton.[54] However, by copying the Erra Pater's characteristics, the Scottish almanac could collaterally avoid potentially dangerous controversy. In the cited example's case, perhaps the author recollected events of 1661-62, an intense period of witch-hunting when discretion may have been vital to a prophet's survival.

Because he was reluctant to engage in serious judicial prophecy, the Scottish almanac author might have been hard pressed to win the wider pseudo-scientific community's approval. Additional late seventeenth-century developments hampered not only him, but his foreign counterparts. Hinted earlier, the watershed for the almanac as prognostication was the middle to end of the seventeenth century, after which, prognostication was increasingly ill-regarded. This phenomenon was not unique to that time: throughout its long history, astrology's popularity flowed and ebbed. Yet only three eighteenth-century astrologers appear in a list of some forty from seventeenth to nineteenth-century London, and the American scene was similarly bleak.[55] There was an explanation for this. By the start of the eighteenth century, the intellectual vitality which stimulated astrology had greatly diminished.[56] The belief in neo-Platonic interdependent harmonies had passed, forcing judicial astrology's obsolescence.[57] Doubt gradually increased, concerning astrology's ability to accurately predict future events, an ongoing process that became acute in the early 1700s:

> ... public attitude to astrology seems already to have been changing while many intelligent and civilised men still supported it ... [T]here was a considerable body of opinion shifting away from the whole proposition – in particular where prediction was concerned.[58]

This shift probably was rooted in the Renaissance, as Copernicus's heliocentric universe would not suffer theories that all celestial influence was directed solely toward Earth. Also the cosmos had become 'crowded' with objects like Haley's comets, and Jupiter's moons, discovered by Galileo. Thus the former influential position assigned to the few heavenly bodies figuring into astrologer's calculations, could be questioned. The Scottish almanac writer may have been

54 Capp, *Astrology and the Popular Press*, 31.
55 Tester, *A History of Western Astrology*, 240-1.
56 Capp, *Astrology and the Popular Press*, 238.
57 Geneva, *Astrology and the Seventeenth Century Mind*, 12.
58 George Parker, 'Familiar to All', in *Eighteenth-Century Popular Culture: A Selection*, ed. J. Mullan and C. Reid (Oxford: Oxford University Press, 2000) 212.

especially hard-tasked, his nation being central for enlightened eighteenth-century thinking. The new discoveries, however, did not force the immediate extinction of astrology solely by showing it to be superstition. Strangely, certain astrologers embraced these revelations, employing them to improve the intellectual standards of their art.[59]

A good example of this latter situation arose thanks to the development of the new Gregorian calendar in 1582. Owing to improved methods for calculating the solar year – the outcome of Renaissance thinking – it was determined that by the sixteenth century, a cumulative error of ten days had resulted through use of the old Julian calendar. Chiefly charged with repairing the error was Copernicus himself. The church had a stake in this work, its outcome having ramifications for the celebration of Easter and Lent – hence Pope Gregory XIII's interest in the matter. This would also produce implications for Scottish astrologers.

Because the new calendar was the product of the Catholic hierarchy, protestant lands such as Britain were reluctant to accept it. The new calendar was not universally accepted there until 1751.[60] Until then, however, debate raged as to which should be accepted, the 'Old Style' or the 'New Style' of determining Easter, with competing almanac authors entering the debate.

Late in the seventeenth century, such a feud erupted between the camp of John Forbes and Duncan Lidel, and that of James Paterson. As for their activities, Forbes had a printing press in Aberdeen, while Duncan Lidel was the nephew of another Duncan Lidel, mathematics professor at Helmstadt, then Marischall College. Duncan the nephew graduated MA from Aberdeen in 1634, before moving to London to teach geometry, gunnery, and navigation. Later, Duncan was appointed chair of maths at Aberdeen, a post at which he was succeeded in 1687 by his son George, who graduated MA at age twenty. George was deposed from Aberdeen in 1706 for immoral conduct, reinstated in 1707, then re-deposed in 1717 for suspected Jacobite affinities, and immorality again!

The conflict between the factions erupted over the dating of Easter and Lent. The arguments are involved, but essentially both parties initially determined Easter's date using the Julian calendar. Paterson subsequently changed his mind, believing that the corrected Gregorian calendar offered greater precision.[61] Unconvinced, Forbes defended the Old Style, precipitating a protracted war in print between the two factions. Paterson struck first with his satirical broadside *Long Lent*:

59 Geneva, *Astrology and the Seventeenth Century Mind*, 12; cf. Parker, 'Familiar to All', 213.
60 F. Marian McNeill, *The Silver Bough*, 4 vols. (Glasgow: W. Maclellan, 1957–1968) vol. 1, 15.
61 McDonald, 'Scottish Seventeenth-Century Almanacs', 276.

> Lent fourty Work dayes ever was,
> With just six Sundayes more;
> But three Horn'd Beasts at Aberdeen
> Intends to make three score.
> For now they want but only six,
> As clearly may appear;
> And if they continue with their old tricks,
> They shall want none nixt year.
>
> But for to know when Pasch should be,
> Their Errors to discover,
> It still should the first Sunday fall,
> After the Jews Pass'over.
> Which falls this year April the seventh,
> As Jews do reckon all
> The fourteen day of Nisan month
> It every year must fall ...[62]

Forbes and the Lidels (the 'three Horn'd Beasts') were quick to retort with their own satirical verse,[63] as there was more than professional reputation at stake. Indeed, in the climate of the 1680s, when more and more almanacs were being published in Scotland, an author could not allow himself to be bettered by a rival. As his credibility rose or fell, so might sales of his almanac, even though evidence from mid seventeenth-century England indicates that it was possible for a fraudulent astrologer to garner a following.[64] Still the Forbes versus Lidle feud illustrates the way in which some almanac authors faced challenges posed by developments resulting from early modern science. The seventeenth century was of course the age of scientific advancement. For purveyors of dated belief systems such as astrology, the question was one of enduring.

Many Scottish almanac authors faced the challenge by re-asserting their intellect. On the subject of prognosticators' relative scholarly credentials, the most frequently-consulted English astrologer of the mid seventeenth century, William Lilly (1602–81), had no mathematical or astronomical training.[65]

---

62 *Long Lent, Or a Vindication of the feasts, Against those three great Horned beasts, John Forbes, Master Duncan Lidel, With his Son George to tune their fidle* (Aberdeen, 1685). The National Library catalogue claims this was printed by John Forbes – a suspect claim for obvious reasons, unless Forbes's conceit concerning his own name got the better of him!
63 McDonald, 'Scottish Seventeenth-Century Almanacs', 278.
64 Curry, *Prophecy and Power*, 91.
65 Geneva, *Astrology and the Seventeenth Century Mind*, 9. A Scottish version of Lilly's English almanac flatters him as an astrologer in training, which is a far cry from being an expert practitioner.

Lilly – in fact well schooled in the Classics, and in Greek and 'a little Hebrew' – learnt his craft from another astrologer, John Evans.[66] Lilly was not isolated in his impromptu knowledge, since in his England, astrologers regularly hired others to do their calculations.[67] However, this did not prevent certain almanac writers from fashioning themselves scholars of considerable skill and elevated credentials, with the intended effect of imparting authority to all they might say or write. Hence the redoubtable Calvin noted that such charlatans:

> . . . couer themselues with this cloke. They name them théselues Mathematiciens whyth is as muche to say as professers of the liberall sciences. But none of thys is newe: for theys forgers haue also pretended the same to ý intent they might deceiue ý world.[68]

Jean Calvin was partially correct in observing the associated effect of gimmickry within astrology. Certainly some practitioners may have possessed expertise of varying levels, even though many others feigned proficiency in the 'liberal sciences'. Yet the Scottish situation might have been marginally different, as it seems certain of its prognosticators were competent mathematicians and astronomers. The first such noted was John Corss, whose *Mercurii Scoti Ephemeris sive Almanack* for 1663 was printed by the Society of Stationers for Edinburgh.[69] Also, owing to the complexity of the material he reproduced, J. A. of Aberdeen might have possessed fair mathematical knowledge.

To help sustain credibility, J. A. self-promoted his own intellectual prowess, producing two or three pages relating numerous astrological and astronomical 'facts'. His information was derived from zodiac lore and calculation involving the seven celestial bodies, or 'planets', from Ptolemy's universe: Saturn, Jupiter, Mars, Sol, Venus, 'Mercurius', and 'Luna'. Of course, Sol and Luna are not planets, and it is hard to imagine that at least some people in latter seventeenth-century Scotland were not aware of this. Apparently the discoveries of Copernicus and Galileo impacted little upon J. A.'s conception of the heavens, or at least that which he thought relevant to worldly and human affairs. What is really being presented by J. A. is sort of an alternative cosmology. This competing or archaic concept of the universe existed outside the realm of learned and authoritative thought. J. A. might have been aware of

---

66 B. Bobrick, *The Fated Sky, Astrology in History* (Simon and Schuster: New York, 2005) 203–5.
67 Geneva, *Astrology and the Seventeenth Century Mind*, 9.
68 Calvin, *An admonicion*, 13–14.
69 Aldis, *Books Printed in Scotland before 1700*; McDonald, 'Seventeenth-Century Scottish Almanacs', 259.

current scientific theories concerning the heavens. Yet, for the purposes of his almanac, he seems to be saying that such recent developments had little place in astrological-based prediction.

Not altogether typical of most almanacs, J. A.'s astrological data serves as a guide for would-be astrologers, emphasising the cryptic symbolism used to calculate and convey prophetic messages, as in the following:

> Astrologers use these two Characters . . . the Dragons head ☊, and the Dragons tail, (which is nothing else but the intersections of the Moons orbite with the Ecliptick) but this Dialect is something too superlative for vulgar Capacities.[70]

This is an example of the astrologer's 'secret language', the ancient art of encryption.[71] J. A. creates an air of elitism, by emphasising that this knowledge is beyond common understanding; only masters such as he could effectively wield it.

Similarly, the almanac author could highlight his own prowess by claiming to possess knowledge passed down by previous masters. In the case of 'Philomathes of Aberdene', the authority of western astronomy's very father is cited: 'Ptolomeus showeth us all the dismal or perillous dayes that come in the Year'.[72] The intended outcome of including any and all such material was to highlight the prognosticator's intellectual capabilities, real or imagined.

Many almanac authors, boasting scholarly pseudonyms, often attempted to feign authority by highlighting their own mathematical 'credentials', real or fictitious. It is doubtful whether all readers were so easily impressed however, owing to increasing levels of scepticism. Yet, it cannot be denied that by the eighteenth century, a new level of professionalism might have entered the Scottish almanac industry. Certain readily-identifiable individuals emerge, boasting seemingly real, and impressive credentials. Patrick Stobie 'Philomathemat' apparently was one such person. Stobie worked out of Perth c.1718, and at least one of his almanacs ran the following:

> Aritmatick Decimal and Vulgar in all its parts, Square and Cub-root, Algebra both Simple and Quadratick, together with . . . Surveying, Geography, Geometry, Trigonometry, Astronomy demonstrated after most plain and easy Method . . . to be taught by Mr. Patrick Stobie second

70 *A New Prognostication*, 1667, 13.
71 Early modern encryption is described by Geneva, *Astrology and the Seventeenth Century Mind*, Chapter 2.
72 *A New Prognostication for . . . 1669 . . .* (Glasgow: Robert Sanders, 1669) 13.

Doctor of the Grammar School of Perth, at Deacon Mitchel's in the Kirkgate, be[t]wixt Six and Eight at Night.[73]

From the same century comes one of Scotland's most readily-identifiable astrologers, also appearing among the most learned. John Man was described as 'Teacher of Navigation to the Fraternity-House of Leith' by almanacs bearing his name. This claim seems genuine, as a piece appearing in the *Edinburgh Gazette* advertised his skills:

> John Man professor of Navigation &c, for the greater convenience of his Schollars is removed to Leith. Whoever would be instructed in the said Art, may repair to his home at the back of Babylon.[74]

Previously, Man lived in Edinburgh, where c.1696 he succeeded his uncle John Paterson (another prominent almanac author 1679–93) as a mathematics teacher. In 1699 Man was in Leith teaching maths at Trinity House. This position was founded in 1680, for which a salary of Scots £20 per annum was allocated for six hours daily teaching March to September, and four daily hours the remaining months. Man received Scots £80 to defray his moving expenses, plus a housing allowance of Scots £40.

In every sense, therefore, Man appeared the professional, an assessment substantiated by his skill at assembling navigational equipment:

> Navigation in all its Parts Taught by John Man at his House near the Tollbooth of Leith, where all sorts of Mathematical Instruments are made, and Sea-Compasses, and Compasses for Coal-Heughs touched . . .[75]

Further suggestive of Man's proficiency was the sophisticated nature of his almanac. For example, he provided scientific explanations as to why certain eclipses would remain imperceptible to earthly onlookers. Displaying a high level of mathematical knowledge, Man instructs his readers in basic navigational techniques, providing 'a table of points & half points for every quarter of the compass to aid in navigation'.[76] Thus John Man probably stood at the forefront of almanac writing, given his abilities related to astrological observation,

---

73 *Perth's True Almanack; Or a New Prognostication For . . . 1718 . . .* (Edinburgh: John Moncur, 1718) 18.
74 *Edinburgh Gazette*, no. 18 (24–27 April, 1699).
75 *Edinburgh Gazette*, no. 212 (27–31 March, 1701).
76 *Leith's True Almanack . . . for . . . 1704 . . . By John Man . . .* (Edinburgh: George Mosman, 1704) 12.

calculation and interpretation. Success often spawns contempt, however. Despite his glowing credentials, Man had his detractors, the most visible being another almanac author, Merry Andrew.

If the number of extant almanacs bearing his name is indicative, Merry Andrew appears to have been one of the most popular prognosticators in Scotland during the first half of the eighteenth century. Not only was Merry Andrew consistently published during that time, at least, but its per annum numbers also could have been substantial.[77] 'Andrew's' first almanac was issued in 1699; his last, seemingly in 1752, possibly the year of his death. All this is difficult to say with certainty, as is ascribing this publication record to any single individual, since it would presuppose a career of over fifty years – which is unlikely, but theoretically possible. Self-styled 'Professor of Predictions', Andrew's credentials are unknown, if he possessed any at all. By his own allegation, Andrew arrived at his calculations through 'Stargazical Art at Tam-tallon' – possibly suggesting that he performed astrological observation at Tantallon Castle near North Berwick.

There is certain evidence that Merry Andrew should be regarded as a Scottish counterpart to the English 'Poor Robin', a seventeenth-century English burlesque, or 'mock almanac'. Originally created by William Winstanley, *Poor Robin's Almanac* was first produced in 1662 by the Company of Stationers, selling 3,000 copies. Winstanley's creation was a commercial success, rivalling the genuine item. After his passing, the Company continued to independently produce Poor Robin. Throughout the course of the seventeenth century, it enjoyed average sales of 7,000 before being dropped in the early nineteenth century. The reason for this publication's success was remarkably uncomplicated:

> Poor Robin's formula was to combine jokes and satire with much of the useful information to be found in the conventional works. It thus contained both a serious and facetious chronology, and a calendar with saints' days as well as one of villains' days – the latter a wonderfully bizarre collection, including in a typical year (1666) the names of ... Robin Hood ... Dr. Faustus, Caligula, Richard III, Tom Thumb, Copernicus[78] ... and the Witch of Endor.[79]

---

77 This assertion reflects upon the surviving numbers currently held by various archival repositories: Scotland's National Library holds no fewer than three copies of Andrew's 1709 almanac, while the British Library possesses a fourth (see English Short Title Catalogue, CD-ROM). These are indeed impressive figures, in view of the fact that an almanac is a 'disposable' piece of literature (a 1709 almanac is valueless in 1710).

78 To the astrologer, Copernicus was a villain, given that his view of the universe clashed with that of Ptolemy – the latter enjoying near saintly status among astrologers.

79 Capp, *English Almanacs*, 40.

The generation of 'both a serious and facetious chronology' was occasionally a feature of Merry Andrew's almanac. In 1703 his 'A brief Chronology of other Things' contained events of a scandalous or satirical nature:

> Since Gargantua combing his Head there fell out of his Hair a Cannon Bullet of 20 pound weight. 5917 [years ago] ... Since A. G. and his Wife walking by a deep Rivers side he wished all Cuckolds were cast into that River. To whom his kind-natur'd Wife replied, Pray Husband first learn to Swim. [5{?} years ago].[80]

The reference to 'Gargantua' is obviously inspired by the writings of François Rabelais;[81] the inspiration behind the other entry, is anybody's guess!

Quite likely Merry Andrew never seriously regarded all aspects of his 'art'. His nonchalant stance might be reflective of wider eighteenth-century attitudes toward the almanac, when the entertainment value of prognostications was beginning to overshadow any of its more 'practical' aspects. Attitudes were changing, to such extent that by the eighteenth century, many who consulted astrologers did so 'in search of fun, not instruction'.[82] Thus intrigues orchestrated by an author may have become an important feature designed to enhance a publication's popularity. As such, Andrew's barbs sent in Man's direction might have been a clever gimmick to sell more almanacs:

> I will not trouble you with answering that Rapsody of illegible Nonsense, Lies, and Mis-representations which Mr Man stufft his last Almanack with: If I should, I could ... show how two of the Tables (which he imprudently calls his own) are stole out of Paterson's High-ways of Scotland ... I will shortly take occasion in a Paper ... and inquire into his pretentions ... But in the mean time ... I'll generously afford him the following ...
>
> > John! may thy Labours never find Restraint;
> > O! may thou still appear a Fool in Print:
> > Hault not to promise finer things each Year,
> > Nor ever fail of being Jock-the-Liar.
> > May thou still stuff the Gazette with Praise[83]
> > Among the Run-aways, who there get Bays;

---

80 *Merry Andrew, 1703* ... (Edinburgh: James Watson, 1703) 2.
81 François Rabelais, *The Lives, Heroic Deeds, and sayings of Gargantua and his son Pantagruel* (1532–34), Book 1, Chapter 37.
82 Capp, *English Almanacs*, 259.
83 Perhaps a reference to Man's advertisements in the *Edinburgh Gazette* (see above).

> Nor e'er a Poet deny the Feats to raise;
> Till it be known with what ado,
> Thou tricks the Mob and Country too.[84]

Anagrams such as this, both laudatory and satirical, were commonly employed by astrologers, as part of their secret language.[85] In this instance, Merry Andrew is using the anagram to satirise both John Man and possibly the art itself.[86]

Merry Andrew laughed at everything and everyone, even those who would consult his almanac,

> Wherein the Reader may find (if he have more Brains than a Butterfly) many remarkable Things, worthy of his Observation:

> Calculated for the Meridian of any Place in Scotland, where they understand an Ape from an Apple and a sucking Pig, from a Hay-Stack. And fitted for the Noddles of most Peoples Understanding.[87]

Like Poor Robin, Merry Andrew was a sceptic's delight. The predictions made by such productions were always highly equivocal, so as to suit virtually any outcome. However, given that audiences were maybe a little less naive, little wonder that a semi-serious almanac such as Andrew's would adopt certain non-serious traits while attempting to win a favour with this increasingly sophisticated readership.

Satirical squibs and poems became a near standard feature of Merry Andrew's almanac. His weather forecasts typified this, as they became the source not of practical meteorological lore, but of questionable moral advice:

> This Month [January] to keep thee from all harm,
> In bed with Cloaths wrap they self warm:
> Three things a woman well will please,
> A Kiss, a Coach, and live at ease;

---

84 *Merry Andrew, 1703*, 3.
85 See Geneva, *Astrology and the Seventeenth Century Mind*, 35–6.
86 In England, at least, duels between astrologers were often the outcome of deep seated rivalries, sometimes political. Such was the case between late seventeenth-century almanac authors George Parker and John Partridge, the former a strong Tory and a Jacobite supporter; see their pieces reproduced in *Eighteenth-Century Popular Culture: A Selection*, ed. J. Mullan and C. Reid (Oxford: Oxford University Press, 2000) 151–78.
87 *A New Almanack . . . For . . . 1750 . . . By Merry Andrew . . .* (Edinburgh, 1750) 1. This greeting was repeated at least once by Merry Andrew, in 1751.

> And three things will a Man content,
> Tobacco, Wine, and Merriment.[88]

As cheap literature, this type of almanac probably had a certain cathartic value for society. By and large the subject matter was non-threatening, and for a few pennies, the reader could be amused by problematical weather lore, numerous pieces of astrological and meteorological trivia, and if lucky, find a laugh in the form of satirical squib or ribald verse. A few would be interested in the practical information contained therein; it stands to reason that information garnered from tide tables, and dealing with the rising and setting of the sun, was probably – in the main – accurate, dependent upon the skills of the compiler of such. There would always remain devotees to the almanac's weather predictions:

> Despite the satirists, it is clear that the public demanded weather predictions ... [for example] and as late as 1708 Jonathan Swift asserted that it was common for country gentlemen to consult the almanac for a fine day before arranging a hunting expedition.[89]

Potentially, therefore, almanacs produced by Merry Andrew, his peers and successors, could find their way into almost every household, largely because they offered something to everyone.[90]

The satirical aspect of the early modern Scottish almanac reached an apogee with Merry Andrew. Yet this publication contained a precocious approach toward astrology. Andrew's attitude seems akin to that of many twenty-first-century devotees: the heavenly bodies might guide, but human perseverance could mitigate, even overcome, the stars' dictates. After enduring official and professional criticism, astrology and the Scottish popular almanac took on a new, very modern persona devoted to sheer entertainment. Regarding astrology thus, readers might consult astrology largely to see *if*, through sheer coincidence, prediction comes to pass, rather than to gain irrefutable insight into the future. Experiencing over two centuries of development, the Scottish popular almanac had sufficiently matured so as to meet modern expectation.

---

88 *Merry Andrew*, 1705, 5.
89 Capp, *English Almanacs*, 63.
90 McDonald, 'Scottish Seventeenth-Century Almanacs', 261. Of course, there is little, if any, direct evidence to say that it did. Yet indirect evidence, regarding numbers printed and subject matter, might lead to the conclusion that the almanac possibly entered most households.

FOUR

From Natural to Supernatural:
The Material Culture of Charms and Amulets

Hugh Cheape

The material culture of charms and amulets, as evidenced in museum collections where they tend to be classified as such, will be found to include a wide variety of material, both hand-made and naturally-occurring, organic and inorganic, and spanning a range of perception from natural to supernatural. They may include gems, crystals and worked semi-precious stones, some mounted in medieval reliquaries or deriving from them, talismanic brooches such as inscribed ring brooches and the later 'heart' brooches, prehistoric 'relics' such as stone and bronze axes, arrowheads, spindle-whorls, jet and amber beads, naturally-occurring objects such as oceanic drift-seeds, fossil material without evident living analogues, 'curiosities' such as pierced stones credited with potency, coins and touch-pieces, and written charms in manuscript and printed form.

The collection of charms and amulets in the National Museums Scotland, for example, includes material in all these categories and is remarkable for its size with approximately 300 items. The collection is self-evidently wide-ranging and representative significantly of areas of medieval and early modern belief. Until recently, this collection had not been seriously examined since George Fraser Black's substantial paper on 'Scottish Charms and Amulets' in the *Proceedings of the Society of Antiquaries of Scotland* in 1893, and the late Dr Robert Stevenson's unpublished presentation at the 'International Conference on Celtic Folklore' held in Stornoway in October 1953. The latter study, available as a four-page handout at the Conference, was more of a detailed listing of a proportion of the collection, offering an intuitive measure of taxonomy and taking the analysis further in the light of more recent studies on the foundations laid by G. F. Black.[1] Charms and amulets as tangible manifestations of popular belief seem to have been neglected with the exception of these two studies, but with a perceptive broadening of

---

1 George F. Black, 'Scottish Charms and Amulets', *PSAS* 27 (1892–93) 433–526; Hugh Cheape, 'Charms Against Witchcraft. Magic and Mischief in Museum Collections', in *Witchcraft and Belief in Early Modern Scotland*, ed. J. Goodare, L. Martin and J. Miller (London: Palgrave MacMillan, 2008) 227–48; Hugh Cheape, 'Touchstones of Belief', *ROSC* 20 (2008) 102–16.

historical enquiry it seems appropriate to bring the surviving material of this culture back into a scholarly historical discourse.

Museum taxonomy and a classification *per se* of 'charms and amulets' imposes a sometimes synthetic framework on highly diverse material whose form and function might have belonged to often unrelated contexts. But taxonomy or the principles of classification are at the core of the methodology of museums in collecting and interpreting the artefacts of human history. Careful observation, measurement and description raised museology above the slur of 'antiquarianism'. In sustaining a taxonomic approach, an argument should be offered for its relevance. At an elementary level, the evidence of provenance and tradition describes an historical role for charms as a class of healing or protective devices although close scrutiny may suggest a too-ready and credulous acceptance of second-hand information and a degree of hyperbole in museum records.[2] Documentary evidence however, describes charms and amulets in contemporary settings, and the surviving material gives us dimensionality and enriches and enlivens the changing angles from which the past is viewed. It may not always be clear in earlier sources what is being described or what is before the writer's gaze; the discriminating Edward Lhuyd, writing to Dublin in January 1700 about his manuscript and folklore research in Scotland, included this class of material in his observations: 'Draughts of their antient amulets; which are surely for the most part the Remains of Druidism: viz . . . adderbead, Cocknee Stone, Toadstone, Eye-button or bead, the Combat Stone, the Snail Stone, the Healing Stone, the Elf Arrow, the Hedgehog Stone, and the Molestone all which have their various virtues and hidden qualities . . .'[3] Examples of these items can be identified approximately in museum collections and, as historical evidence therefore, charms and amulets are significant and worthy of serious note and should impress us both as vehicles and as catalysts of belief.

Charms and amulets were more normally part of the fabric of everyday life and culture in past generations and there has been a strong, extensive and consistent belief in both their curative and protective properties. Early sources suggest that in the medieval period they attained the status of *Materia Medica*, and, with the development of medical science from the seventeenth century, they continued to have a medical role. *Materia Medica* continued to draw on a wide range of materials more likely today to be described as homeopathic or folkloric, or even as prophylactic magic. The physician and naturalist, Sir Hans Sloane (1660–1753),

---

2 See for example Hugh Cheape, 'Charms Against Witchcraft', 228–9, for a creative account of charms and their origins by Joseph Train (1779–1852).

3 Letter dated 29 Jan. 1700 in J. L. Campbell and Derick Thomson, eds. *Edward Lhuyd in the Scottish Highlands 1699–1700* (Oxford: Clarendon Press, 1963) 7. See also Michael Hunter, *The Occult Laboratory: Magic, Science and Second Sight in Late 17th century Scotland* (Woodbridge: Boydell Press, 2001).

whose collections of books, manuscripts and curiosities formed the basis of the British Museum following his death, recorded *Materia Medica* in remedies of the day; moss and a human skull, for example, provided a cure for epilepsy or 'the falling sickness', and the shavings of a rhino horn were to be used as an antidote to poison. The more exotic remedies tend to be repeated in the secondary sources and the less remarkable *Materia Medica* perhaps passed over.[4] Martin Martin's *Description of the Western Islands* gave an account of unremarkable dieting and therapies used in curing in late-seventeenth century Lewis, while the more remarkable 'medicine' was '... for curing diarrhoea and dysentery, they take small quantities of the kernel of the black molocca beans, called by them Crospunk, and this being ground into powder, and drunk in boiled milk, is by daily experience found to be very effectual.'[5] Information about the use of charms and amulets, recorded particularly from the nineteenth century, suggested that they were often used with spoken formulae and symbolic behaviour, relegating them to 'folk medicine'. Talismanic belief then begins more obviously to be marginalised as a pejorative 'folk medicine' and its practice consigned to perceived domains of the ignorant and primitive.[6] Today, however effective orthodox medicine might be, there seems always to be consumer demand for alternative medicine or 'complementary medicine' among which charms and amulets and antique philosophies have their place.

Accepting for the sake of argument classifications imposed in museology, the material culture of charms and amulets offers an area of study (as proposed in this essay), examining the objects and classes of object themselves as a discrete class and moving to context, with linguistic, historical and social evidence. There is a presumption here that such objects have tended to be misappropriated into folklore and cosmological studies to serve preconceived ends, and that anthropological studies and concepts deriving from seminal works such as Sir James Frazer's *The Golden Bough. A Study in Comparative Religion* (1890) have failed to explain the material adequately while boldly proposing a thesis of custom and myth as survival from a 'primitive past'. Finally, it is suggested that museum collection and display may itself become a mythogenic process, capable of inducing changes of 'meaning' in the material culture.[7]

4 On Hans Sloane see A. MacGregor, ed., *Sir Hans Sloane, Collector* (London: The British Museum, 1994).
5 Martin Martin, *A Description of the Western Isles of Scotland* (1703; 1716; rep. Edinburgh: Mercat Press, 1976) 254.
6 See for example J. Sands, 'Curious Superstitions in Tiree', *The Celtic Magazine* 8 (1882–83) 252–4.
7 See F. Marian McNeill, *The Silver Bough. Volume One. Scottish Folk-Lore and Folk-Belief* (Glasgow: William MacLellan, 1957) for an espousal of 'The Golden Bough' thesis; the mythogenic effect of museum collection and display is explored in Hugh Cheape, 'Touchstones of Belief'.

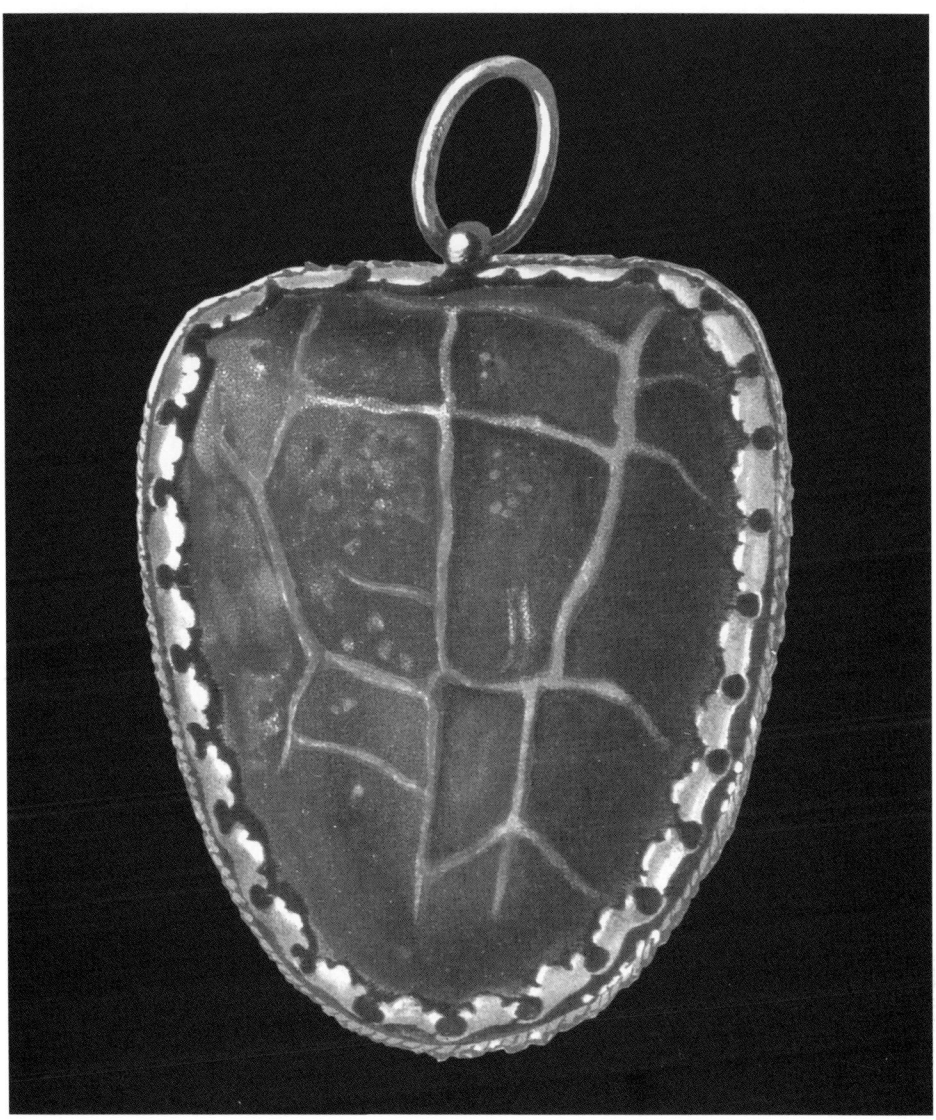

Veined stone mounted in silver and described by its owner, Sir Walter Scott, as: 'Toadstone... sovereign for protecting new-born children and their mothers from the power of fairies.' The 'toadstone' (as supposedly found in the head of a toad) was an amulet frequently mentioned in early accounts of charms and related beliefs.

M. M. Maxwell Scott, *Abbotsford. The Personal Relics and Antiquarian Treasures of Sir Walter Scott* (London 1893), 56.

Talismanic brooch of cast gold of about 1300 belonging formerly to the Bannatynes of Kames, in Bute, showing the underside with an inscription of holy names. In line with widespread belief, the names of Jesus of Nazareth, the Magi and one of the 'Fates' served as a defence against danger and violent death.

NMS H.NGA 437. By courtesy of the Trustees of the National Museums Scotland.

Leug or 'sacred stone' known as the 'Ardshiel Stone' or 'Luck of Ardshiel'. Several crystal spheres of this form survived in the possession of Highland families. The stones were mounted in silver bands and pendant chain, and put to use by dipping into water which was given as a curative drink to man and beast.

NMS H.NO 72. By courtesy of the Trustees of the National Museums Scotland.

Crystal amulet in a distinctive shape described as 'hogback', possibly deriving from the applied decoration on Reliquaries and treasures of the early church. The amulet is mounted in silver to be dipped into water which could be given as a salve to protect against the 'evil eye'.

NMS H.NO 81. By courtesy of the Trustees of the National Museums Scotland.

Status symbol of a large silver-gilt brooch set centrally with a rock-crystal and used to fasten a cloak. The brooch, made by a Glasgow silversmith about 1610, was acquired by the Campbells of Ballochyle as marriage tocher and was regarded also as a protective and good-luck charm.

NMS H.NGA 266. By courtesy of the Trustees of the National Museums Scotland.

George Fraser Black (1866–1948) examining items in the extensive prehistoric collections of the National Museum of Antiquities of Scotland about 1890. As Assistant Keeper of the National Museum, he was the first to study the material culture of Scottish charms and amulets, and published his findings in the *Proceedings of the Society of Antiquaries* in 1893 before emigrating to a career in the New York Public Libraries.

Photo. by courtesy of the Trustees of the National Museums Scotland.

Set of smooth stones formerly used as charms or devices in curing pain, illness and injury. They belonged to a reputed 'witch' who died at Bonar Bridge about 1900.

NMS H.NO 94-96. By courtesy of the Trustees of the National Museums Scotland.

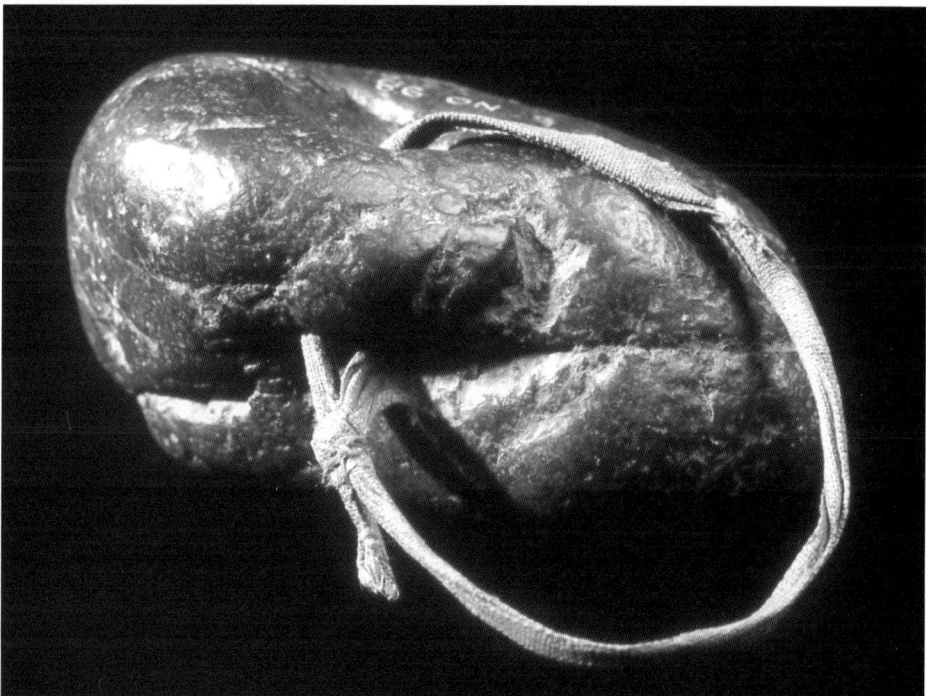

Holed stone with fabric loop used to suspend it as a charm over doors, bedposts, stables or byre-stalls to protect against hurt and harm considered to be caused by human agency. This amulet was described as a 'mare-stone'.

NMS H.NO 21. By courtesy of the Trustees of the National Museums Scotland.

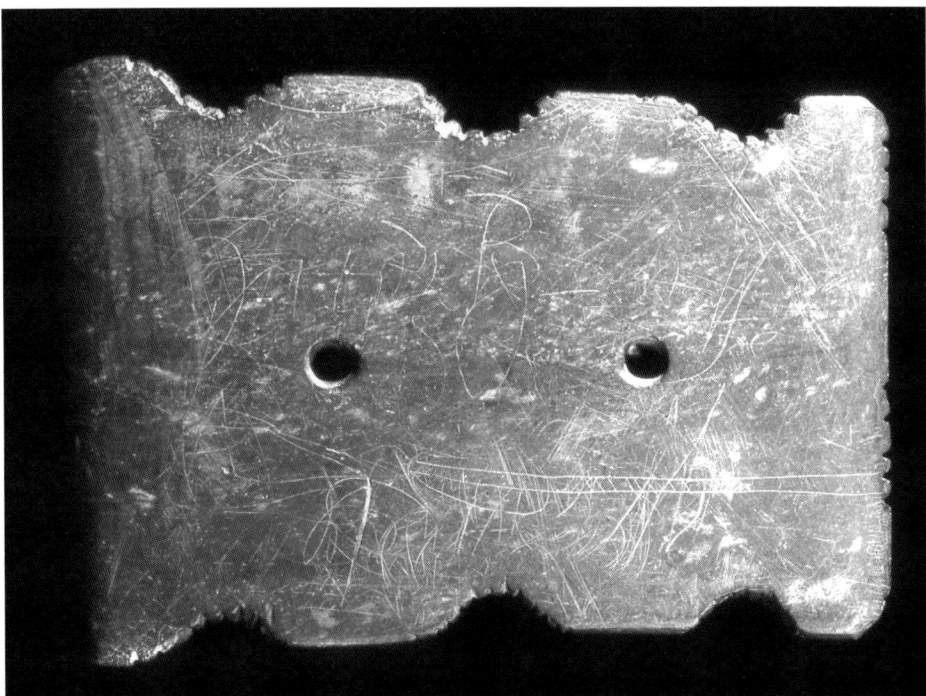

Plaque of slate, approximately 10 × 7 cm, pierced with two holes and carved along the edges, used in Islay until the late-eighteenth century as a charm, presumably together with a 'prayer', for curing disease.

H.NO 1. By courtesy of the Trustees of the National Museums Scotland.

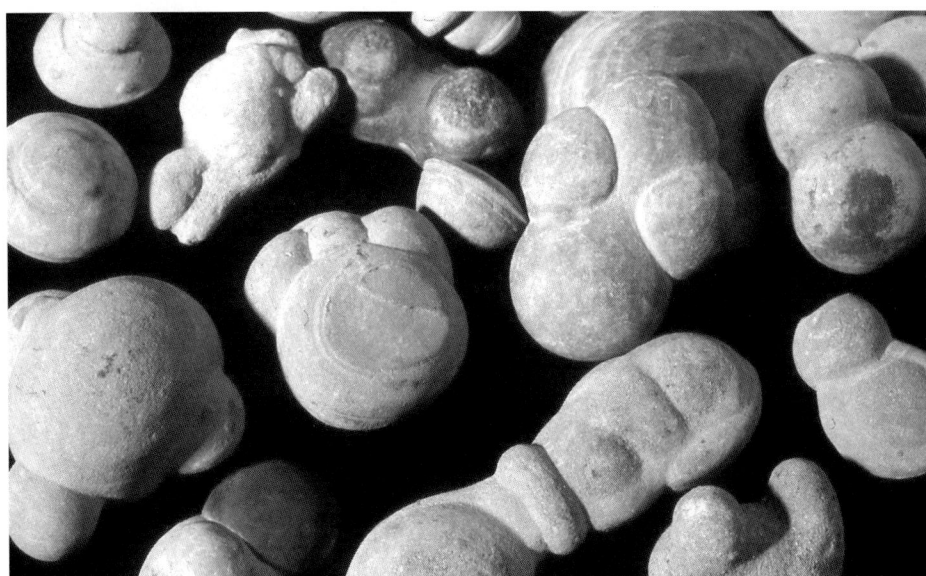

Collection of small natural stone accretions, regarded as potent and formed by supernatural means owing to their extraordinary appearance. They were used as amuletic charms in the repertoire of skills, often inherited within the same family, of practitioners of folk medicine.

NMS H.NO 13. By courtesy of the Trustees of the National Museums Scotland.

If the material is said to be inadequately understood, it may be a consequence of the National Museums' collections not having been examined in detail since the late-nineteenth century while being represented through random and indiscriminate use by scholars seeking token references. In past narrative and analysis, the objects have tended to be used by publishers seeking individual graphic examples for their productions – the token 'charm' to illustrate a study – and perhaps inadequately or indifferently by writers to illustrate disjointed *idées fixes* of folklore and folk belief and, it is suggested, misappropriated and imperfectly understood. For example charms and amulets are treated as a unified group or system and as an identifiable and tangible element of cosmology, without necessarily examining the background of individual pieces. In this process, of course, museums are complicit but silent. The approach tended to be anecdotal and single objects and one-off incidents of use translated into a generalising association with a region or even a country. This is a weakness in popular history where the noting and accumulation of information is generalising, suggesting that the facts being adduced might be universal. A particular piece of information from a single source might be quoted in terms which tend to infer a system of folk belief. For example, an early-twentieth-century treatise on 'everyday folklore and superstition', *The Hand of Destiny*, plays to credulousness and paints a dreary picture of ethnic malaise:

> In the Highlands, where belief in the 'evil eye' still lingers, when anyone was said to be 'ill-wished', they grew sick, had no great pain but began to feel tired and drowsy. They grew thinner and thinner every day until at last they became mere bones. When under the influence, cows ceased to give milk and other cattle had accidents which destroyed them, while fishermen caught very little and ruin threatened the household.[8]

Brooches and jewellery have always been keenly acquired by collectors and museums, reflecting also values inferred to them as dress fasteners and accessories, forms of personal adornment as well as financial assets by their original owners and wearers. Together with gems, often incorporated in them, they were highly valued for their craftsmanship and rarity, and also for amuletic properties. Jewellery of precious metals was clearly an important signifier of wealth and rank, and the materials used in their manufacture and their forms of decoration indicate a variety of symbolic values that they would be seen to express. Brooches with talismanic inscriptions invoking Christ, the Virgin Mary

---

8   C. J. S. Thompson, *The Hand of Destiny: Folklore and Superstition for Everyday Life* (1932; New York: Bell, 1989) 73.

and other 'holy names' were worn to signalise religious devotion and to protect against illness and to ward off perceived dangers of 'witchcraft'. They were worn by women, children and men at all levels of society across most of Europe. They could be costly items of fashion-wear when thirteenth- and fourteenth-century Scots were adopting new dress styles. A silver ring brooch, found with a hoard of coins of late-thirteenth-century date at Canonbie in Dumfriesshire, is inscribed with the typical formula *IHESUS NAZARENUS REX*, for 'Jesus of Nazareth, King of the Jews', and is a good example of the new styles brought from Europe.[9] This form of inscription can be seen to have been common on silver ring-brooches and the brooches to be dateable to the late-thirteenth and fourteenth centuries, in other words to the era of the Wars of Independence. The inscription is also seen in a blundered form, for example on an octagonal silver brooch found in Mull with 'black letter' inscription *ANAN* and *IHCN*, we assume for 'Jesus of Nazareth'.[10] Prophylactic inscriptions with names or formulae appear often in abbreviated form and may reflect the illiteracy of the craftsman-engraver or be designed to be more mysterious or magical by deliberately being made cryptic. The Angelic Salutation, *AVE MARIA GRATIA PLENA*, as the first words of the Angel's message to the Virgin in the Annunciation, was a commonly inscribed and amuletic formula, invoking the protection of the Virgin. Veneration of the Virgin Mary had developed into a cult in the Western Church by the twelfth century. Such inscriptions might be used on other forms of jewellery, such as on a fourteenth-century gold ring found at Weisdale Voe in Shetland.[11] Other inscriptions invoked Caspar, Melchior and Balthasar, the names of the Magi or 'Wise Men'. They were not named in the Scriptures but their names emerged in the early middle ages and were invoked as departed Saints. The names of the 'Three Kings' were venerated throughout medieval Europe, offering protection specifically from a number of illnesses such as epilepsy – 'the falling sickness' – and fevers. One of the most spectacular and lovely of the surviving Scottish talismanic ring brooches is the so-called 'Kames Brooch' of about 1300. It is cast in a gold ring of a diameter of 2.75 cm with the upper surface in the form of a circle in relief of six legendary beasts (dragons or wyverns) each gripping the one in front, and elaborately inscribed on the back: *IHESUS NAZARENUS CRUCIFIXUS REX IUDEORM IASPER MEL PCHIORA* and with *ATROPA*

---

9   NMS H.KO 4/H.NG 19. Reference is made to the catalogue numbers of specified objects in the National Museums Scotland's collections; see J. Graham Callander, 'Fourteenth Century Brooches and other Ornaments in the National Museum of Antiquities of Scotland', *PSAS* 58 (1923–24) 160–84; see also Mary B. Deevy, *Medieval Ring Brooches in Ireland: A Study of Jewellery, Dress and Society* (Wicklow: Wordwell Monograph Series No. 1, 1998).
10 NMS H.NGA 116, H.NGA 242, H.NGA 22.
11 NMS H.NJ 124.

engraved on the back of the pin, being one of the names of the Fates, added to two of the Magi.[12] As in this instance, invocation of the name of Jesus and the Cross was a defence against violent death or sudden harm.[13]

Crystal is naturally clear and bright and these characteristics give an impression of purity which has long been regarded as helping to give protection from disease and illness and to bring good luck. The reputation of rock-crystal as a symbol of purity evolved into treating it as an object with mystical and miraculous powers, little of which can sustain any scientific explanation. Crystals, most often in the form of globes or spheres, were used in curing people and animals and there is frequent mention of this in early sources. These examples typically are mounted in slim silver bands with ring, for a pendant chain; this was designed not for hanging round the neck but to allow the crystal to be dipped into water and the water given to a sick person to drink. As the crystal was dipped into the water, a prayer might be said to increase the effectiveness of the cure and potency of the amulet and to ask for divine help. The so-called 'Keppoch Charm' from Lochaber, described in Gaelic as *leug* or 'jewel', which was taken to Australia about 1854, was seen and described by Rev Dr Alexander Stewart who contributed a column in the Inverness Courier under the name 'Nether Lochaber'. It was 'an oval of rock-crystal, about the size of a small egg, fixed in a bird's claw of silver, and with a silver chain attached, by which it was suspended when about to be dipped'. He recorded the prayer which invoked an impressive pantheon of St Bride, the Virgin Mary, the Trinity, the Apostles and Angels. This and a number of other invocatory charms were recorded by 'Nether Lochaber' and they can usefully be compared with similar material later published in *Carmina Gadelica* whose authenticity has been questioned.[14] The definition of the term *leug* in one of the earliest Gaelic dictionaries (1780) is significant: 'a precious stone. In the Highlands a large crystal of figure somewhat oval, which priests kept to work charms by water poured upon it, at this day, is given to cattle against disease'.[15] The different elements played their own part but

---

12 NMS H.NGA 437, H.NGD 10.
13 Alexander J. S. Brook, 'Notice of a Silver Brooch with Black Letter Inscription and Ornamentation in Niello', *PSAS* 23 (1888–89) 192–9; R. B. K. Stevenson, 'The Kames Brooch', *PSAS* 95 (1961–62) 308–9; William D. Mackay, *Urquhart and Glenmoriston: Olden Times in a Highland Parish* (1893; Inverness: Northern Counties Newspaper and Print and Publishing Company, 1914) 212; see also Ewan Campbell, 'A Cross-Marked Quern from Dunadd', *PSAS* 117 (1987) 105–17.
14 Alexander Carmichael, *Carmina Gadelica* (1900; Edinburgh: Floris Books, 1997). See Domhnall Uilleam Stiùbhart, ed., *The Life and Legacy of Alexander Carmichael* (Port of Ness: The Islands Book Trust, 2008)
15 Rev. Alexander Stewart, 'Notice of a Highland Charm-Stone', *PSAS* 24 (1889–90) 157–8; William Shaw, *A Galic and English Dictionary* (London: W. and A. Strachan, 1780) s.v. leicc, leug.

the object or relic, the water and the prayer together formed a miraculous trinity. The power of these charms was enhanced by a belief in them being ancient and one or two of these have probably been remounted from older pieces of pre-Reformation church jewellery.

The possession of healing crystals bestowed reputed powers and was also, like jewellery, a signifier of status. Rock-crystal spheres of similar character to the charmstones are mounted in the Sceptre of the Honours of Scotland and in the Lord Treasurer's Mace. Several of the leading families in the Highlands had crystals which might form important elements in a paternalistic repertoire of support and protection.[16] They were valued highly, including monetary value, for example 'ane precious stane' of the Campbells of Craignish was valued in 1610 at 100 merks and could be hired out on security for its return while its safekeeping was entrusted to a custodian family.[17] The Central Highland lairds, the Stewarts of Ardvorlich, had a crystal charm called the *Clach Dearg* ('The Red Stone'), which was said to have been brought from the Holy Land by a crusader, *Seumas Beag* Stewart. The charm was famous for the curing of disease in cattle, and people were said to come from distances of up to forty miles to obtain some of the water into which it had been dipped. In these cases, charms against diseases in cattle were more or less identical for humans since the agencies of ill, such as the evil eye, were more or less identical. Another example from the Stewarts, who also had a reputation as successful cattle breeders, is the rock-crystal charm of the Stewarts of Ardshiel.[18] Known as the 'Luck of Ardshiel', it is finely mounted in engraved silver bands with a chain for dipping it into water. Several of the Stewart families had charms and amulets which were resorted to, particularly for curing sickness and murrain in cattle, and equally their success as stock breeders could be explained by their possession of these gems.[19] Traditions of Eastern origins and methods of use are remarkably similar for all the surviving crystal charms, supplying a conventional motif which made for good story-telling and precept. Other examples differ in detail; the *Clach na Brataich* ('The Stone of the Standard') of the Robertsons of Struan was said by the family to have been in their possession since its discovery on the eve of Bannockburn when its appearance out of the ground had been regarded as auguring victory. The MacDougalls of Dunollie had two crystal charms (now

16 See for example NMS H.NO 80-81.
17 John J. Reid and Alexander J. S. Brook, *The Scottish Regalia* (Edinburgh: Neill and Company, 1890); George F. Black, 'Notice of a Charm-Bead from Craignish', *PSAS* 28 (1893-94) 230-3.
18 NMS H.NO 72.
19 See for example Hugh Cheape, 'The Red Book of Appin: Medicine as Magic and Magic as Medicine', *Folklore* 104 (1993) 111-23.

missing) which were described, also under the name *leug*, by John Ramsay of Ochtertyre (1736–1814) in terms which interestingly bring together most of the elements of traditions attaching to crystal charms (see Appendix). Traditional stories also preserve accounts of crystals and their place in systems of belief. The mighty Alasdair MacColla was much given to relying on omens and charms; he had an amulet (*leug buaidh*) which he carried with him and would use to forecast the outcome of an impending battle.[20]

A distinctive group of rock-crystal charms are oval in shape and ridged or 'hog-backed' on one side and may be derived from reliquaries.[21] Similar crystals, for example, are mounted on the shrine of Saint Patrick's Bell in Ireland and on the 'drop' of the silver-gilt case of Saint Fillan's Crozier.[22] Saints' relics such as the hand bells from their missionary journeys and also the reliquaries themselves, created to enshrine the precious relics, were used as charms. One of the better documented of these is the bronze bell of Saint Fillan of Glendochart, placed on the head of persons suffering from insanity and the bell itself cited in the formula for curing.[23]

An early surviving crystal reliquary, possibly of late-twelfth century date, may have been formed to hold a fragment of the True Cross. This is a good example of relic and reliquary as religious object and is in the British Museum. Its elaborate inscription in abbreviated form links it with Saint Ninian and a Premonstratensian religious house either at Whithorn in Galloway or at Fearn in Easter Ross. The reliquary was probably held on a pendant chain which fitted through two loops on its rim. Another example of a possible link between amuletic object and religious belief is the strange 'Barbreck's Bone'. This is a smooth slice of ivory, cut from an elephant's tusk, approximately 19 × 11.5 cm, which was apparently famed in Argyll as a cure for madness and belonged to the Campbells of Barbreck, Craignish.[24] It was given to the National Museums by Frederick William Campbell of Barbreck in 1829. The 'Bone' was considered so valuable that £100 had to be given on deposit as security for its safe return.

20 Sir James Y. Simpson, 'On Some Scottish Magical Charm-Stones or Curing-Stones', *Archaeological Essays*, vol. I (Edinburgh, 1872) 210–12; Black, 'Scottish Charms and Amulets', 439–41; Alexander Allardyce, *Scotland and Scotsmen in the Eighteenth Century from the MSS of John Ramsay Esq of Ochtertyre* vol. II (Edinburgh: William Blackwood, 1888) 452–4; Rev. Dugald Campbell, 'Parish of Kilmore and Kilbride', NSA Argyllshire vol. VII (Edinburgh, 1845) 527; Angus Matheson, 'Traditions of Alasdair MacColla', *Transactions of the Gaelic Society of Glasgow*, vol. V (1958) 54–5, 68–9; cf. Richard Dawkins, *Science, Delusion and the Appetite for Wonder* (Harmondsworth: Penguin, 1998) for a critique of charms and amulets as a retreat from reason and scientific method.
21 NMS H.NO 81, 109, 110, 114.
22 NMS H.KC 13.
23 NMS H.KA 2.
24 NMS H.NO 2.

The amulet may have been held by or rubbed on the skin of the sufferer. As a piece of ivory, it was an unusual sort of object to find in the Highlands at this time. Current thinking attributes its intrinsic character and survival to its prior use as a shrine panel or decorative mounting on a book cover or *còmhdach*, for example on a Bible or Prayer Book. A feeling of its holiness, we might assume, gave it a power. An exemplar for the re-use of reliquary settings is the Glenorchy Charmstone which has been mounted, probably in the late-sixteenth century, by a travelling silver-smith or *ceàrd* in a silver setting with inset pieces of coral.[25] This is assumed to be the same jewel as described in an 'Inventar of Geir' in the Black Book of Taymouth, corroborating the longevity of such traditions.[26]

A small number of 'reliquary brooches' has survived to suggest that large rock-crystal-set brooches were prized possessions in late-medieval Scotland. A magnificent brooch like this was worn to hold a cloak on the shoulders and was also probably regarded as a protective charm. The 'Ballochyle Brooch', of silver-gilt set with a rock-crystal, was traditionally acquired by the Campbells of Ballochyle as marriage tocher with the Lamonts of Lamont, and continued to be used in Cowal as a talisman or charm to protect people and cattle against disease or witchcraft. The sick were given drinks of water into which the brooch was dipped.[27] The brooch has recently been identified as having been made in Glasgow about 1610 by the goldsmith, William Stalker, whose mark or monogram, '*VS*', appears on it.[28] The families of Lorn, Glenlyon, Lochbuie and Ugadale each had a magnificent reliquary brooch kept through successive generations for its prized workmanship and protective potency. The Glenlyon Brooch, 14 cm in diameter, is inscribed on the back with the names of the Magi and '*Consumatum*', alluding to the dying words of Christ. Raised centre sections could open to reveal a little chamber under the crystal, made to contain a relic; this might be a fragment of cloth, wood or even bone, or a written prayer which brought the owner or wearer in some degree nearer the Saint whose protection was sought. The Ugadale Brooch, for example, belonged to the Mackays of Ugadale in Kintyre who claimed that they had been given

25 NMS H.NO 118.
26 David H. Caldwell, *Angels, Nobels & Unicorns: Art and Patronage in Medieval Scotland* (Edinburgh: National Museum of Antiquities of Scotland, 1982) 21–2; Black, 'Scottish Charms and Amulets', 517; Cosmo Innes, *The Black Book of Taymouth* (Edinburgh: T. Constable, 1855) ii–iii; see also Martin, *Description of the Western Isles*, 278, for curing stones formerly in a crucifix.
27 NMS H.NGA 266.
28 George Dalgleish and Henry Steuart Fothringham, *Silver: Made in Scotland* (Edinburgh: National Museums Scotland, 2008) 29–30, 39–40; see also Black, 'Scottish Charms and Amulets', 436, for traditions about the Ballochyle Brooch.

it by Robert the Bruce when he had been given shelter by the family.[29] The Brooch of Lorn, about 9 cm in diameter and perhaps the most famous of the group, is similarly associated with the Bruce and the early fourteenth-century. It was said to have been relinquished by the King with his cloak in order to escape MacDougall of Lorn's followers in the skirmish at Dalrigh by Tyndrum following the Battle of Methven in 1306. This series of brooches incorporating rock-crystals carries vague traditions of being made or refashioned in the Highlands by travelling 'cairds', but more recent research would suggest that they were made by burgh goldsmiths or silversmiths working in the stylistic milieu of the Scottish Renaissance in the sixteenth century. The Highland connection might still be discernable through the crystals that, arguably, were the still-prized heirlooms and relics which their owners had taken to be enshrined by the top craftsmen of the day in styles linking the Highlands to Continental Europe.[30]

The evidence suggests that crystals and less exalted stones were commonly used in curing throughout Scottish society, particularly in the hands of skilled folk. They all formed a recognisable element of medieval *Materia Medica* and seemed to have come into wider prominence as curative and protective devices in the period approximately between the fourteenth and seventeenth centuries, particularly following the exercises by the Christian authors of 'Lapidaries' to refine the medicinal use of precious stones in terms of their amuletic qualities. A standard practice employed by the skilled practitioner might be, for example, to rub the stone on the affected part of the body with a prayer. It is less straightforward to fit individual items into a chronological framework when similar material is recovered in archaeology and speculation offered about function and context. Pebbles of white quartz figured in archaeological reports such as the excavation of chambered cairns although conclusions on their significance or function have been tentative.[31] The aesthetic quality of quartz seems to make it collectable. A small pebble of white quartz which was found in the Culbin Sands is mounted in copper bands and appears to imitate the more spectacular amuletic crystals.[32] Three agate beads of different sizes are strung on blue and white braid and a gold-

---

29 NMS H.NGD 11.
30 [John Mackay] *The Celtic Monthly* 14 (1906) 194–6; see also British Museum Catalogue nos. M&LA 55.12–1.220 for the Lochbuie Brooch (NMS NGD 12) and M&LA 97.5–26.1 for the Glenlyon Brooch.
31 Joan Evans, *Magical Jewels of the Middle Ages and the Renaissance particularly in England* (Oxford: Clarendon Press, 1922); Arthur Mitchell, 'On White Pebbles in Connection with Pagan and Christian Burials', *PSAS* 18 (1883–84) 286–91; *Palace of History. Catalogue of Exhibits Volume II*, forward by John Glaister (Glasgow: Scottish Exhibition of National History, Art and Industry, 1911) 662–8.
32 NMS H.NO 82.

mounted and indeterminate hardstone attached to the braid with a piece of silk ribbon.[33] Distinctively-coloured water-worn pebbles were and still are collected. A good example in the national collections is a heart-shaped and water-worn stone of microgranite acquired from Shetland, having been used in Whalsay as a charm for curing illness in people and latterly in cattle.[34] A small basalt pebble from Polwarth in Berwickshire was used as an amulet and known as the 'Lucky Stone'.[35] Several similarly formed 'charms' in the national collections have comparable attributions and specific references suggest practices amounting to a 'system' of belief.[36] A plaque of slate, approximately 10 × 7 cm, with notched sides and two small symmetrically-placed perforations was among the earliest non-prehistoric antiquities given to the National Museum in 1784 and came into the collections with the information 'formerly used for cure of diseases in Islay'.[37]

These are tangible relics of the 'charmers' against whom the kirk campaigned, or the white or small, round, blue stone reported to have given the 'Brahan Seer' his clairvoyant powers. Apart from aesthetic appeal or modern classification as semi-precious stone, few of these stones are particularly remarkable. This can be borne in mind when considering earlier descriptions of charms; Martin Martin's lengthy description, for example, of the magical *Ball Moluidh* – 'a green stone, much like a globe in figure, about the bigness of a goose egg' – in the custody of a family in Arran.[38] Charms and amulets were caught up in the European-wide phenomenon of the witch-hunts, which escalated in Scotland during the reign of James VI. Accident and sickness could more easily be ascribed to identifiable people wishing or devising ill to others. Those who might be identified as having a power to harm others were looked on as magicians or witches and were imprisoned and put on trial for evil practices and casting spells. Stones with holes in them were considered to give people a power to see into the future or to cast spells, as described in traditions of the 'Brahan Seer', and, to a limited extent, the national collection reflects the way in which the folk healer or 'charmer' was indicted as an enemy of the state. There is, however, a whiff of Victorian creative and imaginative description and interpretation about these objects in museum catalogues. Three stones, two like small birds' eggs and one a grooved quartzite pebble, belonged to a reputed witch who died at Bonar Bridge in 1900. They were said to have been used for charms and it is notable that the grooved stone

---

33 NMS K.2001.853.
34 NMS H.NO 73.
35 NMS H.NO 67.
36 For example, NMS H.NO 54–57, H.NO 91–92.
37 NMS H.NO 1.
38 Martin, *Description of the Western Isles*, 260.

was almost certainly a form of early 'strike-a-light'.[39] The calf's heart pierced with pins found under the flagstone floor of a byre in Dalkeith and given to the National Museums in 1827 by Sir Walter Scott would seem to have been a sinister device formed either to bring about disease and death or to 'transfer' sickness and misfortune.[40] The 'Witch's Cursing Bone' from Glen Shira, Argyll, speaks eloquently for itself.[41] The 'Witches Rope' made of horsehair was said to have been used by a witch to take away the milk of a neighbour's cows; it was dragged across their field during the night. Vindictive impoverishment could be more personal and a small silver heart brooch from Rosehearty, Banffshire, was worn in the early nineteenth century to prevent witches taking away the milk of a nursing mother.[42] Belief in talismanic qualities of heart brooches probably swelled the demand for 'luckenbooths', the trademark of Edinburgh's metalworkers' quarter round the Kirk of Saint Giles.

Other aspects of the material culture of charming which had drawn the ire of pulpit and kirk session can be guessed at although their commonplace character must have ensured their disappearance. The wood of the rowan (formed into tiny crosses) and red thread are much written about, and twisted or knotted thread is the focus of lively traditions of healing or 'turning' malign influences; Rev Alexander Stewart published a healing verse or *rann* which was intoned while worsted thread was tied round an animal's tail. The 'charm of the riddle' or charming and divination by sieve and shears involved farming tools which are visible in museum collections but not known to be interpreted as such.[43] Other material such as fabric is still to be seen at certain locations. Wells and springs have always been regarded as important places because they are the source of life-giving water. It has been estimated that there are over six hundred healing wells in Scotland, many named after different Saints. Wells and springs were regularly visited for healing water for themselves or a sick child or relation. They would (and we still do) leave gifts of metal such as coins or pins to make a wish and bring good luck or perhaps a scrap of clothing from off the sick person's body. These 'clootie wells' are named from the offerings of cloth hung beside them, a well-known example being the Clootie Well of St Boniface at Munlochy in Ross and

39 NMS H.NO 94–96.
40 NMS H.NO 22.
41 NMS H.NO 78.
42 NMS H.NO 48, H.NGA 155, H.NGA 266.
43 Rev. Alexander Stewart, *Nether Lochaber: The Natural History, Legends and Folklore of the West Highlands* (Edinburgh: William Paterson, 1883) 201–3; Robert Chambers, *Domestic Annals of Scotland*, 3 vols. (Edinburgh: William Chambers, 1858–61) vol. 2, 434–5; William Mackay, ed., *Records of the Presbyteries of Inverness and Dingwall, 1643–1688* (Edinburgh: Scottish History Society, 1896) 156; Duncan C. Mactavish, ed., *Minutes of the Synod of Argyll, 1639–1651* (Edinburgh: Scottish History Society, 1943) 84.

Cromarty. A small collection of coins, metal buttons and pins which were left in the Holy Well at Inchadney, Kenmore, by Loch Tay, has been preserved.[44]

Naturally perforated stones which could be strung up and hung in significant spots such as over doors or on bedposts attracted traditions of offering protection against disease in cattle, especially illness inflicted through human agency, and against nightmares. The latter syndrome and its side-effects seem to have been widely recognised and animals so stricken described as being 'hag-ridden' when in fact sick or ill-used. The counter-charm in this case might be described as a 'mare stone' and a few in the national collection have this attribution and were said to have hung in byres or stables.[45]

Stones of different shapes and sizes became amulets in the hands of the user or the eyes of the beholder, according to attributions in museum catalogues. One or two examples, displaying certain characteristics such as a hollowed face defined by sets of concentric circles, have been explained as 'pivot-stones' carrying the vertical axles of the water wheel of a grain mill. Typical also are fossils which have been used decoratively since prehistoric times but not much explained before the late-seventeenth century. Material that came out of the ground could be assumed to have come from an 'otherworld' of the supernatural and as a consequence acted as counter charm. The gift of a jewelled 'serpent's tongue' to Queen Margaret in 1507 was almost certainly a fossil being used as an amuletic 'test' against poison. The interpretation of fossil material is an evolving science and names in folklore recall earlier phases of explanation of such phenomena, including their origins and medicinal as well as magical properties. The bullet-shaped guards of an extinct mollusc, *Bellemnitella mucronata*, were known as 'thunderbolts' and adopted as amulets. They were regarded as being hurled to the ground after violent thunderstorms. Belemnite guards which occur in Jurassic rocks were recorded as 'thunderbolts' by Hugh Miller when he found them in the geologically rich strata at Eathie.[46] Another amulet of fossil material was the 'toadstone', included, significantly with its Gaelic name as *Clach Losgain*, in Edward Lhuyd's listing in 1700. The shiny teeth of the Mesozoic fish *Lepidotus* were believed to have formed as a hard concretion within the head of the toad. The notion of toads' heads containing jewels can be found in Classical sources and the toadstone myth was powerful, including a belief in their medicinal value

44 NMS H.NO 62–66.
45 NMS H.NO 21, H.NO 29, H.NO 98. W. R. Halliday, *Folklore Studies Ancient and Modern* (London: Methuen, 1924) 132–55; J. Geoffrey Dent, 'The Holed Stone Amulet and its Uses', *Folk Life* 3 (1965) 68–78.
46 *The Accounts of the Lord High Treasurer of Scotland*, 13 vols. ed. T. Dickson and J. B. Paul (Edinburgh: H. M. General Register House, 1877–96) vol. 3, 359–60; Hugh Miller, *My Schools and Schoolmasters* (Edinburgh: Nimmo, Hay and Mitchell, 1907) 134, 160, 163.

as protection against or antidote to poison. Where the fossil *Lepidotes* were less abundant, the myth and the name could be readily adopted for other amulets, whether fossil or not. Rev Alexander Stewart described a 'healing stone' (*Clach-Leighis*) seen at Kinlochleven, Argyll, in about 1888 and considered it to be a natural curiosity. He learnt from his informant, the stone's owner, that

> ... it was used in healing of ailments, and that the tradition in the family was that it had originally been found growing on the top of the head of a toad! When questioned as to the *modus operandi* he could only say that sometimes the charm was applied directly to the seat of pain, and at other times it was dipped in water from a running stream, over which an incantation was said, and that the patient was made to drink of the water, and had some of it sprinkled over him.[47]

Amulets as naturally-sourced material have included a class of tropical drift seeds and seed pods from South America and the West Indies, carried across the Atlantic on the Gulf Stream and deposited on the Atlantic seaboard of Ireland, Scotland and Scandinavia.[48] These were described by Martin Martin as forms of *Materia Medica* and rather more sanctimoniously by Alexander Carmichael in *Carmina Gadelica* as an amulet placed in the hands of women in labour by the midwife. The term used in Uist for the drift seed charm was *Airne Moire* ('Mary's kidney'), confirmed by Rev Fr Allan McDonald (1859–1905) in his wordlist, who also added the term *Cnò Mhoire* for the Molucca bean or 'Mary's nut', heart-like in shape and used as a little snuff box after the kernel was taken out.[49]

Three or four classes of recovered prehistoric and historic items seem commonly to have been adopted as amulets. Some axeheads which came into the national collections through private sources were described as 'thunderbolts' and were said to avert evil, for example the effects of so-called 'evil eye'. Sir Arthur Mitchell summarised this in his Rhind Lecture series in 1880, 'The Past in the Present': 'in every part of Scotland these ancient tools or weapons are now treated by the people as possessed of a power to keep away misfortune and cure disease'.[50]

---

47 *Palace of History*, 668; Rev. Alexander Stewart, 'Notice of a Highland Charm-Stone', 157.
48 NMS H.NO 41, H.NO 49, H.NO 53.
49 Martin, *Description of the Western Isles*, 93–4; Alexander Carmichael, *Carmina Gadelica* (Edinburgh: Scottish Academic Press, 1972) vol. 2, 225; J. L. Campbell, ed., *Gaelic Words and Expressions from South Uist and Eriskay* (1972; Dublin: Dublin Institute for Advanced Studies, 1991) 25, 75; see also Rev. John Lane Buchanan, *Travels in the Western Hebrides from 1782 to 1790* (1793; Waternish, Skye: MacLean Press, 1990) 46.
50 Arthur Mitchell, *The Past in the Present: What is Civilisation?* (Edinburgh: David Douglas, 1880) 156; see also Sir John Evans, *Ancient Stone Implements, Weapons and Ornaments of Great Britain* (1871; London: Longmans, 1897) 469.

When Scott visited Shetland in 1814 with the Commissioners for Northern Lights, he was presented with 'the most superb collection of the stone axes (or adzes, or whatever they are) called *celts*. The Zetlanders call them *thunderbolts* and keep them in their houses as a receipt against thunder'.[51] Examples of spindle-whorls, lost or discarded and subsequently picked up, have been termed 'adder stones' with the attribute of treating snake-bites, the association and potency owing to their being described as having been formed by adders.[52] A snakeskin charm appears to be a sloughed-off adder skin, backed with silk and then strung through a discoid stone and a talismanic ring attached with ribbon.[53] As a form of homeopathic medicine or counter-charm for snake-bites and poison, the application of a part of the snake to the wound was always regarded as a sure form of cure. The pierced discoid stones may have been a spindle-whorl and certainly answers the literary and traditional description of the 'adder-stone'. The combination in this instance of the 'adder-stone' with the snakeskin threaded through it reflects the tradition that they were used (or even created) by the snakes themselves in sloughing off their skin when moulting in due season. Amber beads, having been fashionable and desirable items in prehistory, were always gathered up and treasured when found. They were used as protective amulets with a strong and consistent belief in their potential for alleviating eye troubles.[54] A group of amber beads acquired recently by the National Museums is strung together in necklace or bracelet form and called 'Lammer-Beads'. They were described as a protection against supernatural powers for children and infants before baptism or, alternatively and for adult use, as a cure for sore eyes.[55] This was the description of the charms when exhibited at the Glasgow International Exhibition in 1888 and as subsequently published in the record of the exhibited historical and archaeological collections.[56] The descriptions of the charms in 1890 do not throw significant extra light on their provenance except for some traditional and popular anecdotal accounts of their context in folk belief. For example, a tradition that amber or 'lammer' beads were particularly prized by the fishing communities of the East Coast, we might presume was because amber had more frequently been found there on the North Sea rim in the past.[57] Another consistent amuletic belief was in the countercharm potency

51 Walter Scott, *The Voyage of the Pharos* (Hamilton: Scottish Library Association, 1998) 30.
52 NMS H.NO 8–11. Captain F. W. L. Thomas, *PSAS* 4 (1860–62) 119; Mitchell, *The Past in the Present*, 6.
53 NMS K.2001.854.
54 For example, NMS X.FM 1, H.NO 4–7, K.1905.1177.
55 NMS K.2001.851.
56 J. Paton, *Scottish National Memorials* (Glasgow, 1890).
57 Paton, *Scottish National Memorials*, 337–8; see also Robert Chambers, *Popular Rhymes of Scotland* (1826; London and Edinburgh: W & R Chambers, 1892) 328.

of prehistoric arrowheads; known widely as 'elf-arrows', 'elf-bolts' or 'fairy darts'. Many of these have been mounted as pendants. Rev John Fraser supplied Edward Lhuyd with a version of current belief about such arrowheads in 1702.

> It is strange that these elf stones, whither litle or mickle, hes still the same figure, though certainly knowen to fall from the aire; the comonality superstitiously imagine that the fairies both maks them and gives them that shape, and that they doe hurt by them, which we call to be elfshot.[58]

Amulets that were worn or carried on the person as forms of apotropaic jewellery to guard against misfortune could be sought from skilled folk who made them. A remarkable number of 'lead hearts' are now in museum collections, principally due to the contemporary prevalence of metal detecting and the application of Treasure Trove legislation. An example in the national collections acquired through the Treasure Trove Advisory Panel is a rough but unmistakable model of a heart, approximately 5.5 × 4 cm, cast in lead, probably in an earth mould which has given a rough and pitted surface to the convex face of the object.[59] It was found in garden grounds at Silverknowes, Edinburgh. As such, of course, it comes with no supporting information or potential inference to be drawn from the find context of a town garden. The heart-shape suggests an amulet, home-made and intended as a curing or protective device. This belongs conceptually in a medieval context of meagre scientific or medical knowledge and strong spiritual credo. It is almost certainly associated with the belief in placing different parts of the body under the specific protection of an amulet. A 'heart' amulet therefore was made to protect the vital and central organ against the threat of disease or injury. As heart brooches were much treasured for healing virtues, their inferred potency derived from the same association. There is a number of references to the use of lead hearts for curing perceived heart ailments or fevers, and the action of 'turning the heart' in lead on behalf of a person suffering from heart disease. The remedy of 'casting the lead' was known as a cure for insanity when a person's heart was believed to be out of its proper position in the body, and Thomas Edmonston's *Etymological Glossary of the Shetland and Orkney Dialect* of 1866 includes the 'leaden heart' as a 'spell' which was hung round the neck of a patient.[60]

---

58 Rev. John Fraser, 'Notes on the Superstitions, Customs, &c. of the Highlanders, 1702', *Analecta Scotia* 2 vols. (Edinburgh: Thomas G. Stevenson, 1834) vol. 1, 119.
59 K.2000.157.
60 Rev. J. MacDonald, 'Stray Customs and Legends', *TGSI* 19 (1893–94) 274; Thomas Edmonston, *An Etymological Glossary of the Shetland and Orkney Dialects* (London: Asher & Co., 1866) s.v. Leaden-heart; Donald MacDonald, *The Tolsta Township* (Tolsta Community Association, 1984) 71.

A silver medal, awarded in its original form in 1798 to soldiers in the Breadalbane Fencibles but 'clipped' into the shape of a heart, was recovered recently from military training grounds between Ardesier and Fort George. It has been suggested that the object was cut down to act as an amulet for a young man recruited into the army in the course of the Napoleonic Wars. There is sufficient evidence to link this to the Highland practice of intoning a protective charm or *seun* against mortal danger and to ensure their safe return home. This might be accompanied by a talisman which was worn in a hidden place or sewn into the clothing. Formulae of words or prayers chanted over the 'warrior', described by the folklorist as the 'rune of protection', are still well-known in Gaelic, especially in terms of the service of Gaels in the world wars of the twentieth century.[61]

'Charms' and 'amulets' seem almost synonymous and not necessarily mutually exclusive, though etymologically they are. 'Charm', deriving from Latin *carmen*, can be distinguished as a form of word or words, with some implicit power such as protective prayer or sacred formula. This is the sense of the term in the earliest written sources.[62] Collections such as the outstanding *Carmina Gadelica* and other 'folklore' collections made in the nineteenth century and since, illustrate the continuing significance of the spoken and written word. In the medieval perspective, the terms 'charm' and 'amulet' are rarely mutually exclusive and the 'charm' may also be an object, in the form of a piece of manuscript or print worn as an amulet to avert misfortune or as talisman to attract good fortune. Slips of parchment inscribed with passages of Scripture worn on the body were known as 'Phylacteries' and this type of Jewish 'charm' is probably linked culturally with a piece of Scottish medieval *arcanum*, the 'gospel' or *soisgeul* (sometimes also described as *seun*) of pre- and post-Reformation Scotland. The potency of a 'line in Latin' was still recalled in the nineteenth century and examples of written charms preserved. Manuscript forms such as *'in nomine Patris & Filii & S S Amen'* suggest the agency of a Gaelic-speaking priest.[63]

Written charms with names or set formulae were acquired by the sick and

---

61 Hugh Cheape, 'Lead Hearts and Runes of Protection', *ROSC* 18 (2006) 149–55; see also Andrew Lang, ed., *The Highlands of Scotland in 1750* (Edinburgh and London: W. Blackwood and Sons, 1898) 111.
62 Black, 'Scottish Charms and Amulets', 434, 452; see also Chambers, *Popular Rhymes*, 339, Iain Thornber, 'Rats', *TGSI* 55 (1986–88) 128–47, and John A. Morrison, ' "Drumming Tunes": A Study of Gaelic Rat Satires', *TGSI* 57 (1990–92) 273–364, for the art of rhyming rats to death or causing them to migrate by the power of verse.
63 Rev. Dr Donald Masson, 'Popular Domestic Medicine in the Highlands Fifty Years Ago', *TGSI* 14 (1887–88) 312; Donald MacKinnon, *A Descriptive Catalogue of Gaelic Manuscripts* (Edinburgh: Constable, 1912) 6, 9, 10; John MacKechnie, *Catalogue of Gaelic Manuscripts* (Boston, Mass.: G. K. Hall, 1973) 125.

were particularly remedies sought by sufferers of toothache, with the pieces of paper folded and carried on the person. Common elements in these charms were prayers or incantations, besides the mystique of the written word, which were deemed to protect the individual from harm (see Appendix). Protective prayers have survived in classical Gaelic literature from the eighth and ninth centuries in forms recalled by still-practised *lorica* or 'breastplate' hymns. A similar 'cross-poem' or *crosradhach* has been attributed to Columba and the same amuletic and charm motif is included in the nineteenth-century *Carmina Gadelica*.[64] Recent written charms from Presbyterian Scotland invoked pre-Reformation spiritual concepts.[65] The minister of Golspie, Rev James Joass, Fellow of the Society of Antiquaries of Scotland, acquired a folded slip of paper from the employer of a Wester Ross shepherd in 1855. This was a written charm to cure the toothache purchased for half-a-crown from a 'professional witch' at Kishorn, Loch Carron, and worn by the sufferer round his neck. It may be significant that this text from the Scottish *Gàidhealtachd* is written in English and may reflect a taboo against reading the text once it had been bestowed in its folded form on the sufferer. The formula with its non-standard English orthography is known from other examples in Scotland and Ireland:

Petter sate weapn on a marabl stone Christ came Passn by and askne wath Aileth the Petter Petter ansirid and sayd my Lord my God my tothe Christ ansirid and sayd those that will carry those lines in my Name Shall be Heald and whosoever shall carrey these Lines in my Name shall never feel the mouthache. Amen[66]

Medicine may still be, depending on individual circumstances, as much faith as understanding and treatment and cure associated with convictions as well as the skill of the healer, and on charms and amulets as well as prayer. If this is 'superstition', it was an ideological response to uncomfortable facts that people died unexpectedly and in great numbers. In the past and before the more overt distinction between formal and alternative medicine, charms and amulets were core material of popular belief and, in the face of the strictures of the church

---

64 John MacInnes, 'Religion in Gaelic Scotland', *TGSI* 52 (1980–82) 222; Carmichael, *Carmina Gadelica*, vol. 4, 302–3; Jonathan Roper, *English Verbal Charms* (Helsinki: Academia Scientarum Fennica, 2005).
65 NMS H.NO 18–19, H.NO 93.
66 Signed Kate McAulay, NMS H.NO 18. For versions of the toothache charm, both written and spoken, see [John Mackay], 'Highland Medical Lore', *The Celtic Monthly* 14 (1908)149; George Henderson, *Leabhar nan Gleann* (Edinburgh: N. MacLeod, 1898) 171; William Matheson, 'Eòlas an Dèididh', *Tocher* 35 (1981) 311–12.

and its teaching, forms of sub-culture. From the Reformation, the church forced charmers into disrepute and kirk sessions disciplined them. They were the folk who might try to heal with plant concoctions, which more often purged than poisoned, or with charms and symbolic or ritual behaviour, such as applying an amulet to the body and simultaneously uttering prayers or invocations. Experience and history suggest that, more often than not, placebo or otherwise, in the face of authority, this was effective.

Charms and amulets, preserved in museum collections or individual cabinets of curiosities or as personal talismans, were created in a different age by, for the most part, nameless people; they are, perhaps quintessentially, popular culture. We recognise them for their purpose though we may not subscribe overtly to their values; we may also preserve or create our own charms and amulets, thus consciously or unconsciously investing in our inheritance (or heritage) and preserving cultural memory. Many of these take the form of ancient exemplars. This recognition is significant as an intuitive signal for the importance of material culture in the face of neglect, the disdain of learning and science and the condemnation of formal religious teaching. Charms and amulets tend to be removed from context, social, economic and cultural, and treated as the odd and bizarre, the province of the folkloric and primitive. But the objects themselves offer the shock of recognition and a prompt that the material culture is intimately linked to life-experience and can be illuminated by interdisciplinary study.

If we are justified in using and maintaining the cachet of 'charms and amulets', it can serve through the medium of the material itself to illustrate how culture, belief and language change and how people in the past regarded the world around them. This was not, of course, the same as our world nor was it a homogeneous and unchanging past. If the cosmos of a medieval or early modern world was complex and changing, charms and amulets offer unusual, sometimes unique, insights into it. In selecting an insight that can throw light on characteristics or the psyche of an earlier age, it might be suggested that charms and amulets describe an age or stage when Faith and Reason were not yet in conflict, when 'scientific' and folkloric belief were not polar opposites, and varieties of meaning that now seem mutually exclusive – the physical, the metaphysical, the symbolic – coexisted both intellectually and attitudinally. The challenge offered by the material culture is to strip away the accretions of time, the pretensions of scholarship and anthropological explanation, and to strive to see charms and amulets as their creators and users saw them in a Scotland of the past.

APPENDIX

[From the manuscripts of John Ramsay of Ochtertyre –see footnote 20]
The *Leug* – i.e. a sacred stone – is another engine of superstition derived from the Druids, which is used by the Highlanders as well as by some other branches of the Celtae. The Highland ones are generally larger than a hen's egg, and of much the same shape. Some of them are of a substance like crystal, and others of a sort of half-transparent pebble. There are few old families of any consideration that have not one of them in their possession. Various are the virtues ascribed to them – some being accounted efficacious in curing diseases, whilst others are supposed to secure people against dangers. And therefore, not many years ago, it was customary to lustrate persons, who were about to go on a military expedition, with water into which the *leug* had been dipped. Mr McDougall of Dunolly, a gentleman of Lorn, is in possession of one of the most celebrated of these stones. According to tradition it once belonged to McDougall, Lord Lorn, a great family forfeited by King Robert Bruce, of which Mr McDougall is reputed the representative. Its fame for curing the diseases of cattle is still very high with the common people of Argyleshire; and long ago the first people of that country sent for it on extraordinary occasions, and gave their obligation to restore it under a severe penalty. It has a flaw, concerning which they have a foolish tradition. It had been lent, say they, to somebody at a distance, with strict charge to put it in a clean place, instead of which it was put into a sack of wool. This offended it so much, that it gave a loud crack and flew home. Ridiculous as this may seem, the same locomotive powers are ascribed by the Highlanders to other *leugs*, as well as to S. Fillan's bell.

[Copy of Charms said to have been used in Ross-shire about 1890. NMS H.NO 93]
For stopping by the urine of the cow.
Going to the cow holding the Bottle to her water saying the Lord's prayer. Saying I hold this to you in the good name against foes or Enemy, witchcraft or any ill will or Curses or such or ill Eyed witch by any bad turned [i.e. ill-disposed] temporal or spiritual, saying the Creed and the Lord's prayer. I shut you Bottle in the good name that their ill may be turned on themselves saying the Almighty may do his own good will, they all the ill will.

Taking up the Herbs to be boiled.
I take up these Herbs in the name of the Cow & the name of the owners, man & wife by name & surname. I take this up in the good name against foes, ill will, witch-craft, Curses that it may be turned by the Blessed trinity

by which every thing temporal & spiritual is turned and that all our worldly wealth & our neighbours worldly wealth be Blessed. The Herbs & milk new from the cow to be put in the pot on the fire. The good name shuts all holes.

FIVE

The Scottish Enlightenment and the Supernatural

Colin Kidd

The supernatural has been shunted to the fringes of the modern Western world. On the one hand, religion, the officially-approved supernaturalism of the establishment, is increasingly considered to be a private affair which should not encroach upon the secularism-cum-religious neutrality of a laicised public sphere; on the other, the unofficial folkloric supernaturalism of the wider public is perceived as a quaint, but marginal, curiosity in a high technology-driven consumer society whose comforts depend upon a scientific world-view. Indeed, the supernatural is no longer deemed to be of any real political significance, except in anomalous and backward peripheries. Nor, despite vigorous debates over issues of personal morality, abortion, and the limits of scientific experimentation in fields such as embryology, are modern Western political divisions usually underpinned by rival metaphysical systems.

The gulf between the present and the age of the Enlightenment is striking. Three centuries ago the supernatural constituted a major theatre of debate in the battle between orthodox Christianity and its enlightened critics. Moreover, the struggle for this contested terrain had important ramifications not only for the church, but also for the state. In post-Reformation Europe the identity of the state was predominantly confessional. Church and state were inextricably intertwined, with monarchs – many of whom were believed to be invested with miraculous healing powers – deriving considerable spiritual legitimacy either from the Papacy or from their own national Protestant churches.[1] To question the supernatural authority of the Church, as happened in the Enlightenment, was to issue a further implicit challenge to the institutional structure and authority of the state. Strange as it may seem to modern observers, the supernatural was quite properly at the forefront of public discourse in the age of Enlightenment.

Scotland was no exception, though, as we shall see, the peculiarities of Scotland's institutions and the distinctive configuration of the Scottish

---

1 See e.g. Ian Bostridge, *Witchcraft and its Transformations, c.1650–c.1750* (Oxford: Clarendon Press, 1997); Stuart Clark, *Thinking with Demons: The Idea of Witchcraft in Early Modern Europe* (Oxford: Clarendon Press, 1997), part 5; Paul Monod, *The Power of Kings: Monarchy and Religion in Europe, 1589–1715* (New Haven and London: Yale University Press, 1999).

Enlightenment conferred a measure of local colour on what was otherwise a derivative subplot of a much wider British and European phenomenon. To a large extent, discussions of the supernatural in Scotland shadowed debate in England. In the early eighteenth century Thomas Halyburton (1674-1712) claimed that Scotland was as yet 'less tainted' with the 'poison' of infidelity than England, but feared that many were already 'infected'.[2] Scottish discussions of the supernatural still tended to follow English developments as late as the 1730s when some of the major theological controversies raging in the Kirk grew out of the responses of Scottish theologians to the provocations of two heterodox Oxbridge Fellows, Thomas Woolston (of Sidney Sussex) and Matthew Tindal (of All Souls). In 1731 the Reverend William Wilson (1690-1741) of Perth, identified deism as a wider problem of the reformed churches, which had struck at Scotland via England: 'when our neighbour's house is on fire, it is time for us to take the alarm'.[3] Nevertheless, some highly original contributions did stem from Enlightenment Scotland. At an early stage, Enlightened Scotland had played a considerable role in the intellectual formation of the radical Irish-born heretic, John Toland, educated at Glasgow University between 1687 and 1690 and then at Edinburgh University from which he graduated with an M.A. In *Christianity not Mysterious* (London, 1696) Toland set out to challenge the supernatural foundations of Christianity: 'to what end should God require us to believe what we cannot understand?'[4] Scotland derived even more notoriety from the arguments of David Hume in his incisive deconstruction of miracles and the testimony upon which their credit rested.[5] Yet, it was in Enlightened Scotland, too, that the Common Sense school developed a series of sophisticated solutions to the challenges posed by Humean scepticism, including a brave attempt by George Campbell (1719-96), the Principal of Marischal College, Aberdeen, to conserve the authority of certain classes of testimony to miracles.[6]

It is unhelpful to confine definitions of the Enlightenment to those critics who led the assault on ecclesiastical pretensions. The defenders of supernaturalism – in Scotland especially – were as much part of the Enlightenment as materialists, sceptics and deists. The mainstream of the Scottish Enlightenment was to be found on the side of orthodoxy, not among the ranks of those uncompromising

---

2 Thomas Halyburton, *Natural Religion insufficient* (Edinburgh, 1714) 32.
3 William Wilson, *A Discourse concerning some Prevailing Evils of the Present Time: wherein Mr Campbell's Reasonings concerning the Nature and Influence of Religious Enthusiasm are particularly examined* (Edinburgh, 1731) 6.
4 John Toland, *Christianity not Mysterious*, ed. P. McGuiness, A. Harrison and R. Kearney (1696; Dublin: Lilliput Press, 1997) 85.
5 David Hume, *An Enquiry concerning Human Understanding*, ed. E. Steinberg (1748; Indianapolis: Hackett, 1993) Section X 'Of Miracles', 72-90.
6 George Campbell, *A Dissertation on Miracles* (Edinburgh: A. Kincaid and J. Bell, 1762).

traditionalists who were behind the trial and execution of the heterodox Edinburgh student Thomas Aikenhead in 1697,[7] but among a progressive grouping which recognised that science and philosophy provided the only means of convincing sceptics and deists of their errors. Note that George Campbell in his critique of Hume spoke warmly of the learning and sophistication of his opponent.[8] Scotland's clerical Enlightenment operated on two fronts: against notorious heretics to the left, but also to the right against conservatives within the Kirk who believed that to enlist reason in defence of supernaturalism was to concede too much to the opponents of revealed religion, perhaps even to fall some way into the trap of heresy oneself.

Indeed in the age of Enlightenment the boundaries of the natural and supernatural were not located where the modern observer might expect to find them. During this period the emergence of Newtonian science – upon which the Scottish Enlightenment would eventually rest – neither led to a materialistic outlook, nor did it encourage the rejection of the supernatural. The experimental method did not preclude a hinterland of presuppositions about the existence of the supernatural. Isaac Newton, though heterodox in his Christology, was an enthusiastic theologian (with a marked interest in prophecy) and a keen student of alchemy, his alchemical papers amounting to about 650,000 words. To Newton alchemy seemed to belong quite properly to the realm of natural philosophy, rather than – as we might imagine – to the supernatural: if all matter was ultimately of one sort, then transmutation seemed a real possibility. Nor did Newtonian science do anything to dent belief in the immateriality of spirit. Gravity, after all, seemed to some commentators (though not to Newton himself) to provide compelling scientific evidence of an incorporeal force in the cosmos quite distinct from matter.[9]

In the seventeenth century the first stirrings of the Enlightenment had prompted an important realignment of theological debate. Although the clerisies of Europe, including Scotland, continued to wage scholarly warfare over the well-trodden campaign country of grace, salvation and church government, from the mid-seventeenth century onwards the theologians of Christendom faced an additional set of even thornier problems. No longer was it only the

---

7 Michael Hunter, '"Aikenhead the Atheist": The Context and Consequences of Articulate Irreligion in the Late Seventeenth Century', in *Atheism from the Reformation to the Enlightenment*, ed. Michael Hunter and David Wootton (Oxford: Clarendon Press, 1992).
8 Campbell, *Dissertation on Miracles*, vi.
9 B.J.T. Dobbs, *The Foundations of Newton's Alchemy or 'The Hunting of the Greene Lyon'* (Cambridge: Cambridge University Press, 1975); Scott Mandelbrote, '"A duty of the greatest moment": Isaac Newton and the writing of Biblical criticism', *British Journal for the History of Science* 26 (1993) 281–302; J.J. Dahm, 'Science and Apologetics in the Early Boyle Lectures', *Church History* 39 (1970) 172–86.

particular confessional variations found *within* Christianity which were at stake; now from *outside* the established parameters of Christian theology atheists, pantheists, atomists and others were launching various formidable philosophical assaults which threatened the metaphysical foundations of Christianity itself. Collectively, from their different metaphysical standpoints these heretics called into question traditional Christian understandings of the supernatural realm. For example, materialists such as Thomas Hobbes argued against the reality of the spirit world. Spirit, according to Hobbes, was a corporeal substance. On the other hand, pantheists such as Benedict Spinoza and Toland collapsed the distinction between spirit and matter, arguing that God and the cosmos were one and the same. Perceptive Christian apologists saw the implications: to conflate spirit and matter was to undermine the Christian God. A new theology of evidences developed to counter the cavils of these sceptics. In particular, the defenders of Christianity saw the importance of establishing the immateriality of the spirit world as a bulwark against materialism and pantheism. To take a notable example from the Church of England: in his *Sadducismus Triumphatus*, Joseph Glanvill produced an orthodox apology for ghosts and witches, arguing that without such beliefs it was easier to fall into the trap of atheism.[10]

Scots were keenly attuned to the threat to Christianity posed by materialism, and recognised the apologetic potential in paranormal events. In the late seventeenth century George Sinclair (d.1696), professor of natural philosophy at Glasgow University from 1654 to 1666, and later, of mathematics (1691-6), produced *Satan's Invisible World Discovered* (1685), an anthology of real-life diabolism, apparitions and ghostly happenings, as a means of rebutting metaphysical arguments for materialism and pantheism. Some of the examples were drawn from Scottish experience, some were lifted from Glanvill. A man of pronounced Presbyterian commitments, on account of which he was obliged to resign his chair in 1666, Sinclair denounced the new breed of heterodox thinkers as 'a monstrous rabble of men, who following the Hobbesian and Spinosian principles, slight religion, and undervalue the scripture, because there is such an express mention of spirits and angels in it, which their thick and plumbeous capacities cannot conceive. Whereupon they think, that all contained in the universe comes under the notion of things material, and bodies only; and consequently, no God, no Devil, no spirit, no witch'. For Sinclair the existence of the spirit world was 'one of the outworks of religion, which the bold and too much daring infidelity of some have assaulted'. Hence, examples of mysterious

---

10 See e.g. Brian Easlea, *Witch Hunting, Magic and the New Philosophy: An Introduction to Debates of the Scientific Revolution 1450-1750* (Brighton: Harvester Press, 1980) 154-62, 184, 201-5; John Redwood, *Reason, Ridicule and Religion: The Age of Enlightenment in England, 1660-1750* (1976: London: Thames and Hudson, 1996) ch. 6.

and unexplained events drawn from recent Scottish history, such as the account Sinclair related of the Devil of Glenluce, had, as he noted, an obvious 'usefulness for refuting atheism'.[11]

Another preoccupation of Scottish folklore research in the late seventeenth century was the phenomenon of the 'second sight'. Prominent researchers included Martin Martin, the Reverend John Frazer (1647–1702), minister of Tiree and Coll, and the Reverend Robert Kirk (1644–92) of Aberfoyle, himself a seventh son. In his manuscript treatise, *The Secret Commonwealth of Elves and Fairies*, Kirk highlighted the theological significance of his fascination with the 'second sight'. 'The true solution of the phenomenon', argued Kirk, resided in 'the courteous endeavours of our fellow creatures in the invisible world to convince us, (in opposition to Sadducees, Socinians and Atheists), of a Deity; of spirits; of a possible and harmless method of correspondence betwixt men and them, even in this life ... of the orders and degrees of angels ...'.[12]

Materialism and pantheism were not the only new threats faced by the orthodox. To complicate matters further, the authority of scripture was itself under assault. Was the Old Testament really the inspired Word of God, or was it an error-strewn compilation of texts, texts moreover abounding in the superstitious values of the ancient Hebrews? It was no longer enough to combat materialists by pointing to scriptural examples of the numinous. This crisis in authority compounded the threat to Christianity. Halyburton complained that deists made 'a jest upon the scriptures', rejecting the authority of the Bible for 'paganism à la mode'.[13] 'The Old Testament prophecies concerning the Messiah that was to come, are denied', lamented Wilson, 'the miracles of Christ are derided, his Resurrection from the dead impugned, his true and supreme deity assaulted'.[14] Moreover, the rise of deism and natural religion also posed their own particular challenges to Christian theologians. The defence of scripture required a quite different recourse to the supernatural from that associated with the proof of the immateriality of spirit. While miracles and spiritual happenings might help to conserve the authority of Christian metaphysics, they were insufficient in themselves to bolster the divine inspiration claimed

---

11 George Sinclair, *Satan's Invisible World Discovered* (Edinburgh, 1685), 'Preface', A1r, A4v; p. 75.
12 Robert Kirk, *The Secret Commonwealth of Elves, Fauns and Fairies* (MS 1691: London: David Nutt, 1893) 55; John Frazer, *Deuteroskopia, or a brief Discourse concerning the Second Sight, Commonly so called* (Edinburgh: A. Symson, 1707); Martin Martin, *A Description of the Western Islands of Scotland* (London: A. Bell, 1703) 300–35; Shari Cohn, 'An Historical Review of Second Sight: The Collectors, their Accounts and Ideas', *Scottish Studies* 33 (1999) 146–85. See also chapter 1 above.
13 Halyburton, *Natural Religion insufficient*, 25, 31.
14 Wilson, *Discourse*, 6.

for scripture. As George Mackenzie (1630–1714), Viscount Tarbat and 1st Earl of Cromarty, perceived, only prophecy provided a reliable defence of the Bible. Some critics might scoff at miracles, for various reasons, including the possibility of their being mere 'natural effects' or the fact that their impact was limited and short-lived, convincing only direct witnesses. However, Cromarty, a polymathic scientist (one of whose topics of investigation was the second sight), antiquary, latitudinarian theologian and practising politician, sought a secure basis for the defence of scripture in synchronic prophecy, a careful calibration of Biblical prophecies against chronological computations. Cromarty's aim in his *Synopsis Apocalyptica* (1708) was 'to evince, that the gospel of the Old and New Testament, is the word of God; and therefore infallibly true: And that because God hath attested it to man; not only by miracles (which though they were sure yet were only transitory proofs) but also by prophesying of such things, as depended not only on contingent causes; but also on a complication of causes; each of which depended upon the free acts and wills of many, and different free agents; and with that uncertainty which arises from the fortuitous contingencies which render events uncertain oft-times, even to the proximate and immediate agent: these are seals, which none but the omniscient can affix'. In other words, when an event conformed to a prediction, this confirmed the divine inspiration of scripture. The only drawback, as Cromarty saw it, was that the Devil, 'the author of confusion' had introduced various 'achronologies' and other 'falsehoods' into what had become the disputed field of chronology as a means of obscuring this vital evidence for the truth of Christianity. It is revealing that Cromarty managed to combine an Enlightened outlook, whether through his latitudinarianism and his scientific projects, with a strong belief in various areas of the supernatural, including prophecy and the intervention of the Devil in the affairs of men.[15]

The debate over the supernatural had profound practical implications for the church. The deists were not only critical of Christianity as a system of belief, but were also determined to subvert the institutional foundations of Christendom. After all, the deists believed that it was priestcraft – a deliberate project to blind the people with superstition in order to elevate the priests themselves above the vulgar herd – which had corrupted the plain simplicity of natural religion. Tindal contended that priests had 'made it their business to puzzle mankind, and render plain things obscure; in order to get the consciences, and consequently, the properties of the people at their disposal...'[16] In this context, miracles were

---

15 Cromarty, *Synopsis Apocalyptica* (Edinburgh, 1708), Section I, 3, 13–14, 35; Section II, ii.
16 Matthew Tindal, *Christianity as Old as the Creation: or, the Gospel a Republication of the Religion of Nature* (London, 1730) 241.

a particular cause for concern. No miracles, no ecclesiastical pretension. The Christian church rested upon the supernatural miracle of Christ's Resurrection. If the Resurrection were exposed as a fraud, a delusion or a conjuring trick with bones, then the whole institutional apparatus of Christianity – establishments, teinds, the manse and glebe, public rebukes, fines and the kirk stool – lost its legitimacy; for the Kirk drew its authority from the Risen Christ. In Scots presbyterian ecclesiology Christ was recognised as head of the Kirk, a body otherwise governed by a hierarchy of ecclesiastical courts staffed by ministers all of whom enjoyed democratic parity under Christ's headship. On the other hand, deists complained that while mystery empowered the sacerdotal church, mystery was not divine in provenance, but man-made and the contrivance of priestcraft. Stripping the veil of sanctity from mystery, deists revealed its real source in a devious clerical conspiracy to dupe mankind. Moreover, Christ – like the other 'human' founders of the great religions – was implicated in the plot.[17] From the 1690s this vein of Anglo-Continental anticlericalism found a foothold at the freethinking margins of Scottish society. In a letter of 1695 to John Locke, the cosmopolitan Scots patriot Andrew Fletcher of Saltoun wrote that he was busy tracing priestcraft from its origins in Egypt, where he found many other monsters 'but none so abominable'.[18] Similar remarks can be found in the Aikenhead trial. Aikenhead was accused of calling the New Testament 'the history of the impostor Christ', whose charlatanry Aikenhead allegedly traced to Christ's acquisition of magic in Egypt.[19]

The assault on priestcraft also received reinforcement from within the Church of England itself. In a controversial sermon of 1717, Benjamin Hoadly, the latitudinarian Bishop of Bangor, argued that Christ's kingdom was not of this world, but purely spiritual: 'The laws of this kingdom, therefore as Christ left them, have nothing of this world in their view; no tendency, either to the exaltation of some, in worldly pomp and dignity; or to their absolute dominion over the faith and religious conduct of others of his subjects, or to the erecting any sort of temporal kingdom, under the covert and name of a spiritual one.'[20] Hoadly's radical critique of traditional church discipline interrogated the notion that the church possessed any divine mandate to support establishments or to impose upon the consciences of men. Religious establishment, in the eyes

17 J. A. I. Champion, *The Pillars of Priestcraft Shaken: The Church of England and its Enemies, 1660–1730* (Cambridge: Cambridge University Press, 1992).
18 Fletcher to Locke, 22 February, 1695(?), in E. S. de Beer, ed., *The Correspondence of John Locke* 8 vols. (Oxford: Clarendon Press, 1976–89) vol. 5, 275.
19 Hunter, 'Aikenhead', 225.
20 Benjamin Hoadly, *The Nature of the Kingdom, or Church, of Christ* (London; Edinburgh reprinted, 1717) 10.

of Hoadly and his supporters, was a profane perversion of Christ's spiritual legacy. Naturally, Hoadly provoked an apoplectic response in the Church of England, but the Bangorian controversy also reverberated throughout the wider British world. Presbyterians were not immune to the influence of Hoadlian ecclesiology. According to Francis Hutcheson 'a perfect Hoadly mania' swept the Presbyterian dissenters of the North of Ireland, while the Glasites, who broke with the Church of Scotland in 1730, also articulated principles akin – in certain respects at least – to Hoadly's.[21] With ecclesiastical jurisdiction under fire from so many quarters, the supernatural basis of the church's claims to authority inevitably became drawn into the debate. Indeed, the controversy over Christ's miracles which emerged in England in the late 1720s at the instigation of Woolston – and which quickly spilled over into Scotland – starkly posed the question of ecclesiastical authority. Contemporaries were aghast at the apparent implication of Woolston's contention that 'the miracles of healing all manner of bodily diseases which Jesus was justly famed for, are none of the proper miracles of the Messiah, neither are they so much as a good proof of his Divine authority to found a religion'.[22]

Here the debate on miracles intersected with the revival of ancient Christological heresies. Around the turn of the eighteenth century the orthodox Athanasian doctrine of the Trinity was under serious assault – inside and outside the church – from Arians, who contended that Christ was subordinate to the Father, though divine, and Socinians, who argued that while Christ had a divinity of purpose he had not himself been divine.[23] Clearly, this heterodox Christology had considerable bearing on the question of the authenticity of Christ's Resurrection and the other miracles attributed to him. Indeed to critics of the church the Athanasian doctrine of the Trinity was a prime example of a mystery concocted by priestcraft and ripe for deconstruction. Aikenhead was alleged to have denounced the doctrine of the Trinity as 'not worth any man's refutation'; to have ridiculed as a gross contradiction the notion that Christ's nature was both divine and human; and to have scoffed at Christ's miracles as 'pranks'.[24]

---

21 Andrew Starkie, *The Church of England and the Bangorian Controversy, 1716–1721* (Woodbridge: Boydell Press, 2007); Ian R. McBride, *Scripture Politics* (Oxford: Clarendon Press, 1998) 44; D. Murray, 'The Influence of John Glas', *Records of the Scottish Church History Society* 22 (1984) 48; David Mullan, 'The Royal Law of Liberty: A reassessment of the Early Career of John Glass', *The Journal of the United Reformed Church History Society* 6 (1999) 256.
22 Thomas Woolston, *A Discourse on the Miracles of our Saviour* (3rd edn, London, 1727) 4.
23 Maurice Wiles, *Archetypal Heresy: Arianism through the Centuries* (Oxford: Clarendon Press, 1996).
24 Hunter, 'Aikenhead', 225.

However, the threat of deism to supernatural religion had not completely displaced the anxiety felt by moderate Protestants about extravagant and deluded forms of traditional Christian supernaturalism. The mainstream clerical Enlightenment was concerned to establish a rational supernaturalism, a Christianity whose proofs were consonant with the touchstones of science and philosophy. Enlightened Protestants were keen to establish a moderate Christianity which veered neither too much towards the hazard of enthusiasm on the one hand, nor that of superstition on the other. This stance towards unacceptable forms of supernaturalism complicated the attitudes of the enlightened towards deism and scepticism. Ironically, Moderate clerics within the Kirk of Scotland shared a pronounced distaste for superstition and enthusiasm with Hume himself, who composed a celebrated essay on the subject of these twin dangers to religion.[25] Scots Presbyterians were acutely sensitive to the charge of enthusiasm, which had been levelled against them since the mid-seventeenth century by Church of England men and by Scots of an episcopalian bent.[26] The problem lay in differentiating an authentic evangelicalism touched by grace from the excesses of an enthusiasm whose provenance was psychological rather than divine. In the early eighteenth century most discussions of this phenomenon centred on the exiled Camisards, or French Prophets, based in London. In – what was perceived as – a blasphemous parody of Christianity the French Prophets had prophesied the resurrection of one of their number, the quack-doctor Thomas Emes, who died in 1707.[27] The notoriety of the French Prophets spread to Scottish theological circles.[28] Throughout the eighteenth century, moreover, the mainstream of Scotland's clerical leadership attempted to whitewash the Presbyterian tradition of the charge of enthusiasm made by their episcopalian critics. Here the focus was primarily on the political manifestations of enthusiasm, notably the violence associated with the Covenanters, and the available strategies ranged from disowning the later Covenanters as traitors to the true Presbyterian cause to downplaying the offences they committed and setting out the extenuating circumstances.[29] However, some critics such as Thomas Rhind, a defector from the Kirk, questioned whether there was

---

25 David Hume 'Of Superstition and Enthusiasm', *Essays: Moral, Political and Literary*, ed. E. F. Miller (Indianapolis: Liberty Classics, 1985).
26 Colin Kidd, *Subverting Scotland's Past* (Cambridge: Cambridge University Press, 1993) 53–8.
27 Hillel Schwartz, *The French Prophets* (Berkeley and Los Angeles: University of California Press, 1980).
28 Campbell, *Dissertation on Miracles*, 158. An edition of *The wonderful narrative; or a faithful account of the French Prophets, their agitations, exstasies, and inspirations* was published at Glasgow by the Foulis Press in 1742.
29 Kidd, *Subverting*, 67–9, 195–8.

anything genuine about Presbyterian claims that their evangelical ecstasies were supernaturally inspired; rather Rhind identified their 'pretended inspirations' as a 'cobweb of fancy, and the product of animal spirits'.[30] This accusation was reiterated from within the Kirk by Archibald Campbell (1691–1756), Professor of Ecclesiastical History and Divinity at St Andrews, in the course of his attempts to excuse the apostles from the charge of enthusiasm. Campbell denounced enthusiasm as a bogus supernaturalism which could readily be explained in the language of contemporary science: an enthusiast, he wrote, 'is mechanically wrought up unto such extraordinary heats and fervours, that he verily believes he is immediately under the benign emanations of Heaven, and has divine revelations made to him; whilst there is nothing really in the case, but pure mechanism and fiction'.[31] However, when Campbell referred to the enthusiasm of the 'last age'[32] he was understood – not without reason – by his most vehement critic William Wilson (an ally of the Erskines and a founder of the Secession church of which he became the professor of divinity in 1736) to be casting aspersions on the Covenanters.[33] Wilson also noted that Campbell's apparent unwillingness to countenance a third category midway between the extraordinary authentic miracles and enthusiastic pretence left little room for the ordinary supernatural operations of the holy spirit on the hearts of sinners.[34] Enthusiasm remained at the forefront of Scottish discussions of the supernatural, most famously in Hume's essay on miracles which included a deconstruction of testimony prompted by religious enthusiasm, and James Hogg's sustained analysis of the treacherous limits between authentic divinity and the empty – but dangerous – vanity of enthusiastic delusion in *Confessions of a Justified Sinner* (1824).[35]

However, during the eighteenth century superstition provided a much more intractable problem for enlightened Protestants. Critical Protestants mocked the absurdities found in monkish chronicles, the prodigious feats attributed to Catholic saints and, the worst of all Popish impostures, the doctrine of transubstantiation – the supposed transformation of bread and wine at the Eucharist into the body and blood of Christ. Unfortunately, this standard Protestant critique of Roman

---

30 *An Apology for Mr. Thomas Rhind* (Edinburgh, 1712) 202.
31 Archibald Campbell, *A Discourse proving that the Apostles were no Enthusiasts* (1730: 2nd edn, London, 1730) 4.
32 Ibid., p. 7
33 Wilson, *Discourse*, 16–17; Hew Scott, ed., *Fasti Ecclesiae Scoticanae*, 7 vols. (Edinburgh: Oliver and Boyd, 1915–28) vol. 4, 237.
34 Wilson, *Discourse*, 25.
35 Hume, *Enquiry*, 79. However R. A. Houston, *Madness and Society in Eighteenth-Century Scotland* (Oxford: Clarendon Press, 2000) ch. 7, notes the disappearance of diabolism in discussions of madness after *c*.1780.

Catholic superstition paralleled, too closely for comfort, the deist critique of all forms of revealed Christianity, Protestantism included. Indeed, it was probably a quite deliberate strategy on Hume's part to open his deconstruction of miracles with an endorsement of Tillotson's argument against transubstantiation.[36] Hume also denounced the forged miracles associated in Protestant opinion with Roman Catholic priestcraft.[37] Such ironies would not have been lost on contemporaries. Eamon Duffy has outlined the quandary of sophisticated Protestant theologians on the question of miracles: 'The world was rational and wonders had ceased, the profession of Christianity was compatible with the profoundest scepticism about the present possibility of miracles; yet it seemed to demand assent to the notion that the laws of nature had frequently been broken by Moses, Jesus and the apostolic generation'. According to Duffy this was why Anglicans experienced such obvious embarrassment at the miraculous healing powers of Valentine Greatrakes, the Irish stroker who came to England in 1666 (and whose feats were known in Scotland).[38] In effect, Protestants believed that there had been no authentic miracles since the end of the apostolic age in the fourth century AD. Hume cheekily wondered why the 'prodigious events' so common in antiquity never happened in modern 'enlightened ages', forming 'a strong presumption against all supernatural and miraculous relations, that they are observed chiefly to abound among ignorant and barbarous nations'.[39] In other words, within a progressive interpretation of history the miracles of antiquity were – at one level, for Hume also subscribed to a universal propensity of mankind towards the marvellous[40] – the product of social and cultural backwardness. In his response to Hume's essay on miracles George Campbell attempted to deal with the problem of differentiating the miraculous foundations of Christianity from the fictitious miracles attributed to Catholic saints. He moved the discussion of the historical context of testimony away from Hume's chosen ground of social progress towards the particular status of the religion in question. Campbell contended that there was a significant 'disparity' between 'the evidence of miracles performed in proof of a religion to be established, performed in contradiction to opinions generally

---

36 Hume, *Enquiry*, 72.
37 Hume, *Enquiry*, 79.
38 Eamon Duffy, 'Valentine Greatrakes, the Irish Stroker; Miracle, Science, and Orthodoxy in Restoration England', in *Religion and Humanism*, ed. Keith Robbins (*Studies in Church History* 17, Oxford: Blackwell, 1981) 252. Cf. Rob Iliffe, 'Lying Wonders and Juggling Tricks: Religion, Nature and Imposture in Early Modern England', in *Everything Connects: In Conference with Richard H. Popkin*, ed. James E. Force and David S. Katz (Leiden; Boston: Brill, 1999); Jane Shaw, *Miracles in Enlightenment England* (New Haven; London: Yale University Press, 2006); Kirk, *Secret Commonwealth*, 30.
39 Hume, *Enquiry*, 79–80.
40 Hume, *Enquiry*, 78, 81.

received; and the evidence of miracles performed in support of a religion already established, and in confirmation of opinions generally received. Hence also the greatest disparity betwixt the miracles recorded by the evangelists, and those related by Mariana, Bede or any monkish historian'. According to Campbell, the genuine miracles of the New Testament did not suffer by comparison with Popish 'counterfeits'; rather the former's authenticity shone the brighter in contrast to the obvious fabrication of the latter.[41]

As we have seen, there were no clear battle lines in the Enlightenment debate over the supernatural. A fascinating insight into the configuration of the debate on religious supernaturalism in eighteenth-century Scotland appears in the troubled Scottish response to Woolston's *Discourses on the Miracles of Christ*. Woolston argued that Jesus's Messiahship could not be proven from the miracles that were attributed to him. Quite the reverse; read literally, Christ's miracles seemed to be confections of 'absurdities, improbabilities and incredibilities'. To believe in these literally as actual historical happenings – eighteenth-century orthodoxy – was, according to Woolston, 'arrant Quixotism'. To Woolston a literal exegesis of Jesus the healer rendered him no more than a 'quack-doctor' equipped with an effective 'balsam', or worse a 'juggling impostor'. Proclaiming his orthodox adherence to the authentic values of patristic Christianity, Woolston maintained that the solution to this vexing problem was to return to the hermeneutic strategies of the Fathers, who interpreted Jesus's miracles not as literal history, but as 'prophetical and parabolical' allegories. 'The history of Jesus's life, as recorded in the evangelists', proclaimed Woolston, was 'an emblematical representation of his spiritual life in the soul of man; and his miracles are figures of his mysterious operations. The four gospels are in no part a literal story, but a system of mystical philosophy and theology'. For example, the story of Christ curing the blind man should be read figuratively and in spiritual terms as a type of Christ's 'cure of mankind of the blindness of his understanding'. Similarly, the miraculous transformation of water into wine at the marriage feast of Cana should not be read literally, but typologically, as the conversion of the 'water' of the Old Testament law into the new dispensation of the Gospel. However, it was one thing to reinterpret Christ's healing in a mystical sense, it was quite another to subvert the literal historicity of the Resurrection. Woolston contended that the literal story of Christ's Resurrection was 'such a complication of absurdities, incoherences and contradictions, that unless the Fathers can help us to a better understanding of the evangelists than we have at present, we must of necessity give up the belief of it'.[42]

Woolston's conclusion was devastating. Zachary Pearce, one of Woolston's

---

41 George Campbell, *Dissertation on Miracles*, 87, 247–8.
42 Woolston, *Discourse on Miracles*, 57, 59, 65; Woolston, *A Second Discourse on the Miracles of our Saviour* (2nd edn, London, 1727) 3; Woolston, *A Fourth Discourse on the Miracles of our Saviour* (London, 1728) 11, 14, 22, 51.

many clerical critics in England, noted that the Resurrection was 'a point of so great importance that the whole weight of Christianity rests upon it'. Among the more original responses to Woolston's *Discourses* was Thomas Sherlock's *Trial of the Witnesses of the Resurrection of Jesus* (1729). In this pamphlet Sherlock responded to Woolston through the medium of a courtroom drama centred on the question of whether the witnesses of the Resurrection were guilty of giving false evidence. Unsurprisingly, Sherlock's jurors were happy to acquit the apostles of fraud and enthusiasm.[43]

A similar philosophical strategy – unaccompanied, of course, by Sherlock's unusual rhetorical ploy – surfaced in Scotland where Professor Archibald Campbell's *Discourse proving that the Apostles were no Enthusiasts* (1730), although begun, the author claimed, over a decade before, was published as a response to Woolston and Tindal. Unfortunately, Campbell took the line of defence so far that, instead of winning the plaudits of his fellow Kirkmen for his clever anti-deistic manoeuvres, Campbell found himself the victim of a Presbyterian heresy hunt.[44] Campbell's overall argument, to prove that the apostles believed in the Resurrection on 'the irresistible testimony of their own senses', was not itself the focus of controversy. However, in attempting to acquit the apostles from any deception in the matter, Campbell was drawn into arguing that by the time of the Resurrection, the apostles, far from being champions of Christ's cause, had become sorely disillusioned with a figure whom they regarded as something of a con-man. The apostles, according to Campbell, had expected Christ to establish a kingdom on earth, and had no deeper understanding at this time of his real mission, nor of his Resurrection. At the Crucifixion, therefore, the apostles' hopes that Christ would establish a temporal kingdom had been dashed. Furthermore, according to Campbell, seeing their Messiah crucified, the apostles felt enormously let down by him, and assumed that he was in fact some kind of impostor. Far from trying to boost Christ's cult by propagating false stories of his Resurrection, or being so overcome with enthusiasm and zealotry for Christ's cause that they might fall into a delusion of Christ's Resurrection, the apostles were, if anything, disillusioned and somewhat embittered. By recreating the context in which the apostles contemplated Christ's death, Campbell had provided a powerful and persuasive vindication of their testimony of the Resurrection. However, by emphasising the apostles'

---

43 Zachary Pearce, *The Miracles of Jesus Vindicated* (2nd edn, London, 1729) part I, 3; Thomas Sherlock, *The Trial of the Witnesses of the Resurrection of Jesus* (1729: 1746 edn)
44 For the heresy hunt, as well as Campbell's wider career and motivations, see Anne Skoczylas, 'Archibald Campbell's *Enquiry into the Original of Moral Virtue*, Presbyterian Orthodoxy, and the Scottish Enlightenment', *SHR* 87 (2008) 68–100, esp. 93–8.

opinion at the time of the Crucifixion that Christ was a deceiver, Campbell had offended orthodox sensitivities.[45]

Ironically, having tried to defend orthodox Christianity from the subversive arguments of the English heretic Woolston, Campbell found himself the target of his fellow Presbyterians, who believed that he had betrayed the faith that he purported to uphold. The Reverend William Stewart of Perth denied that the apostles had ever considered their crucified Messiah to be an impostor. At the time of the Crucifixion, according to Stewart, 'many signs appeared to support their faith'. Had the vail of the temple not been rent from top to bottom? Had the earth not quaked? Had not graves opened? Had not the saints been resurrected?[46] John Hunter went deeper in his critique of Campbell, arguing that it was wrong *a priori* to support miracles by means of rational argument. Contrary to Campbell, Hunter claimed that the faith of the apostles had not been founded 'on the testimony of their bodily senses': 'Right apprehensions and thoughts of Christ cannot be produced by our natural reason, but must be formed by the supernatural illumination of the Holy Spirit'. Hunter considered Campbell a deistic fifth columnist within the Kirk who seemed to subscribe to something akin to natural religion.[47] Similarly, Wilson accused Campbell of subscribing to the 'pretended rational scheme of religion' set out by Professor John Simson of Glasgow University, a notorious figure who had twice been investigated for heresy.[48] During the same period as the pamphlet controversy over Campbell, the Reverend Robert Wallace (1697–1771), who had attempted to construct an enlightened rebuttal of the heresies propounded in Tindal's *Christianity as Old as the Creation*, also found himself under attack from the orthodox for conceding too much of the supernatural mystery of Christianity. Wallace, like Campbell, had hoped to turn back the 'deluge of scepticism and deism' without resorting to an 'implicit faith and blind obedience' which was, in its own way, damaging to Protestant principles of free enquiry in religion.[49] While enlightened clerics recognised that only by fighting the deists on the neutral grounds of reason and nature could they hope to be taken seriously, their strategies faced considerable hostility within the Kirk.

45 Campbell, *Discourse proving that the Apostles were no Enthusiasts*, xx–xxi, xxiii, 53–4, 67.
46 William Stewart, *A Letter to the Reverend Professor Campbell, Whereto is subjoin'd Remarks on his Vindication of the Apostles from Enthusiasm* (Glasgow, 1731) 11.
47 John Hunter, *An Examination of Mr. Campbell's Principles* (Edinburgh, 1731) 27–8.
48 Wilson, *Discourse*, 9.
49 Robert Wallace, *The Regard Due to Divine Revelation* (London, 1731) 70; H. Sefton, '"Neulights and Preachers Legall": some observations on the beginnings of Moderatism in the Church of Scotland', in *Church, Politics and Society: Scotland 1408–1929*, ed. Norman Macdougall (Edinburgh: John Donald, 1983) 193.

A formal investigation into Campbell was launched by the General Assembly in 1735. In the summer of that year Campbell was visited by James Hadow, Principal of New College, St. Andrews, and two local ministers, Alexander Anderson of St Andrews and James Nairn of Easter-Anstruther. The investigators were concerned with seventeen controversial articles found in Campbell's various writings. The seventh article of investigation was Campbell's thesis that 'during the time our Saviour lay in the grave, the disciples were so far from believing him to be the Messiah promised, that they concluded him to be a cheat and impostor'. Campbell vigorously defended his position, publishing an explanation of his arguments in 1735 and *Further Explications* in 1736. Campbell complained that the private opinions of the apostles had been erected into one of the Kirk's Confessional Standards. Eventually, by Act of the General Assembly in 1736 Campbell's explanation – of his 'honest intentions to serve the interests of religion, and to contribute to the overthrow of deism and infidelity' – was formally accepted and the matter dropped, though ministers were cautioned to be more careful in future.[50]

The Moderate party which rose to prominence in the Kirk during the 1750s went out of its way to avoid the sort of controversy which had dogged Campbell's attempts to construct a rational theology. Above all, the Moderates were establishmentarian, keen to avoid a repetition of the Secession of 1733 and to stifle the continuing divisions over patronage which threatened to rend the Kirk asunder. Nothing could be worse, in Moderate eyes, than to add major theological disputation to the existing tensions which dogged the Kirk. The enlightened Moderates, whatever their private beliefs, were happy to subscribe the Westminster Confession of Faith as the Kirk's standard of doctrine, but to remain silent, otherwise, on the great theological issues of the day. The leaders of the Moderate party were prolific authors in such fields as history, moral philosophy, and belles-lettres, but they tended to eschew directly theological topics.[51] Nevertheless, a very restrained form of supernaturalism is visible in Moderate writings. Against those deistic scoffers who equated mystery with

---

50 Archibald Campbell, *Remarks upon Some Passages in books publish'd by Mr. Archibald Campbell STP Professor of Divinity and Ecclesiastical History in the University of St. Andrews, With his Explications on them* (Edinburgh, 1735) 11–12, 92; Campbell, *Further Explications*, 85; *Acts of the General Assembly of the Church of Scotland 1638–1842* (Edinburgh, 1843) 638–9.
51 I.D.L. Clark, 'Moderatism and the Moderate Party in the Church of Scotland, 1752–1805' (unpublished PhD thesis, University of Cambridge, 1963); Richard B. Sher, *Church and University in the Scottish Enlightenment* (Princeton and Edinburgh: Edinburgh University Press, 1985); John Rattray McIntosh, *Church and Theology in Enlightenment Scotland: The Popular Party, 1740–1800* (East Linton: Tuckwell Press, 1998) 25: 'There was little Moderate interest in doctrine [or] apologetics'.

absurdity, Hugh Blair argued that there were some phenomena which – because they transcended the limits of human faculties – were perceived as through a glass darkly; yet these were nonetheless quite essential components of a rational religion. While most of the Christian scheme – such as the perfections of God and his moral government – was 'perfectly consonant to the most enlightened reason', Blair conceded that certain articles, such as the essence of the Godhead and the redemption of fallen man, remained 'mysterious and dark'. However, this was no excuse for sceptics to attack Christianity. Was not the sceptic bound to admit that nature itself – the very foundation of deism – was equally mysterious? After all, argued Blair, 'how a seed grows up into a tree; how man is formed inside the womb; or how the mind acts upon the body after it is formed, are mysteries of which we can give no account, than most of the obscure and difficult parts of revelation'. By the same token, in answer to sceptics who could see no evidence for the workings of providence in the affairs of men, Blair claimed that providence also constituted a 'system' (compared, tellingly, to a clock) though humans perceived only 'some broken parts of a great whole . . . a few links of that chain of being which, by secret connexions, binds together the present and the future'.[52] Similarly, William Robertson traced the operation in human history of a superintending providence working indirectly through natural secondary causes: 'The Supreme Being conducteth all his operations by general laws'.[53] Robertson's sermon *The Situation of the World at the Time of Christ's Appearance, and its connection with the success of his religion, considered* (1755) concentrates less on Christ's supernatural mission than on the sociological context of the environment in which that message was received. Although a theology of evidences – concentrated on Biblical miracles, and, in a smaller measure, on Biblical prophecy, – persisted within the Kirk,[54] no longer did it embrace the ghosts, apparitions and cases of the second sight which had featured so prominently in late seventeenth century apologetic. Robertson treated superstition as a phenomenon to be explained as a cultural, historical and psychological phenomenon, with God himself apparently bound by the laws of nature, as providence led mankind gradually through appropriate societal forms

---

52 Hugh Blair, *Sermons*, 2 vols. (Edinburgh: Anderson, 1824–5) 'On Our Imperfect Knowledge of a Future State', vol. 1, 40–2; 'On our Ignorance of Good and Evil in this Life', vol. 2, 94; 'On Scoffing at Religion', vol. 2, 73–4; 'On our Present Ignorance of the Ways of God', vol. 2, 185, 187, 190; 'On the Government of Human Affairs by Providence', vol.2, 509.
53 William Robertson, *The Situation of the World at the Time of Christ's Appearance* (1755), in Robertson, *Works* (London, 1831) 43.
54 F. Voges, 'Moderate and Evangelical Thinking in the Later Eighteenth Century', *Records of the Scottish Church History Society* 22 (1985) 148.

from primitive idolatry towards an enlightened unsuperstitious monotheism.[55] Nevertheless, this was not the last word on the topic from the Moderates and their allies. George Campbell, in his sermon *The Success of the First Publishers of the Gospel a Proof of its Truth* (1777), took a very different line from Robertson, indeed stood his argument almost on its head, to make the case that the first apostles – a bunch of lowly fishermen – would not have succeeded in founding the Christian church without the enjoyment of providential favour.[56]

Although the evasion of theological disputatiousness was a necessary plank of the Moderates' establishmentarian policy, it was impossible to ignore the challenge posed by the philosophy of David Hume, whose *Enquiry concerning Human Understanding* (1748) included a self-contained chapter devoted to the subject of miracles. Hume's discussion focused on testimony for miracles. As any miracle was, by definition, a breach of the laws of nature, and these laws were themselves established on the basis of 'a firm and unalterable experience', then, Hume contended, there was an inevitable presumption against the testimony of those who had alleged experience of miracles. Indeed, ruled Hume, 'no testimony is sufficient to establish a miracle, unless the testimony be of such a kind, that its falsehood would be more miraculous, than the fact, which it endeavours to establish'. Hume brought out the subversive significance of his arguments. Some of the examples he deployed, such as that of a dead man returning to life, were deliberately insensitive and provocative. Moreover, Hume made it clear that no human testimony for a miracle would suffice as 'a just foundation for any such system of religion'. Hume's parting shot not only undermined any basis for a rational supernaturalism, but also appeared to question the sanity – or integrity – of every Christian: 'the Christian religion not only was at first attended with miracles, but even at this day cannot be believed by any reasonable person without one. Mere reason is insufficient to convince us of its veracity: And whoever is moved by Faith to assent to it, is conscious of a continued miracle in his own person, which subverts all the principles of his understanding, and gives him a determination to believe what is most contrary to custom and experience.'[57]

---

55 N. Phillipson, 'Providence and progress: an introduction to the historical thought of William Robertson', in *William Robertson and the Expansion of Empire*, ed. Stewart J. Brown (Cambridge: Cambridge University Press, 1997); Colin Kidd, *British Identities before Nationalism* (Cambridge: Cambridge University Press, 1999) 50–1.
56 George Campbell, *The Success of the First Publishers of the Gospel a Proof of its Truth* (Edinburgh: William Creech, 1777); Jeffrey M. Suderman, *Orthodoxy and Enlightenment: George Campbell in the Eighteenth Century* (Montreal and Kingston: McGill-Queen's University Press, 2001) 41, 204.
57 Hume, *Enquiry*, 76–7, 88, 90.

Hume's essay on miracles provoked an inevitable flurry of responses.[58] However, the Moderates were concerned lest the vigorous Presbyterian campaign against infidelity flare up into a public heresy hunt which would expose theological divisions within the Kirk or clog up the business of its courts. In 1755-56 the Moderates organised effectively to frustrate the attempts of die-hards such as John Bonar and George Anderson to see Hume's philosophy formally investigated and condemned by the Kirk. Indeed, Anderson desired Hume's excommunication, on the grounds that the philosopher had been baptised into the Kirk and was therefore technically subject to its discipline.[59] On the other hand, Hume's devastating critique of Christianity was answered in measured terms by George Campbell in his *Dissertation on Miracles* (1762), an influential work which was reprinted, whether in English or in translation, at least twenty-three times between 1762 and 1841.[60] Campbell contended that there were 'in human nature, some original grounds of belief, beyond which our researches cannot proceed, and of which therefore it is vain to attempt a rational account'. Moreover, Campbell identified flaws in the argument that experience alone should be used as a touchstone in judging the authenticity of testimony. On these grounds, reports that there were black people in the world could not be made credible to those white people who had never actually encountered a negro. How, asked Campbell, does an unusual fact – from beyond our immediate experience – differ from a miracle? If a miracle is a transgression of the laws of nature, which are known to us by experience, then by what criterion should we judge when the laws of nature are broken? Indeed, argued Campbell, Hume's sophistry threatened to subvert the achievements of Enlightened scientific discovery. How were the wonders of science different from miracles? Do we not believe in the wonders of electricity and magnetism, asked Campbell, on the basis of expert testimony, before we witness the experiments themselves?[61] Campbell's arguments did enough to blunt the force of Hume's arguments against miracles. Unable to set out a convincing demonstration that miracles occurred, Campbell had at least proposed an array of significant objections to Hume's deconstruction of the testimony that they had taken place.

Supernatural intervention in human history via secondary causes remained an intellectually respectable option for the enlightened. However, the supernatural

---

58 H. Sefton, 'David Hume and Principal George Campbell', in *Aberdeen and the Enlightenment*, ed. Jennifer J. Carter and Joan H. Pittock (Aberdeen: Aberdeen University Press, 1987) 126.
59 Sher, *Church and University*, 66-73; McIntosh, *Church and Theology*, 71-3.
60 Suderman, *Orthodoxy and Enlightenment*, 29-30, 123-35, 209-15, 275.
61 Campbell, *Dissertation on Miracles*, 16, 39, 51-2, 82-3.

rationalism of the Moderates was a desiccated affair. Providence became more generalised and less specific, and there was a declining emphasis upon particular providences. Where previous generations of orthodox Scots Calvinist clerics had celebrated a world apparently teeming with miraculous providences,[62] now the Moderates identified providence rather as an end point, the final mystery which lay beyond the mechanics of naturalistic explanation, whether in science or in history. It would be a mistake, however, to exaggerate the gulf between the enlightened Moderates and the traditionalists who preceded them. George Campbell's own sermon on *The Success of the First Publishers of the Gospel*, and its sharp contrast with the dry sociological message of Robertson's *Situation of the World at the Time of Christ's Appearance*, stands as a reminder that Moderate churchmanship might well be richer and more variegated than has hitherto been suspected. Nevertheless, the Enlightenment had involved a subtle but substantial remapping of the learned world. Domestically, the supernatural was now to be found most regularly in the realm of folklore; and the superstitious practices and beliefs of heathenish peoples overseas, though grist to the emerging science of anthropology, also stood representative of supposedly primitive mentalities. Moderate reticence in the sphere of theology, one aspect of which was a gradual disengagement from the subject of supernatural phenomena, had inaugurated the long process by which the supernatural has been excluded from the mainstream of Scottish life.

---

62 See e.g. Robert Wodrow (1679–1734), *Analecta, or Materials for a History of Remarkable Providences*, 4 vols. (Edinburgh: Maitland Club, 1842–3).

SIX

'Nathaniel Gow's Toddy': The Supernatural in Lowland Scottish Literature from Burns and Scott to the Present Day

Douglas Gifford

This chapter does not pretend to be anything more than an initial overall survey of the supernatural in the broadest sense. It covers the traditional folk supernatural to the contemporary surrealism, and some of the most notable occasions of its use and development since the beginnings of written literature in Lowland Scotland, and with particular emphasis on the last two centuries of Scottish writing in English and Scots. Additionally, I must make clear from the outset that in discussing the 'supernatural', I deal mainly with its non-Christian traditional and contemporary manifestations. Since the Christian supernatural, for all its irrational presumptions, is so ubiquitously accepted as 'normality', I am concerned with it only when it engages with the non-Christian and the surreal or fantastic.

One of the most striking and individuating features of the occurrence of the supernatural in Scottish literature lies in its use in what can be called 'creative ambiguity', juxtaposing, in mutually exclusive terms, traditional folk belief with Christian orthodoxy or rationalism. Some of Scottish literature's greatest achievements depend upon this juxtapositioning, outstanding shorter examples ranging from Burns's 'Tam O'Shanter', Scott's 'The Two Drovers', and Hogg's 'The Brownie of the Black Haggs' to Stevenson's 'Thrawn Janet', Linklater's 'Sealskin Trousers', Barrie's 'Farewell Miss Julie Logan', and Grassic Gibbon's 'Clay'. The use is not confined to short works; Hogg's *The Private Memoirs and Confessions of a Justified Sinner* (1824) is of course the classic example, but supernatural-psychological tension underlies many of the major works of Scott, Hogg, and Stevenson, with many additional writers from Galt and Douglas Brown to Gunn and Gibbon exploiting the possibilities of layers of implication available within the tension. Nor did the usage stop with the fading of the so-called 'Scottish Renaissance' of the 1920s and '30s; with the 1980s contemporary Scottish writing rediscovered the opportunities latent within older traditions, while bending these traditions to suit their over-riding aim of re-presenting Scotland as multi-faceted and open to change.

'Nathanial Gow's Toddy' 111

The title, which is taken from James Hogg's opening to his short story, 'The Mysterious Bride' (1830), calls for explanation. Hogg had produced for *Blackwood's Magazine* in the 1820s a series of tales (many of them published as *A Shepherd's Calendar* in 1829) in which uncanny local events were recounted in his vivid yet matter-of-fact style. Both form and content owed a great deal to the traditions of the Scottish Ballads and of oral story-telling; but Hogg's tales recurrently allowed ambivalent interpretations. On one hand they could be read as supernatural tales employing traditional, demonic and fairy folklore, and on the other they could be read rationally as studies of individual and community psychological hallucination and delusion. Yet for all his artful contrivance of this ambivalence of interpretation, Hogg continually maintained his belief in the validity of the supernatural, in his poetry and fiction, and regretted that traditional belief in the supernatural world was being increasingly discredited and invalidated.

> A great number of people nowadays are beginning broadly to insinuate that there are no such things as ghosts, or spiritual beings visible to mortal sight. Even Sir Walter Scott has turned renegade and with his stories made up of half and half like Nathaniel Gow's toddy, is trying to pour cold water on the most certain, though the most impalpable, phenomena of human nature. The bodies are daft. Heaven mend their wits! Before they venture to assert such things I wish they had been where I have often been; or in particular where the Laird of Birkendelly was on St Lawrence's Eve, in the year 1777, and sundry times subsequent to that.[1]

Hogg's criticism of Scott relates to stories such as his 'The Two Drovers' (1827), with its sub-layer of supernatural possibilities which are left as hints of the lingering yet outdated world of barbarous belief. Hogg himself was influenced by Scott's emphasis on the superiority of the rational over the traditional supernatural. Yet Hogg seems rather to have reversed the hierarchy, so that his insistence on the strength and validity of supernatural possibilities runs uniquely in his work alongside his surprising insight into complex psychological states. This dualism of interpretation is what gives much of its power to that greatest of Scottish novels, *Confessions of A Justified Sinner*. And it is precisely this balancing of the traditional supernatural and modern psychological narratives which underpins what is arguably our best-known and finest period of Scottish literature, from

---

1 'The Mysterious Bride' was first published in *Blackwood's Magazine*; reprinted in James Hogg's *Tales and Sketches of the Ettrick Shepherd* (Edinburgh and London, 1837) vol. 5, 335.

Ramsay, Fergusson and Burns through Hogg and Scott to the great short stories of Stevenson, Barrie and the writers of the Scottish Renaissance such as Eric Linklater and Lewis Grassic Gibbon.

Before coming to this, however, I would suggest that from its beginnings around 1300, there was probably never a period in the history of written Lowland Scottish literature when writers of any real literary significance accepted and wrote about the supernatural in an entirely credulous and straightforward way. Even earlier, Adomnán's *Life of St. Columba* (697) exploited the supernatural in genealogy and event to confer iconic and heroic status on his subject; Boece and Wyntoun used legend and myth to validate Scottish monarchy, and recently James Fergusson has impressively demonstrated this tendency in his study of the uses and importance of mythic lines of Gaelic descent for Scottish kingship. In literature, both Barbour in the 1370s and Blind Harry in the late fifteenth century invoked the predictions of that most legendary of Scots, Thomas of Ercildoune (Thomas the Rhymer). Andrew of Wyntoun tells us that Barbour's *The Brut* and *The Stewarts Original* took the pedigree of the Stewarts back to Banquo and Fleance, and then back to Aeneas of Troy. Harry took the use of the supra-rational much further than making use of unearthly authority; beginning and ending his poem with visions, he adds his famous and fabulous additions to Wallace's exploits, in having the English Queen beg for peace, and Wallace becoming a champion in France.

Tentatively I suggest that there are five distinguishable periods of use of the supernatural in Scottish creative literature. Firstly, there is an age of (qualified) traditional acceptance running from the beginnings of Lowland Scottish literature around the end of the thirteenth century, and arguably continuing till 1707. Secondly, from 1707 on, we find an increased focusing of ideas of the supernatural within Presbyterian religion for parodic, satiric and ultimately political reasons – a focus which arguably persists until the period of the 1914–18 World War. Thirdly, with what has been termed 'The Scottish Renaissance' (and is certainly a period of literary recovery) there is a movement to use the supernatural as part of an exploration of anthropological, linguistic and cultural roots. Instead of seeing the supernatural as pertaining to a debased or inferior folk culture, the supernatural is once again taken as of great significance, as shedding light on the workings of the subconscious and unconscious imagination. Then, following the Second World War, the fourth period sees a phase of scepticism and rejection of such supernatural usage through the 1950s and 1960s. Fifthly and finally, however, this rejection is overturned in the 1980s by Scotland's innovative and eclectic versions of 'magic realism' into new versions of the supra-rational, such as fantasy and surrealism, together with imaginative exploitation of the traditional supernatural.

It would be easy to portray the first period as one of credulous acceptance of the supernatural – and here the world of the ballads would mainly bear this out with its acceptance of supernatural beings from other worlds in, for example, 'The Demon Lover', 'The Wife of Usher's Well', 'The Great Selkie of Sule Skerrie' and 'Thomas the Rhymer'. It is clear, however, that many of the major creative writers saw other possibilities in exploitation of various traditions of the supernatural, for purposes of satire, reduction and didacticism. Moreover, this was a period when the major writers, such as Gavin Douglas, one of the finest translators of *The Aeneid*, or Sir David Lindsay, in his great European morality play, *Ane Satyre of the Thrie Estaitis*, could feel at home with Christian, classical and folk legend and mythology. Robert Henryson could work with both local and European tradition to bring the animal world to life in charming satires on pride, luxury and greed, as in 'The Uponlandis Mous and The Burges Mous' ('The Country Mouse and The Town Mouse') – and savagely, in his tales of wolves and lambs, cocks and foxes, in his enigmatic versions of Aesop's fables. Conversely, his magnificent *The Testament of Cresseid*, with its astonishingly innovative structure of dream within dream within dream, worked effortlessly with pre-Christian classical legend and mythology counterpointing Christian belief and values. Likewise William Dunbar deployed much of the traditional allegorical apparatus of great European literature in his use of elements such as the dream, the Parliament of the Gods or the beasts, and in the use of classical legend. Working closer to home, his 'The Dance of The Sevin Deidly Sins' arranges his nightmare vision so that it ends with the folk reduction of Highlanders and 'Erschemen' fittingly concluding the dance of the sins, their barbaric din proving so intolerable to the Devil that he smoors them in the deepest pot of hell. His 'Ballat of the Abbot of Tungland', with its comic deployment of the dream genre to allow himself to mock gloriously the attempts of the spurious confidence trickster who pretended to be an abbot – and whose ambitions were rudely dashed when he had to make good his claim to be able to fly – shows a splendid talent for grotesque surrealism and typical Scottish reductive idiom, anticipating that of the eighteenth century vernacular poets. David Lindsay's work in poetry and drama, especially in *Ane Satire of the Three Estaitis*, also demonstrates the medieval Scottish writer's willingness to use legend and myth for purposes of political satire. In his great morality play Lindsay's heroic figure of 'John the Commonweil' demonstrates again how the medieval Scottish writer was able to use folk legend and mythology, in its uncanny invocation of the giant John the Commonweal, the archetypal and supernatural hero who comes to rescue Scotland from the corruption of its rulers.

After the Reformation of 1560, The Court poets of James VI and I, and poets who remained in Scotland such as William Drummond of Hawthornden, were less willing, for a variety of reasons, to use traditional lore in their work. But beyond such sophisticated circles and certainly until the end of the seventeenth century, it is clear that there was a general acceptance of the 'other landscape' and the folk supernatural, in all its manifestations from witches and demons to fairies and spirits, as a hidden parallel to this world – for example, in the popular poetry of the time, and in studies such as George Sinclair's *Satan's Invisible World* (1685), Robert Kirk's *Secret Common-Wealth of Elves, Fauns and Fairies* (1691) and Robert Wodrow's *Analecta, Or Materials For A History of Remarkable Providences Mostly Related To Scotch Ministers And Christians* (recorded in the 1720s but not published until 1842).

My second period, running roughly from 1707–1918, is complex in terms of its development and use of the supernatural, and has at its heart a significant shift in literary attitudes towards the supernatural, helping to bring about what I claimed at the opening of this chapter was Scottish literature's characteristically ambiguous use of mutually exclusive interpretations of its narratives, rational and supernatural – and the justification of the chapter's title. Critics have recognised the multiple dualisms inherent in eighteenth-century Scotland. Three poets can be seen as crucial in reflecting and exploiting attitudes towards traditional beliefs. Ramsay, Fergusson and Burns were sympathetic to vernacular traditions, including those of the supernatural – yet they were equally influenced by three forces which steered them in the direction of creative and imaginative ambiguity. The Act of Union of 1707 had left a legacy of uncertainties concerning national identity; the Scottish Enlightenment and its literati, with their North British ideology, tended to disparage vernacular tradition and the languages which sustained it; and of course, behind this, the age of urban and rural improvement with its emphasis on economic, agricultural and scientific rationalism, constantly undermined the validity of tradition and vernacular culture.

An overview of the three main vernacular poets, Allan Ramsay, Robert Fergusson and Robert Burns, shows one outstanding feature which they all share – namely, a liking for ambiguity which allows them to speak with two voices – in one, with a more simple, orthodox and conformist expression, but in the other, with a deeper social, religious or political criticism. And while they develop a subtle satire which focuses on more specific issues than those of the earlier period, on political and social issues, Scottish, British and European, they also owe much to the previous period. Earlier writers too had disguised their true meaning by covering them with the cloaks of classical legend and European allegory – as in Henryson's *Fables* where one suspects that the apparent and orthodox moral is being suggested somewhat ironically, with a more profound and humanistic questioning underlying it. In *The Testament of Cresseid* it is arguable that Henryson's use of the Parliament of the classical Gods is a way of mocking religious belief in his own age, much as Shakespeare argued in King Lear that 'as flies to wanton boys so we to the Gods/they kill us for their sport'. Similarly, it has been argued that Montgomery's 'The Cherrie and The Slae' has concealed within it a satire upon the clash of values of Roman Catholicism and emergent Calvinism. After Union with England in 1707, writers and editors like Alan Ramsay in his collection of older Scottish poets in *The Evergreen* (1724) were rediscovering these models, so that when Ramsay himself came to write poems such as 'The Vision' or 'John Cowper the Kirk Treasurer's Man' or 'Wealth or the Woody', he was developing possibilities that he had inherited from his earlier mentors. 'A Vision' illustrates this perfectly. With its poet brooding on the woes of Scotland, and falling into a dream in which he encounters the guardian of Scotland, William Wallace, it deploys many of the strategies and subtleties of earlier Scottish poets. Ramsay published this poem under the pseudonym of 'A. R. Scott', and in the pretended antique language and style of an older Scottish poet – suggesting perhaps that this was a poem on the subject of the Wars of Independence by the Alexander Scott of the sixteenth century. The poem is, however, clearly Ramsay's, and its ambivalence stems from the fact that while the poet may seem to be talking about the problems of Scotland in the period of the Wars of Independence, the poem's meaning is equally applicable to the period between the two Jacobite rebellions of 1715 and 1745. The dream structure and the supernatural apparatus of Wallace as the guardian of Scotland speaking his message to the poet echoes the dream garden of Scotland so often envisioned by poets like Dunbar, and Lindsay's great John the Commonweal; but now Ramsay combines this with the ambiguity of Henryson or Montgomerie with specific aim of expressing his Jacobite sympathies. Thus the supernatural is now used to evoke the idea of the spirit of Scotland speaking through the ages, yet speaking satirically – and in politically dangerous terms – apparently on events of The Wars of Independence, but in reality on the need for Scotland in the 1700s (and just before the 1715 Rebellion) to be pushed to its limits of tolerance to force the country to rediscover its old strength and independence of spirit. Ramsay thus manages to remain on the surface the respectable Edinburgh burgess, but underneath, and through his subtle use of the supernatural, he articulates his Jacobitism. Wallace's prophecy here may speak of Bannockburn; but his author Ramsay speaks of contemporary Scottish poverty, and his vision of the restoration of the Stuarts. (The language of the poem is Ramsay's version of older Scots.)

> Quhen all your trade is at a stand,
> And cunzie clene forsaiks the land,
> Quhilk will be very sune,
> Will preists without their stypands preach?
> For nocht will lawyers causes streich?
> Faith thats nae easy done.
> All this and mair maun cum to pass,
> To cleir your glamourit sicht;
> And Scotland maun be made an ass
> To set her jugment richt.
> Theyil jade her and blad her
> Afore she brak her tether
> Tho auld yet, she's bauld yet
> And teuch like barkit leather.
>
> But mony a corss shall braithles ly,
> And wae sall mony a widow cry,
> Or all rin richt again;
> Owre Cheviot prancing proudly north,
> The faes sall tak the feild neir Forthe,
> And think the day their ain:
> But burns that day sall rin with blude
> Of them that now oppress;
> Thair carcasses be corbys fude
> By thousands on the gress.
> A king then sall ring then,
> Of wyse renoun and braif,
> Quhase pusians and sapiens
> Sall richt restoir and saif.[2]

Ramsay's use of the supernatural here and elsewhere, as when he evokes the ghostly spirit of John Cowper the Kirk treasurer's man in a pre-Burnsian satire on social privilege ('Elegy on John Cowper') demonstrates well the increasing subtlety of exploitation of its possibilities for social and political satire – especially in the light of his clear-headed scepticism regarding the validity of

---

2 Ramsay's poem, which first appeared in his *The Evergreen* of 1724, carried a spurious note: 'Compylit in Latin be a most lernit Clerk in Tyme of our Hairship and Oppression, anno 1300, and translatit in 1524'. See *Poems by Allan Ramsay and Robert Fergusson*, ed. Alexander Kinghorn and Alexander Law (Edinburgh and London: Scottish Academic Press, 1974) 35.

witchcraft when Sir William Worthy mocks the idea in his play of 1725, *The Gentle Shepherd*.

Ramsay, Fergusson and Burns realised that there were all sorts of possibilities in widening the range of supernatural exploitation, going far beyond traditional folklore. In Robert Fergusson's 'The Ghaists' we find the poet raising the ghosts of the great Edinburgh philanthropists George Herriot [sic] and George Watson, to bemoan Westminster taxation of Scotland through the Mortmain Bill. This clever juxtaposition of older and traditional fears of haunted graveyards with acid political comment was to draw on the 'Habbie Simson' tradition of mock-elegy, and Ramsay's use of the ghost of John Cowper. With an imaginative wit which approaches surrealism, all three poets bring inanimate objects to vivid life in grotesque flytings – Ramsay with the arguments of brandy and whisky, Fergusson with pavement and road, Burns with the old and new bridges of Ayr. In 'The Holy Fair' Burns would draw on Fergusson's 'Leith Races', with its clever personification of Mirth as a fun-loving spirit attending the festivities. In his version of holiday release, Burns brings Fun to life as a winsome peasant girl, taking his hand as they approach the holiday atmosphere of the fair, their light-heartedness contrasted with their two fellow-travellers, the gloomy black-clad personifications, Superstition and Hypocrisy.

Burns also develops the mock-elegy tradition (or indeed looks back to the medieval traditions of the beast fable as used by Henryson), extending the mock-lament beyond humanity to include sheep, as in 'Poor Mailie's Elegy'. And in 'The Twa Dogs' he exploits the possibilities of humanising the aristocratic Newfoundland dog and the homely Collie so that they can discuss the folly of human ways which, in comparison with the ways of simple animals, appear as pretentious, hypocritical, immoral and counter-productive.

Burns's fertile poetic innovation is crucial in moving towards what can be regarded as probably the most significant period in blending together traditional and aesthetically accomplished deployments of the supernatural. His range of treatment runs from the more or less simple recording of traditional folk beliefs in 'Halloween' to his savage satire on the Earl of Breadalbane in which the devil compliments the Earl on his frustrating the designs of Highlanders who 'were so audacious as to attempt to escape from their lawful lords and masters whose property they were', in their plan of emigration to Canada, and his companionable addresses to Auld Nick in 'Holy Willie's Prayer', another variation on the demonic theme, in which in the end Holy Willie can be read as addressing not God but his more sinister master.

It is, however, 'Tam O'Shanter' which points towards the creative ambiguities of the great fictions of the nineteenth century. This poem, with its remarkable blend of traditional lore and contemporary irony, and of racy Scots and elegant literati English, establishes a kind of template for the many ambivalent narratives to follow in Scottish literature, from Scott and Hogg to Stevenson and Grassic Gibbon – and even in America, as in the stories of Nathaniel Hawthorne, with their similar ambivalence of interpretation. At one level, the poem can be read as a simple tale of the supernatural, where, after the witching hour, Tam, in the best traditions of folklore, awakens the wrath of supernatural forces. In this, the most accepted reading, Tam barely escapes with his life and soul, pursued by the legions of Hell irate with his impudence. In a diametrically opposed reading, however, Burn's subtlety, in leaving deeper psychological interpretations available, becomes clear. Tam has yearned for drink, song, human warmth, conviviality and even sexuality; after passing midnight, 'o' night's black arch the key-stane', he dreams or hallucinates, creating, in nightmare, dark versions of the experiences of release for which he yearned. In this reading, Tam becomes a kind of Scottish Everyman, dreaming of holiday and release in ways which his Calvinist upbringing cannot allow to happen in reality; his guilty consciousness must surround these wishes with threats of punishment. How cleverly Burns tells us that drink, 'inspiring bold John Barleycorn', has made Tam face the devil; how slyly he warns us, tongue-in-cheek, that when our thoughts incline to drink, we may buy its joys more dearly than we imagine. The implications of his ironic slyness emerge when one realises that the price that Tam had in the end to pay was the tail of his horse, and the imminent wrath of his wife. Thus Burns wryly comments on dour Scottish distrust of pleasure – as well as more philosophically (and in Enlightenment English, standing high above local matters and dialect) – recognising the all-too-transitory experience of the sensation of pleasure, a moment seen then gone forever, vanishing amidst the storm of life. And with these two opposing readings, the poem points towards what will in the work of nineteenth and early twentieth-century Scottish writers, from Hogg and Stevenson to Gibbon and Linklater, become a recurrent ambivalence of interpretation, between supernatural and rational reading.

It was not to be poetry, however, that carried on this supernatural/psychological duality. From Ramsay to Burns there is clearly identifiable a scaling down of an important tradition in Scottish poetry, that of the national epic, as found from Barbour, Blind Harry and David Lindsay to Ramsay's ambitious 'The Vision' and (admittedly reduced in range) Fergusson's 'The Ghaists'. Burns reduces the scale of his traditional national visionary poetry further in his 'The Vision', where Coila, now a female visionary muse, is simply the muse of the district of Kyle, a part rather than the whole of Scotland. By Scott's time, epic poetry is safely located as the lays of last minstrels and therefore unthreatening to modernity, as in Hogg's *The Queen's Wake* of 1813, with its multiple pastiches and parodies of traditional supernatural, the Lowland high jinks of 'The Witch of Fife' and the Highland Gothic terrors of 'The Fate of MacGregor' and 'Young Kennedy'. Hogg increasingly turned to comic or religious fantasy such as 'The Russiade' or 'Connel of Dee'. And in his more ambitious and symbolic 'Kilmeny' (one of the seventeen poems forming *The Queen's Wake*), critics have continued to disagree as to what Kilmeny represents, and what her visions imply regarding her country. At best, she represents a purity and goodness for which Hogg's Scotland has little time nor place. In her withdrawal from the fallen realities around her she anticipates those recurrent protagonists of Scottish fiction, from Stevenson's David Balfour to Gibbon's Chris Guthrie, and I have argued elsewhere that these figures evidence a nineteenth and twentieth century disillusionment with and disengagement from social and political realities on the part of their authors, speaking perhaps for a much wider detachment.[3]

Hogg's views on the history of supernatural belief in Scotland are important, since clearly, as the self-proclaimed 'king of the mountain and the fairy school', in poems like 'Old David' and 'To the Countess of Buccleuch' he saw his beloved creatures and beliefs in the other and older landscape of folklore withering in what he described as the cold and saturnine light of modern rationalism. For all Hogg's undoubted ability to evoke these older worlds in his poetry, as in his uncanny and elusive portrayal of a creature somewhere between saint and witch in 'Kilmeny', or his lively and concrete evocations of the supernatural in poems like 'The Witch of Fife', it was to be in his fiction that he followed Burns's example of 'Tam O'Shanter'. In *Confessions of A Justified Sinner* he echoed Burns's 'Holy Willie's Prayer' in his sinner's dramatic monologue which claims moral authority from God for what would be regarded by most others as social crime or deadly sin. And echoing the dual readings of 'Tam O' Shanter', he presented a wonderful ambivalence in his picture of what can be read as either a psychologically-disturbed young man, whose burden of Calvinist guilt drives him to invent an *alter ego*, who at first tempts and then seduces him into suicide, thus using this interpretation as a profound satire on extreme Calvinism; or, on the other hand, presents yet another of those many ballad and folklore protagonists who, through pride, arrogance and wicked actions, arouse the wrath of God and the Devil and are thereafter haunted by a demon. Hogg was to use this ambivalence of interpretation in the majority of his stories – in *Winter Evening Tales* (1821), *The Shepherd's Calendar*, in stories like 'Mary Burnet', 'Tibby Hyslop's Dream', 'Robb Dodds', the later 'The Cameronian Preacher's Tale', and many others.

He continually presented situations that could be read as tales of complex psychological and human confrontations on one hand, or as traditional

---

3 Douglas Gifford, 'The Politics of Scottish Fiction', in *The Polar Twins*, ed. Edward J. Cowan and Douglas Gifford (Edinburgh: John Donald, 1999) 284–303.

ballad-style invocations of devils and preachers on the other. I place Hogg before Scott in this respect, although Scott himself in stories like 'The Two Drovers' and throughout his early novels especially, from *Waverley* to *The Antiquary* and *The Heart of Midlothian*, continually deploys a milder version of this strategy, allowing the supernatural possibilities to co-exist with what could be read a simple superstition and coincidence. For example in his classic, 'The Two Drovers', Scott never eliminates the possibility that the spey-wife, Janet of Tomahourich, has had her vision of the tragic fate of Robin Oig. Yet simultaneously, writing as a rational historian and lawyer, and as a product of the Scottish Enlightenment, he allows that the tragedy may be entirely explicable in psychological terms, arising out of Robin Oig's complex clan and family background, and his hidden Highland pride and passions. What is deeply ironic, however, is that Scott, who had used to the full the possibilities of the traditional supernatural in his *The Lay of the Last Minstrel*, in *Marmion*, and whose earlier fiction regularly exploited this kind of creative ambivalence, began in the 1820s to become increasingly negative in his attitude towards such juxtapositioning of supernatural folk tradition and modern rationalism in fiction – for example in his reviews of *The Brownie of Bodsbeck* and his review of Hogg's monumental use of Border folklore in *The Three Perils of Man* in 1824. Nineteenth century treatment of the supernatural – in Europe and America as well as Scotland – was profoundly affected by Scott's reorientation. Nowhere is this more succinctly expressed than in Scott's 1826 review of John Galt's novel *The Omen* (1825). Galt had used traditional supernatural in works such as *The Entail* (1823), but always with a coolly disparaging and rational perspective which tended simultaneously to mock his usage. His novel *The Omen*, which is the story of a sophisticated and sensitive central character's increasing sense, through omen and potent, of his doom, anticipating Poe's *The Fall of the House of Usher* (1839) is singled out by Scott as exemplifying a new kind of supernatural of which Scott completely approves.

> In the elegant little volume, which forms the subject of this article, we find another example of the novel of character and an indisputably good one. The theme which has been chosen as predominating in his hero's mind, a youth of a gentle, melancholy, abstracted disposition, is a superstition as connected with an anxious and feverish apprehension of futurity — a feeling which though ridiculed at one time, reasoned out in another and stubbornly denied upon all has, in one shape or other, greater weight with most men than any is willing to admit of himself or ready to believe in another . . . the reader will easily imagine that we do not allude to the superstition of the olden time, which believed in spectres, fairies and

other supernatural apparitions. These airy squadrons have long been routed and are banished to the cottage and the nursery. But there exists more than one species of superstition entirely distinct from that which these phantoms, a disease, a weakness of the mind . . . amongst which is pre-eminent that which supposes our mind receives secret intimations of futurity by accidents which appear mysteriously indicative of coming events, by impulses to which the mind seems involuntarily subjected, and which seems less to arise from its own reflections than to be stamped and impressed on the thoughts by the agency of some separate being; this constitutes the peculiar superstition of the hero of *The Omen*. The events which he meets are all of a natural and ordinary character in themselves; it is the sensations of the augur by whom they are interpreted that gives them an ominous character.[4]

Scott then goes on to say that many distinguished people have secretly believed in such supernatural possibilities ('Bonaparte secretly believed in the influence of his star – Byron had more than one point of superstitious faith'). What Scott reveals here, and which will have a profound effect on later Scottish writing, is that he has significantly changed his attitude towards traditional folklore ('spectres, fairies and other supernatural apparitions'), to move instead towards the more class conscious hypothesis that sensitive and cultured persons may have more subtle supernatural perception in ways which contrast with what he sees at the naive beliefs of humble peasantry. Again we are reminded of Hogg's argument that Sir Walter Scott had 'turned renegade' so that his stories were made up of 'half and half' – Hogg implying that rationality had now bested the irrational and supernatural.

It can be argued that Scottish poetry, now increasingly cut off from its traditional roots, and increasingly expressing itself in English rather than Scots, as a consequence lost much of its radicalism, as well as its rich traditional embedding in long-held belief. For several decades after Scott's death in 1832 it can broadly be seen moving in two opposing directions. On one hand it aspired to tedious post-Miltonic religious epics like Robert Pollock's *The Course of Time* (1827), and consequent powerful but intensely gloomy anti-religious epics like *The City of Dreadful Night* (1875) and Davidson's *Testaments* at the turn of the century. On the other it diverted itself in comic relief in mock-epics such as those of Hogg's already mentioned, or William Tennant's 'Anster Fair' in 1812 where all the extended supernatural apparatus is clearly deflated by

---

4 Scott's review of *The Omen* appeared in *Blackwood's Magazine*, vol. 30, July 1826; reprinted in *Scott's Miscellaneous Prose Works*, vol.8, (Edinburgh, 1871) 333.

being seen finally – and almost literally – as a storm in a teacup. These were followed by anglicised mockeries of older beliefs by *literati* writers such as John Gibson Lockhart in 'The Ballad of Sir Lancelot Bogle', or the wonderful, neglected but quite consciously anti-irrational mockeries of Scottish religiosity of Dundonian James Young Geddes, in hilarious yet satirically serious and ambitious disclaimers to the prophets of religious doom and gloom in long poems like 'The New Jerusalem' and 'The New Inferno'. In these heaven is revealed as ineffably boring, and hell, with its vitality and industry, the only desirable afterlife, while, more seriously, in 'The Second Advent', Christ returns to our modern world, to be rejected by church and society.[5] In all these the supernatural is a prominent feature, but it is no longer explicitly traditional but now tongue-in-cheek, biblically derived, Gothic romantic, or implicitly parodic of Scottish tradition especially in terms of religious sanctions such as demons, Hell and the prospect of eternal suffering. And fiction illustrates this even more clearly. The wonderful gothic tales of George MacDonald, while still using local traditional supernatural elements, owe even more to newer kinds of fantasy in European Romanticism as found in writers like the German mystics Jakob Boehme and Novalis. Margaret Oliphant's fine supernatural tales, while occasionally using traditional folklore, as in 'The Library Window' and 'The Open Door' (both in *Stories of the Seen and Unseen*, 1885) more often work with a similarly European religious and mystical supernatural, as in *A Beleaguered City* (1879), *A Little Pilgrim in the Unseen*, (1882) and *In the Land of Darkness* (1888). The surreal worlds of Oliphant, and even more those of George MacDonald, lead to the twentieth century fantasies of David Lindsay in *A Voyage to Arcturus* in 1920, and to the later epic fantasies of C. S. Lewis and J. R. R. Tolkien.

Writers such as Oliphant and Stevenson continue to exploit the possibilities of that creative ambiguity found in the work of Burns, Scott, and Hogg. Oliphant's 'The Library Window' and 'The Open Door' can be read either as demonstrating psychological breakdown in their protagonists – or they can be read as genuinely supernatural tales, their protagonists caught up in inexplicable events. Stevenson's short stories and novels are prime examples. Stories and novels such as *The Merry Men* (1881), 'Markheim' (1884), and *The Master of Ballantrae* (1888), with their dark symbolic and demonic figures, suggest opposing possibilities – either that their protagonists, such as the giant black man who appears as a kind of judgement at the end of *The Merry Men*

---

5   The virtually unknown work of James Young Geddes, arguably one of the finest, if not the finest, Scottish poets between Burns and MacDiarmid, was published in three volumes: *The New Jerusalem* (Dundee, 1879), *The Spectre Clock of Alyth* (Alyth, 1886), and *In the Valhalla* (Dundee, 1891).

(refashioned in the giant judgemental figure of Attwater in *The Ebbtide* (1894), or uncanny James Durie in *The Master of Ballantrae*, are genuinely demonic, or they can be explained in rational terms as symbols of abnormal humanity. Perhaps the most striking example of all this is found in 'Thrawn Janet', where the tormented minister Reverend Murdoch Soulis may have awakened the Devil, which possesses his old servant-woman; but equally possible is the reading in which his neurotic mind (with the superstitious aid of his benighted and maliciously gossiping community) invents the witch-devil which turns him crazy – but approved by his congregation as the grimmest of preachers. Stevenson developed the use of ambiguity in Scottish fiction till it profoundly challenged conventional moral reading. More often than not his stories offer not only mutually exclusive perspectives of the rational and irrational, but deepen the implications of their opposition to offer reversible perspectives of morality. For example, we may initially judge Henry Durie as Stevenson's morally approved brother in *The Master of Ballantrae*, with James as his evil opposite; but on reflection we may also come to another conclusion, that Stevenson wishes us to probe deeper. If we question the teller of events, the pious house servant and manipulative manager Mackellar, we can recognise his prejudices and reverse our previous assessment, till we speculate as to whether it might be Henry who is the dark brother, with his brother James maligned by him and Mackellar simply on the grounds of his refusal to live by conventional values. The work of Stevenson is outstanding in developing the late nineteenth-century revival of the use of the supernatural in literature. There is no doubt that, as with his invention of 'Lallans' in his poetry collection *Underwoods* (1887), he (together with writers like Oliphant and Macdonald) initiated the movement of recovery of older Scottish culture and belief which would burgeon in the 'Scottish Renaissance' so commonly associated with MacDiarmid, but which owes much more to previous Scottish writers like Stevenson than MacDiarmid and too many critics have yet allowed. Stevenson's subtle use of the traditional supernatural re-opened possibilities for many writers like Neil Munro (as in *The Lost Pibroch*, 1896) George Douglas Brown (*The House With the Green Shutters*, 1901), and John MacDougall Hay (*Gillespie*, 1914), so that their stories could carry undercurrents of traditional belief, with suggestions of demonic or fairy enchantment, second sight, and the fateful inheritance from the past of a tragic destiny. Writers such as John Buchan (especially *Witch Wood*, 1926) and James Barrie in plays such as *Dear Brutus* (1917) and *Mary Rose* (1920) carried on this use of the traditional supernatural. Barrie's novella *Farewell Miss Julie Logan* (1932) can be read as the ultimate version of the classic Scottish supernatural-psychological tale – and indeed as a conscious farewell on Barrie's part, in a world which he felt was increasingly dismissive of legend and magic, to the classic traditional and ambivalent supernatural tale as begun by Burns and developed by writers like Scott, Hogg, Oliphant, Stevenson, and Munro.

For all Barrie's farewell, however, the use of traditional supernatural elements was thriving. And for all MacDiarmid and the 'Scottish Renaissance' writers' claim that they were returning to rediscover the neglected roots of Scottish culture, we are beginning to recognise how much they owed to writers like Stevenson, Munro, and Davidson, or poets like Violet Jacob and Marion Angus, with their recurrent lyrics of uncanny and haunting rural scenes which fuse traditional supernatural imagery and situations and complex exploration of the repressions and limitations of women throughout history. MacDiarmid was to draw deeply on their achievement in his wonderful collections *Sangschaw* (1925) and *Penny Wheep* (1926).

Yet while this late Victorian and Edwardian recovery of interest in the traditional supernatural contributed massively towards the 'Scottish Renaissance' of the period between the two world wars, there is no doubt that that resurgence in Scottish poetry, fiction, drama, and non-fictional prose marked a new period in the use of supernatural tradition. Between the older writers and the new, lay social and crucial cultural events and developments which changed not just Scottish thinking, but that of the entire world. The epic work of Sir James Frazer in anthropology and myth (ironically, intended by him to prove that religious beliefs were mere superstition, but in literature, instead, allowing writers to recreate spiritual possibilities from the bases of world legend and myth), the revelations of Freud and Jung of the unexplored significance of the unconscious and the sub-conscious mind, in its dreams and intuitions, confirmed the initial and tentative explorations of nineteenth-century novelists. And the Great War of 1914–18 awakened writers all over Europe – but especially in Scotland – to their neglect of their national cultures.

There is no doubting the major role played in this re-awakening by Hugh MacDiarmid (Christopher Murray Grieve). His antipathy towards what he saw as the parochial and sentimentalising tendencies of Scottish culture, in its emphasis on Celtic Twilight and Kailyard introversion, may have ignored the substantial achievements of many of his predecessors, but in his emphasis on the importance of perception beyond that of his five senses, and belief in the supra-rational qualities of language, especially older Scots, he certainly opened up spiritual and immaterial possibilities and visions for many of his contemporaries, outstanding amongst them James Bridie (O. H. Mavor), Lewis Grassic Gibbon (James Leslie Mitchell), Neil Gunn, Eric Linklater, Fionn McColla (Tom Macdonald), Somhairle MacGill-Eain (Sorley Maclean), Naomi Mitchison, and William Soutar. 'I'll aye be whaur extremes meet,' insisted MacDiarmid in the persona of his rural visionary in *A Drunk Man Looks at the*

Thistle (1926), insisting that Scotland's collective psyche had lost its essential devilry, without which it had become neutered and anaemic. The poem is a great cry for personal, cultural and political regenerative vision beyond that of rationality:

> I seek, in this captivity,
> To pierce the veils that darklin' fa'
> – See white clints slidin' to the sea
> And hear the horns o' Elfland blaw ...[6]

Yet, for all MacDiarmid's invocation of the Otherworld of the traditional ballads, it was not his main role to exploit the traditional supernatural, but rather to explore the uncanniness of mind in flux, fragmented in psychology, in an unreality derived from nineteenth century European literature, from Dostoevsky and Gogol to Pound and Eliot. MacDiarmid was Scotland's outstanding Modernist. Roderick Watson and Alan Riach's collection of his pioneering *Annals of the Five Senses* and *Other Stories, Sketches and Plays* (Manchester, 1999), a strikingly unusual mixture of poetry, fiction, drama and sketches, has a baker's dozen of supernatural tales, most of which are in the mould of 'Saki' (Hugh Macdonald), and only rarely – as in 'A'body's Lassie', 'The Visitor' and 'Old Mrs Beattie' – developing the tradition of Hogg and Stevenson as in their ambiguities of supernatural and psychological in tales like 'The Brownie of the Black Haggs' and 'Thrawn Janet'. This is no negative criticism; MacDiarmid in other respects of language and culture marvellously re-worked Scotland. He was not, however, to be limited to the magic of the Scottish past, but worked best in a territory inherited from Romantic poetry and Modernism's recognition of the unknown territories and capabilities of the mind. The re-discovery and refashioning of Scottish (and European) traditional supernatural is most ambitious and satisfying in the work of his contemporary and friend William Soutar, in his magnificent recreations of the dream visions of medieval Makars like Dunbar and Henryson. Poems such as 'Birthday', and 'The Whale' re-work centuries-old traditions of Scottish poetry, combining Pagan and Christian iconography. 'The Auld Tree', explicitly acknowledging the magical quality of MacDiarmid's inspiration, is Soutar's most ambitious poem. With its rich fusion of European myth, as in its root symbolism of Ygdrassil, the great tree which upholds the world, and its Renaissance use of Modernist

---

6 Hugh MacDiarmid, *A Drunk Man Looks at the Thistle* (Edinburgh: William Blackwood and Sons, 1926): *Annotated Edition*, ed. Kenneth Buthlay (Edinburgh: Scottish Academic Press, 1987) 20, lines 205–8.

Wasteland imagery, together with older ballad situations and themes such as the prophecies of Thomas the Rhymer, The Eildon Tree, and the relationship of what Gunn termed 'the other landscape' to the 'real' world, it illustrates a key element in the Renaissance's use of the supernatural. All cultures, mythologies and beliefs can be exploited for the writer's over-riding aim of re-discovering what are held to be essential and archetypal truths of communities throughout history. That said, Soutar's poetry has at its heart a profound opposition, in which the poet identifies the Unicorn as the symbol of his vision of ideal beauty and regeneration, while the Gowk/Cuckoo, the cheating bird, represents illusion and disillusion. Within this dualism Soutar makes traditional magic serve his modern purpose of expressing his oneness with older Scottish life and poetry together with his desire (often frustrated) to see Scotland revitalised in culture and politics. It is this thrust of his work which reaches out to connect with the work of contemporary Scottish writers who share his agenda.

Another of Soutar's poems, 'The Tryst', is arguably one of the most achieved and moving poems in Scottish literature, and it exemplifies another key aspect of the Renaissance's re-working of the traditional supernatural. It manages to work on several levels of interpretation, moving from its surface meaning of a lover's night visitation, to a deeper level in which (as in Keats's 'La Belle Dame Sans Merci') a sinister and magical enchantment and seduction has taken place, to the yet deeper and now psychologically explicable level (in which the poet (perhaps speaking from Soutar's own tragically crippled state) creates and un-creates his dream lover.[7] This ambiguity of interpretation we have noted as one of older Scottish literature's key strategies, albeit for different motives and purposes. From the varying interpretations of medieval poems such as 'The Testament of Cresseid' and 'The Cherrie and the Slae' to poems like Ramsay's 'A Vision', Burns's 'Tam O' Shanter' and Hogg's 'Kilmeny', ambivalence in interpretation of rational and supernatural possibilities is fundamental to the author's purpose – as mentioned earlier in the reversible supernatural-psychological interpretation of so many of the short stories and novels of Scott, Hogg, and Stevenson in the nineteenth century. The Scottish Renaissance continued and developed this traditional ambiguity – but now with the underlying motive of re-uniting past culture with the new consciousness of Modernism.

In this respect it is worth seeing how Soutar's past and present possibilities in 'The Tryst' compare with similar pre-occupations in one of the finest short stories of the period, Lewis Grassic Gibbon's 'Clay'. Here, too, several possibilities

---

7 See *Poems of William Soutar*, ed. William Aitken (Edinburgh: Scottish Academic Press, 1988); also *Into a Room: Selected Poems of William Soutar*, ed. Carl MacDougall and Douglas Gifford (Glendaruel, Argyll: Argyll Publishing, 2000).

are allowed, in this story of a crofter transformed from family man to land-obsessed miser. Is it simply his family characteristics re-asserting themselves in Rob Galt's absorption in the old farm he has just taken over, Pittaulds? Or is he under the spell of some Earth-spirit, transferring his love of family into some grotesque and enchanted love-affair with the land itself, which vampire-like draws his labour and in the end his life to itself? Or is the real enchantment in the call, coming over thousands of years to Rob, of the ancient Pict who once farmed Pittaulds ('the farm of the old Pict'?), and whose grave Rob unearths, only to die on discovery?

All Gibbon's Scottish work exemplifies this, from *Sunset Song*, the first in the great trilogy of novels, *A Scots Quair* (1932–34), to short stories like 'Clay', 'Smeddum', and 'Greenden'. Neil Gunn spoke for the Renaissance and its aims of recovery of lost identity in *Highland River* (1937); 'Our river took a wrong turning somewhere, but we haven't forgotten the source.' In their novels, and, to a lesser extent, in those of Eric Linklater and Naomi Mitchison, there are, recurrently, moments of epiphany when their protagonists stand outside time, and experience epiphany and contact with their ancient past – usually in some ancient place, as they feel the intimations of history from standing stones, brochs, earthhouses. Such moments are not explained in rational terms; nor, however, are they insisted on as supernatural. Both possibilities co-exist; history may be articulating itself through some ancient spiritual bond – or something like Yeats's 'Great Memory' or Jung's 'collective unconscious', it may be making the past known in inexplicable, yet not supernatural, way. These are moments when rationality or the rules of biology and time are set aside. In *Sunset Song* virtually all of the central protagonists relive events from thousands of years before, as for example Chris Guthrie, when she 'sees' the ragged man calling 'the ships of Pytheas', or when Chae Strachan, aided perhaps by drink, 'sees' the carter/soldier from the time of the wars of Calgacus against the Romans. Similarly Gunn will have Kenn in *Highland River* and Finn in *The Silver Darlings* transcend time to allow them to share in ancient pre-Christian experience. Mitchison and Linklater likewise give their protagonists experience and memories beyond that of their own time. And in poetry, MacDiarmid, Muir and Soutar, consistently endow their poetry with this same sense of 'other time', so that the sense of modern Scotland living in the shadow of an older, even timeless, *ur*-Scotland is constantly suggested to the reader.

These writers draw on a common pool of imagery and symbolism. For example, serpent symbolism abounds in the work of Muir, MacDiarmid, Soutar, Gunn and Mitchison, recurrently carrying the same implication of older, pre-Christian, wise knowledge which insists on being heard as a correcting voice or meaning within the various versions of fallen or Wasteland Scotlands their fiction and poetry present. Beyond the pagan serpent, with its implied rebuke of the Christian appropriation of its symbolism for indication of evil, lie an impressive number of animal symbols, carrying varying degrees of the mythical and suggestive – unicorns, white hinds, white or black bulls, salmon, horses, birds of varying sorts from swans and eagles and cuckoos as 'gowks', and, in the work of Gunn a host of humbler animal ideals, from green linnets to black rabbits, to the curlews equally beloved of Gibbon. All these are messengers, speakers of an underlying, if forgotten, union of the world of nature and of man – embodied in Gunn's concept of the strath, so much more than glen or valley, in that it contains a total organic symbiosis of creatures from the animal to the human in a growing place which is also developing in time, with the systole and diastole of its river as its heartbeat.

For all this timeless earth and animal mythology, worked with re-affirmation of the Scottish traditional supernatural to underpin some of Scottish literature's finest imaginative works, such 'renaissance' of what were believed to be older truths and older ideals was not to last for more than two decades. Even within the period of 'renaissance' writers such as George Blake (in his lament for the decline of Scotland's most heroic industry in *The Shipbuilders* (1935), and Ian Niall (as Ian McNeillie) in his mockery of rural idealism in *The Wigtown Ploughman* (1939), McNeillie's foreword asks: 'Would you have me tell you a fairy story?'; he and Blake were attacking what they saw as false rural and urban romanticism. The contrast between the idealistic and nationalistic cultural values of the Scottish Renaissance and the sceptical and anti-romantic attitudes of writers of the period following the Second World War could hardly be more striking. After the German and European failure of ideologies of national socialism, and their supportive mythic traditionalism, a dark reaction emphasising social realism and sceptical materialism took place which was deeply distrustful of Renaissance ideology and mythology, with its respect for the traditional and the supernatural, and its emphasis on essentialism and its belief in an intimate and fundamental relationship between landscape and character. Most of the major poets after the war, like Norman MacCaig and Iain Crichton Smith, for all their caring relationship with their Scottish Highlands and islands, preferred to leave out Scottish Renaissance sub-texts of profound archetypal and mythic meaning, those resonances with the 'collective unconscious' so beloved of MacDiarmid and Muir, Gibbon and Gunn. This reaction culminated in the work of post-1945 writers such as Edward Gaitens, Dorothy Haynes, Robin Jenkins, George Friel, and James Kelman, with their sardonic and reductive attitudes towards older and modern presentations of Scotland as noble and romantic in tradition, with colourful interaction between Highland and Lowland histories, the past seen as endowing the present with dignity and social value. Partly because of the collapse of ideas of national socialism in Europe, but also through belated realisation of the grimness of living conditions in the post-war industrial conurbations and twilight rural despoliations of the Scottish Lowlands, these authors emphasised what they believed to be the spiritual bleakness and hopelessness of modern Scotland, stripping away what they saw as the spurious iconography in all-too-prevalent representations of Scotland past and present. These seemed – and indeed seem to many contemporary writers – utterly irrelevant to the majority of people living in arid non-communities and employed, if at all, in soul-destroying monotony. This is the dominant tendency in Scottish fiction and literature in the 50s till the 70s, and still carries weight in the present-day work of writers like James Kelman, Agnes Owens, Duncan McLean, and Irvine Welsh.

For the next three decades most of Scotland's major writers shared this bleak mood; Robert Garioch's poetry mocked the pretensions and hypocrisies of douce Edinburgh; while in drama Ena Lamont Stewart's *Men Should Weep* (1947) exemplified and focused on an even darker urban Scotland, in its harrowing picture of a dysfunctional family riven by Scottish attitudes accepting male domination, alcoholism, and the *status quo* of poverty and violence. Even Scotland's star of London's West-End, James Bridie, whose earlier plays of the 'thirties like *The Holy Isle* (1942) and *The Forrigan Reel* (1944) had success often subscribed to Renaissance ideas of vital and uncanny intimations necessary to modernity from an ancient past, acknowledged the new mood of disillusion in his Jenkins – like the study of a idealistic schoolteacher in industrial Lanarkshire whose prize pupils turn to crime and prostitution, *Mr Gillie* (1950). And in the 1960s, the ironic deconstructions of Highlands and islands in MacCaig and Crichton Smith (who extended his attacks on the destructive effects of Highland Clearance and bigoted Scottish religion in his first novel, *Consider the Lilies*, in 1967) were accompanied by devastating satires on traditional Scottish icons of value and achievement, the Scottish dominie and the Scottish soldier respectively, in Muriel Spark's *The Prime of Miss Jean Brodie* (1961) and James Kennaway's *Tunes of Glory* (1956). The disillusion with urban Scotland deepened with Archie Hind's *The Dear Green Place* (1966), and with *From Scenes Like These* (1968), in which Gordon Williams graphically portrayed the destruction of childhood innocence in a setting neither urban or rural, but now so typical of what Scotland had become for so many of its inhabitants. These novels exemplified a mood which so many Scottish novelists beyond Robin Jenkins would follow in the 1970s, from George Friel in *Mr Alfred MA* (1972) to William McIlvanney and *Docherty* (1975), and Alan Spence in *Its colours They Are Fine* (1977). Even the work of Orkney poet and novelist George

Mackay Brown, who seemed in his timeless evocations of ancient and heraldic islands to hark back to Renaissance values, has a sub-text of disillusion with what repressive religion, materialism, and so-called progress had done to his islands, outstandingly in his two collections of short stories, *A Calendar of Love* (1967) and *A Time to Keep* (1969). The picture is rounded out when drama and poetry are considered alongside fiction. The plays of Bill Bryden, Hector MacMillan, Roddy MacMillan, Stewart Conn and Donald Campbell, to name but a few, all subscribed to this sense of a dying sense of the communal and the historical. Outstandingly, Bill Bryden's *Willie Rough* (1972) exploited the idea of the protagonist descended from Lindsay's John the Commonweal of *Ane Satyre of the Thrie Estaitis* of the sixteenth century; but Rough by name and rough by nature, Willie, of flinty integrity and the mouthpiece of his dispossessed workers on the shipbuilding Clyde, is a failed visionary, whose poetic perspectives from the heights of the hills above the Clyde gives way to the acceptance of the destruction and devaluation of his community. Like Docherty, all that Willie can show at the end is defiance; and in later plays like *Benny Lynch* (1974) Bryden was to deepen his sense of Lowland Scottish deterioration in his picture of the icon of macho Scotland whose reality was insecurity, fear of the dark, and an utter lack of integrity and awareness of self in time and place. Similarly, *The Bevellers* (1973) by Roddy MacMillan and *Play Donkey* (1977) by Stewart Conn showed variant pictures of Scots whose hard-man mentality had taken over from any genuine sense of society.

Vision and magic – let alone traditional supernatural belief and practice – seemed to have vanished from Scottish writing. But change was in the air; despite – or perhaps because of – the failure of the Devolution Bill of 1979 which proposed a parliament for Scotland, several major Scottish writers were to return to re-evaluation of Scottish history and culture. Our last period of changed usage of the traditional supernatural emerges with the 1980s, with writers like Edwin Morgan, Alasdair Gray, and Liz Lochhead, in poetry, fiction and drama, developing a new kind of imaginative relationship with their country and its culture, a relationship which refused to accept a simple realism of generally bleak and economically-deprived urban character. Instead, the connection of the urban with the rural, and the idea of the future possibility of a whole modern Scotland, linking past with present and future, began to be emphasised; these and many other writers insisted on reintroducing, albeit in different form from Renaissance usage, elements of magic and myth, employed for symbolic and social-political reasons. The changes of these writers in approach and ideology, and of the contemporary writers who follow them, have radically changed the directions of Scottish literature; and what is striking is that this change has generally involved a return to the nineteenth-century strategy of maintaining ambiguity of interpretation – with, of course, post-modern subtleties.

A new grouping of writers has emerged whose novels refuse to accept the premises of Scottish writing either in its Renaissance idealism or post-war scepticism, but nevertheless exploit possibilities of the supernatural surreal and irrational. These writers include Ian Banks, Margaret Elphinstone, Andrew Greig, Sian Hayton, and Alison Kennedy. With similar intent, but through varying strategies, the work of poets such as Liz Lochhead, Edwin Morgan, Douglas Dunn, Robert Crawford and W. N. Herbert, explores such possibilities, while in drama the last fifteen years has seen a range of impressive adaptions in drama of mytho-poetic Scottish fiction, outstanding being Alistair Cording's remarkable adaptation of *A Scots Quair* (1993). Many recent Scottish dramatists now use folk-tradition, myth and legend in their work, and refuse to accept the limitations of strict social realism – as in Liz Lochhead's *Mary Queen of Scots Got Her Head Chopped Off* (1986) and her translation into Scots of Moliere's *Tartuffe* (1990), Edwin Morgan's translation into Scots of *Cyrano de Bergerac* (1990), and plays such as Sue Glovers' *Bondagers* (1990), Rona Munro's *Bold Girls* (1991) and *The Maiden Stone* (1995). Many contemporary dramatists now imagine Scotland in ways which allow the traditional supernatural to be part of an eclectic Scottish culture and identity. Through these new strategies they re-examine issues of gender and the place of women in relationships, in history; with an underlying desire for a multi-faceted Scotland, no longer demanding allegiance to essential Scottishness, but recognising other people's right to perceive Scotland differently.

Three texts stand out from the work of the 1980s as representative of these changes of agenda, and of the new magic in literature. Alasdair Gray's *Lanark* (1981), Edwin Morgan's *Sonnets from Scotland* (1984), and Liz Lochhead's *Mary Queen of Scots* helped initiate and exemplify the change which is still under way, breaking significantly with the scepticism of the urban-fixated anti-historicism of the post-war period. Perhaps Edwin Morgan deserves pride of place in this new development. With *This Second Life* (1968), he had reorganised his perspectives on himself, Glasgow, and – with his remarkable science-fiction poetry – arguably, the universe. 'Does every man feel like this at forty?', he asked, in an awakening which was to be of profound importance for many other Scottish writers. When *Sonnets from Scotland* appeared in 1984, this awakening revealed itself as a rediscovered sense of the limitless imaginative possibilities of the *idea* of Scotland, or Scotlands, a matrix of myths, attitudes, possibilities, histories. In fifty-one linked sonnets, ranging to extremes different from, but every bit as mind-stretching as MacDiarmid's in *A Drunk Man Looks at the Thistle,* Morgan explored the geological formation of Scotland, its pre-historic and wolf-haunted forests, its medieval grimness and grotesquerie, its modern debates. And astonishingly, but on reflection not so surprisingly, given Morgan's record of fine speculative science-fiction poetry, and its concern with humanity's relations with whatever lay out there in space, Morgan went on to show post-nuclear Scotlands – Scotland as a republic, and even Scotland as a kind of time-and-space *doppelganger* in an alternative universe. All this was made the more disruptive of traditional ways of seeing Scotland by making the perspective that of inhuman visitors travelling in space and time. Now his poetry took on the task of creating new attitudes and new mythologies – with one important qualification. These new myths do not pretend to any other source of authority than the human imagination; identity is not perceived as an almost magical creation of past communities and their dreams, handed on through collective unconsciousness, nurtured by a presiding Mother Scotland, but a web of rational and irrational meanings consciously constructed and acknowledged as such, and delicately balancing the claims of Scottish and international cultures, insisting both on international and home focus, and insisting gently on an ultimately more than rational basis for living relationships.

Liz Lochhead's poetry had also been making its mark, from its beginnings in *Memo For Spring* (1972) to collections like *The Grimm Sisters* (1981), and *Dreaming Frankenstein* (1984). In poems like 'Rapunzelstiltskin', and 'Tam Lin's Lady' she updated magical tales and figures from European and Scottish folktale and ballad tradition. These figures and situations were now used as commentary on the modern relationships of men and women; the past informing the present, the present revealed as much more in thrall to the past than sophisticated modernity might imagine. Like Morgan, Lochhead reached a wide audience, who responded to this rich new way of imagining and representing Scotland, in which the prevailing ways of seeing Scotland as urban wasteland were enriched with fantasy, humour, surrealism, and constant interplay with tradition and magic. Lochhead's plays, exploring the subliminal sexuality of the Romantic poets and relishing the multiplicity of meanings inherent in Stoker's *Dracula*, gave this changed perspective even greater influence. *Mary Queen of Scots Got Her Head Chopped Off* is, in this respect, of major significance, as well as being exciting in its novel dramatic presentation and the richness of its language. La Corbie, female crow who presides as commentator and witness to Scotland's history, has something of the presence of Lindsay's John the Commonweal in *Ane Satyre of the Thrie Estaitis* (1552), but simultaneously reminds us of the great modern Renaissance protagonists who represented Scotland – Chris Guthrie, the Drunk Man, Kirsty Haldane. Yet she is different; raucous, shabby, a parody of that renaissance, but still somehow suggesting a sad glory, an endless cycle of tradition and violence. The play insists on breaking the boundaries of present and past, changing queens into guttersnipes, lovers into street urchins of present day Scottish slums. Lochhead's perspectives see myth as protean, unfixed, a range of haunting possibilities which aren't objective and inherited magic or supernatural, but are constantly recreatable by the contemporary mind, a chosen – if not always understood – context and landscape of the imagination and the emotions.

But it was Alasdair Gray's astonishing *Lanark* which most dramatically changed literary creative consciousness in the 1980s and '90s. This astonishing blend of science-fiction, social satire, surrealism and autobiography broke all previous boundaries of Scottish fiction in its account of its protagonist's nightmare existence in a grey city called Unthank, his descent into a weird underworld Institution, his escape from it, and his memories of his previous life in post-war Glasgow. The novel never reveals whether its central character (called Lanark in Unthank, and Duncan Thaw in Glasgow) has died, or whether he has simply suffered nervous breakdown; ambivalence is maintained till the end. Different in so many ways from the work of Morgan and Lochhead, nevertheless, like *Sonnets* and *Mary Queen of Scots*, it thrust the idea of the entirety of Scotland again to the fore, instead of asserting fragmentation – and it emphasised the need to bring back imagination, fantasy, and the supernatural as ways of envisioning new Scotlands. It is true that *Lanark* presents a country fragmented and incoherent. Nevertheless, Gray's full-page panoramic illustrations of land and seascapes of Scotland, with recognisable mountains, glens, cities, castles, cathedrals and factories, show that Gray wishes to see Scotland whole. This attempt at totality of vision is different from what was happening in the 1970s, despite similarities between, say, Jenkins' Fergus Lamont and Thaw, or even between Thaw and McIlvanney's Conn Docherty. Gray goes beyond any previous Scottish writer in synthesising a huge and bewildering variety of literary and pictorial genres in his work. *Lanark* fuses together many varieties of Scottish storytelling and themes with endless examples of American and European literature – but, like Lochhead, does so in order to place Scotland in the wider world context, as well as to re-introduce new layers of mythic meaning and suggestion. And yet once again there are glimpses – fleeting, elusive, insubstantial – of dear green places, and celebrations of landscape, notably in the novel's outstanding moment of epiphany, in the vision Lanark has of his son Alexander climbing Ben Rua, both at peace for once in a day of rare beauty.

This magic was also in the air elsewhere – in Fred Urquhart's stories of ghosts from Scottish history invading the present in *Proud Lady in a Cage* (1980) and *Seven Ghosts in Search* (1983), in Colin Mackay's anthropomorhic and poetic evocation of the spirit of ancient Scotland in *The Song of the Forest* (1986), or in Dorothy Dunnett's *King Hereafter* (1982), with its teasing of Scottish historians in its assertion that the formidable Earl Thorfinn of eleventh-century Orkney was one and the same person as the great Celtic King Macbeth, and a figure of mythic significance, with visions of Scotland's post-Celtic future. Alan Clews created a tale of modern haunting in the rural west of Scotland in *A Child of Air* (1995). And beyond this more recognisably-traditional supernatural writing, all through the 1980s and '90s, strange, dreamlike and unclassifiable texts appeared, ranging from Stewart Hutchison's metaphysical and fantastical eccentricity in *Scully's Lugs* (1979), the bizarre *grand guignol* of Iain Bank's *The Wasp Factory* (1984) and *The Bridge* (1986), by Bank's own admission inspired by Gray's *Lanark*, to the Scottish-Canadian surrealism of Eric McGoldrick's *The Paradise Motel* (1989) or the Scottish-Italian grotesquerie of Donald Mackenzie's *The Truth of Stone* (1991) or the weird American's-eye-view of Edinburgh and Scottish *kitsch* in Todd McEwan's *McX* (1990). Douglas Dunn's *Secret Villages* (1985) cast a very different kind of semi-sinister surrealism over its short stories about strangely unplaceable communities and their elusive inhabitants; Harry Tait's award-winning *The Ballad of Sawney Bain* (1990), re-created the cannibal monster of Galloway as dreamer and community-builder, trapped in a barbaric historical nightmare.

In many ways, however, it was the contemporary writing of women which went on to exemplify this move away from reductive social realism towards the new and non-essentialist use of the magical and the mythic as an imaginatively playful way of exploring possibilities and implying reform. Older writers like Nancy Brysson Morrison in *The Gowk Storm* (1933) had continued to keep echoes of the traditional supernatural in their use of folk-hints, portents and proverbs as suggestive undertone, an older music, in their fiction; a few, like Dorothy Haynes, Naomi Mitchison, and Marion Campbell in *Thou Shalt Not Suffer a Witch* (1949), *Five Men and A Swan* (1958), and *The Dark Twin* (1973), respectively, had continued to work in the tradition of the classic Scottish traditional supernatural tale, albeit with very different emphases and tone. The title story of the collection *Five Men and A Swan* is an outstanding story in the Renaissance manner of, say, Linklater's 'The Goose Girl', only here evoking a woman's perspective on the old legends of the bird-woman, and now deploying tradition to make a strong statement against Scottish male sexual aggression. Mitchison outstandingly posited the existence of actual magic in *The Corn King and the Spring Queen*, with its many other moments suggestive of ancient and genuine earth-magic (amongst many examples of the supernatural, Erif Der's bringing back to life of a dead flower through hand-magic, the significance of oracular prophecy, and the serpent apparitions on the death of Kleomenes stand out). It is significant, however, that some fifteen years later, and after the war, her use of magic is qualified; in *The Bull Calves*, American Indian magic and

Scottish witchcraft are exploited in the light of her reading of Jung's ideas on the re-integration of the broken self, so that on one hand Indian ritual and lore is viewed as psychologically healing, while Kirstie's involvement with a coven is readable as simply a result of her distorted mental state. Thereafter, a strand of Mitchison's fiction, running down from *Travel Light* (1952) to *Images of Africa* (1980) and *What Do You Think Yourself?* (1982) has exploited the supernatural in a variety of ways which illustrate a new eclecticism, as these novels present the supernatural as allegorical fable, as traditional African magic, and as satirical surrealism respectively.

Following the inspiration of Naomi Mitchison, whose *Early in Orcadia* (an attempt to re-create mindsets of the first Orcadians reminiscent of William Golding's *The Inheritors* (1955)) had appeared in 1987, Margaret Elphinstone and Sian Hayton have developed a fascinating vein of quasi-historical, speculative and magical fiction. Mitchison was not the only writer from whom they could gain inspiration. The work of George Mackay Brown since the mid-1960s had ploughed a comparatively lonely furrow, in celebrating Orkney past and present in a way which continued to share much of the Renaissance's emphasis on fundamental human relationship with the past, racial origins, and the land and sea-scapes in which these were formed over centuries. Brown's conversion to Catholicism in 1961 allowed him to keep faith with the Christian supernatural in his fiction and poetry in the '60s and '70s, and it would be fair to say that it was principally his anthropomorphic evocations of Orkney through the ages which kept a sense of the legendary and mythic alive in Scottish literature when most others had turned from it. Aware of the work of Mitchison and Brown, Elphinstone and Hayton have developed their own way of handling the mythic, the non-rational, the edges of experience. Elphinstone has written two novels concerning the wanderings of singer-poet Naomi, as she moves around Galloway and the Lake District – only a Galloway changed, a region of the future after apocalypse, a world returned to basic communities, isolated and unsure. Elphinstone's visionary Green Light in *The Incomer* (1987), and her dark discovery of poisoned lands in *A Sparrow's Flight* (1989), were new slants on modern issues extrapolated into the future, handled with delicacy and power from a quietly feminist position. And magic and myth played an even more central and poetic part in Elphinstone's short story collection, *An Apple on a Tree* (1991) with its encounters in Galloway with the pagan god Pan, its unapologetic supernatural events – used by Elphinstone in a curiously straightforward yet clearly allegorical way. *Islanders* (1994), showed a deliberate change of tack, however; now she portrayed the quiet lives of Fair Isle farmers and peasants with the merest of hints of the magical, yet somehow still managing to embed these lives in a world-view deeply aware of the rhythms of seasons, seas, and the importance of tradition. In this fine epic novel Elphinstone winnowed the concerns and presentation of Renaissance writers like Gunn, Linklater and Mitchison to the bone, almost as though her aim was to see how plain and unromanticised her telling and presentation could be, while setting itself well apart from the predominantly sceptical perspectives of the urban writers. She continues to vary her use of the supernatural; in *The Sea Road* (2000), and in her delightful romantic adventure-fable *Hy Brasil* (2002) in which she brings to modern life Tir-nan-Og, the Celtic paradise, The Green Isle of the Great Deep, as an actual mid-Atlantic nation-island.

It is *The Sea Road*, however, in its blending of history, legend and myth, and feminist perspective which best exemplifies contemporary rediscovery of the possibilities of the supernatural. Gudrid Thorbjornsdottir recalls her sea-voyages to Greenland and Vinland, and her terrible experiences of bloodfeuds and plague. Conveying a sense of otherness of time and place, as in *Islanders*, is Elphinstone's striking achievement. She does this by incorporating elements and attitudes from the Icelandic Sagas – *Eirik's Saga*, *Graenlendinga Saga*, and *Eyrbiggja Saga*; but also through another alien ideology which runs as undertone throughout, in the elusive yet powerful suggestion of Thurid's magical abilities, comparable to those allowed by Naomi Mitchison to Erif Der, The Spring Queen, in *The Corn King and The Spring Queen*. Elphinstone handles this enigmatically; Thurid and others believe she has such powers; more challengingly, a voice belonging to neither Thurid or even the author intermittently comes in, italicised (rather like MacDiarmid's use in poetry of a sub-voice in italics which speaks for deepest meaning), and looking on the protagonists of the novel from a height, yet allowing a supernatural significance to events. The status of this commentary is never clear; but its effect is to push the great voyages, the appalling hardships, the sudden deaths, beyond reason and history to legend and myth, as though the final narrative, beyond the heroic journeys and characters here, is one dimly discerned, in which the Icelanders' discovery of the Americas, of the land of wine, Vinland, with its tragic conclusion in the brutal loss of New World innocence in the killing of the native Skraelings and Icelanders, retells a version of the expulsion from Eden. Mackay Brown had something of this Fall from Innocence in his epic *Vinland* (1992); now Elphinstone triumphantly retells the same story from a woman's view, tracing this crucial woman's witnessing and part in what becomes a sardonic fable on men's dreams and women's endurance.

The work of Sian Hayton in her trilogy, *Cells of Knowledge* (1989), *Hidden Daughters* (1992), *The Last Flight* (1993), is also impressive and original. These stories tell of the Celtic daughters of the giant Uthebhan, women of superhuman powers and great spiritual strength, but doomed to be distrusted by the new male-dominated Christian era. Set around the end of the first millenium, the stories contrive to lose history in myth; places are named in ways which hint at what they are now, but suggest a very different origin and society. Again, a sense of allegory hangs over all; but quite what the allegory means Hayton doesn't clearly suggest. Is it that the old woman-led Celtic society is measured against male-Christian dominance, and found to be greatly superior? Hayton allows no clear narrative to emerge, but permits hints, echoes, and occasional mentions of previous sisters and situations to loosely hold her trilogy together. She also begins in the Christian world, only gradually revealing her lost and hidden magic; then returns to the Christian, posing unanswered questions as to what will happen to the sisters and their descendants. In all this the past is shown to be protean, as flux; but a flux which hints towards the present, with disturbing implications for our values and gender relations.

As Scottish literature approached the millenium, Scottish writing became bewilderingly eclectic, and no more so in its rich and varied ways of exploiting the supernatural and irrational. An essay like this cannot do justice to the rich and exciting variety of recent Scottish literature; in conclusion, I turn to Scottish fiction as best illustrating some of the main changes in the way Scottish writing repudiates generic categories and modes. What is most striking is its sheer unclassifiability, its continual crossover and mixture of genres and modes, the way it uses non-linear narrative and unconventional presentation which refuses to remain in one time scale, and ranges from use of the traditional supernatural with a modern application to post-modern Scottish Gothic, science-fiction and grotesque surrealism. The fictions I now very briefly discuss are often very dissimilar, some employing straightforward supernatural and magical special effects, some allowing these effects to be explained as psychological delusions, while some do not bother to explain these effects as anything other than happenings on the page, subject to no laws but their own.

Broadly speaking, there seem to me to be three main categories. Firstly, there are those novels which use the traditional Scottish supernatural, with the duality of interpretation we have noted as such a feature of Scottish fiction. Novels in this grouping include Christopher Whyte's *The Warlock of Strathearn* (1997), Andrew Greig's *When They Lay Bare* (1999); Andrew Murray Scott's *Tumulus* (1999), Alice Thompson's *Pharos* (2002) and James Robertson's *The Fanatic* (2000). A second grouping moves the traditional Scottish supernatural to meet international fantasy, employing magic realism to create strange conjunctions of recognisable Scotland and world events which break all laws of reason. Outstanding here is of course the later work of Alasdair Gray, in novels *Poor Things* (1992) [where he combines a Scottish inheritance from Stevenson's *Dr. Jekyll and Mr Hyde* (1886) with aspects of Mary Shelley's *Frankenstein* (1818)], and *A History Maker* (1994) which moves somewhere between the Border Tales of James Hogg and modern science fiction. Iain Banks' fiction has ranged from the bizarre but recognisable 'real' world of *The Wasp Factory* (1984) to the twin worlds, real and decidedly fantastic, in *Walking on Glass* (1985) and *The Bridge* (1986), his brilliant homage to Alasdair Gray. Alison Kennedy's *So I Am Glad* (1995) splendidly illustrates the type. Jennifer Wilson is a Glasgow radio announcer, unhappy in her job and her private life. Her saviour is her new flat-mate – who turns out to be Cyrano de Bergerac. Kennedy balances beautifully the two possible readings – one, that Jennifer has created, like Hogg's Robert Wringhim in *The Justified Sinner*, the figure her psyche most desires, and two, that Cyrano really has somehow crossed hundreds of years to become her lover. Other fiction like this is found in Christopher Whyte's hilarious Glasgow fantasy, *Euphemia McFarrigle and the Laughing Virgin* (1995) and John Herdman's series of surreally disturbing novels, the latest being *The Sinister Cabaret* (2002).

A third and very varied grouping would gather together a range of very different types of fiction, related only – but importantly – in their refusal to allow laws of reason and conventions of fiction to stop them from imagining whatever kind of world they wished to bring into existence. The range here is impressive – so a summary listing is all that is possible. Once again the work of Alasdair Gray dominates here, as in the dazzling variety of worlds imagined in very different ways in *Unlikely Stories, Mostly* (1983). Christopher Whyte's *The Cloud Machinery* (2000) is a tale of complex crime and necromancy in Venice in 1761 which mingles elements of detective fiction with historical and Gothic, yet refuses to commit itself, with its supernatural elements only revealing themselves half-way through the novel. Even writers with an established reputation for orthodox fictions moved to use the possibilities of the new supernatural: Alan Massie turned from political novels of classical Rome and modern Europe to present the twelfth-century Scottish wizard-scholar Michael Scott telling his story of the Dark-Age travels of young Roman, Marcus, wandering Europe on a political goose-chase filled with monstrosities and magic. This third group – or should it be a fourth? – extends to contain the most extreme uses of supra-rational and surreal fictions. Alice Thompson's *Justine* (1996) and *Pandora's Box* (1998) create bizarre and surreal narratives to make their statements about the cruelty of male-female relations. Michel Faber created wonderful worlds in the award-winning short stories of *Some Rain Must Fall* (1999), and a gruesome, grotesque yet horribly persuasive tale of Highland abduction of humans by enigmatic aliens for food farming in *Under the Skin* (2000), a Swiftian ironic commentary on human mistreatment of animals and nature. Comparably surreal and bizarre are the stories of James Meek's *The Museum of Doubt* (2000), Magritte-like in their strange landscapes and magical conjunctions of everyday objects and weird transitions. Kate Atkinson's rich mixture of memory, fantasy and comedy in *Emotionally Weird* (2000) deepened her previous complexities of memory and imagination in novels like *Behind the Scenes at the Museum* (1995) and *Human Croquet* (1997) to new extremes. John Burnside's *The Dumb House* (1997) is one of the darkest of these surreal fictions, in its monstrous account of the upbringing of a child without access to language. Andrew Crumey created some of the most tantalisingly complex surreal fictions of the period in *Music in a Foreign Language* (1994), *Pfitz* (1995) and *D'Alembert's Principle* (1996). Outstanding in contemporary work of this kind is the surreal and sardonic irony of Frank Kuppner's generically unplaceable work like *A Concussed History of Scotland* (1990), *Something Very Like Murder* (1996) and *Life on a Dead Planet* (1996).

Is nothing sacred? Even crime fiction has refused to stay within its conventional boundaries, in the work of Paul Johnston and Mathew Fitt. Johnston uses Edinburgh as his crime-base in the series of novels featuring his wayward rebel-detective Quintilian Dalrymple, beginning with *Body Politic* (1997) – yet this is now Edinburgh a few decades from now; devolution has failed, Britain has broken into a fragmentation of little city-states, with roving marauders and gangs outside their fenced perimeters, and Guardians rule in a system derived from Plato's *Republic*. And crossing yet even more borders, in terms of language and fictional conventions is Mathew Fitt's marvellously imaginative and original *But and Ben a Go-Go* (2000), in its even darker and more futuristic vision of a post-Aids-and-global-warming sea-world, where raising the sea-level by two thousand feet has somewhat changed the map of Scotland, with only the tops of mountain ranges surfacing, and the main cities now floating constructions anchored to what used to be Greenock. The main story is the quest of Paolo Broon to release his life-partner Nadia from a living hell in the miles-high storage banks of the Rigo Imbeki Medical Centre, where thousands of super-virus sufferers are kept alive in capsules – but along the way Fitt's imagination creates a roller-coaster journey which becomes not so much a personal quest as an extended satire anticipating where our consumer and hedonistic world may end up. The entire novel is, astonishingly, written in Scots, a feat which works remarkably well in taking the reader in a totally unparochial and ground-breaking journey.

Perhaps it is fitting that such a broad survey of Scottish literature's use of the supernatural should end here, with Scottish fiction (and poetry and drama) maintaining their distinctive voices and languages, still telling of quests for love and identity, but now in altered landscapes and very different ethnic communities, with conditions of life of unimaginable difference. Along the way the older ghosts and nightmares have transmogrified into manifestations of our newer fears and visions; but the magic of the imagination is clearly alive and well in the third millennium of Scotland's writing.[8]

---

[8] It is impossible to give detailed references for the many works cited above. There are few general discussions of the supernatural in Scottish literature; the two most useful are Coleman Parsons, *Witchcraft and Demonology in Scott's Fiction: With Chapters on the Supernatural in Scottish Literature* (Edinburgh and London: Oliver and Boyd, 1964); and Colin Manlove, *Scottish Fantasy Literature: A Critical Survey* (Edinburgh: Canongate Academic, 1994). See also Lizanne Henderson and Edward J. Cowan, 'Writing the Fairies', in *Scottish Fairy Belief: A History* (2001: Edinburgh: John Donald, 2007). With regard to modern Scottish literature, the present author's 'Imagining Scotlands: The Return to Mythology in Modern Scottish Fiction', in *Studies in Scottish Fiction: 1945 to the Present*, ed. Susanne Hagemann (Frankfurt am Main: Peter Lang, 1996) 7–50, gives a fuller discussion of the range of literature discussed in the essay above. For yet fuller discussion and bibliography regarding post-war Scottish writing, see *Scottish Literature in English and Scots*, ed. Douglas Gifford, Sarah Dunnigan and Alan MacGillivray (Edinburgh: Edinburgh University Press, 2002). For the modern novel, Cairns Craig's *The Modern Scottish Novel; Narrative and the National Imagination* (Edinburgh: Edinburgh University Press, 1999) is particularly useful.

SEVEN

Witch, Fairy and Folktale Narratives in the Trial of Bessie Dunlop[1]

Lizanne Henderson

Once upon a time there lived a witch named Bessie. She hadn't always been a witch but since becoming one she found that her neighbours thought her very powerful and they began to visit her in search of cures and advice. A terrible plague and famine was sweeping across the land and Bessie, who was expecting a child, was afraid. Her husband, and her animals, were suffering from the pestilence. Bessie was in labour when a stranger came in through her cottage door. She was a stout woman and she asked Bessie for a drink, and she obliged. The woman then said 'Bessie, your bairn will die, but your husband will mend of his sickness'. With that, she left.

Not long after, Bessie was feeling very sorry for herself and began to cry loudly. A man with a grey beard, who carried a white wand, approached her and said 'Good day, Bessie. What worldly thing makes you lament so greatly and greit so sairly?' She answered, 'Alas! have I not great cause to lament, for our money and possessions are dwindling away, and my husband is sick, and my baby will not live'. The gentleman said 'Bessie, you have crabbit [angered] God, and asked for something you should not have'. The gentleman then went away and she saw him enter a narrow hole in the dyke that no earthly man could have gone through, and Bessie was afraid.

The second time the gentleman appeared, he promised Bessie wealth and clothing, horses and cows, if she would deny her Christianity. Bessie said 'if I should be pulled apart by horses, I would never do that'. The gentleman was very angry with her.

The third time the gentleman appeared, he told her not to speak, or fear anything she was about to see, and when they had gone a little pace forward,

---

[1] Versions of this paper, entitled '"A stout carline who begged for a drink": The Queen of Elfland as Beggar in the Trial of Bessie Dunlop', were presented at Beggars Descriptions: Destitution and Literary Genres International Literary Conference, University of Groningen, The Netherlands (1998), and 'Fantasticall ymaginatiounis': The Supernatural in Scottish History, Literature and Culture Conference, at University of Strathclyde, Glasgow (1999). Thank you to all for the helpful comments given on these occasions.

Bessie saw twelve beautiful people. The strangers bade her to sit down with them and said 'Welcome Bessie, will you go with us?' but she did not answer. When they departed she asked who these people were; 'they are the good neighbours that dwell in the court of Elfland, and they desire you to go with them'. But Bessie replied, 'I see no reason to go with them unless I know why?' 'Look at me Bessie. I have plenty of meat and clothes, and I can offer you the same if you will go with me.' Bessie was stubborn though and again she refused. Then the gentleman became very angry with her.

Bessie continued to meet with the gentleman and he taught her how to make potions and use charms. But she grew curious as to why the gentleman seemed to favour her over anyone else, so one day she asked him who he was and why he came to her. 'Bessie, do you remember when you were lying in childbed and a stout woman came to your door to ask for a drink?' 'Yes,' she said, 'I remember that very well.' 'That was the Queen of Elfland, my mistress, who commanded me to wait upon you and to do you good. As for me, my name is Tom Reid and I died in a great battle near thirty years ago, and now my home is in Fairyland.'

At this point it would be gratifying to state 'and they all lived happily ever after', but that is not possible because there is no happy ending for the heroine of this story. Elizabeth, or Bessie, Dunlop, from Lynn in Ayrshire, tried for witchcraft, sorcery and conjuring spirits, was strangled and burnt on 8 November 1576.[2]

Bessie was only one of the 3,837 persons known to have faced a formal accusation of witchcraft in Scotland; at least 168 of those confirmed cases involved persons from Ayrshire.[3] Exactly how many of the accused were executed is unclear though at least half of that number seems a reasonable estimate; Bessie was, unfortunately, among the unlucky ones. During the period of the European witch-hunts – between roughly 1450 and 1750 – over 100,000 trials and around 50,000 to 60,000 legal executions took place.[4] Scotland was, relatively speaking, one of the European countries worst affected by the witch persecutions and, as on the Continent, there were peaks and troughs in witch-hunting activities[5]

---

2 Trial of Bessie Dunlop, 1576, *Books of Adjournal*, NAS JC2/1 f.15r–18r, and Pitcairn (ed.), *Trials*, vol. 1, part II, 49–58.
3 Ayrshire statistics are based on Alistair Hendry's unpublished 'Witch-Hunting in Ayrshire' and *The Survey of Scottish Witchcraft Database* at www.arts.ed.ac.uk/witches/ which provides the most up-to-date figures on Scottish witch trials.
4 Wolfgang Behringer, *Witches and Witch-Hunts: A Global History* (Cambridge: Polity Press, 2004) 156, Robin Briggs, *Witches and Neighbours* (London: Harper Collins, 1996) 8.
5 For more on Scottish Witch-Hunts see Julian Goodare, Lauren Martin and Joyce Miller, eds, *Witchcraft and Belief in Early Modern Scotland* (Basingstoke: Palgrave MacMillan, 2008); Brian P. Levack, *Witch-Hunting in Scotland: Law, Politics and Religion* (New York: Routledge, 2008); P. G. Maxwell-Stuart, *An Abundance of Witches* (Stroud: Tempus, 2005); Julian Goodare, ed., *The Scottish Witch-Hunt in Context* (Manchester: Manchester

and marked regional differences.⁶ Ayrshire experienced several serious bouts of witch-hunting, the first formal trial and execution occurring in 1572. Thereafter a steady pace of accusations continued in every decade and peaked in the 1650s, tailing off dramatically after 1683. Official action against witches was mainly over in Ayrshire after the 1680s, though there is evidence to suggest that witch belief was still present into the nineteenth century. Isabel or Bell M'Ghie (1760–1836), a resident of Beith, has been described as the 'last of the Ayrshire witches'. Like Bessie Dunlop, over two hundred years earlier, Bell was a healer who had clients of every social standing, including the well-to-do. Her particular forte was dairy problems, healing sick people and animals, and providing counter-magical charms.⁷

An interesting feature in many of the Scottish witch trials, including that of Bessie Dunlop, is the abundance of material relating to fairy belief. This is not exclusively a Scottish phenomenon – similar evidence occurs in other countries such as England, Hungary, Italy and Germany – but it is fair to say that Scotland has a remarkable amount of fairylore interspersed within witch belief contexts.⁸

The confession of Bessie Dunlop is, as already mentioned, not the only one in which evidence of fairy beliefs and traditions is found, but it is one of the earliest and among the most descriptive of the accounts that relate fairy encounters. It is also of interest in that it provides the first clear evidence that fairy belief had become entangled with the demonic, well before the assimilation of continental witchcraft beliefs had taken root in Scotland, a process that has generally been

---

University Press, 2002); P. G. Maxwell-Stuart, *Satan's Conspiracy: Magic and Witchcraft in Sixteenth-Century Scotland* (East Linton: Tuckwell Press, 2001); Laurence Normand and Gareth Roberts, *Witchcraft in Early Modern Scotland: James VI's Demonology and the North Berwick Witches* (Exeter: University of Exeter Press, 2000); Christina Larner, *Enemies of God: the Witch-Hunt in Scotland* (1981; Edinburgh: John Donald, 2000).

6 For Scottish regional studies see for instance, Lizanne Henderson, 'Witch-Hunting and Witch Belief in the *Gàidhealtachd*', in *Witchcraft and Belief in Early Modern Scotland*, ed. J. Goodare *et al.* (Basingstoke: Palgrave MacMillan, 2008) 95–118; Edward J. Cowan, 'Witch Persecution and Folk Belief in Lowland Scotland: The Devil's Decade', in *Witchcraft and Belief in Early Modern Scotland*, ed. J. Goodare *et al.* (Basingstoke: Palgrave MacMillan, 2008) 71–94; Hugh V. McLachlan, *The Kirk, Satan and Salem: The History of the Witches of Renfrewshire* (Glasgow: The Grimsay Press, 2006); Lizanne Henderson, 'The Survival of Witchcraft Prosecutions and Witch Belief in South-West Scotland', *SHR* 75, 1: No. 219 (April 2006) 52–74, Stuart MacDonald, *The Witches of Fife: Witch-Hunting in a Scottish Shire, 1560–1710* (East Linton: Tuckwell Press, 2002).

7 A. MacGeorge, *An Ayrshire Witch* (reprinted from *Good Words* for private circulation, London, 1886) 1–12. See also Edward J. Cowan and Lizanne Henderson, 'The Last of the Witches? The Survival of Scottish Witch Belief' in *The Scottish Witch-Hunt in Context*, ed. J. Goodare (Manchester and New York: Manchester University Press, 2002) 198–217.

8 For a fuller discussion of this see Lizanne Henderson and Edward J. Cowan, eds, *Scottish Fairy Belief: A History* (East Linton: Tuckwell Press, 2001; repr. Edinburgh: John Donald, 2007).

attributed to King James VI's role in the North Berwick witch trials of 1590–1 and the publication of his book *Daemonologie* in 1597.[9]

Embedded deep within Bessie's testimony is the incorporation of a significant amount of narrative plots and motifs that have since become familiar to many of us through the genres of folktale, traditional story, and local legend. Bessie was, in a sense, recounting what we have come to regard as 'fairytale', but what was presumably for her a memorate, a personal experience narrative.[10] James VI was of the opinion that witches made use of tales of the fairies as 'a cullour of safetie' for their crimes so that 'ignorant Magistrates may not punish them for it'. James did not advocate leniency for those who had seen the fairies and thought they should be as severely punished 'as any other witches'.[11] Bessie Dunlop may well have been drawing upon stories known to her via folktale and oral tradition. It could even be possible that she thought the telling of tales of the fairies and the spirit world might save her from a death sentence.[12] It has also been suggested that Bessie was describing a real 'visionary experience' and as such it 'was an expression of a vigorous popular visionary tradition rooted in pre-Christian shamanistic beliefs and practices'.[13] Whatever aspects of the confession Bessie actually believed or did not believe can never be known, though it is clear that her inquisitors believed her story.

This is by no means the only witch trial where such indications of deep rooted folkloric material can be detected. Several other confessions could be examined in this way, notably Jonet Boyman of Edinburgh, executed in 1572, who was accused of raising evil spirits at a fairy well near Arthur's Seat in order to learn how to heal the sick. She conjured a whirlwind that brought forth the shape of a man who stood on the other side of the well and gave her the necessary instructions to heal her patients. On another occasion, she predicted the death of a child because 'it had gottin ane blast of evill wind for the moder [mother] had not sanit [blessed] it well aneuch' before leaving the house, and so the fairies had found it unblessed and took it away with them.[14]

---

9 Larner, *Enemies of God*, 66–7. See also Edward J. Cowan, 'The Darker Vision of the Scottish Renaissance: The Devil and Francis Stewart', in *The Renaissance and Reformation in Scotland*, ed. I. B. Cowan and D. Shaw (Edinburgh: Scottish Academic Press, 1983) 125–40, and Stuart Clark, 'King James's *Daemonologie*: Witchcraft and kingship', in *The Damned Art*, ed. Sidney Anglo (London: Routledge and Kegan Paul, 1977) 156–81.
10 On the memorate, see Chapter 8 below.
11 James VI, *Daemonologie, 1597* (London: The Bodley Head, 1924) 75.
12 Diane Purkiss shares my view that accused witches often drew upon stories they already knew and incorporated them into their own lives and testimonies. See *Troublesome Things: A History of Fairies and Fairy Stories* (Harmondsworth: Penguin, 2000) 88.
13 Emma Wilby, *Cunning Folk and Familiar Spirits: Shamanistic Visionary Traditions in Early Modern British Witchcraft and Magic* (Brighton: Sussex Academic Press, 2005) 243.
14 Trial of Jonet Boyman, 1572, NAS JC 26/1/67, Henderson and Cowan, *Scottish Fairy Belief*, 127–9.

Alison Peirson of Byrehill, executed in 1588, was visited by her uncle, who now dwelled in Fairyland, and came to teach her medicines and charms. Aside from her uncle, she saw other dead relatives and friends in Elfland. Alison claimed to have been tormented by the fairies over many years. They repeatedly offered to do her good and to never want for anything if only she would 'be faithfull and keip promeis' to them. For her refusals to join their company she was, on more than one occasion, temporarily paralysed.[15]

Among those found guilty of treasonable sorcery against King James VI was the schoolmaster John Fian in 1590–1. He was cruelly tortured until he confessed his involvement in a conspiracy of witches to bring down the King, notably raising storms at sea to sink the King's ships. The chapbook *Newes from Scotland* (1591) reported a rather bizarre tale that was circulating about Fian's failed attempt to work a love spell. The object of his affection had spurned his advances and so Fian persuaded the woman's little brother, a pupil in his school, to bring him a sample of his sister's pubic hair. However, the boy's mischief was intercepted by his mother and he was made to explain what he was up to. The mother, wishing revenge for Fian's lewd intentions towards her daughter, concocted a plan. She cut three hairs from the udder of a cow and instructed her son to hand these over to Fian instead. When the schoolmaster received the hairs, he did not hesitate to perform the love spell, the results of which were not quite as he expected. Instead of the woman he fancied appearing at his door was the cow which was seen by many of the townsfolk 'leaping and dauncing upon him' and following him wherever he went. The reporter claimed that this was the moment when John Fian's reputation as a 'notable conjurer' first began to grow 'among the people of Scotland'.[16]

Isobel Gowdie of Auldearn, executed in 1662, went on hunting parties with other witches, was invited to sumptuous dinners hosted by the fairies, and had a spirit who waited on her called the Red Reiver. She described the Queen of Fairies as 'brawlie clothed in whyt linens' and the King as 'a braw man, weill favoured, and broad faced', while other fairies in her company, the 'elf boys', were 'little ones, hollow, and boss baked'.[17] The expression 'boss baked' carries the sense of diminutive and hump-backed, while her usage of the term 'hollow' is strongly reminiscent of another description of a male fairy by Jonet Boyman (1572); he was 'wele anewch cled . . . wele faceit with ane baird [beard]' but wasted away like a stick when seen from behind.[18] The motif of fairies with hollow backs also occurs in German and Scandinavian tales, sometimes called

---

15 Pitcairn (ed.), *Trials*, vol. 2, 161–5.
16 Pitcairn (ed.), *Trials*, vol. 2, 209–23, esp. 221.
17 Trial of Isobel Gowdie, 1662, Pitcairn (ed.), *Trials*, vol. 3, 604.
18 NAS JC/26/1/67.

the 'ellefolk', while the Inuit of Arctic Canada have stories of people who have no back.[19]

Folkloric elements were often apparent in European witch testimonies as well. The notorious *Malleus Maleficarum* (1486) includes several accounts of witchcraft in south-west Germany that similarly have a feel of folktale and traditional storytelling about them. The authors, it might be assumed, were consciously drawing upon the oral traditions of German folk belief, tale and legend, collecting the stories not for their folkloric value but as hard-core 'evidence' of the threat witches posed. For instance, in the town of Waldshut on the Rhine, a woman was up on charges of witchcraft for raising a hailstorm at a wedding. Detested by her neighbours, she was not invited to the nuptial celebrations and so, wishing to be revenged, she summoned a devil to assist her. The devil duly appeared and carried her to the top of a nearby hill where she was seen by some shepherds digging a hole in the ground, urinating into it, and stirring it with her finger. The devil then took the liquid and used it to create a violent hailstorm that rained down on all the wedding guests. While discussing amongst themselves the cause of this terrible storm, they became suspicious when the witch was seen coming into town. The shepherds, having subsequently revealed what they had seen, the guests' suspicions were confirmed and she was arrested. On the basis of eyewitness testimony, and her confession that she acted as she did because she had not been invited to the wedding, she was executed.[20]

This paper will attempt to investigate the interface between memorate, folktale and historical record by examining a selection of folkloristic motifs from Bessie Dunlop's witch trial confession, including one of the more unusual features, the 'beggarly' motifs, and specifically the appearance of fairies as beggars, as encountered by Bessie and others.

There are, of course, some problems with using witchcraft trial records such as this one. Although it is a story told by a convicted witch, relating her alleged experiences, it was recorded and written down through the filter of her inquisitors. This leads to the uncomfortable situation that elements of her story may have been distorted, taken out of context, or forced to fit a preconceived stereotype of witch behaviour. On this latter point, the early date of Bessie Dunlop's trial does not readily support the theory of an imposed learned witchcraft stereotype coming from the judges and examiners for no such stereotype had yet been formulated among Scotland's elite. The so-called 'cumulative concept of witchcraft',[21] as postulated by Brian Levack, was still in

19 Thompson, *Motif Index*, F232.1 fairies have hollow backs, F525.6 Person without back.
20 Heinrich Kramer and Jacob Sprenger, *Malleus Maleficarum*, trans. Montague Summers (1486; 1928; New York: Dover, 1971) 107.
21 Brian P. Levack, *The Witch-Hunt in Early Modern Europe* (1987; London: Pearson, 2006) 32.

its infancy, in a Scottish context at least, and would not fully develop for another decade and a half. While the trial of Bessie Dunlop does indeed indicate a growing awareness of the demonic powers at large in the world, and is, without question, a significant indicator of the demonisation of witches and fairies in sixteenth-century Scotland, Bessie's account arguably reveals more about contemporary folk belief than intellectual witchcraft theory.

On the reliability of witch trial evidence, as Carlo Ginzburg has argued, 'the fact that a source is not "objective" . . . does not mean that it is useless';[22] we must find alternative ways of reading and dealing with such texts. Interesting work has been done by scholars, such as Ginzburg, Diane Purkiss and Marion Gibson, on how to 'read' witchcraft trials, especially the magical or distrustful elements, to arrive at a 'better understanding of the construction of stories of witchcraft and our interpretation of them'.[23] Deconstructing witch confessions is often an exercise in trying to know the unknowable.

So what is known about Bessie Dunlop? She was married to Andrew Jack, with whom she had children, and they lived on a farm on the Boyd estate at Lynn, on the outskirts of Dalry, Ayrshire.[24] Bessie almost certainly hailed from an Ayrshire family as Dunlop is a well-known surname in the region, deriving from the lands of Dunlop in the district of Cunningham.[25] It can be surmised from the evidence that in socio-economical terms, the couple were not poor but of the middling sort (even upper middling); they kept cattle and sheep, had horses, made occasional trips to Edinburgh and Leith for market, and had acquaintances of high social standing. Bessie's age is not recorded at the time of the trial but she was probably in her 30s, at most, based on the fact that she had given birth at least twice within a few years of her execution. She was also a self-confessed charmer and could communicate with the spirit world.

It is not clear how Bessie Dunlop came to be accused of sorcery and witchcraft as the existing records do not plainly state the name of the complainant. However, it can be deduced that problems began for Bessie when a burgess of Irvine, William Kyle, consulted her about a stolen cloak and she told him that the culprit was Mally Boyd, also a resident of Irvine, who had since refashioned

---

22 Carlo Ginzburg, *The Cheese and the Worms: The Cosmos of a Sixteenth-Century Miller*, trans. John and Anne Tedeschi (1976; Harmondsworth: Penguin, 1982) xvii.
23 Marion Gibson, *Reading Witchcraft: Stories of Early English Witches* (London and New York: Routledge, 1999) 6.
24 Pitcairn (ed.), *Trials*, vol. 1, 49. Lynn Glen – variously spelled Lyne, Linn, Lin – is now a local beauty spot on the Caaf Water, close to Dalry.
25 Her husband's surname, Jack, is harder to place and appears to be of no particular provenance. George F. Black, *The Surnames of Scotland: Their Origin, Meaning and History* (New York: New York Public Library, 1946).

the cloak into a kirtle. Though Kyle had promised no harm would come to her for revealing the name of the thief, he renegued on his word and the next time she came to the Irvine market, she was seized and put in the Tolbooth. Bessie was not, however, without influential friends. James Blair, brother of William Blair of the Strand,[26] came to her assistance, having her released from the prison.

Her problems may have deepened when she accused two blacksmiths, Gabriel and George Black, of stealing plough-irons[27] from Henry Jameson and James Baird of the Mains of Watterton and taking the stolen property to their father's house at Locharside. The indignant blacksmiths brought a complaint against Bessie to the Archbishop of Glasgow, James Boyd of Trochrig,[28] to clear their good name. It is implied in the record that Archbishop Boyd was favourable towards Bessie, perhaps believing her claim against the blacksmiths to be well-founded. Nonetheless, irreparable damage seems to have been done to Bessie's reputation. When a third set of charges was brought against her, by person or persons unknown, she was not so fortunate; this time no one would come to her rescue.

Bessie was taken before the High Court of Justiciary in Dalkeith on 20 September 1576 and sentenced to death at Edinburgh on 8 November, a severe verdict considering that she was adamant in court that she refused offers to go to Fairyland or to enter into any ungodly pact.[29] Furthermore, she argued that she herself had no kind of 'art or science' but that all her knowledge was obtained from a man by the name of Tom Reid, whom she maintained had died at the Battle of Pinkie twenty nine years earlier on the 10 September 1547, and who now dwelt in the court of Elfland under the control of the Fairy Queen. Notably, she was not found guilty of practising *maleficium* – harmful magic – or entering into a demonic pact; crimes that were to become standard in witchcraft accusations as the witch-hunts progressed. Her crime lay in the 'using of sorcerie, witchcraft, and incantatioune, with invocatioun of spretis of the devill; continewand in familiaritie with thame, at all sic tymes as sche thought expedient, deling with charmes, and abusing the pepill with devillisch

---

26 The Strand is a prominent street in the town of Beith, Ayrshire, traditionally the spot where market days were held and presumably the home of William Blair.
27 The iron parts of the plough e.g. the coulter.
28 The Archbishop of Glasgow (1572–81), James Boyd of Trochrig (family home in Girvan Parish), born 1534, died 21 June 1581, of whom it was said that he 'strenuously defended the lawfullness of his office against the insults of our first zealots'. He was the second son of Adam Boyd of Pinkill, brother to Robert, Master of Boyd, who was, according to Pitcairn, the landowner of the Lynn estate where Bessie Dunlop resided. Pitcairn (ed.), *Trials*, 55; James Paterson, *History of the County of Ayr: With a Genealogical Account of the Families of Ayrshire*, 2 vols. (Ayr: John Dick, 1847) vol. 2, 79.
29 *Books of Adjournal*, NAS JC2/1 fo. 15r–18r, Pitcairn (ed.), *Trials*, vol. 1, 58.

craft of sorcerie'.³⁰ Bessie was not charged with any form of malefice – she never physically hurt anyone – but rather was convicted for her charming and healing abilities and her supposed close relationship with a ghost and with the fairies, associations that were becoming dangerously unacceptable in sixteenth century Scotland. Only a month before Bessie was incarcerated, intolerance towards magical practitioners was expressed by the Privy Council when they issued a proclamation against 'Egyptians' or gypsies, denouncing them as 'ydle vagaboundis' who live wicked and mischievous lives, committing murders, theft, and 'abusing the sympill and ignorant people with sorcery and divinatioun, to the greit offence of God'.³¹

The fact that many of Bessie's clientele came from the local elite and landowning classes does not seem to have swayed the members of the assize, nor did any of her former clients seemingly appear at court in her defence. Among her customers was Lady Johnstone,³² who sought Bessie's assistance when her daughter, the wife of the Laird of Stanelie,³³ became ill. After consultation with Tom Reid, who diagnosed the young woman had a 'cauld blude [cold blood]' that went around her heart 'that causit hir to dwam [swoon or faint] away', he prescribed a potion of ginger, cloves, aniseed and liquorice mixed with strong ale. Bessie made the medicine as instructed and gave it to Lady Stanelie to drink while she was at the house of her sister, Lady Blackhall.³⁴ Presumably the treatment worked as she was paid a peck of meal and some cheese.³⁵

On another occasion Bessie was asked to visit the Lady Kilbowie³⁶ who was suffering from a crooked leg. This time, Tom Reid advised Bessie that nothing could be done as the leg would never mend because the 'merch of the bane was

---

30 Pitcairn (ed.), *Trials*, vol. 1, 51.
31 'Egiptianis', 27 Aug. 1576, RPC, vol. II, 555–6.
32 Lady Johnstone is almost certainly the wife of Sir William Wallace of Johnstone and Auchenbothie. William M. Metcalfe, *A History of the County of Renfrew from Earliest Times* (Paisley: A. Gardner, 1905).
33 Lady Stanelie is possibly the daughter of William Wallace of Johnstone. There is a Stanelie, or Stainley, in the parish of Ardrossan, though it is more likely a reference to the Maxwell family estate at Stainley Castle in the parish of Paisley, Renfrewshire.
34 Her sister may have been Margaret Wallace, Lady Blackhall, daughter of Sir William Wallace of Johnstone, who was married to James Stewart, 8th Baron, of Auchingoun, Blackhall and Ardgowan. James Stewart received a Royal Charter in 1579 confirming his lands as feudal barony, including the family home of Blackhall, situated one mile south-east of Paisley Abbey. Blackhall Manor is the oldest house in Paisley, dating to the 12th century, and was the Stewart family residence until c.1700. Janet S. Bolton, *From Royal Stewart to Shaw Stewart: Their Story* (Nenufra, 1989); 'Blackhall Manor', www.renfrewshire.gov.uk
35 Pitcairn (ed.), *Trials*, vol. 1, 54.
36 Kilbowie is situated in present day Clydebank, West Dunbartonshire.

consumit [the bone marrow was wasted away]'.[37] Lady Thridpairt,[38] in the barony of Renfrewshire, sent for Bessie to ask if she could reveal the name of the thief who had stolen 'twa hornis of gold, and ane croune of the sone, out of hir pyrse?'[39] After consulting Tom, Bessie named the thief and the stolen money was returned to its owner within twenty days. The chamberlain of Kilwinning, James Cunningham,[40] paid Bessie a visit following the theft of some 'beir [barley] that was stollin furth of the barne of Cragance [Craigends]' and she was able to tell him where it was. When various items of clothing and linens started to go missing from Lady Blair's house, she had the servants beaten, until she consulted with Bessie who discovered, via Tom Reid, that the servants were innocent and rather it was 'Margaret Symple [Semple], hir awin friend [relative]' that was stealing from her.[41]

Another member of the Blair family – but of the Beith branch – William of the Strand, received a visit from Bessie when she was instructed by Thomas Reid to deliver a message to him. William Blair's eldest daughter was due to be married to the young Crawford Laird of Baidland.[42] However, Bessie came to tell him to call the match off otherwise his daughter would go mad and 'die a shameful death', committing suicide by throwing herself off a cliff. Bessie's dire warning was heeded and the Laird of Baidland agreed to marry Blair's youngest daughter instead.[43]

37 Pitcairn (ed.), *Trials*, vol. 1, 54.
38 The lands of Thirdpart, in Renfrewshire, were sold by John Crawford to William, Lord Semple, in 1523. George Robertson, *A Genealogical Account of the Principal Families in Ayrshire*, 2 vols. (Irvine: Cunninghame Press, 1823) vol. 1, 179.
39 The 'two horns of gold' may refer to a unicorn, a gold coin struck in the reign of James III, *Jamieson's Scottish Dictionary*. The 'crown of the sun' (*ecu d'or au soleil*) was a French coin, first struck in the reign of Louis XI in 1475, William Shaw, *The History of Currency* (1895; Boston: Adamant, 2005) 401. In Scotland c.1501, it was valued at 14s 6d. E. Gemmill and N. J. Mayhew, *Changing Values in Medieval Scotland* (Cambridge: Cambridge University Press, 1995) 128.
40 James Cunningham, Laird of Ashinyards (land in Kilwinning parish he acquired in 1567). James's father was Gabriel Cunningham (c.1515-1547), 3rd Laird of Craigends. Aged around 18, Gabriel attended the trial for murder of his father William, 2nd Laird of Craigends, by William, Lord Semple, 17 Nov. 1533. In 1543 the feud between the Cunninghams and Semples was not yet over when Gabriel was accused of the murder of John Semple of Auchinlodmont. Among Gabriel's accomplices was William Wallace of Johnstone. Gabriel was killed in 1547 at the Battle of Pinkie. Pitcairn (ed.), *Trials*, vol. 1, 164, 167; *Register of the Privy Seal*. 8 vols. (Edinburgh: General Register House, 1908-1982) vol. 3: 81, no. 538, 541, 559.
41 Lady Blair is most likely Grizel Semple (1551- unknown), daughter of Robert, 3rd Lord Semple, and Elizabeth Carlisle, who married John, Laird of Blair, on 8 Feb. 1573. Paterson, *History of the County of Ayr*, vol. 1, 414.
42 Possibly Andrew Crawford who, according to Paterson, married a daughter of William Blair of the Strand; see Paterson, *History of Ayrshire*, 419. The Crawfords of Baidland are now of Ardmillan. The most famous Crawford from the period was Captain Thomas Crawford of Jordanhill; see note 63.
43 Pitcairn (ed.), *Trials*, vol. 1, 56.

Bessie does not seem to have been engaged in midwifery, though when asked if she ever provided assistance to women in labour, she disclosed that she could do nothing for them until she had spoken with Tom who gave her green silk lace 'out of his awin hand' and instructed her to tie it around their left arm, underneath their clothing.[44] Bessie further revealed that when she was giving birth to her last child, Tom came into her house, offering words of support, though she does not mention whether he gave her a lace for her own arm.

All of the healing and knowledge that Bessie garnered for her well-to-do patrons she learned from her ghostly associate, Tom Reid, her conduit to the otherworld. Just who exactly Thomas Reid was remains unclear but Bessie's four-year relationship with this man became a central feature of the interrogations. She claimed that she first met him, sometime in 1572, while driving her cows to pasture, at a spot between her home and the yard of Monkcastle.[45] She was crying and distracted with worry for she had very recently given birth but her baby, and her husband, were seriously ill. A man approached and hailed her: ' "Gude day, Bessie"; and she said, "God Speid you, gudeman". "Sancta Marie" said he'. He asked her why she was crying and she told him of her troubles; her property was dwindling, her husband was gravely ill, she knew her baby would die soon, and she herself was at a weak point having recently been in child bed. 'Haif I nocht gude caus thane to haif ane sair hart?' Tom replied that she must have angered God by questioning him. His advice was to make amends to the Almighty for he predicted that before she returned home her child would surely die, as would her cow and two sheep (thus predicting emotional as well as economic loss), although her husband would make a full recovery. Bessie confided that although she was initially heartened by the revelation that her husband would get better, she became afraid when she saw Tom Reid depart through a narrow hole in the dyke that no ordinary man could have passed through. At this point, it seems, she first realised that Tom was not of this world.

The initial encounter, as portrayed by Bessie, is curious in that the stranger called out to her using her first name, though she in turn addressed him politely with 'gudeman'.[46] Of course, this could simply be an accident of the manner in which the evidence was recorded. But, if this is indeed an accurate account of

44 Pitcairn (ed.), *Trials*, vol. 1, 54.
45 Monkcastle House, south of Dalry, Ayrshire.
46 Thompson, *Motif-Index*, N762 Person Accidentally Met Unexpectedly Knows the Other's Name. The term good/guid/gude-man had various meanings in Scots, see *DOST*. Bessie was presumably using it in the sense of politely addressing a person. However, it was also used to denote a woman's husband, the occupier of a mill or keeper of the tolbooth (jailer), or towards an owner or tenant of a property, especially of a small estate or farm, ranking below the 'laird'. It was also used euphemistically as a name for the Devil. The 'gudeman's croft' was a plot of uncultivated land dedicated to the Devil.

how Bessie narrated the meeting, it opens up a number of questions. Was Bessie lying about having never met or heard of Thomas Reid before? If so, why? The confession later reveals that Tom had been sent to wait upon Bessie by the Fairy Queen and so, from Bessie's point of view, the meeting was no accident; he did already know of her.

A further notable aspect of the initial meeting was that Thomas Reid greeted her with a catholic salutation 'Sancta Maria'. It has been suggested, unconvincingly, that perhaps Thomas Reid was actually a catholic priest, 'compelled to live under a feigned character' within the new protestant regime.[47]

The conditions under which they first met are intriguing and further emphasise the folktale quality of the narrative, as well as conforming to standard sixteenth century popular beliefs about fairies. In keeping with Scottish tradition, the period surrounding pregnancy and childbirth was considered a dangerous time for women, not only from a medical point of view, but also from the potential threat of supernatural attack. It is tempting to suggest that Bessie may have secretly believed that her baby had not died of natural causes but was 'taken' by the fairies. The presence of the Queen of Elfland during the birth of her ill-fated child, followed up very shortly by a visitation from the ghostly Thomas Reid – both of whom foretold the death of her child – would suggest such a possibility. Thus Bessie was able to explain to herself, and possibly to her accusers, in meaningful terms, the loss of her child, the beginnings of her relationship with the otherworld, and the onset of her healing powers.

There are countless examples, from the historical and folkloric record, of supernatural powers granted to humans as a result of contact with fairies. There is nothing in the record of Bessie Dunlop's trial to suggest that she was a practising charmer previous to her encounter with the Queen of Elfland and her minion, Thomas Reid, and so it would seem plausible that the explanation for her healing abilities and second-sight was a direct result of this meeting. It is also possible that Bessie turned to charming, sometime around 1572, in order to supplement the family income. By her own admission, things were tough at home with sickness, death and the loss of livestock. She referred to her husband and child lying sick in the 'land-ill', which is an obsolete term denoting famine, a pestilence or plague, or some other epidemic.[48] Scotland in the second half of the sixteenth century was marked by intense periods of famine and economic

---

47 Paterson, *History of Ayr*, vol. 1, 411–12. Paterson accompanies the trial of Bessie Dunlop with a story entitled 'Willie Mackie and the Ward Witches', a local legend dated to the first half of the 18th century. Ward Farm is by Dalry. For an excellent discussion of the religious situation in Ayrshire, during the Reformation era, see Margaret H. B. Sanderson, *Ayrshire and the Reformation: People and Change, 1490–1600* (East Linton: Tuckwell Press, 1997).
48 Pitcairn (ed.), *Trials*, vol. 1, 51 note 4.

inflation. Local shortages were so acute in some places that grain had to be imported to cope with the dearths. There was an outbreak of plague in the later 1560s and severe famine during the years 1570 to 1575.[49] In 1574, infectious disease was so rampant that Edinburgh forbade the traffic of sick persons to and from the city on pain of death; 'being informit of the greit inconvenient liklie to follow be spreding of the infectioun of the pestilence to landwart, throw the departing of seik and fowll personis'.[50]

That Bessie was alone and overcome with worry, crying out loud about her predicament, when Thomas Reid showed up, is reminiscent of the folktale hero's encounter with a supernatural helper. For instance, in 'Rashiecoat', the Scottish variant of 'Cinderella', the protagonist is at a low point when a fairy/animal helper arrives to offer advice.[51] Similarly in 'Whoopity Stoorie' or 'Ceann Suic', Scottish Lowland and Highland variants of 'Rumpelstiltzchen', the hero, usually a woman, is lamenting her misfortune at an impossible task that has been put to her when the supernatural helper appears and offers to do the work for her. However, the offer comes with strings attached, such as the loss of her child if she cannot come up with the helper's name after a designated space of time.[52]

The circumstances surrounding the initial meetings between Bessie, the Queen of Elfland, and Thomas Reid may have had certain resonances with the learned ideas of her inquisitors and their interpretation of these characters as none other than devils in disguise. In sixteenth-century European demonological thought the Devil reputedly appeared in times of trouble in order to lure people into witchcraft. The Devil would offer them assistance with their problems in return for their allegiance, demanding that they renounce their baptism and acknowledge him as their sole master.[53] Jean Bodin, a French lawyer and author of *Démonomanie des Sorciers* (1580), was convinced that people were drawn into witchcraft through their own sins, such as 'avarice, envy, drunkenness,

---

49 S. G. E. Lythe, *The Economy of Scotland in Its European Setting, 1550–1625* (Edinburgh and London: Oliver and Boyd, 1960) 17–18; Alex. J. S. Gibson and T. C. Smout, *Prices, Food and Wages in Scotland, 1550–1780* (Cambridge: Cambridge University Press, 1995) 12.
50 Act 'Anent the Pest', Dalkeith, 31 Oct. 1574, RPC vol. II, 1569–1578, 415.
51 'Rashiecoat' in Robert Chambers, *Popular Rhymes of Scotland* (Edinburgh, 1826), and 'Rashin-Coatie' in George Douglas, *Scottish Fairy and Folk Tales* (1901; New York: Dover, 2000) 86–9.
52 AT 500 'The Name of the Helper'. For 'Rumpelstilzchen/Rumpelstiltskin' see *The Complete Fairy Tales of the Brothers Grimm*, trans. Jack Zipes (New York: Bantam, 1992); for 'Ceann Suic' see A. J. Bruford and D. A. MacDonald, *Scottish Traditional Tales* (Edinburgh: Polygon, 1994) 110–12; for 'Whoopity Stoorie' see Hannah Aitken, ed. *A Forgotten Heritage: Original Folk Tales of Lowland Scotland* (Edinburgh: Scottish Academic Press, 1973) 61–4.
53 See, for instance, Nicolas Remy, *Demonolatry*, trans. E. A. Ashwin (1595; London: Rodker, 1930) Book 1, chapter 1.

wantonness', and 'for reward in this world' the Devil 'forces them to renounce God and to worship him and to kiss his rear in the form of a he-goat or some other foul animal . . .; he transports his slaves at night to commit filthy acts'.[54] The demonologists regularly discussed, in vivid detail, the sexual relationship that many witches allegedly had with the Devil, though there was widespread disagreement as to the exact nature of these intimate encounters. In a Scottish context, the sexual element, though present in elite discourse on the activities of witches, cannot be described as an essential ingredient in witchcraft confessions, but neither was it absent. A Musselburgh woman, Janet Daill (1661), confessed to meeting the Devil whom she said appeared 'in the likeness of ane man with grey clothes who promised to give her money'. She consented to become his servant and give herself to him although she knew who he really was. The next time she met him 'the Devil had carnal dealing with her and caused her renounce her baptism'.[55] In this case, as in others like it, sexual contact was a method of sealing the Demonic Pact as well as demonstrating full obedience to the master.

In keeping with stereotypical witchcraft narratives of encounters with the Devil, Thomas Reid fulfilled at least one characteristic demand; the rejection of Christianity. Tom offered Bessie the promise of wealth and prosperity if she would only 'denye hir Christindome, and the faith sche tuke at the funt-stane [baptism]'. Her refusal to commit such an act of apostasy provoked him to anger, but she would not succumb to his coercions, even if, as she put it, she should be 'revin at horis-taillis'.[56] However, when Bessie was asked if she had carnal dealings with Thomas, or had been in a 'suspect place' with him, she insisted that her relationship with him was purely platonic, though she said that once he 'took hir by the aproun, and wald haif had hir gangand [going] with him to Elfame'. Apparently, this episode had taken place at her own home, while her husband was in the house sitting, for some unexplained reason, with three tailors. Thomas appeared to her, at the auspicious hour of twelve noon, and 'he tuke hir apperoun and led hir to the dure [door], and sche followit, and geid [went] up with him to the kill-end [Kiln], quhair he forbaid hir to speik or feir for onye thing sche hard or saw'.[57] Moments later Bessie was introduced to twelve 'gude wychtis', or fairies. The meaning here is unclear, though there is a hint that Tom's physical gesture of leading her out of the house by her

54 Bodin was complementary of the 'praiseworthy custom of Scotland' called 'Indict', a form of acquiring evidence from informers, via a box that was placed in church into which anyone could deposit a piece of paper with the name of a witch and details of their crime. Jean Bodin, *Démonomanie des Sorciers* (1580) *On the Demon-Mania of Witches*, trans. R. A. Scott and J. L. Pearl (Toronto: Centre for Reformation and Renaissance Studies, 1995).
55 Trial of Janet Daill, Edinburgh, 29 July 1661, NAS JC/26/27.
56 Pitcairn (ed.), *Trials*, vol. 1, 52.
57 Pitcairn (ed.), *Trials*, vol. 1, 52, 56.

apron, away from her husband, may have been regarded as inappropriate social behaviour towards a married woman; a sexual innuendo or come-on.[58] However, from a supernatural perspective, his touch may well have been the method that enabled Bessie to see the otherwise invisible 'good neighbours', a relatively common fairy motif. For instance, Robert Kirk, author of *The Secret Common-Wealth* (1691), stated that one way to see the fairies was to touch a person with second-sight.[59]

Other accused witches, such as Alison Peirson (1588), whose confession bears some similarities with Bessie Dunlop's, also claimed to have had a non-sexual relationship with a male ghost, whom she said was her uncle, the source of her medicinal knowledge, and her primary contact with the fairy world. Of course, there are examples where sexual contact had been confessed to, such as Andrew Man (1598) who claimed a long-term relationship with the Queen of Elfland and had children by her. The union between confessing witches and the Devil was sometimes described as aberrational in some way, such as Margaret Lauder (1643) who stated that when she eventually succumbed to the Devil's repeated advances, he 'lay with hir eftir ane beistlie maner lyk a doig'.[60] What could be said is that in all of these examples the supernatural consort was a figure of some authority; an uncle, a Queen, the Devil, and in Bessie's case, though few details are known about Thomas Reid it can be assumed he had been a man of relatively high social standing.

The Devil was, of course, a notorious liar and deceiver, and so it comes as no surprise that Bessie was questioned as to why she should have believed that Tom Reid was telling her the truth, particularly about having been at the Battle of Pinkie. After all, she claimed 'she never knew him when he was alive'. I have so far been unable to confirm if a Thomas Reid fought and died at Pinkie, though Bessie stated that if she should ever doubt his claim, she should seek out his son, also named Thomas, who had succeeded his father in the household of the Laird of Blair, 'and to certain other [of] his kinsmen and friends', to confirm his identity. At the time of Bessie's trial, the Laird of Blair was John Blair (1547–

---

58 'To hold by the Apron-Strings' carries a sense of property, but neither the *Oxford English Dictionary*, the *Dictionary of the Scots Language*, nor the *Dictionary of Slang* records an explicit sexual meaning for the phrase. However, a song from an English play, *The Comical Revenge, or Love in a Tub* (1664), written by Restoration playwright George Etherege, suggests the phrase may have been popularly understood to have sexual connotations: 'He took her by the Apron/To bring her to his beck; But as he wound her to him/the Apron-strings did break'. Michael Cordner, *The Plays of Sir George Etherege* (Cambridge: Cambridge University Press, 1982) 35.
59 Robert Kirk, *The Secret Common-Wealth*, 1691, ed. Stewart Sanderson (Cambridge: Brewer, 1976) 64.
60 Trial of Margaret Lauder, Edinburgh, 29 Dec. 1643, S. I. Gillon and J. I. Smith, eds, *Selected Justiciary Cases, 1624–1650*, 3 vols. (Stair Society, 1954–74) vol. 3, 611–12.

1609) whose father, also John, did in fact die at the Battle of Pinkie in 1547. Whether or not he died at the side of Thomas Reid remains a mystery.[61]

It should perhaps not go unnoticed that in 1575 John, Laird of Blair, entered into a 'band of mutual assistance' with Robert, Lord Boyd (brother of the Archbishop of Glasgow, James Boyd) who was, according to Pitcairn, also Bessie's landlord.[62] Furthermore, John, and his brother William, were convicted on 21 May 1577 of 'shooting with pistols' at Captain Thomas Crawford, 'and his servants for their slaughter'. They were then taken to Blackness Castle as wards until John paid a fine of five thousand pounds and William two thousand pounds.[63] The feud was of long-standing for in 1510 Humphrey Blair, a cleric, was among several accused before the Archbishop of Glasgow for conspiring in the slaughter of William Crawford of Baidland.[64]

The Battle of Pinkie Cleugh, east of Edinburgh, was the last battle between Scotland and England during the so-called 'Rough Wooing'. Although it featured 'one of the largest Scottish hosts in history', with as many as 25,000 men on the field, it proved a devastating defeat for the Scots, with losses of up to 10,000. According to Bessie, Tom Reid referred to the battle as 'Black Saturday', as it was commonly known in Scotland.[65] Pinkie was undoubtedly the iconic event of the 1540s.

Why Bessie should have described encounters between herself and a man who died at this particular battle is intriguing and raises questions about history and memory. Were these her memories or those of the people around her? As in other parts of the country, Ayrshire lost many men at Pinkie, and a number of Bessie's acquaintances had fought or lost family members on that dark day. Had Bessie grown up hearing stories about Pinkie or was she drawing on personal

---

61 Paterson, *History of Ayr*, vol. 1, 414. Blair Castle, stronghold of the Blair family, is near Kilwinning, Ayrshire. There may have been a family connection between John, Laird of Blair, and the brothers William Blair of the Strand and James Blair who came to Bessie's assistance during her internment at Irvine.
62 Paterson, *History of Ayr*, vol. 1, 414; Pitcairn (ed.), *Trials*, vol. 1, 49.
63 Pitcairn (ed.), *Trials*, vol. 1, 71–2. I have so far been unable to confirm if this is the same Captain Thomas Crawford of Jordanhill (1530–1603) who also resided at Kersland, Dalry parish, Ayrshire. He fought at the battle of Pinkie where he was captured and later ransomed, was a confidant of Lord Darnley, and was actively opposed to Mary Queen of Scots. After Darnley's death, he planned and led the assaults on Edinburgh and Dumbarton castles. In 1577 he became Provost of Glasgow and built the first bridge over the Kelvin River at Partick.
64 Sanderson, *Ayrshire and the Reformation*, 32.
65 See Marcus Merriman, *'The Rough Wooing': Mary Queen of Scots 1542–1551* (East Linton: Tuckwell Press, 2000) 7–10, 233–7, David Caldwell, 'The Battle of Pinkie', in *Scotland and War AD 79–1918*, ed. Norman Macdougall (Edinburgh: John Donald, 1991) 61–94, and Gervase Phillips, *The Anglo-Scots Wars, 1513–1550* (Woodbridge: Boydell Press, 1999) 191–200.

recollections from childhood? Bessie's exact age is unknown at the time of her death in 1576, though, as mentioned above, she was still of child-bearing years. Speculatively, her familiarity with a battle that took place twenty-nine years earlier might suggest that she was a child or young adolescent in 1547. A further possible clue in the confession is that she stated she never knew Tom Reid when he was alive – as opposed to saying he flourished before she was born. Regardless of whether or not Bessie had lived through Pinkie and its immediate aftermath, the dominant presence of one of the fallen soldiers in her narrative is testament to the enduring power and lasting significance Pinkie had on the Scottish psyche. It also gives her story a ring of truth and believability.

Among the qualities that make Bessie's account more 'believable' as a closer approximation to traditional folk belief is, perhaps, the mundane, matter-of-fact, narration of events and personages. There is very little overt 'magic' in a story that is essentially all about magical occurrences; the natural and the supernatural are effortlessly entwined. The Queen of Elfland, who might be expected to be glamorous and sophisticated, is plainly described as a 'stout woman' who asks Bessie for a drink. The eight female and four male 'gude wychtis that wynnit in the Court of Elfame', to whom Bessie was introduced, were all well dressed; 'the men wer cled in gentilmennis clething, and the wemene had all plaiddis [plaids] round about thame'. Their unremarkable appearance was only belied by the fact that they departed in a hideous whirlwind that left Bessie feeling sick. Thomas Reid, though he is a member of the undead, can disappear through a small hole in a wall, and has superior occult knowledge and medicinal abilities, is also described in quite ordinary terms. He was an

> honest wele elderlie man, gray bairdit, and had ane gray coitt with Lumbart slevis [Lombard sleeves] of the auld fassoun; ane pair of gray brekis [trousers] and quhyte schankis, gartanit abone the kne; ane blak bonet on his heid, cloise behind and plane befoir, with silkin laissis drawin throw the lippis thairof; and ane quhyte wand in his hand.[66]

The enigmatic Thomas Reid is a complex and multifaceted character, potentially representing a variety of folkloric motifs. He exists in a liminal world, at the very gates of Elfland, moving freely between the land of the living and the dead. Though ghosts or spirits of the dead are to be considered distinct from the fairies, both are strongly connected with the Otherworld, and Tom Reid is no exception. He acts as Bessie's intermediary between the fairies, the underworld and this world. Alison Peirson shared a similar relationship with the fairies via

---

66 Pitcairn, *Criminal Trials*, vol. 1, 51, 53.

the ghost of her uncle, who taught her medicines and charms.[67] The association in the learned tradition between witches and necromancy was long-standing and of biblical origin. Ever since Saul asked the woman of Endor to raise the ghost of Samuel, witches were credited with the ability to communicate with the dead in order to access secret knowledge.[68] Late Medieval and Early Modern theologians and demonologists debated at length whether such acts of sorcery actually constituted the raising of the dead or merely demons in disguise. Bessie Dunlop claimed that 'sche hirself had na kynd of art nor science' but habitually would ask Tom Reid, who would supply the necessary information to cure the sick or find lost property. From the point of view of her interrogators, was Bessie fulfilling an age-old stereotype – the witch as a raiser of the dead/demons? Among the charges levied against her was sorcery and 'invocatioun of spreitis of the devill'; necromancy is not explicitly mentioned though the charges imply that she was thought to have conjured or invoked Thomas Reid. However, it can be argued that Bessie had an entirely different interpretation of events. According to her testimony, it was Tom who first approached her; she did not claim to have raised or summoned him intentionally. From her perspective, he was sent to 'wait upon hir, and to do hir gude' by his mistress, the 'Quene of Elfame'. The link in the supernatural chain was initially forged by a visitation from a fairy. What is perhaps a little unusual in this story is the casting of the Queen of Fairy in the role of a beggar.

When setting out to study the motif of the fairy as beggar, I initially began by reading through various collections of British and European fairy tales, or more accurately folktales or *märchen*, for what better place to find such examples. However, it quickly became apparent that it is relatively rare to find fairies in the role of beggars. Indeed fairies in fairy tales are rare.[69] Within folktale, beggars are invariably kings in disguise so that they may spy on their subjects, test a princess they wish to marry, or are reduced to begging because they have lost

67 Henderson and Cowan, *Scottish Fairy Belief*, 137–8. In both cases the dead function as supernatural helper figures, Thompson, *Motif-Index*, N810 Supernatural Helpers.
68 'The Witch of Endor' is more correctly a 'woman that hath a familiar spirit', 1 Samuel 28: 1–25. In Latin, *familiaris*, or household servant, expressed the notion that sorcerers had spirits at their command.
69 There is much confusion and disagreement over the correct terminology, and scholarship is inconsistent. There are many terms in usage, e.g. wonder tale, marvellous tale, German *märchen* and *zaubermärchen*. The term 'fairy tale' is a translation of *conte de fée*, originally referring to translations of literary French tales composed from the 1690s onwards, in which the powerful *fée* (a fairy woman) plays an important role. As many tales do not include the presence of fairies proper, 'fairy tale' should be regarded as a subgenre of 'folktale' ('oral narrative'). See Bengt Holbek, *Interpretation of Fairy Tales* (Helsinki: Suomalainen Tiedeakatemia, 1987) FF Communications No. 239, 450–1, and Stith Thompson, *The Folktale* (Berkeley: University of California Press, 1977) 7–10.

the princess they adore. Sometimes the beggar is a saint or Jesus Christ himself, posing in this guise in order to discover the compassion and kindness, or vice versa, of the people from whom he begs. And sometimes the beggar is an evil sorcerer or malignant queen or stepmother who takes on this persona in order to trick the object of their hatred, usually young maidens, so that they may hurt or kill them.[70]

The fairy in the role of beggar does not appear as a tale type in Aarne and Thompson's *The Types of the Folktale*, though AT480 'The Kind and Unkind Girls' sometimes involves a request made by a tester-donor in the shape of an old woman or hag whom the girl meets on her journey and by whom she is rewarded if she complies with the request or is punished if she refuses.[71] Nor does it occur in Thompson's *Motif-Index* though fairy in the form of a hag (F234.2.1), fairy grateful for hospitality (F332) or a loan (F335), fairy recovering a stolen cup by posing as a beggar (361.2.1), and the more general, fairies borrowing from mortals (F391), are included.[72]

In Scottish folktales the motif of the fairy as beggar, while not common, does indicate some sort of discernable pattern. Generally, the narrative involves the appearance of a solitary fairy who requests food, drink, implements, or some other sort of assistance from a human, such as borrowing a mill to grind grain, or a woman to nurse her children or act as midwife. The person to whom the request is made is then either rewarded or punished, depending upon their reaction to the request.[73] W. Y. Evans-Wentz recorded, if the fairies were 'refused milk or meat they would take a horse or a cow' but if they were 'well treated they

70 For examples of a king as beggar see 'The Maiden Without Hands', and 'King Thrushbeard', in guise of a saint or Jesus see 'Brother Lustig', 'The Poor Man and the Rich Man' and 'The White Bride and the Black Bride', and in the form of an evil sorcerer/witch see 'Fitcher's Bird' and 'Snow White' in Zipes, *Complete Fairy Tales of the Brothers Grimm*. The beggar as helper is present in Thompson, *Motif-Index*, N825.3.1 Help from Old Beggar Woman, N826 Help from Beggar.
71 This is a familiar tale type in Scotland. For example, a tale associated with Edin's Hall Broch, an Iron Age fort in Berwickshire, tells of a brother who meets an old woman and shares his food with her. She gives him a gift in return for his kindness. Later, the brother encounters the giant Edin who has turned his two brothers to stone. He uses the old woman's gift, which turns out to be an axe, to slay the giant and release his brothers from enchantment. Joyce Miller, *Myth and Magic* (Musselburgh: Goblinshead Press, 2000) 176-7.
72 Thompson, *Motif-Index*; Antti Aarne and Stith Thompson, *The Types of the Folktale* (Helsinki: Academia Scientiarum Fennica, 1961).
73 Fairy requests a mortal nurse in 'Nurse Kind and Ne'er Want' and milk in 'A Back-Gaen Wean', Aitken, *Forgotten Heritage*, 14-15. A fairy boy requests ale in 'The Laird O' Co', Gordon Jarvie, ed., *Scottish Folk and Fairy Tales* (London: Penguin, 1997). Fairy requests meal in 'The Goodwife and the Fairy', Philippa Galloway, ed. *Folk Tales From Scotland* (Glasgow: Collins, 1945) and in two unnamed stories in J. F. Campbell, *Popular Tales of the West Highlands*, 2 vols. (1860-1; Edinburgh: Birlinn, 1994) vol. 1, 425-9.

would repay all gifts'.[74] Sometimes the request is only made after the human has been deceived into trusting the fairy who has offered to help, but once the help has been given, the fairy demands a hefty reward, such as the person's child or even the person's life. The only way for the person to get out of the bargain is to trick the fairy themselves or meet other imposed conditions such as guessing the name of the fairy; e.g. tale types of 'Rumpelstiltzchen', or in Scotland 'Whoopity Stoorie'.[75] In a Scottish context, it would seem that the fairies could occasionally become dependent upon their human neighbours, for some things at least.

So if the begging fairy is relatively elusive and hard to find within the genre of folktale, where else can she or he be found? There are, of course, other sources in which information about fairies has been transmitted, for instance, legends and traditional tales. Legends, unlike folktales, are typically set in a definite time, in worldly, rather than otherworldly, places, and although marvels may take place they call for the hearer's belief in a way that a folktale which incorporates magic does not.[76] Traditional tales, though in many ways they can and often do resemble folktales, are not bound by the same formulaic rules which apply to the latter. It should be stated that these terms are used with a great deal of caution as there is much overlapping between these categories, and one cannot even be sure if the folk who originally told these stories would recognise the desire or the need, which the academic constantly has, for classification and categorisation.

That aside, these kinds of narratives yield more direct examples of fairies in the shape of beggars, and closer parallels to the experience related by Bessie Dunlop. The most frequent patterns to emerge are as follows: a woman is singing and rocking her child / or she (sometimes he) is alone in the house when a female stranger, dressed in green or something unusual or distinctive, enters the cottage and asks the woman to nurse her baby / or asks for milk for her baby / or asks for a bowl of oatmeal. If she obliges she is rewarded but if she does not she is punished. If the fairy woman comes to see a man it is mainly to ask for an implement or tool, or for permission to use his mill or farm equipment. The issue that is central in these kinds of stories is hospitality.

Recorded from an informant in Kirkcudbright, is the story of a miller's wife who was sitting 'rocking her baby to sleep' when she was surprised 'to see a lady

---

74 Walter Yeeling Evans-Wentz, *The Fairy Faith in Celtic Countries* (1911; New York: Citadel, 1990) 95.
75 'Whoopity Stoorie' is one of the few occasions when personal names of fairies are divulged; Scottish fairies are frequently nameless. Henderson and Cowan, *Scottish Fairy Belief*, 14–17.
76 On the difference between folktale and legend see Max Lüthi, *Once Upon a Time: On the Nature of Fairy Tales* (Bloomington: Indiana University Press, 1976).

of elegant and courtly demeanour, so unlike any one she had ever seen in that part of the country, standing in the middle of the room'. She had not heard the lady enter the house and 'rose to welcome her strange visitor' who was 'very magnificently attired' in a green dress with gold embroidery and a 'small coronet of pearls' on her head. She offered her a seat, but the lady declined. Rather, the lady asked, 'in a rich musical voice, if she would oblige her with a basin of oatmeal' on the promise that the meal would be returned to her. A generous portion of oatmeal was given to the lady who then departed. A little while later, the oatmeal was indeed returned, not by the same lady but by 'a curious little figure with a yelping voice; she was likewise dressed in green'. Before leaving, the second visitor advised that all the family should partake of the meal. However, 'one servant lad spurned the fairy's meal' and died shortly after, confirming the suspicions of the household that the first visitor 'was no less a personage than the Queen of the Fairies'. Only a few days later, the miller himself received a visit from the shrill-voiced stranger who asked him politely to start up the mill as she wished to grind some corn, promising that everything would be as he left it the next day. The miller did not dare refuse and in the morning, she had kept to her word and he found everything in the mill as she said he would.[77]

As already mentioned, the humans are generally rewarded if they give the fairy what s/he requests and punished if they do not. In stories where the human has been offered food or drink by the fairy, refusal will result in a punishment, such as blindness, having to perform impossible tasks, or death. On the other hand, the acceptance of the offer will be rewarded, or sometimes simply ignored. The fairy will not harm a human who shows respect and good manners.[78]

However, there is another dimension involved here. Acceptance of fairy food, drink or any other kind of gift can, and often does, lead to enchantment. It is frequently the way in which fairies gain control over humans. Similarly, if the human does not recognise that the stranger who asks for assistance is a fairy and helps without taking any kind of precaution, such as blessing oneself or remaining silent, they too may find themselves enchanted. This, presumably, is the explanation behind Bessie Dunlop's alleged enchantment. Bessie, who was in childbirth, a time when fairies were considered dangerous to both mother and

---

77 Story related by Johnny Nicholson, Kirkcudbright, Feb. 1859, in J. F. Campbell, *More West Highland Tales*, 2 vols. (1960; Edinburgh: Birlinn, 1994) vol. 1, 425–6.
78 J. F. Campbell observed that in some tales the refusal by a guest to accept hospitality until the host has complied with his or her demand was a way of compelling the host to do what would otherwise not be done. Also, in some stories such as 'Fear Gheusdo', the fairies are similarly bound by the laws of hospitality, and in many cases a mortal coerces the fairy to execute their commands by simply refusing fairy hospitality until the wish has been fulfilled. Campbell, *More West Highland Tales*, vol. 2, 147, 166.

newborn,[79] particularly before they had been churched or baptised, presumably took no precautions against possible fairy attack. When the fairy arrived at her own bedside she was unable to recognise her as such, understandably enough, given that descriptions of the Queen of Elfland are usually more grandiose and elegant than the 'stout' beggar-woman that paid a visit to Bessie. When Bessie gave the Fairy Queen a drink this had the effect of putting her under a spell; she was then visited on a regular basis by another otherworldly creature, Tom Reid, who was also under enchantment.

A similar story of the failure to recognize a fairy in the shape of a beggar was recounted by folklorist Walter Gregor.

> A fisherwoman had a fine thriving baby. One day what looked like a beggar woman entered the house. She went to the cradle in which the baby was lying, and handled it under pretence of admiring it. From that day the child did nothing but fret and cry and waste away. This went on for some months, when one day a beggar man entered asking for alms. As he was getting his alms his eye lighted upon the infant in the cradle ... 'That's nae a bairn; that's an image; the bairn's been stoun [stolen]'. He immediately set to work to bring back the child ...[80]

The fisherwoman, as in Bessie's story, did not recognise the beggar woman to be a fairy, nor did she take precautions to protect her newborn from such an attack. In counter-magical fashion, it is the 'genuine' beggar man who breaks the fairy's spell, returns the changeling from whence it came, and restores the human child which 'throve every day afterwards'.

So what is going on in Bessie Dunlop's narrative? How do we classify it, if indeed it should be classified at all? Is this a memorate? Was Bessie, under the influence or threat of torture, drawing upon native folk traditions in her desperation to please her inquisitors? Were the witch hunters imposing such ideas upon her? Or was Bessie recounting a 'visionary encounter experience'[81] not unlike that of a shaman or witch-doctor? Judging from the trial evidence Bessie appears to have believed that her experiences were true supernatural

---

79 A woman was considered particularly susceptible to fairy enchantment during and after childbirth, until she had been churched and the baby baptised, and precautions, such as placing iron under the woman's pillow, were quite common. For examples see Robert Kirk *The Secret Common-Wealth*, and Martin Martin, *A Description of the Western Isles of Scotland* (1703; 1716; Edinburgh: Mercat Press, 1976).
80 The beggar man successfully restored the human child by holding a black hen over a blazing fire, thus frightening away the fairy imposter. Walter Gregor, *Folk-Lore in North-East Scotland* (London, 1881) 61.
81 Wilby, *Cunning Folk and Familiar Spirits*, 243.

encounters, as did her accusers. The level of detail she supplied certainly implies her strong conviction in the reality of these experiences. It is unclear whether or not torture was actually used to illicit her confession; though unlikely, the possibility exists that Bessie was under no duress to say what she did.[82] Basically, it does not really matter whether or not her account is 'true'; what is important is that her contemporaries, and possibly she, herself, believed it to be true. The question is, how do we reconcile Bessie's sixteenth century story with later collections of folktales and legends which appeared in printed form in the eighteenth and nineteenth centuries, basically the period when people started to collect such folk material for the first time? Bessie's story can clearly be related to folktale, the difference being that she evidently lived the experience while those who told or heard similar stories in the nineteenth century were participants in a form of entertainment. At what point in time the orally-communicated medium of folktale came to be regarded and classified solely as 'fiction' is unclear but such was certainly the widespread opinion by the end of the nineteenth century. It has been suggested that in earlier times the storyteller, and indeed the listener, may not have drawn such 'a sharp line between truth and fiction in their narratives'. Tale-tellers 'could not always make a clear distinction between truth and invention in the folktale' and may have actually believed, in some cases, what they narrated. On the other hand, it has been argued that the artistry and distinctive structure and form of the folktale, as opposed to legends that are based on 'fact', are indicators of the folktales' fictional status.[83]

There is another fundamental question that needs to be addressed; the role of the beggar in this narrative. The beggar is a key element in Bessie's story. It is where her story begins, it is the explanation she gives for the onset of her special powers, and, sadly, it is the reason for her demise.

Folktale scholarship has suggested a variety of ways to interpret these stories, and many are reductionist, that is they offer a single explanation e.g. psychological, mythological, anthropological, ethnographical, socio-historical or feminist. But, rather than support one model of interpretation, folktales should perhaps be read, as suggested by Satu Apo, as multi-dimensional; all aspects apply as 'the fictitious world and its meanings in folk tales spring from

---

82 On the use of torture in Scottish witch trials see Stuart MacDonald, 'Torture and the Scottish Witch-Hunt: A Re-examination', *Scottish Tradition* 27 (2002) 95–114; MacDonald, *The Witches of Fife*, 123–42; Brian Levack, 'Judicial Torture in Scotland during the Age of MacKenzie', *Miscellany* IV (Edinburgh: Stair Society, 2002) vol. 49, 185–98; Levack, *Witch-Hunting in Scotland*, 21–4;

83 Andreas Johns, *Baba Yaga: The Ambiguous Mother and Witch of the Russian Folktale* (New York: Peter Lang, 2004) 45. On the difficulties of classifying supernatural tales see also Alan Bruford, 'Problems in Cataloguing Scottish Supernatural and Historical Legends', *Journal of the Folklore Institute* 16/3 (1979) 155–66.

the totality of human life and culture, and not from one of its component areas'.[84] However, in Apo's opinion, not even a multi-dimensional examination 'can hope to reveal more than a few of their potential meanings'.[85] There is ultimately a duality within folktales. They deal with the fantastic and the realistic, with the hopes and fears of their tellers, thus tying them in with reality. Although many of the individual elements may be unrealistic, folktales nevertheless, as Lutz Röhrich contends, look at 'real problems' that are relevant to everybody, and 'the reason for the widespread use of the tale of magic lies in its everyday relevance'.[86] Folktales are complex; 'while they might seem naive, straightforward, or simple at first, a closer examination reveals a rich variety of potential meanings and messages'. Furthermore, the persistence of 'certain folktale plots (tale types) and images (motifs) across time and space is due to the universal nature of the problems or questions addressed'.[87] Though folktales can be heard and enjoyed as entertainment, they can also provide a glimpse into the interests and concerns of both tale teller and listener.

Folktales, on the one hand, often depict community members helping one another out, albeit in lieu of some form of compensation, but they can also portray tensions and jealousies within those same social groups. Furthermore, the folktale, through the use of 'fictitious' characters and events, can express 'real' feelings and emotions which otherwise would be socially unacceptable to disclose:[88] envy, resentment, lust, and hatred. The folktale 'sublimates' reality by stylising frightful or unsavoury things, and turning them into ornamentation, abstraction, and direct action.[89]

Bessie Dunlop's extension of hospitality to the beggar woman may similarly reflect such a dichotomy. Within Bessie's society, toleration of beggars was decreasing and they were being viewed with increasing hostility and resentment.[90] Accused witches were themselves often stereotyped in the role of a beggar, harassing their neighbours and cursing them when they did not indulge their demands for assistance.[91] One of the charges levied against convicted witch

---

84 Satu Apo, *The Narrative World of Finnish Fairy Tales* (Helsinki: Academia Scientiarum Fennica, 1995) *FF Communications* No.256, 144.
85 Apo, *The Narrative World of Finnish Fairy Tales*, 149.
86 Lutz Röhrich, *Märchen und Wirklichkeit. Eine volkskundliche Untersuchung* (Wiesbaden: Steiner Verlag, 1956) 195–6.
87 Johns, *Baba Yaga*, 44.
88 Holbek, *Interpretation of Fairy Tales*, 394.
89 Lüthi, *Once Upon a Time*, 93, 124, 146.
90 On beggars in sixteenth-century Scotland see E. J. Cowan, 'Scotching the Beggars: John the Commonweal and Scottish History', *The Scottish Nation: Identity and History: Essays in Honour of William Ferguson* (Edinburgh: Birlinn, 2007) 1–17.
91 Larner, *Enemies of God*, 21, 89–102. Alan MacFarlane developed a model for the beggar as witch in his work on the Essex witch-hunts, *Witchcraft in Tudor and Stuart England:*

Catherine MacTargett from East Lothian (1688) was begging. When she was displeased with the alms given, she was said to have used threats to get what she wanted. On one such occasion, Catherine cursed a woman who refused to give her any more alms and predicted that the woman would not recover her health until either she died or her newborn baby died. A month later the woman's suckling child passed away and, just as Catherine had stated, the woman made a full recovery.[92] In this instance, Catherine's aggressive begging, and subsequent cursing, was directed at a nursing mother. The woman had obeyed the rules of hospitality, offering the beggar a handful of meal, but she did not or could not protect herself from the witch's curse.

Bessie was faced with a similar paradox: she had a social obligation to the beggar and was under pressure to extend hospitality, but she was also governed by conventions involving encounters with the supernatural and otherworldly beings. Perhaps this part of Bessie's story is a sublimation of inner conflict and resentment generated by the 'stout carline who begged for a drink'.[93]

Another aspect to the beggar motif that seems to be relatively common is the revelation of secrets; the beggar has second-sight or can see things that others cannot. The prognosticative ability of beggars is a feature within both Bessie Dunlop and Catherine MacTargett's confessions and is a relatively common motif within memorate, legend, and folktale in Scotland as elsewhere. A Norwegian tale relates the story of Lasse who went into the forest to cut trees but failed to protect himself from supernatural attack and was transformed into a wolf. Many years passed and his wife assumed Lasse was long dead until one day, a beggar-woman came to her door. The good wife took the unfortunate woman in and gave her food and treated her well. Before the beggar left, she told the wife that her husband was not dead but transformed into a wolf and that she would see him again. That night the wife left out a piece of meat to tempt the wolf to the door and when she saw him approach she said 'If I were sure that you were my own Lasse, I would give you a bit of meat', which instantly broke the spell and the wolf-skin fell off, revealing her own husband.[94] Kindness to the beggar has been rewarded with access to supernatural knowledge.

A Regional and Comparative Study (1970; London: Routledge, 1999). However, Lauren Martin has challenged this model as not widely applicable in a Scottish context, in 'The Devil and the Domestic: Witchcraft Quarrel's and Women's Work in Scotland', in *The Scottish Witch-Hunt in Context*, ed. J. Goodare (Manchester: Manchester University Press, 2002) 73–89.

92 Trial of Catherine MacTargett, 30 May 1688, *RPC*, 3rd ser., vol. 13, 245–62.
93 J. A. MacCulloch, 'The Mingling of Fairy and Witch Beliefs in Sixteenth and Seventeenth Century Scotland,' *Folk-Lore* 32 (1921): 227–44.
94 Sabine Baring-Gould, *The Book of Werewolves* (1865; New York: Causeway Books, 1973) 108–9.

No corpus of folktales from sixteenth-century Scotland has survived to provide direct comparisons with Bessie's remarkable story, recounted in horrific circumstances, but other stories like hers would, in the course of time, evolve as a diversion for the nursery or the parlour, a whimsy to send children to sleep, transformed from the wretched reality that 'once upon a time' had sent Bessie to a horrible death.

She has, however, been remembered in other ways. For instance, this particular trial has attracted the attention of scholars through the centuries, dating back to Sir Walter Scott, Charles Kirkpatrick Sharpe, Robert Chambers, J. A. MacCulloch and Katherine Briggs.[95] A stage play based around her life, written by John Hodgart and Martin Clarke, *Bessie Dunlop: Witch of Dalry* (1977; rewritten 1995), was first performed in 1977 at Garnock Academy, in Kilbirnie, Ayrshire; a fitting tribute to a local lass.[96] There is a street in Ardrossan called 'Witches Linn' in recognition of local traditions surrounding Bessie's former home. That said, the visitor to Ayrshire today is most likely to be directed to sites associated with the more famous, albeit literary witches, of the Robert Burns poem 'Tam O'Shanter' than to the former haunts of Bessie Dunlop. And there are people still living who claim that, growing up in Ayrshire, Bessie was used as a threatening figure by their parents to encourage good behaviour.[97]

One of the fascinating things about the stereotypical Scottish witch is that there is no stereotype. Each case and every trial has its own dynamic and particular set of circumstances, and every individual person convicted of witchcraft has their own unique story to tell. The confession of Bessie Dunlop reveals that while she may have drawn in part upon local legend and folktale under the duress of the questioning of her inquisitors, rare glimpses of her own life and attitudes shine through.

---

95 My own relationship with Bessie Dunlop has been a long one. I first encountered her while researching my undergraduate dissertation in 1989–90 and was inspired to continue investigating her trial, among others, for my Masters thesis in 1993. See also Henderson and Cowan, *Scottish Fairy Belief: A History* (2001; 2007).
96 John Hodgart and Martin Clarke, *Bessie Dunlop: Witch of Dalry* (London: Hodder and Stoughton, 1995) xiii.
97 Oral communication.

EIGHT

Stories of the Supernatural: From Local Memorate to Scottish Legend

Margaret Bennett

'Now I'm telling you a true story of what I know was there . . . and that's true . . . That was in my own family . . . '

Most stories we have come to regard as *legends* are set in the distant past. Scotland, with its accounts of saints, witches, fairies, monsters, Highland clans, Border feuds, placelore and so on, has a considerable wealth handed down by generations of storytellers. Such legends continue to reinforce images of the country and its people and, while they may not always be entirely accurate, they are 'told as true'.[1] They are highly significant, not only to the tellers and their immediate audience, but also to a much wider public. By no means does this one small country have a monopoly on such a tradition, however. If I speak (or write) as one who has never been to, say, Norway or to Greece, I admit that my *imagined* pictures of both countries are as much influenced by the legends I have read as by any travel brochures I have seen.

The majority of legends now conserved in print no doubt began life in oral tradition. The function of telling and re-telling them was not merely to entertain but to preserve the past in the consciousness of the present. Whether written or told, they inevitably influence the perception of readers or listeners, even to those with no personal connection to the original location of the legend.

Even though I belong to a culture that places storytelling at the heart of its traditions, I have generally left any formal discussion on *function* or *classification* of tales, legends, or simply 'stories' to a few specialists.[2] I have preferred, instead,

---

1 Within narrative scholarship, folklorists summarise the definition of legend as 'a story that is told as true' as opposed to a folktale which makes no such claim but is simply 'told as entertainment'.
2 My training in narrative scholarship was via the thorough schooling of Professor Herbert Halpert, Memorial University of Newfoundland. He introduced me to the major works, beginning with John Francis Campbell of Islay, John Lorne Campbell, and the collectors at the School of Scottish Studies in Edinburgh. Later, during my 14 years on the staff of the School, I was inspired by my colleagues, the late Dr Alan Bruford and Donald Archie MacDonald who were the true specialists on the Scottish narrative tradition.

to enjoy the storytelling as an observer-participant, leaving others to draw the lines of classification around my own tradition, or, if they were so inclined, to advocate some strict category, such as 'true legend' on a narrative still in circulation. This paper compels me to consider the stories I have heard, told (or read) about the supernatural and to propose where this repertoire might be placed in the context of folk narrative scholarship.

On the Isle of Mull a story is told about a headless horseman, said to make its appearance before any of the MacLeans of Lochbuie are close to death. The spectral horseman, known in English as 'Hugh of the severed Head', is said to ride past the house, or even stop at the door. So far I have never met a MacLean who has actually seen him, or even a MacLean whose grandfather has had the experience, but if I did, I would not call him a liar. Though the origin of the story is said to date around the fourteenth century, Rev John Gregorson Campbell, writing just over a hundred years ago, noted:

> About fifty years ago a Mull woman . . . insisted she had often, when a young woman, heard him galloping past the house in the evening and had seen the sparks from his horse's hoofs as he rode down the shore on his way to Tiree.[3]

The more recent account places the legend within three or four generations – 'living memory' some would say – thus giving both teller and listener a more direct contact with the original subject. It is in this way such stories are perpetuated.

In his many books, Hugh Miller from Cromarty (1802–1856), the noted stone-mason, geologist, naturalist and writer, provided invaluable insight into the place of traditional narratives in the life of the town or community and in the life of the man himself. Unlike modern folklorists, anthropologists or psychologists, Miller made no attempt to classify his stories, or even explain them; he simply wrote them down as he heard or observed them, in the context in which they occurred. Long passages in his books centre on the supernatural and, though his stories are considerably more recent than 'Hugh of the small (or severed) Head', Miller's chronicles have much in common with older legends about death-warnings. None is more striking than his first memory of such, when, in November 1807, he saw a spectral arm, the forerunner of the drowning of 'one of the best sailors that ever sailed the Moray Firth':

---

3 John Gregorson Campbell, *Superstitions of the Highlands and Islands of Scotland* (Glasgow: Maclehose, 1900) 118.

My mother was sitting . . . beside the household fire, plying the cheerful needle, when the house door, which had been left unfastened, fell open, and I was despatched from her side to shut it. What follows must be regarded as simply the recollection, though a very vivid one, of a boy who had completed his fifth year only a month before. Day had not wholly disappeared, but it was fast posting on to night, and a grey haze spread a neutral tint of dimness over every more distant object, but left the nearer ones comparatively distinct, when I saw at the open door, within less than a yard of my breast, as plainly as ever I saw anything, a dissevered hand and arm stretched towards me. Hand and arm were apparently those of a female; they bore a livid and sodden appearance; and directly fronting me, where the body ought to have been, there was only blank, transparent space, through which I could see the dim forms of the objects beyond. I was fearfully startled, and ran shrieking to my mother, telling what I had seen; and the house-girl whom she next sent to shut the door, apparently affected by my terror, also returned frightened, and said that she too had seen the woman's hand . . . And finally my mother going to the door saw nothing, though she appeared much impressed by the extremeness of my terror and the minuteness of my description. I communicate the story, as it lies fixed in my memory, without attempting to explain it. The supposed apparition may have been a momentary affection of the eye. but . . . its coincidence, in the case, with the probable time of my father's death, seems at least curious.[4]

As with any story of the supernatural, Hugh Miller's account takes the form of a factual report of an occurrence, or experience, which validates belief in supernatural powers. The main difference between Miller's narratives and the earlier ones that have come down through several centuries is that the older ones are told in the third person, whereas Miller's are personal.

If, like Hugh Miller, I turn my focus to my own community's stories of the supernatural, I would have to conclude that virtually all of them fit the same grouping as his. Consider the following transcription, a typical example of the genre, video-recorded in 1994 from one of my uncles, Murdo MacLean, who was born and brought up in Skye.[5] The background to this story is that he and his family had moved to Croy on the mainland in the 1960s, and my grandparents

---

4 Hugh Miller, *My Schools and Schoolmasters* (1871; Edinburgh: Nimmo, 1907) 24–5.
5 Murdo MacLean was video-recorded at his home in North Kessock by the Glasgow-based film company Caledonia, Sterne and Wylde (now know as Caledonia TV). The transcription given is verbatim; words in square brackets are added for clarification. His wife, Effie, had died by the time this was recorded, and he maintained that he would not have told it as long as she was alive.

later lived beside them in a little self-contained 'granny-flat' attached to their house. Granny and Seanair (as we called them) stayed only a few years before returning home to Skye. Later Murdo and his wife, Effie, moved to the Black Isle where this recording was made:

> Murdo: Now Granny lived with us, Granny and Seanair, as you know, and when they went back to Skye, we were letting the [main] house [to summer tourists]; we were in the wee end. And this night, I don't know how long after she died [in Skye], maybe weeks, and we were in bed [in Croy], and I woke with a cold wind, oh, very, very cold and I could feel something queer. And Mam was sleeping beside me, now I didn't wake her up, and I looked over and here was Granny, the grey hair, now she had it longish [though she only ever brushed it out before she went to bed], and the black cardigan she always wore, sitting beside Mam on the bed. So I woke her, I don't think she [Effie] seen anything, but it put the scare in me. Now a few nights after that I woke again, this cold air, oh, you can't – [imagine how cold]. It was a really weird cold, you could feel it in the room, and I shouted over to Mam 'We're not alone'. But I didn't see anything that night and Mam says, 'We're not'. She felt it too, and that was Granny. And we don't know how did she come back, was her spirit at rest, or did she want to tell something to her [Effie]. But we never solved it except she was there [as] in true life, as if she was living and I could see her sitting beside Mam on the bed . . . Well, I didn't want to be living in Croy after that. I was glad to be away from it . . . It changed my life . . .

Such was the significance of this story that concluded with 'it changed my life'. Murdo immediately launched into a second story, this time much lighter in tone, even amusing, about the neighbours beside their next home. Both experienced a poltergeist and Murdo was also connected to this account by virtue of the fact that they had both called on him to show him the evidence. In this relatively short session Murdo told me a series of personal narratives, all concerning some aspect of the supernatural, and, presumably to ease the dramatic tension, or catch his listeners unaware, he slipped in a joke and an amusing 'catch tale'.

The context of stories such as these was usually within what was commonly called the *taigh ceilidh*, or house visit. From my own childhood in the 1950s, through my adolescence, and indeed to this day, entire sessions of stories with a supernatural theme occur within my family and community. The geographic location of 'community' need not be one of the islands in which I spent my life – Skye, Lewis, Shetland – but any place where the tradition is familiar to those present. I found it to be just as common when I lived in Newfoundland and

Quebec, or visited descendants of Scottish emigrants in North Carolina and New South Wales.[6] As in Scotland, the narratives are localised to these parts of the world, and are specific to the tellers or named individuals in their kenning. Duncan McLeod from Scotstown, Quebec was seated by his neighbour's kitchen stove when he told this story about 'an old fellow by the name of A. D. Morrison' who was said to have had the second sight:

> The day that [Peter MacRae] was killed, he walked into the post office on his way to work, and the AD [sic] was in there talking to the postmaster, Jack Scott, and he saw a halo around Peter's head. And after Peter stepped outside he told Jack that there was going to be a death, a tragedy of some sort . . . I don't know what his job classification was, but he worked in a quarry, and he was down in the lower depths of the quarry when a stone, a loose stone, hit him on the head and killed him.[7]

No matter where such accounts were related, storytelling was never planned, but simply evolved out of general conversation and, depending on the number of people in the group, would usually take the form of an exchange, with one person's story triggering the memory of the next.[8] A typical session in our family would begin towards the end of a day, usually when we were visiting each other. For example, in his own house Murdo MacLean would sometimes begin the session after Effie had gone to bed. Most of his stories were from his younger days in Skye, not only from his own recollection but also from the experiences of previous generations who told them in the first place. This, and the fact that all the stories were located in places where he had lived, made him personally *connected* to all of them. Topics in a typical session covered premonitions of death, ghosts, revenants, poltergeists, wraiths, phantom funerals, the phantom car, second-sight and witchcraft; the time-span ranged from the mid–1800s (his grandmother's memories) to within the decade of his telling. Several of Murdo's stories from the 1950s covered incidents familiar to my own generation, such as the ghost car in Skye. The following story goes back to the early 1930s:

6 The years were: Newfoundland, 1969–75, Quebec, 1975–76 and return visits from 1991 to 2007; North Carolina, regular visits from 1988 to 2009; New South Wales, Dec. 1988 to Nov. 2005.
7 Margaret Bennett, *Oatmeal and the Catechism* (Edinburgh and McGill-Queen's, Montreal: John Donald, 1998) 88.
8 I describe and discuss the dynamics of an actual session in *Oatmeal and the Catechism*, Chapter 6. See also storytelling among the Gaelic settlers in Newfoundland in Margaret Bennett, *The Last Stronghold: Scottish Gaelic Traditions of Newfoundland* (St John's, Newfoundland: Breakwater Books, 1989; Edinburgh: Canongate Press, 1989) chapters 3 and 6.

The true one, and that was the witchcraft, and that happened, oh, about half a mile out of Portree. There was a quarry – there's all houses on it now – but [when I was young] there was this quarry, and [before my time] there was this witch supposed to live in it. She used to put curses on people. She used to read the cups, and she used to read cards. People used to call on her, and the ruins were still there in my time, and I knew the little quarry. Now this is the story of the horse [you asked me for] – it *has* come to me. Now I used to come three miles, I walked from Portree while I was going with a lassie – she was a waitress, and she wouldn't be off duty till about ten, in the hotel, you see. And well, I wouldn't be going home until about 12 or so, ehm maybe 2 in the morning – only very young at the time [laughs].

And there was this fellow, a neighbour of ours . . . I'll mention no names – he was always home at 10 o'clock, and this was on a Monday night, about Forsyth's corner in Portree, about 8 o'clock. And I was going to meet this lassie, and he was standing at the corner, and he says to me 'Murdo, what about coming early with me tonight?'

Well I says to him, 'Yes', I says, 'one in the morning is early for me, or 12'.

'Oh', he pleaded with me.

'No', I says, 'I'll be here at 12 if you want to wait for me, we'll go home together'.

So he was there [waiting] when I seen the lassie home, and standing at the corner. It was after 12 and we started walking up the road. And this is the story he gave me. Now this is a true story as I've been told it, and I thought he was trying to get me to go home early. No, this was the story. He went to church on Sunday night, and he came out of church, and the corner of Portree, the Royal Hotel was always, the fellows there you know, where they met, and there were blue stories and all the filth of the day, and he enjoyed it after being at church . . . And eh, he stayed there for quite a while, and then after he enjoyed himself he started to walk home. And he was telling me this before he reached the quarry, you see, where the horse came out. And I says to him, 'Well, Johnnie', I says to him, 'if you're trying to frighten me for me to be going home early with you at 10 o'clock you're making a mistake'.

So I thought that was why he was telling me the story, that he made it up, and we were just near the place and he caught a hold of me, and he was shivering like that [demonstrates with hands]. Well he told me that this horse came out of this quarry and he could hear the chains on him. And there was a wee house where this woman stayed, along there, and he started running, and he thought if he could manage to reach this house he would escape the horse. Now this was at night, and he was getting puffed and the horse was nearly at him, and he put a hand on the Bible – he had a Bible he had had in church – and the horse went right off the road down the bank. Now it's the state he was in that I believed him, and eh, I told him 'Well, if it was a right horse there'll be marks'. So we looked in daylight and there was no marks. But the fellow left that place, he couldn't – he left Achachoirc and went to Portree. And that's the story of the horse. It was the devil, that him being in church, we made out [concluded] and instead of going home, as he should have, the devil got the better of him. Now we're not talking of it as a ghost *story*, we're talking of it as the fellow told me, and I wouldn't believe him until [I saw] the state he was in when we reached [the place]. He was frightened to pass it he took a grip of me and he was shaking like a leaf. And that is true about the horse . . .

Just a very small proportion of Murdo MacLean's repertoire has been recorded, even though these fireside sessions often kept us out of bed till three in the morning. It is only when I look at the transcriptions, however, that I realise that almost all his stories were punctuated with comments such as 'Now I'm telling you a true story of what I know was there . . .', 'That's true . . .', 'That was in my own family . . .' Such phrases may suggest that, although the teller believes implicitly, he does not necessarily expect all listeners to share his conviction. The same might be said of Hugh Miller's account (above) where he concludes with what may be a concession to the non-believer, in this case a reader. Miller seems to second-guess the doubters by acknowledging that his vision 'may have been a momentary affection of the eye' but leaves them to consider that the coincidence with his father's death 'seems at least curious'. The technique of the writer differs from that of the speaker, but the effect is the same: both acknowledge the option of doubt while pressing the case for belief in supernatural power.

At times Murdo would add 'Now that's not a *story* – that's true'. He would use the word 'story' in two very distinct ways: in phrases such as 'I remember this story. . .' or 'There's a story about. . .' the word simply refers to any narrative. When Murdo emphasised the word, however, he implied there was no truth in it. 'Oh, that's only a *story* he told you . . .' He would also keep this usage for local gossip he wished to discourage: 'Oh, don't listen to that *story*'. There is nothing idiosyncratic about his usage, as children all over Scotland are familiar with a similar phrase used when an adult suspects someone is not telling the truth: 'Now stop telling stories'.

There is no doubt whatsoever that all Murdo MacLean's stories about the supernatural are 'told as true'. That being the case, do these stories I grew up hearing (and sometimes telling) fit into the category of 'legend'? Looking at the entire corpus of material, I would hesitate to regard them as legends *per se,* but would emphatically state that they are not folktales. Perhaps the general listener or participant might refer to such stories simply as anecdotes, if only based on the notion that none of them are very long. Nevertheless, that label is also much too general. These types of narratives suggest to me a sort of 'pre-legend' for they are 'told as true' but are not yet in the distant past as they belong to people in living memory.

By no means am I the first folklorist to struggle with terms, and so I turn to the important work of Swedish folklorist, Carl W. von Sydow.[9] More than fifty years ago, he coined the term 'memorate' for stories of personal happenings which are usually told to give credence to folk beliefs. Folklorists on both sides of the Atlantic readily adopted von Sydow's term, and although *memorate* is now treated as a separate genre from *legend* there are surprisingly few studies that deal with it. Despite the fact that the leaders in folklore scholarship, such as Richard Dorson, Alan Dundes, Herbert Halpert and Jan Brunvand, have all trained new generations of folklorists to be at least familiar, if not comfortable, with the term, there is (as far as I know) no major work in English or Gaelic devoted to the memorate.

On the subject of the supernatural, Brunvand proposed that belief in certain phenomena is largely perpetuated through the telling of memorates. His proposed categories of the supernatural are well covered in Scottish tradition, as the few examples I have listed in the right-hand column will illustrate:

Brunvand	Some Scottish examples
• supernatural creatures	monsters, trolls, brownies, fairies
• returning spirits of the dead	ghosts, revenants noises, smells
• magical happenings	cures that work for 'no reason'
• supernatural signs	warnings of death, omens of bad luck

Although the narratives discussed in this paper are all from Gaelic Scotland that is not to say that such traditions must be relegated to the Highlands, or the label 'superstitious' reserved for the Highlander. The examples of *memorate* cited in this paper are from the Highlands only because that is where I grew up – my family's personal memories are obviously of places or areas in which they lived. There is no doubt, however, that Lowlanders can hold their own in this field: Robert Burns and Walter Scott can match any Highland repertoire.

---

9 Carl W. von Sydow, *Selected Papers in Folklore* (Copenhagen: Rosenkilde and Bagger, 1948).

Furthermore, today's tabloid newspapers carry as many reports of haunted city houses and tenement flats as they do of Highland castles. Some have even been the subject of songs, such as Matt McGinn's 'Dundee Ghost', which, for all its humour, is enough to set off a serious session of urban ghost stories, 'told as true, an' that's a fact'.

Growing up in the 1950s and 60s, my contemporaries and I were more conscious of living in the 'religious' Highlands than in the superstitious. We learned all the 'Thou-shalt-nots' off by heart but there was none, as far as we noticed, that dealt with superstition. Not that the ministers didn't rail against it; some have done so for centuries. It seems that most of the nineteenth-century ministers who produced books of folklore and local traditions could not resist adding their own moral view or judgement on the superstitions of their parishioners. Out of these collections, several important works were published, some with the encouragement of the Folklore Society, and, while the actual lore itself forms a priceless record of the time, it is equally interesting to consider the views of the collectors.

The Rev John Gregorson Campbell was born in Argyllshire in 1836, and at the age of 10 was sent to school in Glasgow, the only Highland boy in his class. He then attended Glasgow University where he studied law and later divinity.[10] Campbell was much interested in oral tradition, and he corresponded with the great folklore collector, John Francis Campbell of Islay (b. 1822), today regarded as the father of folk narrative scholarship in Scotland.[11] The Duke of Argyll then appointed the Rev Mr Campbell to the parishes of Tiree and Coll, requesting that he should, in the style of his namesake, interview his parishioners, and write down as much as possible from living oral sources. Though his books were not published till after his death (1891), Campbell's own opinion becomes quite clear. The minister concludes: 'Superstition shuts out the light, makes the mind unhealthy, and fills it with groundless anxieties'.[12]

His Lowland contemporary, the Rev James Napier from Paisley, a self-styled 'antiquary', published his collection of folklore in 1879. He begins his book with a discussion on superstitious beliefs in which he lays his cards on the table. Having studied previously published definitions of superstition, he quotes several of them before establishing his own: 'Beliefs and practices founded

---

10 See John Gregorson Campbell, *Superstitions of the Highlands and Islands of Scotland* (Glasgow: Maclehose, 1900) and *Witchcraft and Second Sight in the Highlands and Islands of Scotland* (Glasgow: Maclehose, 1902). Both texts republished, *The Gaelic Otherworld*, ed. Ronald Black (Edinburgh: Birlinn, 2003).
11 See John Francis Campbell (of Islay), *Popular Tales of the West Highlands*, 2 vols (1860-1; Edinburgh: Birlinn, 1994) and *More West Highland Tales*, 2 vols. (1960; Edinburgh: Birlinn, 1994).
12 Campbell, *Superstitions of the Highlands and Islands of Scotland*, 229.

upon erroneous ideas of God and nature'.[13] His tone comes across as a sort of admonitory prose, which he maintains throughout the book. Despite Napier's treatment of the subject of superstition and the supernatural I am not convinced that the minister could differentiate between conventional faith, as expressed in the teachings of his church, and other aspects of the supernatural. God, after all, is supernatural. So also are the angels, the Devil, wraiths, fetches, ghosts, fairies and so on. Discussion aside, the Paisley minister seems as fascinated by 'supernatural' episodes in the lives of his parishioners as he is by explaining them away.

> I was sitting once in the house of a newly married couple, when a loud knock was heard upon the floor under a chair, as if some one had struck the floor with a flat piece of wood. The young wife removed the chair, and seeing nothing, remarked with some alarm, 'It is hasty news of a death'. Next day she received word of the death of two of her brothers, soldiers in India, the deaths having occurred nearly a year before. There was no doubt in the mind of the young wife that the knock was a supernatural warning. The natural explanation probably was that the sound came from the chair, which, being new, was liable to shrink at the joints for some time, and thus cause the sound heard. This cracking sound is quite common with new furniture.[14]

Napier seems to flit from belief to disbelief, one minute lending credence to the possibility, and the next moment demolishing it:

> It is not surprising that the solemn period of death should have been surrounded with many superstitious ideas, – with a great variety of omens and warnings, many of which, however, were only called to mind after the event.

Despite the fact that his 'natural explanation' might suggest that he does not believe in such phenomena, Napier continues to report many examples of local or personal narratives. Eventually he manages to draw comparisons between his own Paisley traditions and beliefs from the Holy Land:

---

13 James Napier, *Folk-Lore: or, Superstitious Beliefs in the West of Scotland within this Century* (Paisley, 1879; Wakefield: E.P., 1973) 4.
14 Napier, *Folk-Lore*, 55. See also Margaret Bennett, *Scottish Customs from the Cradle to the Grave* (Edinburgh: Polygon, 1992) where I have drawn comparisons between Napier's account and more recent recordings from oral tradition.

In my native village a wraith seen during morning, or before twelve noon, betokened that the person whose wraith was seen would be fortunate in life, or, if unwell at the time, would recover; but when the wraith was seen in the afternoon or evening, this betokened evil or approaching death, and the time within which death would occur was considered to be within a year. This belief in wraiths goes back to a very early period of man's history. The ancient Persians and Jews believed that every person had a spirit or guardian angel attending him, and although generally invisible, it had the power of becoming visible and separating itself for a time from the person it attended, and of appearing to other persons in the guise of the individual from whom it emanated. An excellent example of this superstitious belief is recorded in the Acts of the Apostles. When Peter, who was believed to be in prison, knocked at the 'door of the gate' of the house where the disciples were met, the young woman who went to open the door, on recognising Peter's voice, was overjoyed, and, instead of opening, ran into the house, and told the disciples Peter was at the door. Then they said 'It is his angel' (wraith). Thus the whole company expressed their belief in attending angels.[15]

By linking his own collection of stories about supernatural happenings to scriptural evidence of similar beliefs, Napier validates not only the belief-stories themselves but also his own preoccupation with the subject.

Writing in the twentieth century, the Rev Alexander MacGregor opens his collection *Highland Superstitions* (1922) by stating: 'It is lamentable that mankind in all ages of the world have been prone to the most degrading superstitions.' With that disclaimer, he then goes on to give a fascinating account of the very superstitions he laments.[16]

The ministers' remarks on the subject prompt me to turn my attention to broader questions of faith: What is faith? Do people actually *believe* what they claim to be fundamental to their faith? And if faith is the 'acceptance of things unseen', is the *faith* required to believe in God the same as the faith required to believe in ghosts or the fairies? Or might there be boundaries between different compartments of belief or faith, say, religious beliefs and 'traditional' beliefs? If so, where could the line be drawn? I suspected that any discussion with the clergy or the folk familiar with the tradition might immediately put them on guard and would not necessarily reveal the truth about such matters. On one of my visits to Skye, however, it occurred to me, that observation rather than

---

15 Napier, *Folk-Lore*, 56.
16 Alexander MacGregor, *Highland Superstitions* (Stirling: E. MacKay, 1922).

pointed questioning would be the better starting place for anyone wishing to discover how faith operates. My quest began with the following incident that took place in the autumn of 1993:

> I was spending a week with my aunt and uncle in Skye, the last of my mother's family to live in Glenconon. Sunday arrived, so it was 'church as usual', for the entire household. That particular morning was crisp, clear and sunny, so, as soon as I was ready for church, I went outside to enjoy what I could of it. My uncle had already beaten me to it, for he was standing at the gable end of the house having a last cigarette before church. In no hurry, we stood admiring the scenery – Beinn Eadra to our left, the Fairy Glen directly opposite us, adjacent to us the croft my grandfather had worked all his life, and beyond that, Uig Bay where he and his father before him had fished.[17]
>
> Looking around us, I began to sense that this might be the moment to shed some light on my questions of faith. No direct interrogation, of course – that would have taken him aback. Besides, I already knew that he went to church twice a week, read the Bible daily in family worship and had a strong, steady, faith in God. This uncle also had undying faith in nicotine – he lit up another cigarette.
>
> Looking out over the landscape towards Uig Bay, I enquired about several ruins, some on his own croft.
>
> 'Oh, yes,' he said, 'they were cleared by Captain Fraser . . . Now that would date them . . .' He tells me the local history. I listen, then point to two ruined houses on his own croft.
>
> 'Not much left of them,' he says, and I remark on how we loved playing in them as children.
>
> He laughs, 'In my day we played there too . . .'
>
> 'Isn't it amazing,' I add, 'how the rowan trees are still growing there – look at all the berries. The trees are alive years and years after all the people who lived there are dead and gone.'
>
> 'Oh, yes,' he inhales another puff. 'That's to keep away the witches.'
>
> He smiles, stubs out the cigarette and off we go to church.

---

17 These landmarks are all connected to accounts of the supernatural. There is a story and a song about a headless spectre who haunts Beinn Eadra (the mountain at the end of the glen); there are 365 hillocks in the Fairy Glen where local tradition names the man who saw the fairies there; and there are accounts of second sight that concern local people. These traditions are so familiar to me that it was not until I had finished this paper that I noticed the association.

On the one hand, this conversation suggests there are no lines to separate mental, psychical or emotional departments of faith. Thus, in the one mind (or society) implicit faith in God can happily co-exist with belief in witches and the power of the rowan tree against witchcraft. On the other hand, however, the same discourse raises more questions surrounding whether people actually *believe* every concept within a so-called belief system.

The rowan tree is as rooted in Scottish tradition as it is in the soil that maintains it. In twenty-first-century Scotland, there is still a strong taboo against cutting this sacred tree even though serious talk of witches is seldom heard. Not only in rural areas, but also in the major cities, many a new house has a rowan sapling planted in its garden. This does not necessarily mean that the person or family who adheres to this custom will actually know why it was practised; it is, rather, a confirmation that tradition is important and that a link to our forebears still plays an invaluable part in daily life.[18]

A community whose way of life incorporates such a wide range of traditional belief has no need of labels to separate one category from another as the entire system is simply taken for granted. Within my family and locality, such traditions range over an extensive continuum of belief: in God, the Holy Spirit, the Devil, angels, saints, fairies, ghosts, spirits of the dead, phantom lights, smells, wraiths, fetches, tokens, doubles, witches, warlocks, and so on.[19] In the course of conversation, any one of these subjects may be acknowledged or discussed.

From the perspective of someone outside the culture, however, the point of view may be more objective. Everyday sayings such as, 'if you break a mirror you'll have seven years bad luck' that are part of daily life may alert listeners from other cultures. If they have never heard the saying before, it will sound curious; and if they do have it, then the same feature may reassure both parties that people the world over like to share hopes, fears, dreams, sorrows, laughter and companionship.

In the early 1960s, American folklorist Kenneth S. Goldstein made a collection of 'popular beliefs' or superstitions in the North-East of Scotland.[20] A

---

18 In a similar vein, many a Scottish bride will insist on having a sprig of white heather in her bridal bouquet, Bennett, *Scottish Customs from the Cradle to the Grave*, 128.

19 See also my discussion on fairy belief in '1690–1990: Balquhidder Revisited', in *The Good People: New Fairylore Essays*, ed. Peter Narváez (New York and London: Garland Press, 1991) 94–115.

20 From its first year of publication, 1888, the American Folklore Society has maintained a strong interest in the subject of the supernatural. (The first AFS article on Scotland appeared in the 1890s.) Goldstein was one of many North American folklorists who took part in a project to contribute to a dictionary of beliefs in the USA. In his time, the call to collect was due largely to Wayland D. Hand who had been working on the subject since the late 1930s. Professor Hand became internationally known for his contribution to the monumental *Frank C. Brown Collection of North Carolina Folklore*. The strong ties

newcomer to the tradition, Goldstein not only attempted to record as many as possible but, at the same time, to determine the actual level of belief held by his informants. As he lived in the North-East for a year he was able to note those taken for granted by local folk such as, 'if you drop a teaspoon you'll have a visitor', or (a more serious one) 'you should never hold a baby up to a mirror or its spirit might be taken away'.

His article, 'The Collecting of Superstitious Beliefs', outlines the project and urges folklorists not only to note the context of their collections but also to address some of the questions that arise. Goldstein proposed, therefore, that collectors should consider a 'scale of belief' to assess the 'degree to which these items are actually believed'. The one he devised bears consideration for it is as applicable to 'belief sayings' as it is to complete narratives and memorates:

1 Whole-hearted acceptance [total belief]
2 Partial acceptance [superstition rationally rejected but not abandoned in practice]
3 Humorous incredulity [superstition rejected and abandoned in practice but passed on]
4 Total rejection [total abandonment in practice, and disassociation or forgetting][21]

Based on his invaluable collection, he also found that [in Scotland] 'superstition existed almost equally at all levels of educational achievement'. Coming from a society 'where affluence is related to educational attainment' as he did, Goldstein admits surprise at this conclusion drawn from his North-East study.[22]

In considering the stories, or memorates, that are the subject of this paper, it may seem paradoxical that in the very part of Scotland where fundamental Calvinism is the strongest, staunch 'believers' (as the church calls them), readily make reference to the supernatural. Even church elders tell second sight and ghost stories. Understandably, we may wonder why these stories of the supernatural persist? What are they really about? And why do some people encounter unexplained experiences or circumstances? Perhaps the only ones

---

of emigration between North Carolina and Scotland make this collection particularly relevant to studies in Scottish tradition. See Wayland D. Hand, 'Popular Beliefs and Superstitions from North Carolina', *The Frank C. Brown Collection of North Carolina Folklore*, vols. 6 and 7 (Durham, North Carolina: Duke University Press, 1961 and 1964).

21 Kenneth S. Goldstein, 'The Collecting of Superstitious Beliefs', *Keystone Folklore Quarterly* (Spring, 1964) 17–18.
22 Goldstein, 'The Collecting of Superstitious Beliefs', 20.

qualified to answer are those who tell of the experiences. When asked, Murdo MacLean explained:

> I believe myself in my own experience in life, that there is, there are signs given before death. And there are signs given after death. And I believe there are signs given for the living too. Now it's only a story I've been told about the living part of it –

Then, without drawing breath, he continued:

> And there was this man he used to go for a walk – he was a banker and every evening he went. Now I don't know where it was, was it on Skye or where, but this is the story as he told it . . . every time he went for a walk he would stop at this point spot, and he would hear laughing, crying and running and he couldn't fathom what it was. So he went abroad and it still was on his mind, how always when he went to this place it had the laughing, crying and running. And [years later] when he came back from abroad he went for his usual walk and what was built there but a school – now that's the story I've heard.

Perhaps many people had this kind of experience, or maybe it is sheer coincidence that I recorded a very similar story in Quebec, from a descendant of immigrants from the Isle of Lewis, Alex MacIver. His story was about a Lewisman, one the first settlers, who, in the mid-1800s, was homesteading near Alex's grandparents. This old man used to tell people that he could hear the sound of singing, like a whole congregation, as if it were coming from the backwoods near where they lived. Years later, when the land had been cleared and settled, that was the very place the church was built.[23]

When Alex MacIver told his story in 1992 he did so as a personal narrative, a memorate, featuring people of his family and community. Alex's generation were the last to speak Gaelic and today (2009), his wife Jean is the only fluent speaker left. The entire district is now French-speaking and the only Scottish narratives told are ones that now survive because they have been recorded or published in books and translated. If this particular story is to survive in Quebec it will not be in the form of a memorate, but as a local or 'placelore' legend.

If the question arises of 'When, if ever, does memorate turn into legend?' the Quebec example might offer insight into the process. In considering well-known

---

23 Any notion that the church was built there because of the old man's experience was out of the question. Quite simply, he was known to have had second sight.

historical legends about Scotland, in particular narratives that are not based on 'official' records of government or church, but on oral tradition, it stands to reason many of them must have entered circulation as personal memories, told as memorates.

In his diary, Sir Walter Scott noted that 'the good thought came into [his] head to write stories for little Johnnie Lockhart [his grandson] from the history of Scotland'. The result was Scott's publication of *The Tales of a Grandfather* in 1827. Many of these stories from history are now regarded as legends but perhaps this has only happened with the passage of time, for, in Scott's day, the more recent eighteenth-century accounts were told to him as personal experiences. Considering he was born in 1771, less than twenty-five years after Culloden, it should be no surprise that he recounts the memories of those who experienced the conflict. In his introduction to the 1898 edition, F. W. Farrar writes 'When writing of the '45 [Scott] could rely on evidence derived from those whose relatives had fallen at Culloden, and even those who could speak of the Chevalier from personal knowledge.'[24] Scott himself concludes his account of Culloden with:

> I should make these volumes thrice as long as they ought to be, were I to tell you the stories, which I have heard (sometimes from the lips of those who were themselves the sufferers) concerning the strange concealments and escapes which the Jacobites were reduced to for the safety of their lives after their cause was ruined.[25]

Nowhere does Scott rely on oral tradition more than in telling about the history of the Borders. Farrar continues:

> He abounded in rare local information. His tastes and pursuits had been in great measure formed by his love for the old songs and tales [stories] which, in the happy days of his early boyhood, formed the amusement of a retired country family . . . he could draw largely upon stories of Border depredations which were still matters of recent tradition. . .[26]

Scott's knowledge of both Highlands and Lowlands extended to all facets of traditional knowledge. His prolific output was impressive and few could rival his curiosity about the many aspects of the supernatural: fairies and witches were as much the subjects of his writing as were kings and queens.

24 F. W. Farrar's introduction to Sir Walter Scott's, *The Tales of a Grandfather* (London, 1898) ix.
25 Scott, *Tales of a Grandfather*, 1170.
26 Farrar's intro. to Scott, *Tales of a Grandfather*, ix.

But what of today? Television has ensured that the sessions we once knew and loved will no longer be the order of the day – or night either. Even in the Islands, the 'soaps' need not be in Gaelic to get people hooked. Nevertheless, accounts of supernatural happenings have not gone out of fashion, even among those who have long since left the 'superstitious Highlands' to take up sophisticated careers in the cities. Furthermore, there is ample evidence both from local and national press that religion can still monopolise discussion. It can creep uninvited into any conversation.

In October 1999, I was having dinner with old friends, one of whom I had known from school days in Lewis. Before long, the conversation turned to the Free Church. The fact that some of us had lived outside Scotland for thirty years, and did not attend any church, seemed to make no difference to our perception of what is 'true' as far as religious belief was concerned. Since it is notoriously difficult for anyone to discard the indoctrination of youth, it became clear that some of the group still held a certain disdain for holy medals and other such 'Roman Catholic notions'. Texts about 'graven images' that had been learned in youth were still quite intact. I was just about to offer, tongue-in-cheek, a quotation from my grandmother – 'life is but a vale of tears . . .' when a remark from the other side of the table changed the subject completely.

The National Mod was the topic of the month. 'I hear your choir swept the boards. Congratulations!' said one of the party, looking straight at the man whom we knew to be the Gaelic tutor.

'Four trophies. Gaelic and music! Now there's something to put on the mantelpiece,' he beamed. 'And the amazing co-incidence is, that last month . . .' and he went on to tell about meeting an elderly woman who had given him a Mod Gold Medal that had been won by a Lewis worthy more than fifty years earlier.

'Priceless. Anyway, I put it in my sporran,' he added, 'and I'm going to do the same thing next year, for this is the first time in years the choir has swept the boards.'

Holy medals are out of the question, but Mod Gold Medals apparently have hidden powers. Each may be only a piece of metal, but faith is beyond explanation, little to do with logic, more to do with indoctrination. Or, could there be something deep within the human psyche that craves belief in the supernatural?

At the turn of the twentieth century, the Rev Mr Campbell suggested that: 'Superstition shuts out the light, makes the mind unhealthy, and fills it with groundless anxieties.' At the dawn of the twenty-first century the opposite is still true for many, as it lights up the person who believes, heightens awareness of dangers, guides in decision-making and allays anxiety.

Worried about winning at next year's Mod? Not a bit! The gold medal in the sporran will take care of that.

NINE

The Church and Traditional Belief in Gaelic Society[1]

John MacInnes

This chapter looks at certain aspects of traditional belief in Gaelic society and the relationship between these and the attitudes and practices of the church. The Christian church in all its branches is naturally wary of any system of belief which might enter into competition with it; the greater the threat of this happening, the greater the church's hostility. On the other hand, it is prepared to tolerate what might be called 'harmless superstition'. Superstition is of course a loaded term of immense denotative range, but if we bear that caution in mind it can be used without any particular bias.

In this short discussion, I shall use it to denote a wide range of beliefs which can be harmless or harmful from the point of view of the church. The materials I have assembled here (a small part of work in progress) are drawn from oral sources in Gaelic society, with the focus on Presbyterian communities.[2] In this connection, I do not believe there is any fundamental division between communities of different denominational allegiances: between, say, Roman Catholic and Protestant or between different Protestant denominations. Throughout this spectrum there may indeed be degrees of tolerance and intolerance; or noticeable differences may exist in the evaluation of non-Christian beliefs. And certain individuals everywhere, whatever their denominational background may be, are prepared to interpret these beliefs typologically, as if by extension of the doctrine that events which belong to the Christian dispensation are foreshadowed symbolically in the Old Testament. Indeed, the medieval Gaelic explanation of the existence of the *Sìdhichean* ('fairies' is the common if inadequate translation) has a partial bearing on that process. In essence, the legend runs as follows.

When Lucifer rebelled against God and was driven out of Heaven, those angels who took his side were banished also; those who opposed him are still angels of God; but those who stayed neutral, being judged to be neither good

---

1 A version of this paper entitled 'Supernatural/Preternatural: Faith, Flesh and the Devil', was presented at 'Fantasticall ymaginatiounis': The Supernatural in Scottish History, Literature and Culture Conference, at the University of Strathclyde, Glasgow (1999).
2 See also Michael Newton, ed., *Dùthchas Nan Gàidheal: Selected Essays of John MacInnes* (Edinburgh: Birlinn, 2006).

enough for Heaven nor bad enough for Hell, were sent down to the mountains and remote places of this earth, there to remain until the Day of Judgment.[3] That legend is still known, if not actually believed, throughout Gaelic society.

Some storytellers, professing members of the church, will point out that many of our traditional beliefs are not really mere superstition, but rather that they show how the human imagination retained a grasp, in however dim and distorted a fashion, of processes and events that are fully explicable only in the truth of divine revelation in the Scriptures. Others again, nominal members of the church at least, hold ecclesiastical and non-ecclesiastical beliefs in curious equipoise. It is obvious in many fields of enquiry that human beings can accommodate more than one system of ideas simultaneously in the mind, even if they are in logical terms mutually exclusive. In Gaelic society it was believed that the last person to be buried (or in most accounts the last male) had to take on the duties of the watcher and guardian of the churchyard and was not relieved of his task until the next burial came. A member of the Church of Scotland, a woman in the Isle of Skye, who died some fifty years ago, believed that all the dead in the graveyard were alive, waiting with eager longing until the last of the future generations should join them, whereupon their society would be complete. At the same time, she accepted implicitly the teachings of the church.

In the seventeenth century, the Rev Robert Kirk (1644–92), who published the first complete edition of the Gaelic metrical psalms and organised the publication of the Irish Bible in roman type, believed that a human being has body and soul, as the church teaches, but also an astral counterpart of the physical body, which at the moment of death goes to the dwelling-place of the *Sìdhichean*, the Fairy Knoll or *Sìdhean*.[4] In this respect, Kirk is regarded as something of a maverick clergyman, but he was probably not unique. It is safe to say, given what we know of Gaelic tradition, that the teachings he set out in detail in his *The Secret Common-Wealth of Elves, Faunes and Fairies* (1691) would be perfectly comprehensible to his entire congregation, and perhaps also, though with certain important reservations, to the great majority of the Scottish Gaelic Protestant clergy of his time. Kirk's theories cannot be entirely dissociated from the strongly held belief that every individual has a doppelgänger (known in Gaelic as a *samhla* 'appearance, apparition' or *co-choisiche* 'co-walker'). To the present day, there are those who vehemently deny

---

3 Variations of this story can be found in Alexander Carmichael, *Carmina Gadelica*, 6 vols. (Edinburgh: Oliver and Boyd, 1928–71) vol. 2, 352–3; W. Y. Evans-Wentz, *The Fairy Faith in Celtic Countries* (1911; New York: Citadel Press, 1990) 113; and Earnest W. Marwick, *The Folklore of Orkney and Shetland* (London: B. T. Batsford, 1975) 46.

4 Robert Kirk, *The Secret Common-Wealth*, 1691, ed. Stewart Sanderson (Cambridge: Brewer, 1976) 52, 61; Michael Hunter, ed. *The Occult Laboratory: Magic, Science and Second Sight in Late 17th-century Scotland* (Woodbridge: The Boydell Press, 2001) 77–117.

the existence of ghosts of the dead but nevertheless believe strongly in apparitions of the living. It is worth putting on record, too, that the only individual I have known in the Gaelic community who gave a personal testimony of a vision of the fairies was a dedicated evangelical minister, the late Rev Donald MacLeod of Strath in the Isle of Skye.

We must not, then, so far as the Gaelic society is concerned, try to make a clear-cut distinction between the church and the rest of the community. There are certain beliefs about which all Gaels are at most agnostic, Second Sight being probably the foremost of these. In general, portents and omens, whether experienced by particularly endowed individuals or not, are very rarely dismissed as entirely without substance. At the same time, and running counter to what has been put forward up to now, it has to be emphasised that there are certainly professing Christians who are inclined to believe that some or perhaps all such beliefs are ultimately of the Devil – which emphatically does not make their manifestations unreal. Furthermore, all sections of the church are strongly opposed to any deliberate pursuit of the occult; and that may extend to divination from séances to telling fortunes from tea-cups or even to reading horoscopes in the popular press.

None of this need surprise us: demonisation of pagan deities and the whole gamut of heathenish rites and rituals is a commonplace in the expansion of Christianity. Yet in Gaelic society Christian believers are by and large less hostile to superstition than they are to thorough-going rationalism and atheism. A person whose mind is open to the mysteries of one system, it is argued, is by that token more malleable, more likely to be persuaded into acceptance of the one true faith, than the person who is implacably opposed to any system of belief that is not scientifically established, and to whom all religion is superstition.

The word 'superstition' (derived from Latin *superstitio* 'standing over') has no exact equivalent in Gaelic. The Gaelic terminology has its own clarities and semantic overlaps and ambiguities, but any detailed analysis of those problems would take us beyond the scope of the subject now. I shall only at various points comment briefly on what seems to be the most relevant items.

The nearest to 'superstition' is *geasachd* (with variants such as *geasalachd*, etc.), a generic term of wide connotation ranging from enchantment and augury to the practices of witchcraft, and belief in all such activities. The diminutive or hypocoristic form *geasag* (again, with variants *giseag*, etc.) signifies a particular belief. A person described in English as 'superstitious' would in Gaelic be 'full of *geasagan*' (plural). The linguistic ancestry of this group of words is ancient, going back to pre-Christian times. In medieval Irish literature the term *geis*[5]

---

5 *Dictionary of the Irish Language*, sv. geis (Royal Irish Academy).

has a prominent role as 'a tabu, a prohibition, the infraction of which involved disastrous consequences'. It also has the meaning of 'a positive injunction or demand; something unlawful or forbidden; a wrong; a spell, or incantation'.

In modern Gaelic usage the semantics have been much reduced. *Geasag* for instance can have rather a dismissive ring to it: 'harmless superstition' conveys the idea well enough. But that can certainly not be said of some other terms, which still retain a sinister quality, the most egregious of them expressive of witchcraft and certain forms of divination. It should be added that belief in witchcraft is pervasive and still strongly entrenched in Gaelic society.

The last witch to be put to death in Scotland was burnt at the stake in Dornoch in 1727. This has apparently led to the view that the *Gàidhealtachd* of the Highlands and Islands of Scotland was as notorious for witch-burning, or persecution of witches in general, as the Lowlands. And it would follow that the Gaelic clergy were actively involved in the process. But while there is evidence of clerical hostility to the use of charms and incantations and related activities, the record is strangely silent on more excessive persecution. (The same, incidentally, appears to be the case in Gaelic Ireland.)[6]

The oral tradition presents a somewhat different picture. There are two strains of information. First, almost every traditional storyteller has a story about witches. The majority are concerned with a particular event brought about by witchcraft and often describe how the machinations of witches are brought to nothing. A minority have a dénouement in which punishment is meted out, which may be death by burning. Second, there are less formally structured narratives that comment on the execution of witches (or women who were taken to be witches) as a mere item of information. Frequently there is a connection with cattle. For example, women were observed going into a cattle-fold at dawn or evening twilight (those in-between phases of daylight) in order to strip the cows of their milk. They were denounced as witches, summarily executed, and buried in the liminal site of the entrance to the fold.[7]

Oral tradition seems to be telling us, then, that the killing of witches was as common in the *Gàidhealtachd* as elsewhere. If we accept this as evidence at all, it is, nevertheless, of considerable interest that there is virtually no mention of judicial execution or the active involvement of the church. While ministers may

---

6 See also Lizanne Henderson, 'Witch-hunting and Witch Belief in the *Gàidhealtachd*', in *Witchcraft and Belief in Early Modern Scotland*, ed. Julian Goodare, Lauren Martin and Joyce Miller (Basingstoke: Palgrave MacMillan, 2007) and Edward J. Cowan and Lizanne Henderson, 'The Last of the Witches? The Survival of Scottish Witch Belief', in *The Scottish Witch-Hunt in Context*, ed. Julian Goodare (Manchester: Manchester University Press, 2002) 198–217.
7 From family tradition.

appear as protagonists in the tales, wrestling in prayer, for instance, against the powers of darkness employed by the witches, they do not work in conjunction with secular authorities. Punishment is dealt out by resolute individuals without ecclesiastical assistance.

Paradoxically, in view of the strength of belief in witchcraft, there is no native Gaelic word for a witch. In the past, the canonical term was *amaid*,[8] known in medieval Irish in two senses: 'a woman with supernatural powers, witch, hag, spectre' and secondly 'a foolish woman'. It has survived in Gaelic, but only in the second sense, and even at that is exceedingly rare. The word which displaced it is *buidseach*, the agent noun; *buidseachd*, with regular formation, is the abstract, 'witchery, witchcraft', from English 'witch'. This has important implications. It may mean that at some stage a new kind of 'witch' came into Gaelic society, bringing new practices. Or a new concept of witchcraft, blending with the old and fitting into a pre-existent system, while doubtless modifying it, may have been introduced from England and the Lowlands of Scotland. It may mean only that a new term came into the language, leaving belief and practice unaltered. We cannot really tell. Nor can we tell at what precise stage the word was introduced. Given that the Witchcraft Act of 1563 must have provoked no little discussion, it is reasonable to assume a date in the second half of the sixteenth century or in the early part of the seventeenth. There is at any rate no objection to those dates on phonological grounds.

Buidseach is specifically 'male witch', but in that sense the word (along with its rarer variant *buidsear*) is now largely confined to folktales. The common word is *banabhuidseach* (with feminine prefix). That is to say, the main focus has been on females. But an overall survey makes it clear that the women did not all belong to one homogeneous class. There were healers of humans and animals, counsellors, makers and users of incantations, 'wise women' as well as those who were held to have malign powers: in summary, 'black' and 'white' witches in English terminology. The word *banabhuidseach*, it is clear, has gradually been extended in meaning, and used loosely, so that now, for many people, it covers all those categories and more.

Some of the women may have been the female shamans of Gaelic society. The evidence here is very meagre but one item is of the greatest interest. If news of events at a distance was required – the fate of a human being or that of a missing ship, for instance – a strong-minded, virgin woman of mature years was consulted. She lay down and went to sleep, and while she slept her spirit left her body and sought the missing person or object. Her spirit returned, she woke up and provided the requisite information. But if the wind changed while her spirit

---

8 *Dictionary of the Irish Language*, sv. ammait

was out of the body, she was in peril and might lose her reason. This account is close to descriptions of shamanic trance.

There was also what we might call a 'Christianised' version of this. A woman would lie down to rest, with or without sleep, having previously prayed for divine guidance. On getting up she would go outside and take auguries from the flight of birds or from the appearance and movement of the first living creatures she happened to see. Divination from agencies, Christianised or not, was called making a *frith*. This is a native Gaelic word, not a loan from Norse as it usually claimed in dictionaries and elsewhere. Its basic meaning is 'finding' and the 'find' may be a person or an object, but the word is nowadays known only in this specialised sense in the context of divination and largely confined, it would seem, to parts of the Hebrides. In some eastern mainland dialects, those of Perthshire, for instance, the act of searching is covered by the term for Second Sight.

Although there were indeed male diviners, women seem to have dominated these rituals. At the same time, interpreting – literally 'reading' – the flight and cries of birds was in fact observed by men and women alike. No particular ritual was necessary nor was the exercise identical with making a *frìth*.

From such practices, however, there developed a remarkable transfer of meaning of the word for a flock of birds, *ealta*, with oblique case *ealtain*. In some dialects of Gaelic *ealtain* signifies the skies or the firmament. This is not only secular usage; in its extended meaning *ealtain* was accepted without comment in ecclesiastical contexts as well, so that one could hear it used in evangelical sermons and extempore prayers: for instance in the phrase 'God who created the land and the sea and the heavens above'. This easy assimilation, a smooth transition into Christian worship of a term with ultimately pagan connotations, is probably unique in Gaelic tradition.

There were naturally other activities, even those designed to cure sick animals or human beings, that the Church viewed with suspicion or treated with overt hostility, depending on denominational attitudes. For example, the well-known practice of binding a thread on an injured limb or some other stricken part was not accepted by everyone as merely a harmless, possibly ineffectual, attempt at healing. Indeed, the very term for 'thread' in this context was slightly different from the common word and it carried almost sinister overtones for austere Christians. The curative act was accompanied by arcane incantations, the practitioners were usually women who possessed mysterious powers, and the whole procedure obviously smacked of witchcraft. However, more tolerant believers took such measures to be 'white magic' – although that term is unknown in Gaelic.

In another sphere of activity, not curative but destructive, that of the Evil Eye, it was men who dominated. Even if the Church was disposed to believe that their practices were of the Devil, an important qualification was allowed: the power of the eye was not always exercised out of ill-will or evil intention. Some men were actually believed to be born with a malign ability that could harm animals (though not humans) simply by looking at them. This was true to such an extent that some of them could not stare at their own flocks and herds. And any man who had very deep-set eyes came under suspicion.

There were 'wise men' too. *Fiosaiche*, which can be translated roughly as 'seer', is based on *fios*, 'knowledge, information, etc.' (its Indo-European root connects it with English 'wise, wit', and perhaps indirectly with 'witch' itself). Although there is a feminine counterpart *ban-fhiosaiche*, the masculine is more common in modern Gaelic. No doubt this is because there are a number of male seers who have that appellation in Gaelic tradition, the most outstanding of them being *Coinneach Odhar Fiosaiche*, called in English, though never in Gaelic, 'The Brahan Seer'. It is interesting that his legend makes his birthplace an ancient Christian foundation, Baile na Cille in Uig, Lewis, and that his gift came from the phantom of a dead woman returning to her grave within the consecrated ground of the churchyard. But Christian centres are not uncommonly located in places that had once been sites of pagan worship – which may give a rather different slant to the story.[9] According to traditional lore, the *fiosaiche* has greater control over his visions, than, say, an individual who has Second Sight and whose visions, being involuntary, are rarely welcome.

Obviously Second Sight itself, even if believed in and tolerated, has always been regarded with mixed feelings by the church. A cataclysmic conversion can remove the power completely and permanently; short of that, the use of a Bible merely as a physical object (snapping it shut so that it fans the seer's head, for example) can blank out the vision. And reflective comments on the powers of *fiosaichean* (pl.) — as opposed to anecdotes of their prophecies — are a mixture of admiration and dubiety, for these powers may ultimately be of the Devil.

There is no dubiety at all concerning the most horrific means of divination that we hear about in the whole of Gaelic tradition. This was done as follows. A cat was impaled on a spit and roasted alive. Its cries attracted hordes of other, unearthly cats to the scene. Finally, the master of them all, the Devil himself, appeared in the guise of an enormous cat, who, in order to secure the tortured animal's release, provided the required arcane knowledge or conferred prosperity. This ritual was apparently known as *taghairm*,[10] a term applied also to a couple

---

9 The fact that the phantom was that of a Norse princess may illustrate the belief that preternatural knowledge not infrequently comes from 'other' or 'former' peoples. For more on seers see also John MacInnes, 'The Seer in Gaelic Tradition', in *The Seer in Celtic and Other Traditions* ed. Hilda Ellis Davidson (Edinburgh: John Donald, 1989) 10–24.

10 The word *taghairm* was taken up by the editors of the *Oxford English Dictionary*, with the first citation from Thomas Pennant, *A Tour in Scotland and Voyage to the Hebrides* 1772

of other procedures designed to put the participants in touch with the powers of the otherworld. The word, which is literally a 'calling towards', i.e. 'an invocation, a summons', is probably not a specific designation for the two or three examples we know about,[11] but rather a term for divination in a more extended sense, at least when supernatural agencies were invoked. Although I have heard the ritual described, the word itself seems to be unknown now among genuine oral tradition-bearers. If, as seems likely, the ritual has roots in ancient, pre-Christian ceremony, it has been appropriately demonised within the conceptual framework of Christianity. The Devil takes the part of a pagan deity or some such being. When 'The Great Cat' appears he utters (in Gaelic) the chilling pronouncement: 'Whomsoever I piss upon shall never see the countenance of the Trinity.'[12]

The church of course condemned such practices unequivocally and anyone who indulged in them was threatened with excommunication. Even the terminology associated with the rites could hardly fail to retain a suggestion of menace. Perhaps this helps to explain the absence of the word *taghairm* from conventional Gaelic literature. It is also absent from the Gaelic Bible. There are numerous prohibitions, in the Old Testament in particular, concerning 'divination' where *taghairm* would fit nicely. But even for denunciatory purposes, it was never used. The learned translators, who deployed a copious lexicon, and who must surely have heard of the word, invariably select other terms. *Fiosaiche*, *ban-fhiosaiche*, already commented on; the abstract *fiosachd*; *druidheachd* from *drui(dh)*, 'druid'; and *geasachd*, also noted above, which appears once, are the chosen equivalents of what the English translators represent as diviners, wizards and witches, divination, enchantment, witchcraft, and the like.

The belief in witchcraft, pervasive in Gaelic society, is endorsed by the Biblical texts, with the so-called 'Witch of Endor' as the paradigmatic figure. In fact, she was 'a woman that hath a familiar spirit' (Authorised Version: 1 Samuel, 28.6; 'witch' only appears in a rubric). The Gaelic, however, puts it differently: 'a woman who has a fairy lover'. It seems a curious choice in the context of Old Testament narrative, yet it passes without comment among Gaels to the present day. Since the churchmen could easily have found an alternative to express the

---

(1774–6) although the reference is not to the cat-roasting rite. Since *taghairm* continues to appear in other dictionaries also, to the present day, this may give the erroneous impression that the word is common in Gaelic Literature or even that it is still in use.

11 In one divinatory ritual, the seer was wrapped in a cow's hide (which connects it with poet-seers' rites of seeking inspiration, and less directly with the 'bull-feast' – or perhaps 'bull-sleep' – of ancient Ireland). The other involves divination by water and the spirits of water. Both of these may well be forms of shamanic divination.

12 See also Ronald Black, ed., *The Gaelic Otherworld: John Gregorson Campbell's Superstitions of the Highlands and Islands of Scotland and Witchcraft and Second Sight in the Highlands and Islands* (Edinburgh: Birlinn, 2005) 167–70.

notion of a helping or tutelary spirit, we may well ask what precisely were their motives in settling on this particular term.

In Gaelic oral narrative the fairy lover was, of course, commonplace. All who were able to read the Bible in that age (over two centuries ago), or have it read to them, would be perfectly familiar with legends of fairy lovers. Was it, therefore, no more than the familiarity of the word and concept that made it seem more attractive, more appropriate, than a culturally strange term? Fairies did indeed impart secret information to their human lovers, giving warning perhaps of impending danger. But they could also be malevolent: all trysts with fairies were hazardous undertakings. So with familiar spirits in other cultures.

Obviously this line of enquiry, which I hope to pursue in greater detail elsewhere, poses a number of intriguing questions as well as some problems that translation from one language and culture to another makes inevitable. For the moment, one may suggest that the Gaelic Presbyterian divines accepted the reality of the traditional beliefs of Gaelic society, although probably not quite in the same way as the majority of the laity interpreted them. They could give them credence, acknowledging their potential for good and evil, and fit them without awkwardness into the framework of Christian cosmology. Furthermore, we may offer as a conjecture that they chose their language not only with care but also with a certain degree of diplomacy. Take their use of the words *fiosachd* and *fiosaiche*. *Fiosachd* was not in itself wholly reprehensible: they therefore occasionally qualify it with *bréige*, 'of a lie'; that is, 'false or lying divination'. (After all, one of their own clerical contemporaries, the Rev John Morrison of Petty, who died in 1774, was a notable *fiosaiche*, known in English as 'The Seer of Petty', and his predictions were by no means limited to strictly spiritual experiences.)[13]

But the translators never at all use *buidseachd* or its congeners, although these loan-words were certainly well established in Gaelic when the Scriptures were being translated (from the 1760s to 1800). There is also, however, the question of linguistic and literary register. *Banabhuidseach*, *buidseachd* and the rest are common register words and might have been deemed inappropriate for the dignified style (in part derived from Classical Gaelic) adopted for Holy Writ. Only in the Vulgate translation of the New Testament of 1875, with its more colloquial language, do they appear.

The Evangelical Revival which followed the translation of the Scriptures radically altered the life of Gaelic Presbyterianism. It inspired intense personal devotion and created, or consolidated, a religious cosmology in which all things were made new. That is to say, in a sense it mirrors some of the concepts we

---

13 For more on Morrison see Derick S. Thomson, ed., *The Companion to Gaelic Scotland* (Oxford: Blackwell Reference, 1983) 224.

have touched on; in another sense, it offers a stark contrast to the universe in which traditional 'superstitions' flourished. In the nineteenth century, a noted evangelical leader of the Free Church of Scotland, the Rev Dr. John Kennedy, accepted the existence of Second Sight. But far more certain and demanding of our attention is the mysterious foreknowledge granted to some men and women who are redeemed in Christ. These experiences, he said, are quite different from the direct inspiration of Biblical prophecy: 'And it is to simple and uneducated people, unable to appreciate the standing evidences of the Gospel, we might expect the Lord to give such tokens of His presence . . .'[14]

Kennedy, like other Gaelic ministers, subscribed to the notion of a secular-sacred division, yet appears to see experiences from both sides of the divide as points on an axis of continuity. In this cosmological shift, traditional clairvoyance and divination were not so much set aside and destroyed as converted and sanctified. But the sacred diviners and their audience would vehemently reject the idea that they had Second Sight. That remained secular. The most famous of all clerical sages was the Rev Lachlan MacKenzie (1754–1819); in oral tradition he was occasionally described as having *fiosachd*; far more often he was referred to as *fàidh*: the word used of Biblical prophets.[15]

It is easy to see how a society that unquestioningly accepted preternatural phenomena and accorded seers and soothsayers, men and women alike, social status and prestige, could accommodate the notion that there were specially-gifted individuals within the church as well. At the same time, the existence of social and theological divisions must never be lost sight of.

A word now in passing about the status of women. In Gaelic culture and literary history, the contribution of secular women poets is very striking; so, equally, is that of women poets, especially within the Evangelical Movement, as composers of sacred songs and hymns. And though both groups may have functioned in a male-dominated society, and sometimes been confined by it, their influence has been far from negligible. The clergy could be rebuked by – and stood in awe of – women of strong character and Christian fervour, the most notable of whom was Peggy MacDiarmid in the nineteenth century, known as *Bean a' Chreidimh Mhóir*, 'The Woman of Great Faith'. Women who were seers, counsellors, and healers in earlier ages could be seen as counterparts of those who became luminaries of the church. If there was indeed a tradition of shamanism in Gaelic Scotland, social anthropologists might be tempted to trace continuities which theologians, with equal justification, would deny.

---

14 John Kennedy, *The Days of the Fathers in Ross-shire* (1861; Inverness: Christian Focus, 1979) 157.
15 For more on Lachlan MacKenzie see Kennedy, *The Days of the Fathers in Ross-shire*, 57–66.

There is one particular form of divination within the ecclesiastical community which survives to the present day. A verse of scripture, read or recalled, can give prophetic insight. In Gaelic, the Bible is frequently referred to as 'The Truth'; in the same context, a portion of scripture is 'A Truth'. People say 'X received A Truth' or 'A Truth came to X'. A reader's eye may light upon a particular passage and that communicates a personal message. More often, however, A Truth comes from the store of memory – an enormous amount of the sacred text was, and still is, carried in memory – to a believer's attention, involuntarily and with peremptory power. The recipient may not know immediately what the significance of the scriptural message may be, but sooner or later its import is revealed. Let me give two simple examples.

A family is leaving their community; a woman friend, much distressed, comes to bid farewell. The person addressed receives A Truth: 'Weep not for me, weep for yourselves. . .' (Luke 23:28). Some years after that, the grieving woman was killed tragically.

A boat fails to return to port at its appointed time; all search proves fruitless; it is presumed lost. A Truth comes to a relative of one of the crew: 'The earth shall yield her increase and they shall be safe in their land' (Ezekiel 34:27). It turns out that the boat had been stormbound in a distant harbour and eventually returns safely.

There are many more complex examples with the interpretation involving apparently extraordinary coincidences and synchronicities. They are, of course, nothing of the kind to those who believe in Providence.

There is presumably a continuity here leading back to beliefs and practices in the early church and beyond that to pagan rites. In Roman religion the Sibylline books were consulted for the oracular statement found by chance. Taking the *sortes Virgilianae* continued the tradition: Virgil's *Aeneid* was opened at random and the lines on which the eyes first fell, or on which a finger was placed, were regarded as prophetic. The early Christians followed the practice, for Virgil was honoured as one of those who were 'natural' Christians before the Incarnation. St Augustine, in the fourth century, and other leading churchmen after his time, consulted the Bible in the same way. Although this kind of divination was banned by church councils of the fifth and sixth centuries, the prestige of St Augustine among Protestants and his influence on the theology of Calvin certainly encouraged the practice in Gaelic Presbyterianism. It still surfaces in a variety of Christian denominations from time to time, but nowhere more consistently than in the *Gàidhealtachd* of Scotland. There it is a commonplace of spiritual experience. No matter how many other factors, anthropological and theological, have played a part, the background of belief which we have sketched makes it almost a predictable outcome.

TEN

Lewis Spence: Remembering the Celts

Juliette Wood

Reassessing the past has always been a popular, if somewhat contradictory-sounding, pursuit and the current resurgence of interest in all things Celtic aptly embodies the ambiguities inherent in this Janus-like activity. Inevitably, perhaps, it has created a gap between hopes for a 'created Celtic past' and ideas about historical accuracy and become something of a battleground between historians and popular writers.[1] Lewis Spence embodies these ambiguities very well. A journalist rather than a full-time historian, he wrote during a period when disciplines such as folklore were still in the formative stage. The images of Celtic civilisation he created seem more like utopian blueprints for the future, but what they reveal about society's changing views of itself is well worth studying. In a broader context, these romantic pseudo-traditions have interesting implications for our understanding of changing group identities, and they emphasise, if only by their inaccuracy, the 'constructedness' of so many cultural concepts.[2]

The belief that a mystery religion was practised in pre-Christian Britain has become commonplace in the contemporary image of the Celt. As an idea it incorporates elements of nineteenth-century anthropology, concepts of cultural diffusion and renewed interest in occult subjects. Since the latter half of the twentieth century, it has also absorbed elements from modern revival celebrations and ecological concerns.[3] In the writings of the Scottish journalist and folklorist, Lewis Spence, this rather disparate set of influences created a powerful image of the past which coincided with Spence's view of politics in Scotland and with his interpretation of man's role in culture.[4] Today, Spence's

---

1 Simon James, *The Atlantic Celts: Ancient People or Modern Invention* (London: British Museum Press, 1999); Review by Amy Hale, *Folklore* 111 (2000) 150–52.
2 Edward J. Cowan, *Alba: Celtic Scotland in the Middle Ages* (East Linton: Tuckwell Press, 2000) 1–23.
3 Ronald Hutton, *The Pagan Religions of the Ancient British Isles: their nature and legacy* (Oxford: Blackwell, 1991; reprinted 1995) 141–2; Juliette Wood, 'Secret Traditions in the Modern Tarot: Folklore and the Occult Revival', *3rd Stone Archaeology, Folklore and Myth* 39 (2000/2001) 26–31; Juliette Wood, *Eternal Chalice: the Enduring Legend of the Holy Grail* (London: I.B. Tauris 2008) 96–102.
4 Derrick McClure, *Language Poetry and Nationhood: Scots as a poetic language from 1878*

writings on Celtic religion, which account for about half a dozen books among the more than thirty he wrote, are influential texts for New Age thinking.[5] Spence himself was a fascinating character. Born James Lewis Thomas Chalmers Spence in Broughty Ferry in 1874, he studied at Edinburgh University where he qualified as a dentist, before becoming an editor with *The Scotsman* in 1899. A committed and active proponent for Scottish nationalism, he was a founder member of the National Party of Scotland in 1928. He fought a parliamentary election as a Scottish nationalist candidate, possibly the first to do so. He wrote a number of books on Native American,[6] Inca and Aztec mythology,[7] as well as ancient Egyptian and Mesopotamian culture.[8] There are volumes on the folk narrative traditions of Germany, Spain, and Brittany and an idiosyncratic study of the origins of London folklore.[9] He edited two dictionaries, one on non-classical mythology and one on romance writers and their work,[10] plus an encyclopaedia of the occult which included a substantial amount of Scottish material.[11] His interest in mythology, specifically for what it could reveal about the ancient past and the workings of the human mind, continued throughout his career, and he returned to the subject several times.[12] He was a member

---

    to Present (East Linton: Tuckwell Press, 2000) 52–66; Richard J. Finlay, *Independent and Free: Scottish Politics and the origins of the Scottish National Party 1918-45* (Edinburgh: John Donald, 1994) 38–40.

5 Spence is an important name on many Internet sites devoted to fairies. To cite but one example, the website Witcheye/stuff2 includes notes from individuals citing Spence as significant in their personal experience. Many sites on Atlantis (www2.kenyon.edu) also refer to Spence's work.

6 *Myths and Legends of the North American Indians* (London: G.G. Harrap, 1914).

7 *The Civilisation of Ancient Mexico* (Cambridge: Cambridge University Press, 1910). *The Mythologies of Ancient Mexico and Peru* (London: Archibald Constable, 1907); *The Popul Voh. The Mythic & Heroic Sagas of the Kiches of Central America*, Popular Studies in Mythology, Romance and Folklore (London: David Nutt, 1908); *Myths of Mexico and Peru* (London: Harrap, 1913); *Mexico of the Mexicans* (London: Counties and peoples series, 1917); *The Gods of Mexico* (London: T. F. Unwin, 1923); *The Magic and Mysteries of Mexico or the arcane secrets and occult lore of the ancient Mexicans and Maya* (London: Rider and Sons, 1930); *The Religion of Ancient Mexico* (London: Watts, 1945).

8 *Myths and Legends of Ancient Egypt* (London: Harrap, 1915); *The Mysteries of Egypt, the Secret Rites and Traditions of the Nile* (London: Rider and Sons, 1929); *Myths and Legends of Babylonia and Assyria* (London: G. G. Harrap, 1916).

9 *Hero Tales and Legends of the Rhine* (London: Harrap, 1915); *Legends and Romances of Spain* (London: Harrap, 1920); *Legends and Romances of Brittany* (London: Harrap, 1917); *Legendary London: Early London in Tradition and History* (London: Robert Hale, 1937).

10 *A Dictionary of Non-classical Mythology* (with Marian Edwardes) (London and New York, 1914); *A Dictionary of Medieval Romance and Romance Writers* (London: Routledge and Sons, 1913).

11 *An Encyclopaedia of Occultism* (London: Routledge and Sons, 1920).

12 *An Introduction to Mythology* (London: Harrap, 1921); *The Outlines of Mythology* (London: Watts, 1944); *Myth and Ritual in Dance, Game and Rhyme* (London: Watts, 1947).

of the Scottish Anthropological and Folklore Society,[13] with strong interests in occult philosophy.[14] Although there is no clear evidence that Spence actively participated in any occult practices, he wrote several articles for the *Occult Review*.[15] For him, the occult impulse was a psychic power inherent in human nature, stronger in some cultures and at particular periods, but which could be activated in all people by various means. This was by no means an uncommon view at the time.[16]

Concepts about the nature of the occult and of mystery religion are fundamental to Spence's thinking. By occultism, Spence meant the revelation of hidden wisdom, but a wisdom which included knowledge of eternal truth and true knowledge of science.[17] This attitude characterised deistic interpretations of religion, especially druidic religion, which stretch back at least to the writings of John Toland. It emphasised the individual's capacity for intellectual and religious experience without the intervention (and control) of an elitist priesthood.[18] Somehow, and this is where his arguments become a little strained, the druids were an exclusive group (Spence favoured the terms 'sodality' and 'brotherhood') but at the same time accessible and liberal whose 'philosophy' could be apprehended by all. In Britain, Spence believed, the druids preserved the ancient belief in a cult of the dead which was a type of ancestor worship associated with belief in eternal life to be shared with our forbears in the blessed isle of the West. However druid magic was not originally shamanic. This only happened after breakdown of the old order (under Romans and under Christianity).[19]

Added to the core beliefs about ancestor spirits was the more complex system of beliefs designated in the literature of the time as a mystery religion which centred on the seasonal and vegetative cycle of growth, decay and regeneration. It took as its central myth, the image of a fertility deity who died annually and was reborn with the spring vegetation. In primitive societies the deity was embodied

---

13 According to the *Proceedings of the Scottish Anthropological and Folklore Society* Spence became a member in 1938, just before the ten-year hiatus caused by the war. In 1948 when it began to meet again, he appeared as vice-president, member of the executive committee and chief reviewer. Vol. 1, no.1 (1935) to vol. 5, no. 3. (1955).
14 *Cornelius Agrippa, Occult Philosopher* (London: Rider and Sons, 1939).
15 'Fairy Folk and Second Sight', *The Occult Review* Jan 1939, 11–16; 'The Secret Tradition in Britain: its Sources and Affinities', *The Occult Review* April (1940) 99–103; 'The Arcane Cult of Arthur', July (1940) 145–9; 'Occult Centres of Scotland', *The Occult Review*, October (1940) 196–8.
16 *The Magic Arts in Celtic Britain* (London: Rider and Co., 1945) 7–13.
17 Spence, *Mysteries of Egypt*, 9.
18 Spence outlines this argument a number of times. See, for example, a particularly passionate version in '*Will Europe follow Atlantis?*', 18–20.
19 Spence, *Druids and Druidism*, 12–14, 146–8, 172–8; Ronald Hutton, *Shamans: Siberian Spirituality and the Western Imagination* (London: Hambleton, 133–6).

in the figure of a divine king whose 'death' through sacrifice (either literally, through a substitute, or metaphorically) brought about the continued fertility of the vegetative cycle and, by extension, of the kingdom. '... Broadly speaking, this belief is associated with the idea that in the king, the son of heaven, is enshrined that magical vitality by virtue of which the forces of life in the region under his jurisdiction function regularly and satisfactorily – the growth of vegetation, of the crops, the production of animal life and even the fertility of human beings.'[20] However, in nineteenth and twentieth century contexts, the impulse became a purely metaphoric one. The motifs of death and regeneration became a personal initiation into some ancient system whose secret had been preserved by some disguised or hidden form.[21] The re-instatement of this 'mystery' would have global implications, often as the only way in which to avert an apocalyptic disaster. For Spence the conservators of this mystery were not a cabal (which was certainly the case regarding the historical mystery religions which his books described), rather the 'mystery' which would save mankind was preserved by an untainted Celtic peasant world of fairy belief and second sight. This was the main thesis of several books on mystery religion, which he considered a positive manifestation of these occult impulses, seeing them in Egyptian, Central American[22] and Celtic culture. However, occult knowledge could produce negative effects in human society. These he explored in two short millennial tracts, *The Occult Causes of the Present War* and *Will Europe follow Atlantis?*, and in a full length study of the connection between Atlantis and the practice of the occult.[23] He was convinced of the reality of Atlantis – a position influenced to some extent by his ideas about cultural diffusion – and wrote several books on the subject,[24] and one on Lemuria as well.[25]

20 *The History and Origins of Druidism* (London: Rider and Co, 1945) 13. See also *British Fairy Traditions*, 53–64, 84–95; *Second Sight*, 159–72.
21 The scope of this paper is limited to the work of Lewis Spence. However, the transformation of ideas on divine kingship into contemporary rituals can be found in the writing of a number of late Victorian and Edwardian writers, among them W. Y. Evans Wentz, Margaret Murray, Jessie Weston, A. E. Waite and Aleister Crowley. Some of them influenced Spence and vice versa, but the broader development of these ideas and, in particular their contemporary ramifications would need further study.
22 Spence, *Civilisation of Mexico*, 49, describes a god-substitute being sacrificed, but instances of this are spread throughout the books, see also *Magic Arts in Celtic Britain*, 115–20.
23 *Will Europe follow Atlantis?* (London: Rider and Sons, 1942); *The Occult Causes of the Present War* (London: Rider and Sons, 1940); *The Occult Sciences in Atlantis* (London: Rider and Sons, 1943).
24 *The Problem of Atlantis* (London: Harrap, 1924); *Atlantis in America* (London: E. Benn, 1925); *The History of Atlantis* (London: Rider and Sons, 1926); *The Occult Sciences in Atlantis*.
25 *The Problem of Lemuria, the sunken continent in the Pacific* (London: Rider and Sons, 1932).

The sum total of his political pamphlets, plays and journalistic writings is enormous.[26] He edited the writings of his friend, the art and literary critic, Blaikie Murdoch,[27] and wrote poetry, short stories, and a popular biography of William Wallace.[28] Often his poetry and short stories drew on Scottish subjects. Spence was attracted to 'the strange remoteness of the ballads and of Celtic poetry, that "otherwhereness" so characteristic of the weird and supernaturally beautiful Scottish verse of the past'.[29] Several poems are written in Scots (more specifically a revived version of it), while many other poems employ vaguely medieval devices as a kind of ornamental conceit. For example, the title of the poem 'Le Roi D'Ys' refers to the famous version of the drowned city legend in Brittany, but it has as its subject a young king called 'Paragon' whose story of shipwreck on a mysterious island is frankly more like an Arabian Night's tale than a Celtic one. His short stories incorporated motifs from Scottish history. *The Archer in the Arras* is a tale of magical revenge in the manner of M. R. James and, although set in France, incorporates the murderous statue with a crossbow which features in the Scottish chronicle account of the death of Kenneth II.[30] The use of revived Scots as a language is embedded in the literary and national renaissance of the twentieth century. The Scots poetry which Spence (and other writers at this time) imitated was associated with the idea of a free and independent Scotland under the Stuart kings whose literature acquired a symbolic value as that of a free people.[31] It would be unfair to give too negative a view of Spence's output. He had his moments. Scotland provided an important image for Italy during the Risorgimento, and this image had a political as well as a romantic dimension. Spence recognised this in the preface to his biography of

26 Many of these publications reflected his strong Scots identity and his interest in its past. For example *Roman Cramond* (Cramond, 1950), David Grant, *A Fengside Fairytale* with an Introduction by Lewis Spence (Aberdeen: Bon Accord Press, 1937), 'Programme for a Masque depicting the life work and times of the Scottish poet William Dunbar', performed in Edinburgh on 13 June 1933; See National Library of Scotland, Inventory of Manuscripts Acc.5916.
27 Lewis Spence, ed., *W. G. Blaikie Murdoch, Man of Art, Man of letters: Selections from his essays on art and literature* (Edinburgh: Gray, 1935).
28 *Le Roi D'Ys* (London: Vigo Cabinet Series, 1910); *Songs Satanic and Celestial* (1913); *The Phoenix and Other Poems* (Edinburgh: Porpoise Press, 1923); *Plumes of Time* (London: Allen and Unwin, 1926); *Weirds and Vanities* (Edinburgh: Porpoise Press, 1927); *Collected Poems* (Edinburgh: Serif books, 1953); *The Archer in the Arras and Other Tales of Mystery* (Edinburgh: Grant and Murray, 1932); *The Story of William Wallace*, 'Little Stories of Great Lives' (London, 1919).
29 Spence quoted by McClure, 60.
30 Juliette Wood, 'Folkloric Patterns in Scottish Chronicles', in *The Rose and the Thistle*, ed. Sally Mapstone and Juliette Wood (East Linton: Tuckwell Press, 1998) 120–3; *The Archer in the Arras*, 9–14.
31 McClure, chapter 4, 53–66.

William Wallace which quoted both Mazzini and Garibaldi.[32] He often had these startling perceptions, but never really worked through them, and unfortunately this very lively, but quirky, intellect became more rigid with time.

The books most frequently read and reprinted are those Spence wrote on supernatural aspects of Celtic culture. These date from the latter period of his writing and draw together many of his interests.[33] For Spence the Celts represented the last vestige of an ancient strain of culture whose belief systems combined a complex idea of divine kingship and ancestor worship.[34] If Scots provided a focus for national sentiment, Celtic provided the moral structure. Reverence for the past could regenerate personal as well as political life.

An initial impression of Spence's list of publications suggests a somewhat bizarre intellect, but his interests were not quite so quixotic as they seem. His early books attempted to articulate the essence of 'New World' and ancient cultures by looking at their mythology and applying what were then current techniques of anthropology and folklore. At this time he wrote several popular accounts of folklore in Germany, Spain and Brittany which combined travelogue descriptions interspersed with summaries of narratives. During the 1920s he began to write on Atlantis, suggesting that certain cultural features found on the European and American continents dated back to a common (and now drowned) predecessor. His interest in occult subjects dated from an early period, but the two fused in the two millennial tracts which he wrote during the First and Second World Wars, *The Occult Causes of the Present War* and *Will Europe follow Atlantis?* In many ways his national consciousness drove his other interests, and he maintained a lifelong dedication to Scottish national politics until his death in 1955. It is only when he discussed the occult and the War, or the links between the fate of Atlantis and European history that his writing went over the top. In regards to the former he was jingoistic, anti-German and took the position that National Socialism was the result of the misuse of occult power.[35] He believed Atlantis was destroyed because it misused the occult arts, but that the 'good' Atlanteans who escaped were the source of Cro-Magnon culture in Europe, a culture that the Celts ultimately inherited. Writing at the opening of the Second World War, Spence was convinced that only the revival

---

32 Spence, *Wallace*, 3–4.
33 *The Mysteries of Britain* (London: Rider and Sons, 1928); *Boadicea, Warrior Queen of the Britons* (London: Robert Hale, 1937); *The Magic Arts in Celtic Britain* (London: Rider and Sons, 1945); *British Fairy Origins* (London: Watts and Co., 1946); *The Fairy Tradition in Britain* (London: Rider and Sons, 1948); *The Minor Traditions of British Mythology* (London: Rider and Co., 1948); *The History and Origins of Druidism* (London: Rider and Sons, 1949); *Second Sight, Its History and Origins* (London: Rider and Sons, 1951).
34 Spence, *The History of Atlantis*, 195–200.
35 Spence, *Will Europe follow Atlantis?*, 17–18.

of Celtic religion (a legacy of Atlantis) would turn back the tide of the 'dark Germanic cultus' and save Europe.[36] The message of 'repent and be saved' is inherent in this genre, and Spence followed a long line of writers who used the image of a failed utopia to draw attention to shortcomings in contemporary civilisation.

When Spence was not riding these hobby horses, he was a lucid writer, although Richard Finlay, in his analysis of Scottish nationalism, suggested that he was inclined to see 'secret conspiracies' everywhere.[37] There is some truth in this, but the bulk of Spence's writing, even on such unorthodox subjects as Atlantis, is closer to the classical tradition of persuasive rhetoric than to paranoid conspiracy prose. He marshalled his proof, however eccentric, and drew his conclusions, however bizarre, in a logical and ordered way. The most effective way to destroy a hypothesis, he tells us in a book on Lemuria, 'is to advance it dogmatically and in that manner of pompous assurance and intolerance for the views of others which compares so evilly with the attitude of honest conviction.'[38] This pious and worthy position was sometimes more in the breach than in the observance, as, for example, when he interpreted the Lion and the Unicorn on the British arms as a survival of the Great Goddess, by linking the lion to Cybele and the unicorn's horn to the crescent moon![39] His consistent attempt at clarity and persuasion, however, are worth noting because many writers in this area became so emotionally tangled in what they were saying as to be almost incoherent. A. E. Waite wrote about many of the same topics as Spence, and influenced the latter's notion of mysticism and the meaning of the Grail, but Waite's prose is often impossibly dense.[40] Spence read very widely and was very catholic in his use of sources. If anything he was a little too readily influenced, and ultimately he is more interesting as an illustration of the mixture of nationalism, occult belief and the appropriation of Celtic culture as a paradigm for social harmony, than for any lasting contribution to the fields in which he wrote. However it is this very mixture which makes him so important for the creation of the Celtic past.

There is no single influence which characterised Spence's writing or the development of his ideas. His commitment to the cause of Scottish nationalism, and his interpretation of Scottish heritage formed the background to his folklore books. Many of his more extreme positions fit into this framework, even if they never quite convince. At the beginning of the 1920s, some members of the newly-

36 Spence, *Will Europe follow Atlantis?*, 167–85.
37 Finlay, *Independent and Free*, 46–7.
38 Spence, *The Problem of Lemuria*, preface 7.
39 Spence, *Myth and Ritual in Dance, Game and Rhyme*, 188–9.
40 A. E. Waite. *The Hidden Church of the Holy Grail* (London: Rebman, 1909).

formed Scots National League, and Spence was among them, viewed the pre-Union history of Scotland as a struggle between a democratic, progressive and *Celtic* people on the one hand, and an authoritarian, imperialist Teutonic people on the other. They argued for the re-interpretation of Scottish history especially during the Celtic period. This romantic 'Celticism' provided a paradigm which accounted for the differences between the Scots and the English. Celtic language, culture and attitudes were defined as quintessentially Scots, and those aspects of Scottish culture which had become tinged with 'Anglo-Saxon Teutonism' were rejected. His pamphlet *The English Peril in Scotland* (1922) accused the Saxons (i.e. English) of attempting to colonise Scotland.[41] Leaving aside the rather simplistic racial typing and the fact that 'Celtic' was being applied to medieval Scottish history,[42] Spence, and others, advocated the idea that Scottish national Celticism would act as a regenerative force to transform and save the British nation.[43] The idea that the British character combined both Anglo-Saxon and Celtic racial characteristics was not new. Matthew Arnold had used this distinction in his brand of romantic Celticism, seeing the Celts as the source of the imaginative impulse in the British nation while the Saxons supplied the logic. In a specifically Scottish context, Skene's *Celtic Scotland* had suggested much the same thing.[44]

Spengler's pessimistic view of western history made a strong impact on some early Scottish nationalists. Lewis Spence was one of them. Under the influence of Spengler's *Decline of the West* which had been available in English since the early 1930s, his tone became one of moral fervour which later seemed to find a reality in his hatred of German national socialism. 'We must re-establish our noble, Celtic ideas in place of Teutonic Kultus and its military despotism now trying to rule our nations'.[45] His later writings called for a Celtic revival as a way to reverse the moral decline of Europe, but his earlier work showed extensive reading in archaeology, anthropology and folklore. The last provided the ideas and the methodology through which Spence attempted to reveal and restore the idea of sacred kingship and mystery religion. The influence of Frazer and Hocart and Cook were important in forming his ideas about kingship and ritual, while John Rhys and D'Arbois de Jubainville provided the mainstay on Celtic culture.[46] His approach to folklore drew on ideas found in

41 Finlay, *Independent and Free*, 35–9, 45.
42 Cowan, *Alba*, 4.
43 Finlay, *Independent and Free*, 38–40.
44 Cowan, *Alba*, 1–4.
45 Finlay, *Independent and Free*, 40, 68 n.2.
46 Although the bibliographies in any of Spence's books are extensive, he relied heavily on a small number of thinkers for his theoretical material. James Frazer, himself, repeatedly makes reference to John Rhys, *Hibbert Lectures*, and H. D'Arbois de Jubainville, *Les Druids*, in J. G. Frazer's *Golden Bough*, especially The Magic Art Vol. II.

the writings of Alfred Nutt and Lawrence Gomme. These two folklorists, both leading lights of the Folklore Society at the end of the nineteenth century, were advocating ideas of cultural diffusion somewhat against the prevailing trend of cultural evolution and savage survival.[47] Even at the earliest period in his writings, 1914–18, these syncretic and highly speculative theories were already giving way, in anthropology and archaeology, to field studies and, in the field of folklore theory, to the historic, geographic research. The effect of this in a specifically Scottish context can be seen in the journal of the Scottish Anthropological and Folklore Society. During the presidency of Herbert J. Rose, the articles and lectures were mainly concerned with the origins of culture and religion. Margaret Murray, for example, spoke to the society about her theory of Neolithic religion in 1948. Once Kenneth Jackson's influence began to be felt in the 1950s however, the speakers and articles veered more towards collecting and analysis.[48] What characterised Spence, and many of the writers of this period who have become important for the contemporary pagan and Celtic revivals, was their willingness to move beyond speculation and to seek concrete contemporary reality for theories such as divine kingship. Margaret Murray, who is often quoted by Spence and whose re-issued title he reviewed in *Proceedings,* is indicative of the direction the more popular writers were heading.[49] Spence is at his most interesting theoretically at the early stages of his folklore writing, but he never really moved on and was still using the same theoretical models in the 1950s at the end of his career.

In 1915 he produced a popular illustrated account of the *Hero-Tales and Legends of the Rhine*. This is one of three such travelogue-cum-folk narrative books; the other two are on Spain and Brittany. His attitude to Germanic tradition here is much less antagonistic. Basically this is a jolly travelogue on the Rhine with stories at every turn. He contrasts Teutonic mystery with Celtic glamour and Egyptian gloom and calls it a thing of shadow and ponderous fantasy, but there is none of the threatening Germanic darkness he finds later in the tracts he wrote during the Second World War.[50] However, the attitudes to culture that would later infuse his call for the revival of Celtic religion were implicit as early as 1912 in one of several books on Mexican culture. He focused on the ideas of divine kingship and godhead linked to the cycle of vegetative growth.[51] Spence believed in a universal mythology which underpinned religion, but accepted

---

47 Richard Dorson, *The British Folklorists: A History* (Chicago: University of Chicago Press, 1968) 220–9.
48 *Proceedings of the Scottish Anthropological and Folklore Society.*
49 Spence's review of Murray's *God of the Witches*, vol. 5, no. 1 (1954) 46.
50 *Hero Tales*, preface 179.
51 *Civilisation of Mexico*, 44.9.

that in the New World, traditions differed from those of Europe. Equally clear is his tendency to draw a moral lesson from history à la Spengler.

> That a faith so virile, so ancient so entrenched in the love of a people as that of Babylonia should fall into an oblivion . . . is a solemn and impressive reminder of the evanescent character of human affairs . . . Must our civilisation . . . fade into the shadow . . . the answer . . . depends upon ourselves. If we quit ourselves as civilised men . . . though the things of our hand may be dust, the works of our minds of our souls shall not vanish but shall remain in the consciousness of our descendants so long as human memory lasts. The faith of ancient Babylon went under because it was built rather on the worship of frail and bestial gods than love of truth.[52]

Spence habitually wrote charmingly disingenuous prefaces to his books using his version of the modesty topos which reflected the classical models of rhetoric which he esteemed so highly.[53] In the absence of a real expert, he listed his own limited qualifications, although never so limited that he is not confident of his subject. Even in his popular books, his prefaces, despite the apparent modesty, were keen to set out his credentials. For his works on Egyptian culture, he laid claim to expertise and familiarity with hieroglyphics,[54] but when he started to write on Celtic subjects, he presented himself quite differently. He admitted that his knowledge of the language consisted of 'extensive lists of words in the modern dialects' but, and he stated this vigorously, he was a Celt and that was sufficient.[55] Spence began writing on Atlantis in the 1920s, and at this point various elements in his thinking began to coalesce. Atlantis provided a context in which Spence could historicise the ideas embodied in Frazer's study of the dying god and divine kingship. Here he could locate a cult administered by a priestly caste and centred on a divine king, which viewed the growth of crops as symbolic of bodily resurrection.[56] For him it provided a link between the New World mythologies of Incas, Aztecs and native Americans, and the Old World Egyptian and Celtic traditions with which he identified. According to Spence, waves of immigrants from Atlantis

---

52 *Myths of Babylonia And Assyria*, 378–9.
53 *Babylonia and Assyria*, preface 5–6, 299.
54 *Myths and Legends of Ancient Egypt*. The preface is keen to indicate his familiarity with hieroglyphics. Andrew Lang (for the survival theory) James Frazer (for the central religious ritual of Egypt) are quoted as authoritative. These he reviewed in the light of the science of modern mythology.
55 *The Magic Arts in Celtic Britain*, preface iii–iv.
56 *The History of Atlantis*, 87–100; 145–59.

entered Europe by way of North Africa. Egyptian civilisation passing on occult mystery religions to the Greeks was one result, while other Atlantean immigrants moved North to Spain where they became the dark Iberians who brought the druid cult to Celtic Britain.

Most of his Celtic writings date from the 1940s and by this time the cultural implications of the Atlantean immigration had become more refined. The earlier, darker Iberian type brought the cult of ancestor worship. The taller, fairer Celts were later bands of immigrants, a warrior elite. Atlantis provided a neat device by which Spence excluded anything 'oriental' (in particular anything Teutonic).

> When we come to distinguish between the systems of the Teuton and the Briton we discover so sharp a difference in imaginative quality and idealistic propensity as reveals the immense superiority of British legend as a donation to humanity. British lore has a beneficent complexion. In Germanic folklore it is rather exceptional to encounter a supernatural figure of benevolent propensity.[57]

By employing a diffusionist model, he explained away anything unpleasant as late corruption, such as cannibalism among the Aztecs or human sacrifice among the druids.[58] He saw the Celts as the quintessential inheritors of the Atlantean tradition.

Spence's study of Boudicca (whom he insisted on calling Boadicea) is interesting as an early modern study of the Queen of the Iceni, but, more tellingly, it illustrates how Spence's cultural interests became more and more politicised. He saw Boudicca as typifying Celtic womanhood, a member of a culture where men and women were treated as equals and individual human life respected.[59] This romantic view of the warrior queen contrasted supposed Celtic gender tolerance with Germanic culture where men dominated women and people were enslaved. It recalls some of the notions of 'Celtic communism' which characterised aspects of nationalist thinking in Scotland.[60] There are of course, problems with this approach, since the massacres depicted in the classical accounts of Boudicca's story are not the best examples of human tolerance. Spence, however, offered an archaeological justification for the violence by suggesting that the Belgae were a mix of Gaulish (i.e. pure Celtic) tribes and La Tene invaders ominously described as 'half Celtic, half Teutonic

---

57 *Minor Traditions*.
58 *Magic Arts in Celtic Britain*, 126–7; *History of Atlantis*, 97–100.
59 *Boadicea*, 44–7.
60 Finlay, *Independent and Free*, 35–6, Occult causes, 56.

whose ancestors met and mingled on the lower Rhine'. The idea is still present in popular studies, but not elsewhere.[61]

His ideas about second sight, druids and fairy traditions form the core of his thinking. For him, they were intrinsically related and provided irrefutable proof for his theories. His study of Second Sight contains a great deal of first hand information and is a thorough search of the Scottish sources available in English. As always he is thorough and perceptive as far as he goes. He noted, for example, similarities between some second sight experiences and various witchcraft and fairy traditions.[62] Witchcraft, for example, was the survival of an Aurignacian cult of nature worship.[63] However the conclusions looked beyond the contemporary phenomena to the survival of a stone age cult in which a primitive religious priesthood used trance techniques to contact ancestor spirits (what today goes under the name of shamanism).[64] 'What we call Second Sight was a species of supernormal vision latent in man sometimes induced by fasting and other causes in which certain people more disposed to such vision than the generality of folk actually beheld such apparitions ... an art definitely cultivated by a priestly sodality of a shamanistic type associated with the worship of ancestral spirits'. According to Spence, the ancient spirit guides invoked in these rituals became known as the fairies, and this very primitive cult was eventually absorbed into the druid religion.[65] On the actual nature of second sight Spence was less clear, but it was linked in his mind with his belief, a belief he shared with his friend and fellow writer on matters Celtic, W. Y. Evans Wentz, in mankind's potential for spiritual and moral goodness.[66]

Not surprisingly Spence thought that second sight was a disappearing phenomenon and that its present form was a somewhat debased remnant of what it had been in the heyday of Celtic culture.

> The alteration appears to have consisted chiefly in a departure from the use of the sight as it related to matters of high policy connected with the fortunes of the tribe, and its employment for the baser purposes of mere personal 'fortune-telling' by priests robbed by an invading faith of their long-continued ascendancy as tribal augurs.[67]

---

61 Peter Beresford Ellis, *Celtic Women: Women in Celtic Society and Literature* (Constable and Robinson, 1995) 135. Christianity accelerated the decline of the status of women in Celtic society. D. R. Dudley and G. Webster, *The Rebellion of Boudicca* (London and New York: Routledge and Kegan Paul, 1962).
62 *British Fairy Traditions*, 66–7.
63 *Atlantis in America*, 122–3.
64 *Second Sight*, 165.
65 Spence, *Second Sight*, 162–6.
66 *Second Sight*, 460–86, 170. Spence discusses the theories of W. Y. Evans Wentz in some detail.
67 Spence, *Second Sight*, 170–1.

Spence drew many ideas about pagan Celtic religion from John Rhys and Alfred Nutt. But unlike them, these were not just speculations on the origin of culture, rather this was an attempt to find modern survivals of an ancient religious system and through these modern survivals re-establish ancient certainties. There were nationalist implications, as well, for the ethnic groups defined by these theories. Spence believed he could call back a past in Scotland when it had been part of a Celtic unity and even trace its heritage back through Cro-Magnon man to Atlantis. 'If a patriotic Scotsman may be pardoned the boast, I may say that I devoutly believe that Scotland's admitted superiority in the mental and spiritual spheres springs almost entirely from the preponderant degree of Cro-Magnon blood which certainly runs in the veins of her people.'[68] The moral and religious certainties of the past had not died. They survived in the world of popular belief.

However one more element was needed to complete the link between current folk traditions and the mystery religions of the past. Spence believed that only by reviving the practice of Celtic magic could mankind hope to escape the ultimate fate of Atlantis, and central to Celtic religion was a mystic vessel known as the Holy Grail of Arthurian literature. The Grail, Atlantis and the fairies may seem bizarre bedfellows, but the theory becomes at least comprehensible (although perhaps not convincing) if one understands the sources. Spence combined his belief that the western European culture had an ancient pedigree that distinguished it from anything 'oriental' (by which he meant anything north of ancient Greece except ancient Gaul).

> Atlanteans have been proved by the labours of archaeologists to have been of a physical type superior to any at present existing to have possessed that greater cranial capacity which is the undoubted mark of distinguished mental ability ... the first wave of the Atlantean race, the Cro-Magnons, were instrumental in bringing to European soil the seeds of its present civilisation, and, ... this culture progressed not from East to West, as has been asserted so frequently and with such blind and positive dogmatism, but from West to East.[69]

This alternative view of history looked west instead of east for cultural origins. Spence linked A. E. Waite's speculation on the Grail as the non-corporeal endpoint for this mystical search with Alfred Nutt's suggestion that it was a cult object among the Celts. The idea that the Grail provided occult experience

---

68 *The Problem of Atlantis*, 230.
69 *The Problem of Atlantis*, 230.

of the divine, open to ordinary men, was merged with assumptions about the Celtic nature of the Arthurian cycle and produced a neat and tidy origin for Celtic mystery religion. It also reflected the notion that the occult (i.e. mystic) impulse in man was a protest against the manipulations of orthodox religion. Never one to shy away from the absolute, Spence declared that the 'whole of European mysticism and much of European occultism is a protest'.[70] The result of linking occult theory with folklore and anthropological speculation produced a Celtic mystery religion, and the pivotal point was a mystic experience, expressed through the metaphor of a divine king and a cult vessel.

> Arthur was one of the central figures of the great British cult of the dead, the British Osiris, who was associated with the drama and ritual of agriculture and of war and who 'died' ritually with each succeeding Winter . . . as time went on . . . arcane idealism took the place of mere mechanical and mimetic ritual.[71]

Spence localised this ideal of kingship linked to nature cycles in the ancient harmonious world in Atlantis. By applying diffusionist principles, although not very rigorously, he found this myth in all the civilisations with which he felt a kinship, namely Celts, Egyptians, Aztecs, Mayans and native North Americans, and he managed to exclude it from those civilisations of which he disapproved. In Britain this

> military and arcane Arthurian cultus had for its purpose the preservation and maintenance of the sacred isle of Britain from destruction by the invading barbarians from the North and from Germany. Also the conservation of British ideals and civilisation and the cherishing of that Secret British Celtic Tradition which had flourished in our island from time immemorial. Central to that cult was an arcane initiation in the underworld preserved in poems such as the Spoils of Annwn, the motif of the Cauldron of Inspiration and eventually in the context of Christian chivalry, the Holy Grail.[72]

As this civilisation decayed and corrupted just as Spengler predicted, the survivors of Atlantis were absorbed into other civilisations, and the Celts inherited this ancient mystery religion which was not lost but went underground

---

70 *Will Europe follow Atlantis*, 18–19, 160, 166–85.
71 'The Secret Tradition in Britain, Its sources and Affinities', *Occult Review* 99–103.
72 'Arcane Cult', *Occult Review* 146–7.

to escape the domination of Normans and Anglo-Saxons (i.e. Germanic) conquerors. Spence drew a parallel between the position of the Atlantean Celts and the present position of Britain at the beginning of the Second World War. Both were facing a choice between decadence and salvation. The Holy Grail, the centre piece of an ancient Celtic Atlantean mystery religion according to Spence, became the means to save the world.

Atlantis has become something of a joke, but when the theory of plate tectonics was relatively new, the possibility of a sunken continent was less absurd. Nutt speculated on the subject, so did D'Arbois de Jubainville.[73] Spence, however, took the problem into a more political register or rather combined it with the political moral lesson which was a part of the classical Atlantean fables. He not only saw elements of Celtic tradition as survivals of Atlantean civilisation, but claimed they introduced the worship of nature and natural forces; the prototype of ancient mysteries which in his opinion, influenced the practice of all mystical societies to the present day. For Spence it was the druid priesthood who preserved the ancient belief. One can still observe the reverberations of this in attitudes to the Templars, Masons, etc. and the general interest in anything which can be classified as shamanism. This preference for highly poetic concepts of mythology has been a feature of the Celtic revival since the second half of the twentieth century. It is a tradition which lies between didactic and academic views of history, or to put it another way, between a sacred or a secular view of history. Part of the attraction of this approach is that a system of complex myths, beliefs and rituals aimed at benefiting a highly-valued society, such as the Egyptian or Celtic or Atlantean becomes attainable once again to those who can open their hearts and minds.

Spence never really achieved a coherent theory, rather he endlessly (and somewhat repetitively) combined bits and pieces of theories. It is an emotional and vigorous position. He addresses the reader passionately and emotionally as a proud and loyal Scot[74] and for the most part he presented an imaginative vision of Celtic nationalism. He saw patriotism in religious terms. As, for example, in the introduction to Wallace's biography in 1919. 'In olden days the land they lived in was sacred to them, and to defend it was a part of their religion. Their patriotism and their faith were as one.'[75] And he sees his particular brand of patriotism in other cultures he admires. For example, the Mexican revolution was a fight 'for the possession and free exercise of that liberty towards which the spirit of man in all climes and ages had so painfully yet so persistently aspired.'[76]

73 *Atlantis In America*, 24–5.
74 McClure, *Language Poetry and Nationhood*, 64–5.
75 Spence, *Wallace*.
76 *Civilisation of Mexico*, iii.

His rhetoric harks back to the libralism of the French Revolution rather than the religion of the ancient Celts, and his contemporaries noted that he was good-hearted if politically naïve.[77] For him the Celts encapsulated first in a Scottish, then in a European and ultimately in a global context, the qualities of Egyptian and New World culture, and the revival of Celtic religion would somehow magically make things right.

> Even yet does it (the Arthurian myth) serve that grave and good purpose more chivalrously than ever as a beacon to British spirituality for the maintenance of a great Commonwealth founded on truth and justice, an Empire which shall continue under God's grace to illumine the world out of that vessel of the inspiration of righteousness the ideal of which was conceived in the first freshness of time's dayspring.[78]

---

77 Finlay, *Independent and Free*, 51–3, 73–5, 80–1.
78 'The Arcane cult of Arthur', *Occult Review*, 149.

ELEVEN

The Wicker Man: Virgin Sacrifice in Dumfries and Galloway[1]

Valentina Bold

The aboriginal inhabitants of . . . stern and wild Caledonia . . . [brought] from the East . . . their reverence for Baal. Fire was his earthly symbol, and from his name, Baal, Lord, and the Celtic *tein*, fire, comes Beltane . . .[2]

The rites were the same in North Britain as in Tophet, the Valley of Slaughter, when the Lord complained they broke the law . . . The Druids . . . decreed that a huge wicker cage in the form of a colossal mortal should be woven, and in it were cast a holocaust of human victims. These were not only prisoners . . . parents gave their best beloved. Rude music made by striking tightly-stretched hides deadened their dolorous cries. When they had thus paid sanguinary homage to their god, when the lurid flames, lit in his honour, had devoured the giant cageful of their choicest and fairest, the assembled company held high revel, danced and caroused.[3]

This sensational, judgemental account of Caledonia – at once 'stern' and 'wild' – is typical of the highly speculative, pagan survivalist studies of traditional customs, which were common from the eighteenth century onwards. *The Wicker Man*, a film first released in 1973, both flirts with, and subverts, this type of alarmist, and alarming, folklore.

The film, initially, showed as a B feature, and was neither widely successful nor well distributed; it was pulled, for instance, from the Cannes film festival – despite a Wicker Man erected on the sea front there. The 1977 review of the film in the American science fiction magazine *Cinefantastique* is widely credited

---

1 A version of this paper was delivered as an introductory talk to a showing of *The Wicker Man* at The Robert Burns Film Theatre, Dumfries, in 1999.
2 Eve Blantyre Simpson, *Folk Lore in Lowland Scotland* (1908; London: EP Publishing, 1976) 1–3.
3 Simpson, *Folk Lore in Lowland Scotland*, 4–5. Since this chapter was first written, of course, there has been a newer version of the film: 2006, dir. Neil LaBute, and starring Nicholas Cage; here, I am discussing solely the 1973 first version.

with turning round the film's fortunes and encouraging its wider showing; now, of course, it has become a cult classic.[4]

The Wicker Man, as is widely known, was filmed in Galloway, and the timeless qualities and perceived remoteness of this area is a major factor in the film's success. In the 1998 Ex-S documentary, celebrating the 25th anniversary of the first release, Edward Woodward commented, 'This is a timewarp . . . We shot this 25 years ago . . . and nothing's altered'.[5] It does look superficially the same, and there are still stumps of wood visible from the film's climactic scene. The enduring beauty of this area is one of the most appealing aspects of the film. As two American fans commented in the documentary, 'We're going to visit the West Highlands or the West wherever the hell it is, we're going to check that out'.

The setting is an amalgam of real Galloway places: Burrowhead, with its schoolhouse; the streets of Kirkcudbright; the pub in Creetown where, to quote Woodward again, 'the best scenes in the movie' were shot. Logan Botanical Gardens were used for the gardens of the Big House and Gatehouse of Fleet also features.

A large part of *The Wicker Man*'s success is due to imaginative casting. Woodward was chosen as a 'box office name': television's Callan. He represents an anti-establishment 'different kind of detective'. This was reshaped into the role of, to quote the director Robin Hardy, the 'Virgin Christian copper' Sergeant Neil Howie of the West Highland Police. Howie is a target for fun from early on but, ultimately, achieves dignity. Britt Eckland as the physically-pliable and manipulative Willow is the perfect foil to Woodward, and, again, 'box office'. Even so, a Galloway body double, Jane Jackson stood in for intimate scenes. Miss Peter, a Soho stripper, doubled for Eckland during the erotically-charged 'Willow's Song'. The choreographer, Stewart Hopps, was disappointed as he had hoped for 'a very magical dance . . . luring him' and instead he got 'bump and grind'. Christopher Lee was cast to subvert audience expectations, as an 'icon of the great Hammer films . . . we thought it would be wonderful to take him from that sort of horror film and put him in something quite as scary but not, perhaps, as hackneyed'. Lee was eager to be involved, recallling 'the part was

---

4 On the history of the film and its reception see the following publications, which post-date this chapter's writing: Benjamin Franks *et al.* (eds), *The Quest for the Wicker Man: Historical, Folklore and Pagan Perspectives* (Edinburgh: Luath Press, 2006); Jonathan Murray *et al.* (eds), *Constructing the Wicker Man: Film and Cultural Studies Perspectives* (University of Glasgow Crichton Publications, 2005); Allan Brown, *Inside the Wicker Man: The Morbid Ingenuities* (London: Sidgwick and Jackson, 2000).
5 *Ex-S The Wicker Man* PSMM53SD (16/12/98) Series Editor May Millar, Director Simon Parsons. Since this chapter was written, the Wicker Man festival has become a fixture of the Scottish music festival scene. See http://www.thewickermanfestival.co.uk/ for further information.

written for me and that doesn't happen very often ... when you've got an author of the calibre of Shaffer what more can you ask for?'

The screenplay, by Anthony Shaffer, is a cumulatively terrifying experience. Shaffer sought to go beyond the Hammer model, to explore 'the origins of this sort of black arts which really was a perfectly straightforward Celtic religion that all of us who live in the British Isles once had'. A Stukeley engraving of a wicker man, apocryphally, was an inspiration. Despite its re-imagining such tradition in a creative way, strangely, this respectful viewpoint invests the film with some authority.

The film works, creatively, in several ways. It is part Hammer Horror, part conventional murder and part supernatural thriller. Aspects of this are reflected in the setting in an isolated place and the cast reference implicit in using Lee. The theme of a virgin at risk – initially a little girl and later, 'Virgin Copper', is an inspired subversion of the chosen genres. In addition, *The Wicker Man* flirts with Hollywood notions of Scotland (the notion that we have supernatural affinities, prevalent from the comic *Ghost Goes West* onwards; in later films this could be called the second sight of *Braveheart* phenomenon. On one level, the film is an anti-*Brigadoon*, but the strangeness of the Galloway village does have echoes of the legendary village accessible to outsiders only once every hundred years. Then again, the filming draws on the style of ethnological documentary, like Robert Flaherty's staged documentary of customs and beliefs in *Man of Aran* (1934) and Werner Kissling's *Eriskay – A Poem of Remote Lives* (1935). The concern for a remote rural area, for character types as well as psychology; the filming techniques, particularly in following the procession, and viewing the contents of a baker's window, gives the illusion of reality. As Sharon Sherman notes, 'All folkloristic films isolate ... examples ... elements of culture, and aspects of human behaviour'. Furthermore, films that 'attempt to reconstruct the past, or view folklore as text/object typically are narrated and rely on a montage of images'.[6]

So, too, *The Wicker Man* has Woodward as the narrator and discoverer of the traditions we encounter. This device allows the film to present a montage of traditions, through a naif character, and to identify aspects of human behaviour in responses to traditions. The traditions Woodward encounters are unfamiliar to him, but integral to the community he encounters. *The Wicker Man* proclaims itself to be a 'researched' amalgam of Scottish (or perhaps British) traditions. The 'group solidarity' of shared customs and beliefs is one of the key factors

---

6 See *Man of Aran* (1934) videorecording (Burbank, Calif.: Hollywood's Attic, 1996) and *Eriskay – A Poem of Remote Lives* (1935) videorecording (Glasgow: Scottish Screen, n.d.); Sharon R. Sherman, *Documenting Ourselves: Film, Video and Culture* (Lexington: University Press of Kentucky, 1998) introduction xi.

in the film; we can see how local identity is created and maintained through celebration and traditional practices, to the exclusion of outsiders.

One of the key motifs is that of Midsummer celebration. Jake Wright, the first director, commented that 'the bedrock of this script was the Beltane fire-festival fertility rite'. Beltane is traditionally a time of celebration, of 'singing and the soundis' of Peblis to the Play in *The Kingis Quair* by James I (1424). Fires were lit on hill tops and traditional food was consumed, including the Beltane bannock, an oatcake baked on the evening before Beltane, made of oatmeal 'watered' with a thin batter made of whipped egg, milk or cream and oatmeal, in places including Daviot and Kingussie. Sometimes pieces of oatcakes were broken off to offer protection to horses and sheep against foxes and eagles. On other occasions, oatcake lots were cast; drawing a charcoal-blackened piece of oatcake meant leaping through the fire three times. Fathers might also carry their children over the fire for their future protection.[7]

Beltane was, equally, the chief festival of witches, along with Halloween. As Mary MacLeod Banks said, in *British Calendar Customs* (1941), the time when 'new members of the community were introduced, and various rites and practices of magical forms were prescribed'. On the night before May Day (1 May), traditionally, witches travelled as hares to take milk from cows; fairies danced on this night too and conducted raids on human beings.

John Glover noted that in Galloway 'no one would give fire or water out of a bowl on May Day – to do so was unlucky', although washing your face in the dew ensured beauty for the coming year.[8] In Kirkmaiden, as recorded in the 1897 *Ethnographic Survey of the United Kingdom*, it was recommended to 'take a snail on the morning of May Day and shut it up in any kind of dish. Omens are drawn from the figures made by the slime'. Strangely,

> In the north of the Stewartry, there is a green howe dipping down to the joining of two hill streams, on the face of the hill stands a great white stone and it was a matter of belief that every May this stone came down to wash itself at the meeting of the waters, and then returned to the hillside to stand guard over the sleeping valleys for another year.[9]

In nineteenth century Scotland it was considered unlucky to marry or be born in May; but it was a good time for visiting wells and shrines for healing.

---

7 Simpson, *Folklore in Lowland Scotland*, 8–9.
8 John Glover, *Dumfries and Galloway: Notes and Queries,* ed. C Mackie (Dumfries: Courier and Herald, 1913).
9 Mary MacLeod Banks, *British Calendar Customs* (London: William Glaisher, 1941) vol. 3, 231, 219.

Revels at this time of year were regulated to some extent, with traditional figures like Robin Hood, Little John, the Abbot of Unrest (Peebles), Abbot of Unreason (Inverness), Prior of Bon Accord (Aberdeen), and so on, in charge. This is part of the European tradition of charivari: licensed – often masqued – misrule is permissible at certain times of year as a safety valve for conventional behaviour at other times.

There is, then, a selective use of traditions in *The Wicker Man*, creatively adapted to enhance the plot and its development. In the film, incidentally, the Beltane shots were set up. Shooting took place in October and November, with the occasional shower of snow and sleet. Fake apple trees were brought in to give a summery feel to the shoot. In the naked dancing scenes, the director describes 'a sort of wandering Dunsinane Wood'. In other scenes Woodward was pursued by a trolley with trees, which ran in front of him as he passed by a section of blossom.

Fire festivals, of course, were significant in Scotland at various times of the year. Still, on Hogmanay, fire-balls are swung at the sea in Stonehaven, and a bonfire is lit in Biggar. On Old Style New Year, 11 January, the tar barrel of the Clavie is lit in Burghead, near Elgin, and carried around this coastal town by a crew of twelve, before reaching its final resting place on Doorie Brae. Then there is Up-Helly-Aa in Shetland.[10]

There are parallels to the Wicker Man idea of burning effigies in the customs associated with Guy Fawkes. Other parallels include Burning Bartle (an above life-sized effigy) at West Witton, Wensleydale, Yorkshire, on the Saturday near St. Bartholomew's Day (24 August). The effigy is soaked in paraffin and thrown onto a bonfire and fireworks are lit. Burning Judas, traditionally took place on Good Friday at Liverpool docks where, representing Judas Iscariot, straw effigies were burnt by groups of children.

Calendar customs have various functions within community traditions, and the film does a good job of implying many of these exist in the practice of customs in their fictional place. Calendar customs are often related to the passing of the year (harvest and term days, for instance). They often involve ideas of death and rebirth and may be closely related to beliefs (for example, in the context of Halloween customs). Customs are related to community identity, creating and reinforcing it for 'us' while excluding 'others'. They demarcate time, making it accessible to our minds and memories.

The Wicker Man uses several elements drawn from 'real' customs. In Scotland,

---

10 See Valentina Bold and Thomas A. McKean, eds, *Northern Folk: Living Traditions of North East Scotland* (Aberdeen: University of Aberdeen's Elphinstone Institute, 1999) on the Burning of the Clavie, and Callum G. Brown, *Up-Helly-Aa: Custom, Culture and Community in Shetland* (Manchester: Manchester University Press, 1998).

May Games were common, and an early reference to the king and queen of May, and summer sports, is found from the wife of Robert Bruce; she found her husband's coronation at Scone in May 1306 a bad omen.[11] May was a popular time for dancing and carolling, as referred to in Gawain Douglas' translation of the *Aeneid*. Dancing round the Maypole is mentioned as a popular custom in James Brown's *History of Sanquhar* (1891). This was, traditionally, often a time for riding the boundaries or waulking cloth, although later this took place in June. The treatment of Mayday in the movie is reminiscent of celebrations in Padstow, Cornwall, with its Mayday horse, or at Abbots Bromley, Staffordshire – Violet Alford called it the most primitive dance in Europe. Carnival behaviour and cross-dressing, as at Abbots Bromley, was also associated with the Maytime festivals, as it is in *The Wicker Man*.

The festivities in the film, too, have international parallels: the gruesomely spectacular coffin and sun breads, for instance, are reminiscent of the *pan de muerte* (bread of the dead) associated with Latin American Halloween traditions. The erotic song, encouraging that 'parts of every gentleman do stand up to attention' seem to draw on a notion that Scottish music is at once primitive and strange. Christopher Lee, in the Ex-S documentary, commented 'it's like going to a really fine opera . . . The [Wicker Man] music is meant to lull you if you like into a sense of security'.

Scotland, of course, has a long-standing tradition of folk drama, as described by Brian Hayward in *Galoshins: The Scottish Folk Play* (1992). His study includes a Castle Douglas version of Galoshins, a resurrection drama, featuring Bold Hector (aka Bold Slasher) carrying a sword and pistol against King Beelzebub, armed with a frying-pan and a club, and a miraculous cure by Doctor Brown.

The film also features a rather gruesome traditional cure. William George Black, in *Folk Medicine* (1883), described how, in late nineteenth century Cheshire, a young frog was held for a few moments, head-first, in the mouth of people suffering from aptha, or thrush. It was thought that the frog took on the patient's illness by the established traditional medical process of transference. An old Shropshire woman recalled seeing this done and noted to Black 'I assure you . . . we used to hear the poor frog whooping and coughing, mortal bad, for days after'.[12]

Such traditional cures, as Lauri Honko has noted, allow lay practitioners, such as the one we briefly see in the film, to act as shaman, medicine man, and psychologist. He 'awakens the collective faith, and promotes the integration of

---

11 Banks, *British Calendar Customs*, vol. 3, 206.
12 William George Black, *Folk Medicine: A Chapter in the History of Culture* (London: The Folklore Society, 1883) 35.

the group ... the myths, the religious dogmas, the group feeling of solidarity and the patterns of role behaviour'.[13]

There are traditional characters here too: Willow is the archetypal witch and seductress; implicitly in league with the Devil, in the tradition of Tam o'Shanter's Cuttie Sark. Dumfries and Galloway has a wealth of traditional tales about witch rides and night flights. Locally, the notorious Hallowmass Rades, with its gathering hymn invoking a 'gray Howlet [owl]', 'grinning cat' and yowling 'tod [fox]', were presided over by the Gyre Carline, Nicniven, the head witch of Scotland.[14] The Gyre Carline was an evil woman to cross. She turned the Lochermoss, then a place for anchoring ships, ranging from Solway sea to Locher-brigg Hill, into a myre, provoked by a tide during a Rade, swept away by her steeds. Of course, Galloway also suffered witch persecutions during the seventeenth century and associations like this, perhaps, enrich the supernatural feel of the film.[15]

The Wicker Man certainly makes use of witch traditions. Witches, for instance, apparently enjoy ceremonial ring dances, accompanied by songs, and there is an example of this in the film. New witches can be initiated by renouncing their faith, being re-baptised, marked in a secret place and given a new name. The policeman could choose this option, perhaps through sexual baptism, but his refusal, unwittingly, encourages his fate. As one critic noted in the *Ex-S* documentary this inverts the usual relationship between sex and death in the most popular horror films.

Christopher Lee as the evil laird, Lord Summerisle, is inherently demonic. Traditionally, the Devil comes in various forms but often, as in *The Wicker Man*, as a tall man in black, who walks as if he has no joints (see for instance, his incarnation in James Hogg's *Private Memoirs and Confessions of a Justified*

---

13 Laurie Honko, quoted by Don Yoder, 'Folk Medicine', in *Folklore and Folklife*, ed. Richard Dorson (Chicago and London: University of Chicago Press, 1972) 191–215.

14 Thomas Davidson, *Rowan Tree and Red Thread: A Scottish Witchcraft Miscellany of Tales, Legends and Ballads; together with a description of the witches' rites and ceremonies* (Edinburgh: Oliver and Boyd, 1949) 8. The hymn is as follows:

> When the gray Howlet has tree times hoo'd,
> When the grinning cat has three times mewed,
> When the Tod has yowled three times I' the wode,
> At the red moon cowering ahind the clud;
>
> When the stars hae cruppen deep I' the drift,
> Lest cantrips had pyked them out o' the lift,
> Up Horsies a', but mair adow.
> Ryde, ryde, for Locher-brigg knowe.

15 Witchcraft in Scotland was first legally punishable by an Act of Parliament, 1563.

Sinner of 1824). Perhaps, though, Lee's character is more like a traditional Druid. Notions of them, popularly, as strange creatures presiding over 'foul orgies of heathen darkness'. Jameson commented that at the end of the eighteenth century, Highlanders were still calling God 'the Arch Druid'.[16] Druids have been defined as,

> One of a class of priests, teachers, diviners, and magicians of ancient Celtic (perhaps pre-Celtic) religion . . . They were physicians, historians, mathematicians, astronomers. Their rank was next to the king, but their decisions were final in all matters . . . They functioned at all rituals of naming, burial and sacrifice. Old Irish texts mention the druids in connection with the terrible human sacrifices associated with Beltane and Cromm Cruac and also Tara.[17]

The film plays, too, with notions of established religion. Christianity, of course, came early to Dumfries and Galloway, and we see some evidence of it, in the churchyard scenes of the film, subverted. Its co-existence with an essentially older culture is one of the major themes of the film (just as, in a real site like that of Whithorn, Pictish symbol stones are found side by side with Christian monuments).

The hero's experiences are, of course, meant to be paralleled with the experiences of Christian martyrs. The film plays, in this respect, with the notion that the truly religious are those prepared to suffer for their faith. The notion is, in some respects, reversed, as here the sufferer is punished for refusal to accept the Old Religion. As Christopher Lee's character says, 'We are talking here about conflict . . . of belief . . . between organised religion for the lack of a better faith, and . . . paganism'. The film reflects both neo-paganism and 'Celticism'. Intriguingly, as the 1998 special issue of *Ethnologies* on 'Wicca' has discussed, modern pagans, typically, reclaim Midsummer for their own, symbolic of a pure, pre-Christian religion.

In a sense, like the audience, Woodward is as much cultural tourist as he is victim. He observes local customs, but his misssion – to solve a crime – prevents his real participation in this society. He does not appreciate the nature of the villagers' belief, as a phenomenon which both invests the mundane world with order and is self perpetuating, because of his complete upholding of an unyeilding Christian belief.

16 Simpson, *Folk Lore of Lowland Scotland*, 5.
17 Funk and Wagnall's *Standard Dictionary of Folklore, Mythology and Legend*, ed. Maria Leach (London: New English Library, 1972) 325.

Christopher Lee has drawn attention to the unsettling qualities of the film, and particularly its morally ambiguous ending:

> *The Wicker Man* is one of the most remarkable films ever made, let alone made in this country . . . The great thing about *The Wicker Man* is not only that it is very amusing, very romantic, very erotic but it's also a very disturbing film and a very frightening film. And the end of course is a tremendous shock.

Ultimately, *The Wicker Man* is a very chilling amalgam of Scottish traditions, convincing acting and skilful writing which goes far beyond the Hammer model it experiments with.

Index

Aberdeen 53, 55, 56, 58, 61, 63, 92, 216
Aberfoyle 1, 95
Abrahams, Roger xv
adder stones 84
Adomnán, of Iona 14, 112
Aesop's Fables 113
Africa 135
Aikenhead, Thomas 93, 97, 98
alchemy 93
Alexander III 10
Alford, Violet 217
almanacs xx, 47–69
amber 84
America 19, 120, 134, 136, 171, 179, 213
American Folklore Society 179
amulets xx, 70–90
Anderson, Rev Alexander 105
Anderson, M. O. 10
angel 31, 38, 43, 44, 45, 74, 75, 95, 177
Anglesey 7
Angus, Marion 124
animals 12, 13, 15, 17, 21, 22, 39, 75, 76, 78, 80, 81, 82–3, 84, 89–90, 100, 113, 117, 126, 127, 128, 134, 141, 143, 145, 147, 151, 154, 155, 159, 162, 165, 188, 189, 190, 191–2, 202, 215, 217, 218
    dog 117, 155
    cat 191–2, 218
    cock/hen 113, 162
    cattle 21, 22, 75, 76, 78, 80, 81, 82, 89–90, 128, 145, 147, 151, 159, 188, 192, 215
    cuckoo 126, 128
    dove 13, 39
    fox 113, 215, 218
    frog 217
    goat 154
    hare 215
    horse 21, 22, 128, 147, 154, 159, 215, 217
    lion 13, 15, 202
    mouse 113
    owl 218
    sheep/lamb 13, 113, 117, 147, 151, 215
    serpent 13, 82, 84, 127, 134
    toad 82–3
    wolf 13, 113, 165

Anne, Queen 53
Apo, Satu 163–4
apocalypse 1
apparitions 4, 23, 31, 94, 106, 121, 134, 207
Ardrossan 166
Argyll 77, 81, 83, 89, 175
Arran 80
Arthur, King 6, 16, 17, 208–9, 211
astrology xx, 8, 47–69
astronomy 48–9, 53
atheism xv, 22, 94, 95, 187
Atkinson, Kate 139
Atlantis 199, 201–2, 205–10
Aubrey, John xvii, xx, xxii
Ayr 117
Ayrshire 142–3, 147, 151, 152, 156, 166

Bacon, Francis xvii, xviii, 15
ballad xiv, xxi, 15, 111, 113, 119, 122, 126, 132, 200

Ballochyle brooch 78
Balquhidder 1
banabhuidseach 189, 193
Banff 3
Banffshire 81
Banks, Ian 131, 134, 138
Banks, Mary MacLeod 215
Bannockburn 16, 76, 115
Barbour, John 6, 8, 112, 118
Barrie, J. M. 112, 123, 124
Bascom, William xvi
Bass Rock 13
Bede 6, 7, 9, 10, 12, 102
beggars xiii, 51, 146, 158–65
Behringer, Wolfgang 31, 40, 43, 142
Beith 36, 143, 150
Beltane 212, 215, 216, 219
Bennett, Margaret xvii, 167–84
Berlington 12
Berwick 9
Berwickshire 80
Bible 1, 11, 78, 95, 96, 102, 106, 158, 185, 186, 191–5
Biggar 216
Black Isle xxiii, 24
Black, George Fraser 70, 78
Black, William George 217
blacksmiths 148
Blair, Hugh 106
Blair, William of the Strand 150, 156
Blake, George 128
Blind Harry 112, 118
Bodin, Jean 18, 31, 153–4
Boece, Hector xvii, 112
Bold, Valentina xxiv, 212–20
Bonnar Bridge 80
Boswell, James 24
Bothwell Brig, battle of 5, 32
Bower, Walter 1, 2, 5, 6, 8, 9, 10
Boyd, James of Trochrig, Archbishop of Glasgow 148, 156
Boyle, Robert 19
Boyman, Jonet 144, 145
Brahan Seer (Coinneach Odhar) 5, 24, 26, 80, 191
Brand, John xxi, xxii
Bridie, James 129

Briggs, Katherine 166
Brittany 7, 197, 200, 201, 204
Broughty Ferry 197
Brown, George Douglas 110, 123
Brown, George Mackay 129–30, 135, 136
Bruce, Robert (see Robert I)
Brunanburh 7
Brunsden, George xx, 48–69
Brunvand, Jan Harold xviii, xix, 174
Brutus 8
Buchan 4
Buchan, John 123
Burke, Peter xvii, xx
Burns, Robert 110, 112, 114, 117–22, 124, 126, 166, 174

Cadwallader 16
Caithness 13, 24
calendar customs xiv, 43, 61, 212, 215–17, 219
Calvin, Jean 50, 51, 52, 63, 195
Cameronians 39, 40
Camisards 99
Campbell, Archibald, 8th Earl and Marquis of Argyll 4, 33
Campbell, John Francis, of Islay xv, xxii, xxiii, 159, 161, 167, 175
Campbell, Rev John Gregorson 22, 168, 175
Campbell, John Lorne 167
Campbell, George 92, 93, 102–5, 107, 108, 109
Campbell, Marion 134
Canada 15, 117, 134, 146
Canterbury 48
Carmichael, Alexander 75, 83, 186
Cary, Grace 33
Castle Douglas 217
celticism 203, 219
Celtic Twilight 124
Charlemagne 8
Charles I 56
Charles II 24, 31, 37, 56
Charles V, Emperor 8
Charles VIII, of France 8
Chambers, Robert xxii, 84, 86, 153, 166

Index

chapbook 13, 15, 53, 145
charming/charmers xiii, xx, 51, 80, 143, 147–2
charms xx, 70–90, 143, 145, 148–51, 158
Cheape, Hugh xx, 70–90
childbirth 141, 147, 151–2, 161–2
Christ, Jesus 1, 73, 74, 75, 78, 87, 89, 95, 97, 98, 100, 101, 102, 103, 104, 106, 122, 159, 194
Christsonday 38
Cicero 10, 11
Clach Dearg 'red stone' 76
Clach na Brataich 'Stone of the Standard' 76
Clodd, Edward xiii
Coll 22, 95, 175
Colville, John 14
Constantine the Great 12
Copernicus 60, 61, 63, 66
Cornwall 7, 217
Corss, John 63
covenant 15
Covenanters xx, 4, 5, 20, 29, 32, 99, 100
Cowal 78
Cowan, Edward J. xvi, xvii, xx, 1–28, 54, 140, 143, 144, 164, 188, 196
Craignish 77
Crawford, Captain Thomas 150, 156
Creetown 213
Cromarty xxiii, 168
Crossford 5
Culloden 23, 182
Cunningham, James, laird of Ashinyards and chamberlain of Kilwinning 150

Daemonologie (1597) 3, 15, 18, 144
Daill, Janet 154
Dalkeith 81, 148
Dalrymple, David, Lord Hailes 11
David, Duke of Rothesay 10
Davis, Robertson 15
Dégh, Linda xvi
deism 92, 95, 96, 97, 98, 101, 105, 106
demonic pact 3, 41, 148, 154

demons xv, 1, 114, 158
Descartes, Rene 18
Deuteroscopia 20
Devil/Satan 1, 3, 15, 18, 30, 31, 40, 41, 42, 52, 94, 95, 96, 113, 119, 123, 146, 148, 151, 153–5, 158, 176, 179, 185, 187, 190, 191–2, 218
divination 31, 81, 187, 188, 190, 191–2, 195
doppelganger 186
Dornoch 188
Dorson, Richard xxi, xxiii, 174, 204
Douglas, Gavin 113, 217
Douglas, Mary xix
dragons 1, 6, 13, 64, 74
druids 71, 89, 192, 198, 207, 210, 219
Drummond, William of Hawthornden 114
Dublin 71
Duffy, Eamon 101
Dumbarton 13
Dumfries (shire) 32, 40, 74, 218, 219
Dunbar, William 113, 115, 125
Dundes, Alan xiii, xv, 174
Dunlop, Bessie 38, 44, 141–66
Dunnett, Dorothy 133–34

Earlston 14
Easter 61
Easter Ross 77
Eathie 82
Edinburgh xxii, xxiii, 56, 58, 63, 81, 85, 92, 115, 117, 129, 144, 147, 148, 153, 156, 197
Edington, John 34
Edmonston, Thomas 85
Edward I 10, 16
Edward VI 13
Egypt 97, 197, 199, 204, 205, 209–11
Eildon Tree 15
elf-arrow 71, 85
Elizabeth I 13, 14, 17,
Ellon 3
Elphinstone, Margaret 131, 135–6
Ember Days 43
England 9, 15, 68, 92, 98, 143, 156

Index

Enlightenment xx, 2, 11, 18, 91–3, 99, 101, 102, 108–9, 114
'Erra Paters' 59, 60
Evans-Wentz, W. Y. 159, 160, 186, 199, 207
evil eye 73, 76, 83, 89, 190
exorcism 42

Fair Isle 135
fairy xv, xvi, xx, xxii, 18, 19, 38, 39, 40, 41, 43, 44, 111, 114, 119, 120, 123, 141–66, 167, 174, 176, 178–9, 182, 185–7, 193, 197, 199, 207, 208; *see also* elf-arrow
fairyland (Elfland) 15, 125, 142, 145, 148, 154, 157
Fairy Queen 15, 142, 145, 148, 152, 153, 155, 157, 158, 161, 162
Falkirk 4
Farrar, F. W. 182
Fergusson, Robert 112, 114, 117, 118
Fian, John 145
Finlay, Richard 197, 202, 206, 211
Fiore, Joachim of 7
Fletcher, Andrew of Saltoun 97
Flodden, battle of 10
folk belief xiv, xv, xx, 73, 84, 88, 110, 146, 157
folk custom xiv, xvii, xviii, xix
folklore xiii–xxiii, 71, 72, 73, 95, 117, 122, 144, 146, 168, 174, 203–4, 214
    legend xv, xvi, xvii, 113, 124, 136, 144, 146, 160–1, 163, 165, 167, 168, 174, 182, 185
    The Folklore Society xiii, 175, 204
folktale xiv, xv, xx, 132, 144, 146, 152, 153, 158–66, 174, 189
Fordun, John of 5, 10
Fort George 86
France 1, 112, 158, 200
Fraser, Rev John 20, 85, 95
Fraser, Jonet 32, 34, 39, 40, 41, 42
Frazer, Sir James 72, 124, 203, 205

Gàidhealtachd xvii, xxiii, 4, 18, 87, 143, 188, 195

Galileo 49, 60, 63
Galloway 32, 77, 134, 135, 213, 214, 215, 218, 219
Galoshins 217
Galt, John 110, 120
Garioch, Robert 129
Gataker, Thomas 51
Gatehouse of Fleet 213
Geddes, James Young 122
Germany 1, 128, 143, 145, 146, 158, 197, 201, 203, 204, 206–7, 209–10
ghost xxii, 21, 94, 106, 116, 117, 133, 149, 152, 155, 158, 171, 174–6, 179–80, 187
Gibbon, Lewis Grassic 110, 112, 118, 119, 124, 126–8
Gibson, John of Lockhart 122
Gibson, Marion 147
Gifford, Douglas xxii, 110–40
Gildas 9, 10, 12
Ginzburg, Carlo xvii, 147
Gladsmuir 23
Glanvill, Joseph 18, 94
Glasgow xiv, 1, 5, 19, 56, 78, 84, 92, 94, 131, 133, 138, 148, 156, 175
Glenluce 95
Glenluce visionary 29–31, 33, 34, 39, 42
Glenlyon brooch 78
Glenorchy charmstone 78
Glover, Sue 131
God xv, xxiv, 2, 3, 7, 9, 18, 29, 31, 34, 37, 38, 48, 49, 50, 51, 87, 92, 94, 95, 96, 106, 117, 119, 149, 154, 176–7, 179, 185, 190
Goldstein, Kenneth S. 179–80
Gomme, G. L. xiii, xviii, 204
Gordon, Patrick of Ruthven 4
Govan 13
Gowdie, Isobel 145
Graham, James, Marquis of Montrose 4
Grail (Holy) 202, 208–9
Grant, Elizabeth 25
Gray, Alasdair 130–1, 133, 137, 138
The Great Prophecy of Britain (Armes Prydein Vawr) 7
Greatrakes, Valentine 101
Greenland 136

Greenock 139
Gregor, Walter 162
Gregory XII, pope 61
Greig, Andrew 131, 137
Gunn, Neil 110, 124, 127–8, 136
Guy Fawkes day 216
gypsies xiii, 149
Gyre Carline 218

Hadow, James 105
Hag-ridden 82
Haldane, Issobell 38, 39
Halloween 3, 117, 215, 216, 217
Halpert, Herbert 174
Halyburton, Thomas 92, 95
Hart, Andrew 54
Hartland, Edwin Sydney xiii
Hay, John MacDougall 123
Haynes, Dorothy 128, 134
Hayton, Sian 131, 135–7
Hayward, Brian 217
healers 3, 80, 87, 143, 144, 151–2, 189
Henderson, Lizanne xiii–xxiv, 40, 41, 140, 141–66, 188
Henderson, William xiv, xv
Henry VII 17
Henry VIII 12, 13, 17
Henryson, Robert 49, 50, 113, 114–15, 117, 125
heresy 1, 104
Higden, Ranalf 9
Highland Host 5, 32
Hoadly, Benjamin 97–8
Hobbes, Thomas 18, 94
Hogg, James 100, 110, 111–12, 118–22, 124–6, 138, 218
Hogmanay 216
Holland 22
Hone, William xxii
Honko, Lauri xvii, 217, 218
Hufford, David xvi
Hume, David 92, 99, 100–1, 107–8
Hungary 143
Huntingdon, Henry of 9
Hutcheson, Francis 98
Hutcheson, Margaret 32

Icelandic sagas 136
Inverness 216
Ireland 1, 7, 12, 77, 83, 87, 98, 101, 192, 219
Irvine 38, 147, 148, 156
Islay 80
Isle of Man 22
Italy 1, 15, 143, 200

Jacob, Violet 124
Jacobite 23, 53, 58, 61, 68, 115, 182
James I 215
James III 150
James IV 12, 17
James V 12, 17
James VI and I 3, 12, 14, 15, 18, 52, 80, 113, 144, 145
Jenkins, Robin 128, 129, 133
Jew/Jewish 18, 59, 62, 74, 86, 177
Joan of Arc 10
John, Duke of Albany 12
John the Commonweal 113, 115, 130, 132
Johnson, Samuel 21, 24
Johnston, Archibald of Wariston 29

Kames brooch 74
Kelman, James 128–9
Kenmore 82
Kennaway, James 129
Kennedy, A. L. 131, 138
Kennedy, Rev John 5, 194
Kenneth II 200
Keppoch charm 75
Kidd, Colin xx, 91–109
Kilbirnie 166
Killearnan 5
Killing Times 5, 15, 32
Kintyre 78
Kirk, Rev Robert xv, 1, 19, 95, 114, 155, 162, 186
Kirkcudbright 160, 161, 213
Kirkmaiden 215
Knox, John 7, 17, 51

lammer beads 84
Lang, Andrew xiii, 205
A Large Description of Galloway 20

Leith 65, 147
legend (see folklore)
Leslie, John xvii
Lesmahagow 5
Levack, Brian 142, 146, 163
Lewis 72, 170, 181, 183, 191
Lewis, C. S. 122
Lhuyd, Edward 71, 82, 85
Lidel, Duncan 61
Lilly, William 51, 62–3
Lindsay, Sir David 17, 113, 115, 118, 130, 132
Linklater, Eric 112, 118, 124, 127, 134, 136
Llewellyn 16
Loch Carron 87
Lochhead, Liz 130–3
Lochwinnoch 36
Locke, John 97
Lomond Hills 13
London xiii, 99, 129
Lothian 13
Louis XIII 29
Love, Grizell 29, 31, 33, 35, 38, 39, 41, 42
Luck of Ardshiel 76
Luther, Martin 50

MacCaig, Norman 128, 129
MacColla, Alasdair 4, 77
MacCulloch, J. A. 165, 166
MacDiarmid, Hugh 122–5, 127–8, 131, 136
McDonald, Rev Fr Allan 83
MacDonald, Allan of Flodigarry 23
MacDonald, George 122, 123
MacFarlane, Alan 164
M'Ghie, Isabel (Bell) 143
MacGregor, Alexander 177
McIllvanney, William 129, 133
MacInnes, John xxiv, 5, 19, 26, 185–95
MacKenzie, Alexander 26
MacKenzie, Sir George, of Rosehaugh 1, 20
MacKenzie, George, Lord Tarbat and 1st Earl of Cromarty 1, 19, 20, 96
MacKenzie, Mary Frederica Elizabeth 25

Maclean, Sorley 124
MacPherson, John 22
MacTargett, Catherine 165
magic 3, 147, 148
maleficium 148–9
Malleus Maleficarum (1486) 146
Man, John 65–6
Mann, Andrew 38, 44, 155
Margaret, Queen 82
Martin, Lauren 165
Martin, Martin 19, 20, 21, 22, 24, 72, 78, 80, 83, 95, 162
Mary Stewart, Queen of Scots 14, 17, 51, 156
Mary Tudor 13, 17
Maxwell, Hew of Dalswinton 39
May Day 215, 217
medicine 3, 72, 87, 145, 158, 217
memorate xvi, xvii, 144, 146, 165, 174, 180, 182
Merlin 6, 7, 8, 9, 10, 12, 16
Merry Andrew 58, 66–9
Methven, battle of 79
Midsummer 215
midwife 83, 151, 159
Miller, Hugh xxiii, 82, 168–9, 173
miracles 6, 92, 95, 96, 97, 98, 101, 102, 104, 106, 107, 108
Mitchell, Margaret 29, 37
Mitcheson, Naomi 124, 127, 134–6
Monmouth, Geoffrey of 7, 17
Montaigne, Michel de 10, 11
Montgomery 115
Moray, Sir Robert 19
More, Henry 18
Morgan, Edwin 130–33
Morrison, John 'Seer of Petty' 5, 193
Mull 74, 168
Munlochy 81
Munro, Neil 123, 124
Murray, Margaret 199, 204
music 4, 183
mythology 113, 124, 125, 128, 136, 197–8, 201, 204–6

Na Duine 'the men' 5
Nairn, Rev James 105

Napier, James Rev xiv, xv, xxiv, 175–7
Napoleonic wars 86
necromancy 158
Netherlands 33
Newes from Scotland (1591) 145
Newfoundland 170, 171
Newton, Isaac 7, 93
Niccoli, Ottavia 16
Niall, Ian 128
North Berwick Kirk 3
North Berwick witch trials 144
Norway 165, 191
Nutt, Alfred xiii, 204, 208

occultism 198–9, 201
Occult Review 198
Oliphant, Margaret 122, 124
oral tradition xiv, xix, xxi, xxii, xxiii, 111, 144, 146, 163, 167–84, 188, 192, 193
Orkney 85, 129, 134, 135

Paisley 35, 149, 175, 176
Paterson, James 61
Pearce, Zachary 102–3
Peebles xxii, 216
Peebles, Barbara 29, 31–8, 42
Peirson, Alison 38, 44, 145, 155, 157–8
Pennant, Thomas 24, 191
Perth 64, 65, 92, 104
Petronius 6
Philip of Spain 13
Pinkie, battle of 23, 39, 148, 150, 155–7
Poe, Edgar Allan 120
poltergeist 30, 170, 171
Polwarth 80
possession (demonic) 42, 43, 44
Prestonpans 23
prodigies 4, 5, 101
prophecy xiii, xx, 1, 4–12, 14, 16, 17, 23, 26, 43, 45, 49, 53, 93, 95, 96, 106, 115, 134, 152, 191, 194, 195
prophets/prophetesses xx, 31
Purkiss, Diane 144, 147

Quebec 171, 181

Rabelais, Francois 67
Ramsay, Allan 112, 114–17, 118, 126
Ramsay, John of Ochtertyre 77, 89
Reeves, Marjorie 2
Reid, Thomas 148–58, 162
Remy, Nicolas 153
Renaissance 10, 60, 61, 79
Rhymer, Thomas 10, 11, 12, 14, 15, 112, 113, 126
Rhys, John 203, 208
Riach, Alan 125
Richelieu, Cardinal 29, 33
Robin Hood 216
Robert I (Bruce) 8, 14, 16, 54, 79, 89, 217
Robertson, James 137
Robertson, William 106–9
Röhrich, Lutz 164
rowan 81, 178, 179
Royal Society 1, 19, 26
Rullion Green, battle of 32, 36

Sadduceeism 2, 18, 19, 95
Sadducismus Triumphatus 94
saints 6, 8, 75, 77, 87, 112, 195
  St Augustine 195
  St Bride 75
  St Bridget 8
  St Columba 6, 87, 112
  St Ninian 77
Sanquhar 217
Satan's Invisible World Discovered (1685) 19–20, 30, 94, 114
Scone 56, 217
Scot, Reginald 18
Scotsman, The 197
Scott, Michael 138
Scott, Sir Walter xxi, xxii, 5, 25, 81, 84, 110–12, 118, 120–2, 124, 126, 166, 174, 182
Scottish nationalism 201–3, 206, 208
Scottish National Party 197, 201
Seaforth MacKenzies 'doom of the MacKenzies' 24–6
second sight xv, xx, 1, 6, 15, 18, 19, 20, 21, 22, 23, 24, 26, 95, 106, 123, 152, 155, 165, 171, 180–1, 187, 190–1, 194, 199, 207

The Secret Common-Wealth (1691) 19, 95, 114, 155, 186
seers 3, 14, 19, 20, 21, 22, 191
Seneca 6
seventh son 95
Shakespeare, William 115
shamanism 144, 189–90, 192, 198, 207, 210, 217
Sharpe, Charles Kirkpatrick 166
Shaw, Christian 41, 42
Shelley, Mary 138
Sherlock, Thomas 103
Shetland 74, 80, 84, 85, 170, 216
Sinclair, George 1, 19, 30, 94, 95, 114
Sinclair, William of Freswick 24
Skye 20, 22, 169, 171, 177–8, 186, 187
Sloane, Sir Hans 71
Smith, Iain Crichton 128, 129
sorcery 51, 142, 147–9
Soutar, William 124–7
Spain 197, 201, 204
Spark, Muriel 129
Spence, Alan 129
Spence, Lewis xxiv, 22, 196–211
Spinoza, Baruch de 18, 94
St Andrews 100, 105
Stalker, William 78
Stevenson, Robert Louis 110, 112, 118, 119, 122–6, 138
Stewart, Rev Alexander 81, 83
Stewart, Prince Charles Edward 23
Stewart, Ena Lamont 129
Stewart, James Francis Edward 'Old Pretender' 53
Stewart, John 38
Stewart, William Grant xxii, xxiii
Stewart, Rev William 104
Stoker, Bram 132
Stonehaven 216
Strathclyde 7
superstition 2, 87, 117, 121, 124, 175–7, 180, 186, 187–8
Swift, Jonathan 69
Sympson, Andrew 20

'Tam O'Shanter' 110, 117, 118, 119, 126, 166, 218

Tantallon Castle 66
Tarbat, Lord (see George MacKenzie)
Tennant, William 121
Theophilus Insulanus 22, 23
Thompson, E. P. xvii, xviii, xix, xx
Thoms, William xiii
Tindal, Matthew 92, 96, 103, 104
Tiree 95, 175
Tir-nan-Og 136
Toland, John 92, 94, 198
Tolkein, J. R. R. 122
torture 3, 162–3
Treasure Trove 85
Tweed 13
Tyndrum 79

Ugadale brooch 78
Uist 83
unicorn 126, 128, 202
Union of 1707 114, 115

Virgil 195
Virgin Mary 73, 74
von Sydow, Carl W. 174

Waite, A. E. 202, 208
Waldhave, Abbot of Melrose 12
Wales 7, 9, 10, 16
Walker, Patrick 4, 5
Wallace, William 54, 112, 115, 200, 201, 210
Wars of Independence 16, 74, 115
Watson, Roderick 125
Wedderburn, Robert 11
well (healing or holy) xvii, 81, 144, 215
Welsh, Irvine 129
West Indies 83
Wester Ross 87
Westminster 117
Weyer, Johann 18
Whalsay 80
Whithorn 77
The Whole Prophecie 12, 27–8
Whyte, Christopher 137, 138
Williams, Raymond xv

Wilson, Rev William 92, 95, 100
witch xx, xxii, 31, 35, 40, 41, 42, 44,
    46, 80, 87, 94, 114, 118, 141–66,
    167, 179, 182, 188–9, 192, 215,
    218
  witch's cursing bone 81
  witch of Endor 158, 192
  witch-hunt 3, 80, 142–4, 148
  witches rope 81
  sabbat 3
  witch trials xvii, 31, 142, 144

witchcraft xx, 18, 45, 74, 78, 89, 117,
    135, 142, 146–8, 153, 154, 171–2,
    179, 189, 190, 192, 207
Witchcraft Act 189, 218
Wodrow, Robert 1, 5, 20, 32, 46, 109, 114
Wood, Juliette xxiv, 196–211
Woolston, Thomas 92, 102–4
Wycliffites 1
Wyntoun, Andrew of 5, 112

Yeoman, Louise xx, 29–46